Praise for *Hermeneutics as Epistemology*

The decisive way to counter error in biblical understanding is to outflank it at the level of its own arbitrary first principles, and to set biblically based first principles in their place. Dr. Roach shows us very fully how Carl Henry did this, by setting current hermeneutical fashions in the corrective frame of an Augustinian, Bible-based, cognitive-propositional account of how God reveals, and how we receive, his word of truth. As Henry was masterful in doing this on the grand scale, so Roach is masterful in vindicating Henry against those who would critique or ignore him. This is a very valuable piece of work.

— **J. I. Packer,** Professor of Theology, Regent College and Co-founder of ICBI

Carl F. H. Henry was a theological titan—a man whose theology is worthy of careful academic investigation. William Roach's assessment of Henry's hermeneutics is both stimulating and illuminating. Readers will find this book a well-researched and careful investigation of Henry's theology and a welcome addition to existing scholarship on Carl Henry.

—**R. Albert Mohler, Jr.,** President of The Southern Baptist Theological Seminary

During a century when liberal and neo-orthodox theologians were insisting upon non-cognitive and modified cognitive views of propositional revelation; Carl F. H. Henry helped to define and defend the classic evangelical stance of the Bible as cognitive-propositional revelation. During our time serving together on the International Council on Biblical Inerrancy, Henry and the rest of the ICBI leaders, sought to clearly articulate the evangelical view and resist all opposing views. However, sadly, in our day, there has been a resurgence of liberal and neo-orthodox theology among evangelical theologians. In his work, *Hermeneutics as Epistemology*, William Roach evaluates Henry's views and reintroduces him into the current dialogues in hermeneutics. You will find his work to be well-researched, faithful to Henry, and a powerful defense of evangelical bibliology and hermeneutics.

—**Norman L. Geisler,** Former President of ETS and Co-founder of ICBI

Carl F. H. Henry was one of evangelicals' premiere thinkers in the latter half of the twentieth century. He guided and shaped the movement as much, if not more so, than any other person, especially in terms of rigorous theological reflection. For him to vanish into the dustbin of history would be a tragic loss for the twenty-first century. A number of scholars have sought to ensure this does not happen. William Roach is one such individual. This book is a welcome addition to the growing scholarship on Henry. I am delighted to welcome and commend it.

—**Daniel L. Akin,** President, Southeastern Baptist Theological Seminary

Carl Henry's legacy will undoubtedly continue to influence evangelical Christianity in the United States, though the worry arises that future writers may treat him on a rather superficial level. William Roach has given us a book that demonstrates the depth of Henry's thought, and how his understanding of knowledge is thoroughly integrated into his theology. In this book, Roach carefully analyzes, not only the background and method of Henry's epistemology, but also how Henry thereby directly addressed the issues of his day. William Roach rightfully points out how the Christian world of today would benefit by emulating him, not simply by repeating Henry's words, but by letting our understanding of the world also be guided by the fact that knowledge begins with the God who has freely revealed himself.

—**Win Corduan,** Professor Emeritus of Philosophy and Religion, Taylor University

William Roach has done Evangelicalism and the wider world of Christendom a great service by reintroducing the incredible combination of keen mind, towering scholarship, and personal piety that was Dr. Carl F. H. Henry to a new generation of Christian scholars. I knew Dr. Henry well and had the privilege of calling him mentor and friend. As I read

Hermeneutics as Epistemology, I was reminded yet again of what a magnificent gift to the church Dr. Henry was and how he still gives us crucial guidance and direction in rightly dividing God's inerrant revelation of himself in Holy Scripture.

—**Richard Land,** President, Southern Evangelical Seminary

When I was in graduate school and lived in the Washington, D.C. area, I got to know Carl F. H. Henry well and spent time with him and his wife at his house. At the time I lamented that fewer and fewer Christians knew of him and his work. That is why I am thrilled that William Roach has written a book on Carl F. H. Henry's epistemological approach to hermeneutics. I am grateful for William Roach introducing Carl Henry to a new generation and into the current discussions in hermeneutics.

—**Kerby Anderson,** President of Probe Ministries and Host of the Point of View Radio Talk Show

William Roach presents an insightful examination of the philosophical and theological thought of one of the great evangelical thinkers of the twentieth century who has much to say to evangelical hermeneutics today. A well-written and thoroughly researched book that makes a major contribution to a proper understanding of Carl F. H. Henry. Well done.

—**Bruce A. Little,** Senior Professor of Philosophy at Southeastern Baptist Theological Seminary and Director of the Francis A. Schaeffer Collection

William Roach's assessment of Carl Henry's epistemology is provocative, insightful, and encouraging. In an increasingly confused world that is rapidly jettisoning the historic doctrine of biblical inerrancy (and its myriad implications), Carl Henry's calls for theological consistency are timely for Christians in every corner of the globe. No doubt the path forward for evangelicals desiring to remain stalwart in their faith is, in fact, not new at all. Carl Henry, through William Roach's careful study, confidently points us back to that path.

—**Cameron D. Armstrong,** Church Planter, International Mission Board (Southern Baptist Convention), Bucharest, Romania

William Roach's, *Hermeneutics as Epistemology: A Critical Assessment of Carl F. H. Henry's Epistemological Approach to Hermeneutics*, is a groundbreaking work. Masterfully articulated, the work presents evangelical scholarship at its finest regarding one of the twentieth century's most influential theologians, especially among the Southern Baptist faith. Roach is to be highly-commended in his reasoned, balanced approach toward unpacking Henry's approach to interpretation of the biblical texts. The work should be in every theologian's library and sets the standard for research on Henry for years to come. The work also serves as a growing basis for a needed discussion of a critical hermeneutical issue facing evangelicalism today (i.e. grammatico-historical vs. historical-critical hermeneutics).

—**F. David Farnell,** Professor of New Testament, The Masters Seminary and Co-author of *The Jesus Quest*

Hermeneutics as Epistemology

Hermeneutics as Epistemology

A Critical Assessment of Carl F. H. Henry's
Epistemological Approach to Hermeneutics

WILLIAM C. ROACH

WIPF & STOCK · Eugene, Oregon

HERMENEUTICS AS EPISTEMOLOGY
A Critical Assessment of Carl F. H. Henry's Epistemological Approach
to Hermeneutics

Copyright © 2015 William C. Roach. All rights reserved. Except for brief quotations in critical publications or reviews, no part of this book may be reproduced in any manner without prior written permission from the publisher. Write: Permissions, Wipf and Stock Publishers, 199 W. 8th Ave., Suite 3, Eugene, OR 97401.

Wipf & Stock
An Imprint of Wipf and Stock Publishers
199 W. 8th Ave., Suite 3
Eugene, OR 97401

www.wipfandstock.com

isbn 13: 978-1-4982-2277-8

Manufactured in the U.S.A.

*This book is dedicated to four people whom God sovereignly
brought into my life:*

Molly Roach, my wife, whose labor of love
and service editing this project,
will be eternally remembered;

Bill and Laura Roach, my parents, who more than anyone else,
modeled before me hard work and perseverance,
along with parental love and dedication;

Bruce Little, my doctoral mentor, who oversaw this project,
and represents to the superlative degree,
what it means to be a pastor-theologian.

CONTENTS

Preface | ix

1   Modern and Contemporary Hermeneutics | 1

2   Carl F. H. Henry's Revelational Epistemology | 59

3   Carl F. H. Henry's Revelational Epistemology and Language | 113

4   Carl F. H. Henry's Revelational Hermeneutic as Epistemology and Methodology | 172

5   Negative Responses to Carl F. H. Henry's Cognitive-Propositional Hermeneutic | 231

6   Carl F. H. Henry's Revelational Hermeneutic in the Current Conversation | 256

Bibliography | 285
Index | 295

PREFACE

I NEVER MET THE man, but I feel like I know him better than some of my closest companions. I relate to the man, because we both came from homes split over religious views (i.e., semi-Protestantism and Roman Catholicism), and we both received Bibles from a local church as teenagers (he stole his from an Episcopalian church, while I received mine as a gift from the wife of a Quaker pastor). We both had conversion experiences to Christianity, so profound, that it set the trajectory of our lives and we dedicated ourselves to full-time Christian service, so we might by God's grace and providence, evangelize the lost and disciple those whom God has graciously chosen to save. Upon reflection, both of us would agree, Scripture knows nothing of a "sinful humanity with immediate access to the holy God in man's own right or on man's own terms; communion with God presupposes the God who speaks and saves." God has revealed himself normatively through the inspired prophets and apostles set forth in the inspired text of Scripture. It is the task of the theologian, especially one who believes an authentic and personal relationship with God actually exists, then to rightly understand the revelation of God in the terms God has chosen to reveal himself, and proclaim *that message* to the watching world.

Now, the question many of you might be asking is: Who is this man? With no further ado, the man is: Dr. Carl F. H. Henry. Henry is considered to be the "dean" of American evangelicalism. Henry was chosen as the first editor of *Christianity Today*, selected among the founding faculty of Fuller Theological Seminary, and served as a professor at top evangelical institutions such as Trinity Evangelical Divinity School. Henry received highest praise from some of the most influential figures of the evangelical movement. Charles Colson once said, "When the history of the evangelical movement is finally written, Carl Henry will emerge as its dominant figure." Kenneth Kantzer remarked, "Carl Henry is the ablest defender of evangelical doctrine in the last half of the twentieth century. He stands firmly and boldly for the full-orbed Biblical and evangelical faith." Consequently, one must be prepared to engage Henry if they are going to understand rightly twentieth-century evangelical theology and hermeneutics.

Before pressing on into the study itself, I shall avoid distracting questions later if at the outset I sketch briefly the importance of this study, and acknowledge the limitations placed upon myself. First of all, a study of hermeneutics is important to anyone claiming to believe the Bible is the inspired and revealed Word of God. It is the task of the Christian theologian to know and rightly interpret the Word of God, because it is the source-criterion for knowledge of God and Christian theology. Second, for those committed to the study of evangelicalism and evangelical theology, an investigation of Henry's hermeneutic is of top priority due to the magnitude of Henry's influence and the gravity of his theological conclusions.

Lastly, this book recognizes a distinction between hermeneutics and exegesis. Hermeneutics is concerned with the nature of the interpretive practice. Exegesis is concerned with the actual interpretation of any particular text. Because this is not a study of Henry's exegesis, I have not provided examples of his interpretation of various passages of Scripture. I have chosen to focus exclusively upon issues related to Henry's epistemology and hermeneutic, along with any other areas his hermeneutic may touch or affect. I also make no claims to comprehensiveness concerning an extensive study of hermeneutics. I do not present a complete history of hermeneutics, nor do I interact with every pressing issue in hermeneutics. Figures discussed in this book have been chosen because of their role and influence in philosophical hermeneutics and methodology. I have tried to be evenhanded in my selection of theologians, philosophers, and issues. I have cited both evangelical and non-evangelical figures, both well-known and less well-known. By in far, I have attempted to select materials and quotes from their most popular literature. The figures chosen may reflect more of an evangelical bent, mainly because it reflects the audience for which this material has been prepared. Finally, the vast majority of the individuals were chosen due to their specific interaction with Henry or views related to topics addressed by Henry.

In the final analysis, I am indebted to the life and work of Carl F. H. Henry. There are few figures who have had such a profound impact upon my life and doctrine. Henry's commitment to Christ, the local church, international missions, and evangelical theology; serves as a model for all Christians, evangelicals first and foremost. May his works be remembered and read, not for the exaltation of Henry *qua* Henry; but unto the glory of God alone, who has the ability to save lost sinners, and use their lives to alter the course of human history by proclaiming the message of Jesus Christ to the lost and dying world.

William C. Roach

1

Modern and Contemporary Hermeneutics

INTRODUCTION

HISTORIC PROTESTANTISM, AS ILLUSTRATED by the Westminster divines, has always been interested in the proper interpretation of Scripture, and the task of hermeneutics. The *Westminster Shorter Catechism*, question three, asks, "What do the Scriptures principally teach?" It answers, "The Scriptures principally teach, what man is to believe concerning God, and the duty God requires of man."[1] J. I. Packer in his article titled "The Puritans as Interpreters of Scripture" writes,

> Consider the implications of this answer [Q. 3.]. First, Scripture teaches us what to believe about God—that is, it sets before us spiritual truths concerning spiritual realities, truths beyond the grasp of fallen reason which only the Holy Spirit can enable us to discern. Therefore we must distrust ourselves, confess our natural inability and blindness in this realm, and invoke the aid of the Spirit to interpret Scripture to us. . . . He who would interpret Scripture aright, therefore, must be a man of a reverent, humble, prayerful, teachable and obedient spirit; otherwise, however tightly his mind may be 'stuffed with notions,' he will never reach any understanding of spiritual realities.[2]

1. Schaff, *Creeds of Christendom*, 3:676.
2. Packer, *A Quest For Godliness*, 99–100.

Packer reminds his readers of the Puritan insistence for individuals to know God in, and through, the Holy Scriptures. Evident also in his comments is a word of exhortation about the great difficulty it is to "interpret Scripture aright."[3] According to Packer, there seem to be natural inabilities, albeit cognitive inabilities due to either sin or human feebleness, that keep even the honest seeker of truth from properly interpreting the Scriptures. To address those inabilities, Protestant theologians such as the Westminster divines and the Puritans, developed hermeneutical principles or methods to guide their interpretations of Scripture.[4]

Two centuries later, some theologians abandoned many of the Protestant principles of interpretation, favoring new trajectories in modern epistemology and methodology.[5] In his classic book titled *Protestant Biblical Interpretation*, Bernard Ramm lists four of the main Protestant principles abandoned by modern theologians.[6] The four principles they abandoned are: (1) The clarity of Scripture; (2) Scripture interprets Scripture; (3) The analogy of faith; and (4) The unity of meaning of Scripture.[7] The "clarity of Scripture" serving as an example of hermeneutics as epistemology, and the latter three as examples of hermeneutics as methodology.

In 1976, Carl F. H. Henry opened the first volume his magnum opus *God, Revelation and Authority* with a chapter titled "The Crisis of Truth and Word." In that chapter, he spoke to the epistemological shifts in modern and contemporary philosophy lamenting their effects on Western society, claiming,

> No fact of contemporary Western life is more evident than its growing distrust of final truth and its implacable questioning of any sure word. . . . So widespread is the current truth-and-word crisis that, according to some observers, the night of nihilism—a new Dark Ages—may be swiftly engulfing the civilized world, and particularly the West which long has vaunted itself as the

---

3. Ibid.

4. George, *Reading Scripture With The Reformers*; Ramm, *Protestant Biblical Interpretation*.

5. For a definition of Modern philosophy, see, Copleston, *A History of Philosophy*, 4:1.

6. Ramm, *Protestant Biblical Interpretation*, 93–162. It should be noted that Ramm does not claim they abandoned them; however, in the following sections, it will become evident that Palmer believes later approaches to hermeneutics abandoned these Protestant principles of interpretation.

7. Ibid., 93–113.

spearpoint of cosmic progress.... The breakdown of confidence in verbal communication is a feature of our times.[8]

Henry uses the term "feature of our times" in order to refer to the general attitude of the West during his life-time.[9] He believes these epistemological shifts in the West (e.g., rationalism, skepticism, agnosticism, etc.) created a "night of [epistemological] nihilism" and "hermeneutical nihilism."[10] In particular, Westerners have been eye-witnesses to the philosophical and cultural breakdown of final truth and verbal communication.[11]

Henry responds to this breakdown of the acceptance of final truth (e.g., "night of [epistemological] nihilism") and any sure word (e.g., "hermeneutical nihilism") setting the tone for the rest of his work, claiming,

> On the one hand, the God of Judeo-Christian revelation, whose truth and Word nullified pagan deities in the ancient past, still holds modern secular man wholly answerable to the theistic exposition of human life. The living God of the Bible inescapably and invincibly shows up and speaks out; the divine Logos is the round-the-clock and round-the-world channel of supernatural revelation. The self-disclosing God attributes human defection from truth and wobbling with words solely to man's devious ways, and continuingly implores a disaffected humanity to life hearing ears and seeing eyes to his proffered revelation and redemption.[12]

The key phrases and concepts from Henry's quote are "human defection from truth," "wobbling with words solely to man's devious ways," and "disaffected humanity." The history of religious hermeneutics indicates that interpreters of Scripture, whether they be Old Testament prophets heralding a message before the nation of Israel, or Jesus Christ correcting the interpretation of the first century Jews, or the apostle Paul opposing

---

8. Carl F. H. Henry addresses these two issues in his magisterial work: *God, Revelation and Authority*, Henry, 1:17; 24. He also addresses them in numerous other publications and articles unto the time of his death in 2003. His view has come to be known as "Cognitive-Propositionalism." A standard work defending the traditional understanding the Bible in terms of cognitive-propositionalism can be found in the article by J. I. Packer titled, "John Owen on Communication from God," in Packer, *A Quest For Godliness*, 81–96.

9. Henry, *GRA*, 1:17; 24.

10. Ibid. 4:296.

11. Schaeffer, *The God Who Is There*.

12. Henry, *GRA*, 1:17–18.

the Judaizer's view of salvation, or the Patristic Fathers interacting with Roman and Greek philosophy, or the Reformers insistence upon *Sola Scriptura* in opposition to the Roman Catholic synthesis of Scripture and tradition, or the modern rationalistic insistence on the superiority of reason over Scripture, or contemporary reader-response theories; theologians have been attempting to overcome a variety of "hermeneutical problems,"[13] for centuries.[14]

For example, in Henry's chapter titled "Are We Doomed to Hermeneutical Nihilism," he notes,

> For two generations Western Christianity has echoed with reverberations of the 'hermeneutical problem.' Contemporary theologians formulate this problem in various ways that reflect the disagreements of modern theology and require a prejudicial solution. As a consequence, the problem itself is worsened rather than overcome. The term *hermeneutics* derives from the Greek word *hermēneutikos* meaning 'to interpret'; hermeneutics, in other words, is the science of interpretation and explanation. In Christian circles the term has especially signified the understanding and exegesis of the text of Scripture.[15]

From this quote, it is apparent Henry believes epistemology is one of the foundational disciplines affecting hermeneutics.[16] In light of the philosophical influences on hermeneutics, this book will consider the classic evangelical scholar Carl F. H. Henry, and his contribution to religious epistemology and hermeneutics. This book will argue that Henry's epistemology is foundational to his hermeneutic offering present-day evangelicals an epistemologically justified approach to hermeneutics as epistemology and methodology. The following chapter will discuss the

13. The term "hermeneutical problems" in this context refers to any general appeal to hermeneutics during any era of church history (e.g., interpreting the Pentateuch, New Testament use of the Old Testament, relationship between: philosophy and Scripture, Scripture and tradition, reason and revelation, etc.). It is not specifically referring to the epistemological aspect of the "hermeneutical problem" prevalent in modern and contemporary epistemology. The only time it does refer to the "hermeneutical problem" in modern and contemporary epistemology is when it refers to "rationalistic insistence on the superiority of reason over Scripture, or contemporary reader-response theories."

14. Mueller, *The Study of Theology*; Franke, *The Character of Theology*; Wolterstorff, *Divine Discourse*; Kaiser and Silva, *An Introduction to Biblical Hermeneutics*, 257–320.

15. Henry, *GRA*, 4:296.

16. As will be shown in subsequent chapters, Henry also believes language, truth, and so forth are other foundational issues affecting the discipline of hermeneutics.

transition in hermeneutics from a theory of biblical exegesis to the present-day notion(s) of the "hermeneutical problem." It will also address the way(s) hermeneutics as epistemology and methodology has influenced many of the current dialogues in evangelical hermeneutics.[17]

HERMENEUTICS AS EPISTEMOLOGY

In *The Blackwell Guide to Epistemology*, Merold Westphal has a chapter titled, "Hermeneutics as Epistemology."[18] The purpose of Westphal's chapter is to put forth the case that many of the modern and contemporary theories of hermeneutics reflect the general mood and corresponding trends in modern and contemporary epistemology.[19] Westphal claims, "As is clear from the above citations, the three of them [Descartes, Locke, and Kant] contribute toward identifying epistemology with the broad generic task of reflecting on the nature and limits of human knowledge."[20] He believes the Enlightenment project, or to be more precise, epistemological "foundationalism," set the parameters for the discussions in modern and contemporary hermeneutics.[21]

Westphal transitions his discussion from modern epistemology to the idealistic epistemology of postmodernism. In particular, he addresses the influence of Richard Rorty, claiming,

---

17. This book is going to make a distinction in the discipline of hermeneutics. The first distinction will be the notion of "hermeneutics as epistemology." This term attempts to communicate the idea that generally speaking, hermeneutics is a form of epistemology. The second distinction will be the notion of "hermeneutics as methodology." This term attempts to communicate the idea that generally speaking, hermeneutics operates according to certain methodological criteria. For example, narrative theology of the grammatical-historical method of interpretation.

18. Westphal, "Hermeneutics as Epistemology," 415–435.

19. Ibid.

20. Ibid., 415.

21. By the "Enlightenment project," the phrase describes the foundationalist view of knowledge, starting with Rene Descartes. Westphal, in "Hermeneutics as Epistemology," describes "foundationalism" on page 432 fn. 6 as, "By 'foundationalism' I shall always mean the strong variety which requires foundational apodicticity from privileged representations "which cannot be gainsaid." In fn. 9 he says, "For example, in his critique of classical foundationalism, Al Plantinga identifies three types of privileged representations. 'The only properly basic propositions [according to classical foundationalism] are those that are self-evident or incorrigible or evident to the senses.'"

> Over against foundationalist epistemologies of modernity, whose twentieth-century paradigms are to be found in Russell's knowledge by acquaintance and Husserl's intuition of essences, Rorty offers a paradigm shift to an understanding of understanding that he calls hermeneutics. It is holistic, historicist, and pragmatic; it construes truth as conversational agreement, rationality as practical, self-corrective capacity, and intuition as linguistic capacity.[22]

The important concept to consider from Westphal's quote is that many people believe present-day hermeneutics is in some respects a response to foundationalism and aspects of the hermeneutical project is to have an "understanding of understanding." This term "understanding of understanding" refers to an epistemological approach to interpretation in which hermeneutics is no longer confined simply to texts,[23] but it construes all acts of cognition as "interpretation,"[24] and it sides with Westphal's claim that, "*hermeneutics is epistemology*, generally construed."[25]

In the concluding sections of his chapter, Westphal discusses Martin Heidegger, Hans Georg Gadamer, and Jacques Derrida. The overview of these philosophers indicate, generally speaking, as Westphal notes, "... at least initial plausibility to the claim that although they [Heidegger, Gadamer, and Derrida] do not describe themselves as epistemologists, they are addressing some of the same large questions discussed by those who do."[26] However, as the following section of this chapter will illustrate, the discipline of hermeneutics cannot be restricted to the definitions of these particular philosophers (e.g., Heidegger, Gadamer, Derrida, and so forth) and their views of epistemology as hermeneutics (e.g., existential and postmodern views, etc.). Instead, the discipline of hermeneutics reflects the influence of a much broader corpus of philosophers and operant epistemologies (e.g., Kant and Hegel; Agnosticism and Dialecticalism).

22. Ibid., 416.
23. Ibid.
24. Ibid.
25. Ibid.
26. Ibid. Westphal explains, "But hermeneutics, so conceived, is a reflection on the nature and limits of human knowledge; for it is no longer limited to the interpretation of texts but interprets all cognition as interpretation. In terms of the nature of knowledge, it emphasizes the embeddedness of knowledge in historically particular and contingent vocabularies (Rorty calls them 'optional'); in terms of the limits of knowledge, it emphasizes our inability to transcend that embeddedness in order to pure reason or absolute knowledge or rigorous science." Ibid.

Richard Palmer in his book titled, *Hermeneutics*, notes, "As it has evolved in modern times the field of hermeneutics has been defined in at least six fairly distinct ways."[27] Palmer lists six definitions of hermeneutics to explain the history of hermeneutics from a theory of biblical exegesis to the present-day philosophical approaches of interpretation. Palmer's six definitions of hermeneutics in a roughly chronological order are:

> (1) the theory of biblical exegesis; (2) general philological methodology; (3) the science of all linguistic understanding; (4) the methodological foundation of *Geisteswissenschaften*; (5) phenomenology of existence and existential understanding; and (6) the systems of interpretation, both recollective and iconoclastic, used by man to reach the meaning behind myths and symbols. Each of these definitions is more than an historical stage; each points to an important 'moment' or approach to the problems of interpretation. They might be called the biblical, philological, scientific, *geisteswissenschaftliche*, existential, and cultural emphases. Each represents essentially a standpoint from which hermeneutics is viewed; each brings to light the different but legitimate sides of the act of interpretation, especially text interpretation. The very content of hermeneutics itself tends to be reshaped with these changes of standpoint. An outline of these six moments will illustrate this point and serve as a brief historical introduction to the definition of hermeneutics.[28]

Since Palmer's book and his six definitions are one of the key textbooks Henry uses to explain the history of hermeneutics, those same definitions will be used as a paradigm to illustrate how hermeneutics transitioned from a theory of biblical exegesis to the "hermeneutical problem."[29] In addition, this overview will substantiate the idea that generally speaking, hermeneutics is at least a sub-discipline of epistemology.[30] The following section will discuss Palmer's six definitions of hermeneutics according to the following five headings: (1) Theory of Biblical Exegesis; (2) Philological Methodology; (3) Science of Linguistic Understanding; (4)

---

27. Palmer, *Hermeneutics*, 33.
28. Ibid., 33–34.
29. Henry, *GRA*, 4:311ff.

30. It ought to be noted that Henry does not agree with every point made by Palmer; however, he generally agrees with his six definitions of hermeneutics. For that reason, Palmer's book is paradigmatic to the discussion of Henry's hermeneutic as epistemology and methodology.

Geisteswissenschaften-Phenomenology-Existentialism; and (5) Hermeneutics as a System of Interpretation.[31]

Theory of Biblical Exegesis

Palmer's first definition of hermeneutics is titled, "Hermeneutics As Theory of Biblical Exegesis."[32] This first approach to hermeneutics sought to find principles or methods in order for the interpreter to interpret Scripture aright.[33] Palmer claims that the word "hermeneutics" probably came into existence to set forth rules for the proper exegesis of Scripture.[34] He goes on to note,

> While the term 'hermeneutics' itself dates only from the seventeenth century, the operation of textual exegesis and theories of interpretation—religious, literary, legal—date back to antiquity. Thus, once the word is accepted as designating theory of exegesis, the field it covers is generally extended (retroactively, one might say) in biblical exegesis back to Old Testament times, when there were canons for properly interpreting the Torah.[35]

Palmer does not go into extensive detail to explain this point; however, he claims this first definition serves as an example of hermeneutics defined as a "Theory of Biblical Exegesis." He claims,

> Without going into details, it is interesting to note the general tendency of biblical hermeneutics to rely on a 'system' of interpretation out of which individual passages can be interpreted. Even in Protestant hermeneutics, there is the search for a 'hermeneutical principle' which will serve as a referential guide. The text is not interpreted in terms of itself; indeed, this may be an impossible ideal. The scriptural text in the Enlightenment, for instance, is the vessel of great moral truths; yet those truths were found there because an interpretive principle was shaped to find

---

31. It ought to be recognized that in the presentation of Palmer's views, this book is combining his fourth and fifth definitions into one. This is because there is a strong connection between the notion of methodical *Geisteswissenschaften* and the concepts of phenomenology and existentialism.

32. Palmer, *Hermeneutics*, 34–38.

33. Ibid., 34.

34. Ibid.

35. Ibid., 35.

them. In this sense hermeneutics is the interpreters system for finding the 'hidden' meaning of the text.[36]

Palmer's first definition of hermeneutics is important because it illustrates the operant trends and trajectories of early forms of Protestant hermeneutics. In particular, his comments reveal that individuals during this time period, including many of the Protestant Reformers, understood hermeneutics in terms of explicit "theorizing principles" and "rules of exegesis."[37]

In summary, Palmer suggests that hermeneutics first sought to develop principles to help guide biblical interpretation. Whether he is right or not about every point is another question; however, Palmer is correct when he claims that this era of hermeneutics sought to explain hermeneutics according to certain "principles" or "rules of exegesis."[38] Palmer goes on to note that subsequent scholars found the "principle approach" to hermeneutics to be too narrow, and unable to address certain philological problems. Therefore, some scholars developed a "philological" approach to hermeneutics in order to address the linguistic characteristics of both biblical and non-biblical texts.

Philological Methodology

Palmer's second definition of hermeneutics is titled, "Hermeneutics as Philological Methodology."[39] Palmer claims,

> The development of rationalism and, concomitantly with it, the advent of classical philology in the eighteenth century had a profound effect on biblical hermeneutics. There arose the

---

36. Ibid., 36. Note: Not all Protestant's look for the "hidden meaning" of the text. For example *The London Baptist Confession of Faith* from 1689 sections 1.7 and 1.9, serve as counterexamples to Palmer's point.

37. Palmer, *Hermeneutics*, 36.

38. It ought to be noted that not all interpreters during this time period sought to find the "hidden" meaning of the text. Palmer defines hermeneutics as an "understanding of understanding." That being said, he seems to be reading his particular views back into this approach in order to find the underlying epistemological and ontological phenomena to their approach. In short, it seems a bit reductionistic to claim that this era was seeking "hidden meaning," when, in fact, many of the Protestant Reformers intentionally opposed Catholic theories of allegorical interpretation, and hidden meanings. Ramm, *Protestant Biblical Interpretation*, 93–162.

39. Ibid., 38.

historical-critical method in theology; both 'grammatical' and 'historical' schools of biblical interpretation affirmed the interpretive methods applying to the Bible were precisely those for other books.[40]

After illustrating his point by reviewing the "grammatical" and "historical" schools of interpretation,[41] Palmer discusses the influence of epistemology on hermeneutics pointing out that,

> With the rise of rationalism, interpreters felt duty-bound to try to overcome advanced judgments. 'The norm of biblical exegesis,' according to Spinoza, 'can only be the light of reason common to all.' 'The accidental truths of history can never become proofs of the necessary truths of reason,' said Lessing; thus, the challenge for interpretation is to make the Bible relevant to the enlightened rational mind. . . . It is enough here to say simply that the conception of hermeneutics as strictly biblical gradually shaded into hermeneutics as general rules of philological exegesis, with the Bible as one among other possible objects of these rules.[42]

In chapter two titled, "Two forerunners of Schleiermacher," Palmer describes the views of two influential proponents of the philological approach: Friedrich Ast and Friedrich August Wolf.[43] Wolf generally believed interpretation should be a practical discipline; hence, hermeneutics is not just a "collection of rules."[44] However, because the more influential of the two figures is Ast, the following section will expound upon his views in greater detail.[45]

Palmer suggests that Ast's key contribution to hermeneutics is he helped to change the aim of hermeneutics from a "collection of rules" to a "philosophical" and "philological discipline." Palmer claims Ast's project can be summarized in three parts: (1) the 'historical,' that is, understanding in relation to the content of the work, which could be artistic, scientific, or general; (2) the 'grammatical,' that is, understanding in relation to the language; and (3) the '*geistige*,' that is, understanding the work in relation to the total view of the author, and the total view (*Geist*) of the

40. Ibid.
41. Ibid.
42. Ibid., 39–40.
43. Ibid., 75–83.
44. Ibid., 81.
45. Ibid., 75–83.

age.'[46] According to Palmer, Ast's most important, and lasting contribution to hermeneutics is the third part because the role it played in forming Schleiermacher's views on hermeneutics.[47] However, from Palmer's overview it seems like Ast is not offering a purely philological, but both a philological and philosophical approach to hermeneutics. This is because his third part incorporates the role of the author and the *Geist* in hermeneutics.

In summary, Ast and Wolf worked to change the definition of hermeneutics from a principle to a philological and philosophical approach.[48] They were not alone in their efforts because Schleiermacher also encouraged the discipline of hermeneutics to focus on the *psychology* of the interpreter, and the *operations of human understanding* in dialogue known as the "Science of Linguistic Understanding."[49]

Science of Linguistic Understanding

Palmer's third definition is titled, "Hermeneutics as the Science of Linguistic Understanding."[50] The primary figure he addresses in this section is Friedrich Schleiermacher. Schleiermacher's key contribution to hermeneutics is he developed the project of "general hermeneutics," mainly because he desired to emphasize the role of cognition in the act of interpretation.[51] Palmer suggests that Schleiermacher attempted to change the definition of hermeneutics from a principle-philological approach to the "art of understanding the conditions of all understanding

---

46. Ibid., 77.

47. Ibid., 77–78. Palmer notes, "The third level of the hermeneutic of the spirit, seeks out the controlling idea (*Grundidee*, foundational idea), the view of life (*Auschauung*, viewpoint, especially in 'historical' authors), and the basic conception (*Begriff*, especially in philosophical works) which finds expression or embodiment in the work. In the case of seeking the 'view of life,' there is a multiplicity in the unfolding of life; when the 'basic conception' is sought, however, we find the unity of form behind the multiplicity. For Ast, the concept of a controlling idea represents a combination of both the other moments of meaning, but only the greatest authors and artists achieve this full and harmonious synthesis in which conceptual content and view of life stand in balanced complement within the controlling idea." Ibid., 79.

48. Ibid., 82–83.
49. Ibid., 40–41.
50. Ibid., 39–40.
51. Ibid., 84–97.

for all dialogue."[52] He also claims, "The result [of this understanding in all dialogue] is not simply philological hermeneutics but a 'general hermeneutics' (*allgemeine Hermeneutik*) whose principles can serve as the foundation for all kinds of text interpretation."[53] Specifically, Palmer notes that Schleiermacher helped to thrust hermeneutics from a form of naïve ontological and epistemological realism to a type of subjective idealism.[54]

Hans Frei agrees with Palmer, claiming, "All commentators are agreed that biblical hermeneutics underwent a sea of change in the early nineteenth century. The transformation was, of course, the result of the romantic and idealist revolution that was sweeping philosophy and historical study as well arts and criticism."[55] According to Frei, Schleiermacher is the figure head pioneering this idealist revolution in hermeneutics.[56] He influenced hermeneutics by synthesizing the discipline with the new developments in German thought such as Kant's agnosticism and Moravian pietism. Schleiermacher's work also signals a new trajectory and definition of hermeneutics by transitioning it away from former principle-philological approaches to a robust philosophical approach (both ontology and epistemology included).

Frei addresses this definitional transition, suggesting, "But once one notes the change in the meaning of the term hermeneutics, from determination of the rules and principles of interpreting texts to inquiry into the nature of understanding discourse and what is manifest in it, the dearth of titles is not really significant or surprising."[57] Schleiermacher is a pivotal figure in the history of hermeneutics because he more than any other individual brought interpretation into the era of "general hermeneutics." Palmer summarizes Schleiermacher's concept of "general hermeneutics," noting,

> This conception of general hermeneutics marks the beginning of the nondisciplinary 'hermeneutics' so significant to the present discussion. For the first time hermeneutics defines itself as the study of understanding itself. It might almost be said that

---

52. Ibid., 85.
53. Ibid.
54. Ibid., 91–97.
55. Frei, *The Eclipse of the Biblical Narrative*, 282.
56. Ibid., 243, 287–306.
57. Ibid., 282.

hermeneutics proper here emerges historically from the parentage in biblical exegesis and classical philology.[58]

The question that naturally arises at this point is: Why did these changes take place in hermeneutics?[59] While an assortment of historical, social, and political answers could be offered to answer this question; the following section will answer the question by focusing on the role epistemology played in the development of "general hermeneutics."

Noted philosopher of hermeneutics, Jean Grondin, in his book titled, *Introduction to Philosophical Hermeneutics*, helps to explain the epistemological transition in hermeneutics from pre-critical interpretation to the Romantic era and Friedrich Schleiermacher.[60] He does this by addressing the influence of epistemology on the discipline of hermeneutics from the Enlightenment period through Kant, up to the post-Kantian era. Grondin goes on to highlight the underlying philosophical changes during these periods, claiming, "The fundamental presupposition of Rationalism was that the human mind, though finite, could by means of thought come to penetrate the logical, and regular construction of the world. Thinking was guided by the principle of reason (*nihil est sine ratione*) that is inscribed in our mind."[61] So far, Grondin seems to be reiterating what Palmer and Frei have already said about modern philosophy and hermeneutics; however, he goes beyond their claims by noting the *way* Kant's philosophy revolutionized the discipline of hermeneutics.[62]

For example, according to Grondin, Kant's epistemology is the *sine qua non*[63] for explaining the revolution in hermeneutics, pointing out that,

> Because the Satz vom Grund [Principle of Reason] stems from *our* reason, Kant concludes that the order it produces or discovers is valid only for the world of phenomena, things as they appear to us and framed by us. Thus the world of things in themselves disappears into pure unintelligibility.[64]

58. Palmer, *Hermeneutics*, 40.
59. Ibid.
60. Grondin, *Introduction to Philosophical Hermeneutics*.
61. Ibid., 64.
62. Ibid.
63. According to the *Dictionary of Ecclesiastical Latin*, the phrase *sine qua non* means, "Without which there is nothing, an essential." Stelten, *Dictionary of Ecclesiastical Latin*, 248.
64. Grondin, *Introduction to Philosophical Hermeneutics*, 64.

Consequently, Grondin believes Kant's critical philosophy, in which he distinguishes between phenomena and things-in-themselves, is a fundamental epistemological premise of Romanticism and Schleiermacher's theory of "general hermeneutics."[65] This is because Schleiermacher incorporates the paradigm of Kant's critical philosophy into his theory of "general hermeneutics."[66]

William F. Lawhead in his book titled, *The Voyage of Discovery*, discusses the innovations of Kant's critical philosophy claiming,

> In opposition to 'dogmatic philosophy' that preceded him, Kant referred to his own thought as 'critical philosophy.' Accordingly, his major work took the form of three critiques. His most important work, dealing with epistemology and metaphysics, was the *Critique of Pure Reason*. By calling his approach 'critical philosophy,' Kant was not calling for a mean-spirited, negative attitude in philosophy that rejects everything. On the contrary, the word *critique* comes from a Greek word that means 'to sort' or 'to sift out.' Thus, Kant's goal was to set out the legitimate claims of reason and filter out all groundless claims.[67]

The significance this observation has for the history of hermeneutics is subsequent philosophers and theologians felt they had to wrestle with the innovations of Kantian epistemology. As a result, Schleiermacher was compelled to synthesize Kantian epistemology and his hermeneutic; thus, creating his theory of "general hermeneutics."[68] It was against this Kantian framework Schleiermacher attempted to answer the question, "What does it mean to understand?" Consequently, this is one of the epistemological situations that gave rise to Schleiermacher's version of the "hermeneutical circle."[69]

---

65. Ibid.

66. Kant's critical philosophy insists that all of reality is filtered and structured by the categories of the mind; hence, reality is not known directly. (See also Körner, *Kant*; Caygill, *A Kant Dictionary*, 384–385). Kant labels his new approach as "critical philosophy," because he claims that humanity can only have a "filtered" knowledge of reality. See Lawhead, *The Voyage of Discovery: A Historical Introduction to Philosophy*, 334.

67. Ibid., 327.

68. See Palmer, *Hermeneutics*, 40–41; Grondin, *Introduction to Philosophical Hermeneutics*, 67–71.

69. Anthony C. Thiselton in the *Dictionary for Theological Interpretation of the Bible*, helps to explain that the "hermeneutical circle," sometimes synonymous with spiral, ". . . has two separable but closely related meanings. One concerns the relation between the 'parts' of the text and understanding of it as a 'whole.' A circle arises

According to Palmer, Schleiermacher posits many levels at which the "hermeneutical circle" operates in order to understand the dialogical relationship between the speaker, the reader, and their given communities.[70] In order to explain these various levels, Palmer includes sections on the conversational, dialogical, and linguistic levels of the hermeneutical circle. However, for the purposes of this project, since Schleiermacher's grammatical and psychological aspects of the hermeneutical circle are the most important for understanding his hermeneutic; only the grammatical and psychological levels will be explained.[71]

Schleiermacher's first type or level of the hermeneutical circle is the "grammatical" moment in interpretation. The second is the "psychological" or "technical" moment directed toward understanding the discourse as a product of a thinking being.[72] Frei notes, "The 'grammatical' moment in interpretation is directed toward understanding the discourse as a focus within a language as a whole, characterized by its relation to the total linguistic stock."[73] This grammatical process is simply the act of coming to know the individual parts of the text in light of the whole, then

---

because each process depends reciprocally upon the other. . . . These two processes together form a progressive dialectic. Hence, a 'spiral' might be less misleading than 'circle.'" Thiselton goes onto say, "A second version of this principle traces a parallel dialectic between the two poles of a 'preliminary' understanding or (reflecting the German) of *preunderstanding* (*Vorverständnis*), and a fuller understanding (*Verstehen*), for which this beginning can pave the way." Finally, ". . . this process does not stop here. The fuller (or more accurate) understanding 'speaks back' to the preunderstanding to correct and reshape it. This revision contributes to a better understanding. Hence, to reread a 'difficult' book, or even to undertake successive readings, may bring about a deeper understanding of it." See Thiselton, "Hermeneutical Spiral," 281.

70. Ibid.

71. Ibid., 88–90. A third type could be the conversational. Anthony Thiselton lists a fourth type of hermeneutical spiral in Schleiermacher's work. It is a subset of the psychological, and dialogical. Thiselton suggests Schleiermacher appropriates both the grammatical and psychological forms of the hermeneutical circle, with philosophers of hermeneutics labeling this aspect of his work as the "comparative pole." Another pole or axis incorporated by Schleiermacher is the "divinatory." Thiselton quotes Schleiermacher saying, "'The divinatory (*divinatorische*) method seeks to gain an immediate comprehension of the author as an individual.' 'Divinatory knowledge' is the *feminine* strength in knowing people; comparative knowledge, the *masculine*." Thiselton uses Schleiermacher's book, *The Celebration of Christmas*, to illustrate this axis, claiming, "After the Christmas service, the women of the household sing hymns to Jesus, while the men debate the conceptual difficulties of the incarnation." Thiselton, "Hermeneutics," 285.

72. Frei, *The Eclipse of Biblical Narrative*, 292.

73. Ibid.

to understand the whole in light of the parts. It is characterized by an inductive method of interpretation. By incorporating an inductive method, Schleiermacher's project does not signify anything new in the discipline of hermeneutics; however, the psychological aspect or level does signify a new direction in the field of hermeneutics.

Frei goes on to say, "The 'psychological' or 'technical' moment is directed toward understanding the discourse 'as a fact in the thinker.'"[74] Schleiermacher maintains that in order to interpret any piece of literature, one must understand both the text and the author.[75] Frei explains *how* this process operates in Schleiermacher's hermeneutic. He writes,

> The unitary act of understanding [in Schleiermacher's hermeneutic], composed of both aspects, is more nearly an artistic than a systematic scientific act because there is no further method or precise prescription for the way these two moments are united: a certain 'oscillation' between them has to be involved. Similarly, of course, there is no further statement concerning the unity of language and thought in the speaker. They are constituted into a unity by himself in such a way that he himself is each moment and also the unity of both; there is no further stable factor or aspect of him that binds to two together. Unity of discourse and unity of understanding correspond: each involves something like a unity-in-duality, and hence the understanding's unitary grasp of the unity of the content is something like an artistic act. Moreover, interpretation is artistic rather than scientific because it involves, in regard to the discourse both as a sample of the universal and as an individual act, an infinite or indefinite approximation; understanding can therefore never be complete. Summarizing both the complex and approximate nature of the unitary act of understanding, Schleiermacher says: 'If the grammatical aspect were to be completed for itself alone, there would have to be a complete knowledge of the language, and in the other case [the technical] a complete knowledge of the person. Since both can never be given, one must always pass from the one to the other; and for the way to do this there can be no rules.'[76]

---

74. Ibid. Note, the final section of this block quote is Schleiermacher in his own words discussing the different levels of hermeneutics. In particular, he distinguishes between the grammatical and the psychological aspects of interpretation.

75. Ibid.

76. Ibid.

Frei acknowledges that Schleiermacher intentionally differentiates himself from earlier hermeneutical approaches, such as "principle approaches," because he believes they have misunderstood hermeneutics according to "axioms" or "rules" that serve to guide and determine the meaning of a text.[77] Consequently, Schleiermacher claims that interpretation requires knowledge of both the "author" and the "text." He also claims this "knowledge event" between the author and the text is a never complete and unending "dialectical process." Finally, Schleiermacher believes this "dialectical process" entails that an interpreter only has "approximate knowledge," never "perfect" or "complete" knowledge of reality or any text.[78]

In summary, both Frei and Palmer suggest that Schleiermacher's most influential contributions to the discipline of hermeneutics are: (1) His notion of "general hermeneutics" (also known as the "Science of Linguistic Understanding"); and (2) His incorporation of the dialectical method into subsequent theories of interpretation.[79] Frei and Palmer's observations are important because they illustrate *how* hermeneutics has been influenced by new trajectories in modern epistemology. In particular, Schleiermacher's synthesis of Kantian epistemology and the dialectical method into a "general hermeneutic" and "hermeneutical circle," are the starting points for those individuals found in Palmer's fourth and fifth definitions of hermeneutics.

Geisteswissenschaften-Phenomenology-Existentialism

Palmer's fourth and fifth definitions of hermeneutics are titled, "The Methodological Foundation of *Geisteswissenschaften*" and "Phenomenology of Existence and Existential Understanding."[80] These two definitions are

---

77. Ibid.

78. Ibid. Schleiermacher also taught there is no such thing as a perfect correspondence between the written text and the mind of the author. The implication of this denial of correspondence in his work is an interpreter is no longer claim to know the mind of the author solely from the text, nor can they claim to the text apart from the mind of the author. Both the text and the mind of the author are required for interpretation; however, each of these two poles cannot be fully known. This dialectical process between the text, author, and reader, creates the so-called "circle" in Schleiermacher and subsequent philosophers of hermeneutics.

79. Ibid., 282–306.

80. Palmer, *Hermeneutics*, 33.

18 HERMENEUTICS AS EPISTEMOLOGY

combined because of the philosophical similarities between *Geisteswissenschaften*, German Phenomenology, and Existentialism.[81] According to Palmer's fourth definition, the notion of *Geisteswissenschaften* refers to ". . . all disciplines focused on understanding man's art, actions, and writings."[82] *Geisteswissenschaften* attempts to incorporate Schleiermacher's psychological aspects of interpretation into a general "humanistic" hermeneutical methodology.[83] Palmer believes one of the pivotal philosophers of hermeneutics, who stood upon the shoulders of Schleiermacher and worked to develop hermeneutics into a "human science" by focusing on the nature of "historical understanding," is Wilhelm Dilthey.[84]

According to Thiselton, Dilthey desired to incorporate hermeneutics as a type of "human science;" consequently, placing hermeneutics on the same playing field as the other so-called social sciences.[85] Palmer summarizes the influence of Dilthey's project and the notion of "historical understanding," claiming,

> To interpret a great expression of human life, whether it be a law, literary work, or sacred scripture, calls for an act of historical understanding, Dilthey asserted, an operation fundamentally distinct from the quantifying, scientific grasp of the natural world; for in this act of historical understanding, what is called into play is a personal knowledge of what being human means. What was needed in the human sciences, he believed was another 'critique' of reason that would do for the historical understanding what Kant's critique of pure reason had done for the natural science—a 'critique of historical reason.'[86]

In summary, according to Palmer, Dilthey's most enduring contribution to the human sciences is his emphasis on the notion of "historical understanding."[87] Palmer suggests that Dilthey not only pioneered a new

81. Ibid., 33. This section corresponds with Daniel Treier's section titled, "After Schleiermacher," Daniel Treier claims, "Despite disagreements, Schleiermacher set the paradigmatic terms for decades—particularly in the German university, where hermeneutics became a way of rejuvenating the humanities, relative to the natural sciences, as sources for knowledge." Trier, "Scripture as Communication," 75.

82. Palmer, *Hermeneutics*, 41.

83. Ibid.

84. Ibid.

85. Thiselton, *Hermeneutics*, 285.

86. Palmer, *Hermeneutics*, 41.

87. The personal aspects of knowledge such as one's place in history make up their "historical understanding." The term "historical understanding" is being used to

definition of hermeneutics;[88] he also strove to emphasize the "historical interpretation" of the interpreter and all "historical understanding" of any text, the biblical text included.[89]

Palmer's fifth definition focuses on "Hermeneutics as the Phenomenology of *Dasein* and of Existential Understanding."[90] He alludes to Martin Heidegger's book, *Being and Time*, where Heidegger attempts to use Edmund Husserl's phenomenological method to study the nature of humanity's *being* [ontology] in the world. According to Palmer, in *Being and Time*, Heidegger presents a "hermeneutic of *Dasein*."[91] This innovative ontological approach radicalizes the historical situatedness or "historicality" (*Geschichtlichkeit*) of the interpreter. Thiselton explains the "hermeneutics of *Dasein*," claiming, "He [Heidegger] used the term 'being-there' (*Dasein*) in contrast to Being (*Sein*), viewing *Dasein* as 'thrown' into a *pregiven* 'world,' which bounded its horizons of meaning."[92] For Heidegger, the temporal nature of the world (the physical and ontological world included), determines the various "possibilities" of human understanding. The effect of this new "ontological approach," is hermeneutics must now accept the premise that all *being* and human *understanding* is conditioned and grounded in fore-conception, and it is never without presuppositions.[93]

For Heidegger and other existentialists, this innovative metaphysical approach to knowledge entails that all interpretation is *ontologically subjective* and all pursuits towards objectivity are futile.[94] Lawhead helps to explain the subjective tenets of existentialism, claiming, "[Existentialism] . . . focuses on the nature of human existence as understood from the subjective standpoint of the subject. Repudiating the notion of a fixed human nature, existentialists claim that we are continually creating the self."[95] This is because according to existentialism, "existence *precedes*

---

emphasize the effects one's place in history has on their overall interpretation of texts and events.

88. Ibid.
89. Thiselton, *Hermeneutics*, 313–343.
90. Palmer, *Hermeneutics*, 41.
91. Ibid., 42.
92. Thiselton, *Hermeneutics*, 285.
93. Ibid.
94. Ibid.
95. Lawhead, *The Voyage of Discovery*, 574.

essence."[96] Lawhead goes on to explain this principle (e.g., that existence precedes essence), claiming, "They [existentialists such as Heidegger] stress the priority of subjective choosing over objective reasoning, concrete experience over intellectual abstractions, individuality over mass culture, human freedom over determinism, and authentic living over inauthentic living."[97] In brief, according to existentialism, an individual might exist prior to subjective actions; however, the totality of those actions collectively and subjectively determine that particular individual's essence and mode of existence.

Palmer suggests that existentialism and its insistence on the ontological ramifications of *Dasein*, affect the discipline of hermeneutics by stressing the priority of the subjective over the objective. He writes,

> So Heidegger's 'hermeneutic' of *Dasein* turns out, especially insofar as it presents an ontology of understanding, also to be hermeneutics; his investigation was hermeneutical in content as well as method. . . . At one stroke hermeneutics is connected with the ontological dimensions of understanding (and all that this implies) and at the same time is identified with Heidegger's special kind of phenomenology.[98]

Here Palmer claims that Heidegger's innovations in metaphysics and hermeneutics synthesizes the discipline of hermeneutics with existential philosophy.[99] In particular, Heidegger's hermeneutic focuses upon the notions of "understanding" and "interpretation" viewed as modes of "humanity's very existence."[100] Another key feature of Heidegger's innovative metaphysic is it creates a new kind of "hermeneutical circle," that emphasizes the subjective *ontological* aspects of humanity (e.g., each of the individual actions that make up the totality of someone's essence).[101]

---

96. The *Oxford Dictionary of Philosophy* defines "existence precedes essence" as, "The central slogan of existentialism, indicating that a person has no predetermined nature or range of choices, but is always free to choose afresh, and thereby reconstitute himself or herself as a different person." Blackburn, *Oxford Dictionary of Philosophy*, 129. The dictionary goes on to define existentialism as, "A loose title for various philosophies that emphasize certain common themes: the individual, the experience of choice, and the absence of rational understanding of the universe with a consequent dread or sense of absurdity of human life." Ibid.

97. Lawhead, *The Voyage of Discovery*, 574.

98. Palmer, *Hermeneutics*, 42.

99. Ibid.

100. Ibid.

101. Trier, "Scripture as Communication," 76.

Westphal believes Heidegger's ontological account of the hermeneutical circle is more extreme than Kant's; however, it should not be considered a vicious circle.[102] The term "vicious circle" typically refers to a type of faulty logical argument. In this context, however, it refers to the idea that all interpretation is futile or pointless.[103] Westphal goes on to suggest that ". . . [Heidegger] is simply abandoning the Euclidian, syllogistic models of knowledge (194–5/152–3). Rather, we are to see in the circle 'a positive possibility of the most primordial kind of knowing (195/153)."[104] Furthermore,

> . . . Heidegger thinks the deepest levels of preunderstanding do not consist of knowledge or belief or representation. For this reason his account of the hermeneutical circle in terms of fore-having, fore-sight, and fore-conception 'includes, but goes beyond, the insight of theoretical holism that all data are already theory laden.' He signals this by presenting knowing as a 'founded mode' of being-in-the-world . . . If knowing is 'founded' and assertion is 'derivative,' theoretical cognition has precognitive presuppositions that can nevertheless be called understanding and interpretation.[105]

---

102. Westphal, *Hermeneutics as Epistemology*, 418. Schleiermacher's version of the hermeneutical circle seems to have been grounded in Hegel, whereas Westphal believes that Heidegger's view is grounded in Kant's theory of knowledge. For Heidegger, all understanding, including intuition and thinking, are derivatives from the *a priori* categories of thought. This notion of the *a priori* categories is an essential part of Kant's epistemology. By adopting Kant's epistemology, Heidegger suggested that understanding must be understood in light of "pre" understanding, because all understanding is derived from a priori categories of thought. Westphal goes on to say, for Heidegger, preunderstanding must be understood in terms of fore-having, fore-sight, and fore-conception (*Vohabe, Vorsicht*, and *Vorgriff*). Westphal concludes his point by quoting Heidegger, who claimed, "Interpretation is never a presuppositionless grasping of something previously given . . . . Any interpretation which is to contribute understanding, must already have understood what is to be interpreted." Ibid., 418. Unlike Kant, who gave the forms and categories a fixed and final character, Heidegger makes it clear that the forms and categories no longer have that fixed status and are no longer simply given. Ibid., 418–419. This new status to the categories affects the discipline of hermeneutics because not only does all interpretation necessitate presuppositions, but those presuppositions are now constantly in flux. For that reason, there can only be changing and subjective interpretations. The search for objectivity ought to be considered a useless quest.

103. At times, the literature in hermeneutics does not distinguish between the hermeneutical spiral and circle. In this context, they are synonymous.

104. Ibid., 419.

105. Ibid.

Grondin elaborates on Heidegger's ontological hermeneutical circle, claiming,

> [For Heidegger] [t]he fore-structure of understanding is the philosophical description of the pre-predicative level of existence. This is consonant with the fundamental effort of hermeneutics to reach what is be-fore (or better, in and behind) statements—in brief, the mind and the soul that expresses itself in the word.[106]

In summary, within Heidegger's ontological hermeneutic, *Dasein* is an ontological approach to understanding; whereby, existential metaphysics grounds his version of the hermeneutical circle.[107] For example, existential metaphysics affect Heidegger's hermeneutic by making the nature of language dependent upon pre-linguistic (e.g., ontological) interpretation.[108] In his later works, Heidegger modified some of his theses, even dropping the term "hermeneutics," however, the ideas developed in his earlier works influenced later philosophers of hermeneutics, such as Hans Georg Gadamer.[109]

Following the lead of Heidegger, Gadamer interacts with existential philosophy in his book, *Wahrheit und Methode* [Truth and Method].[110] In *Truth and Method*, Gadamer presented a systematic overview of the developments in hermeneutics, providing an historical account of Heidegger's contribution to the field of hermeneutics.[111] Palmer claims,

> But *Wahrheit und Methode* is more than a history of hermeneutics; it is an effort to relate hermeneutics to aesthetics and to the philosophy of historical understanding. . . . Hermeneutics is carried one step further still, into the 'linguistic phase, with Gadamer's controversial assertion that 'Being that can be understood is language.'[112]

Palmer suggests that Gadamer's approach to hermeneutics recognizes different historically situated "horizons of understanding."[113] According to

---

106. Grondin, *Introduction to Philosophical Hermeneutics*, 94.
107. Ibid.
108. Westphal, *Hermeneutics as Epistemology*, 420.
109. Thiselton, *Hermeneutics*, 313–321.
110. Ibid.
111. Westphal, *Hermeneutics as Epistemology*, 420.
112. Palmer, *Hermeneutics*, 42.
113. Ibid.

Gadamer, reading a text requires an appropriate dialogical conversation with the text, in which there is a negotiation between what the text says and the way a reader responds or answers the text.[114] He labels this process as the "fusion of horizon."[115] Gadamer claims,

> Projecting a historical horizon, then, is only one phase in the process of understanding; it does not become solidified into the self-alienation of a past consciousness, but it is overtaken by our own present horizon of understanding. In the process of understanding, a real fusion of horizons occurs—which means that as the historical horizon is projected, it is simultaneously superseded. To bring about this fusion in a regulated way is the task of what we called historically effected consciousness. Although this task was obscured by aesthetic-historical positivism following on the heels of romantic hermeneutics, it is, in fact, the central problem of hermeneutics. It is the problem of *application*, which is to be found in all understanding.[116]

Treier summarizes Gadamer's "fusion of horizon" approach, claiming, "A 'fusion of horizon' results: overlap between what the text addresses and what the reader seeks in an existential situation. Again, the text has its say, while a dimension of understanding remains relative to the later context."[117] Research indicates that Gadamer's approach to hermeneutics mirrors aspects of the "hermeneutical circle" in Kant, Schleiermacher, and Heidegger's approaches because of its dialectical and dialogical nature; however, he goes beyond these philosophers by insisting on the role of application, which is central to all understanding and historical consciousness (e.g., fusion of horizon).[118]

Anthony Thiselton in his book, *New Horizons in Hermeneutics*, however, observes that post-Gadamarian theories do not always agree with Gadamer's historical-situatedness approach.[119] In particular, he notes that E. D. Hirsch warned "... about the radical consequences of too readily surrendering humanist paradigms without remainder in exchange for post-modernist assumptions to be noted. In the case of certain *kinds*

---

114. Gadamer, *Truth and Method*. See also: Treier, "Scripture and Communication," 76.

115. Ibid.

116. Gadamer, *Truth and Method*, 306–307.

117. Treier, *"Scripture and Communication,"* 77.

118. Gadamer, *Truth and Method*, 306–307.

119. Thiselton, *New Horizons in Hermeneutics*, 10–16.

of texts many but not all of his arguments can be sustained."[120] Thiselton points out another critique of Gadamer's hermeneutic, claiming it,

> ... also provides a starting-point for a third possible direction of development. Habermas and Apel criticize Gadamer for insufficient sensitivity towards the socio-ethical implications of hermeneutics. Habermas and Apel argue that *given social interests* and not merely bare, finite contextual contingencies, lie behind different actualizations of texts or of truth.[121]

Evidently Thiselton believes it is apparent that instead of establishing more unity around the notion of "historical understanding;" post-Gadamarian's show signs of disunity in the way they approach the various facets of "human understanding."[122] With these signs of disunity in place, while retaining some of the same terms (e.g., "human understanding" and "historical understanding"), post-Gadamerian hermeneutics cannot be considered a monolithic movement.[123]

In summary, the works of Heidegger and Gadamer set the stage for a renaissance in philosophical hermeneutics by incorporating existential metaphysics and epistemology into the discipline. Palmer believes Heidegger and Gadamer develop a paradigm of thinking by which ". . . [h]ermeneutics is put in the center of the philosophical problems of today; it cannot escape the epistemological or the ontological questions when understanding itself is defined as an epistemological and ontological matter."[124] In these respects, Heidegger and Gadamer's projects represent the height of existential philosophical hermeneutics and their works also help to set the stage for the rise of 20th century post-modern hermeneutics.[125] Palmer defines this era in hermeneutics as, "Hermeneutics as a System of Interpretation: Meaning *versus* Iconoclasm."[126]

---

120. Ibid., 13.

121. Ibid., 12.

122. According to Thiselton, "A further distinctive feature of post-Gadamarian hermeneutics emerges from the increasing attention which has been given to psychoanalytic models in formulating what Ricoeur and others term 'a hermeneutic of suspicion.'" Ibid., 13–14. Ricoeur's view claims that both language and the human mind are not transparent or straightforward. Ibid., 14. Instead, both language and the mind are always affected by social and psychological conditioning that affect understanding.

123. Ibid.

124. Palmer, *Hermeneutics*, 43.

125. Caputo, *Radical Hermeneutics*.

126. Palmer, *Hermeneutics*, 43.

Hermeneutics as a System of Interpretation

Palmer's sixth definition is titled, "Hermeneutics as a System of Interpretation: Recovery of Meaning *versus* Iconoclasm."[127] This final system focuses on the relationship between understanding and language. It pays special attention to the nature of propositions, the role of symbols, and the place of figurative language. The central figure of this movement is Paul Ricoeur, who according to Thiselton, ". . . is the most creative hermeneutical theorist of our time."[128] Preeminent Ricoeur scholar, Kevin Vanhoozer, claims,

> He [Ricoeur] mediates between disciplines as diverse as psychology, social theory, history, literary theory, and religious studies—by demonstrating previously unseen connections, formal and material, between them—and he mediates between diverse interpretative approaches by finding a place for each in his hermeneutical arch, which spans explanation and understanding.[129]

Ricoeur's project recovers the power of creative language in metaphor and narrative in order to develop a hermeneutic that is existentially deep.[130] Treier notes that, "Ricoeur speaks of a threefold hermeneutical arc [which seems to have many similar features of the hermeneutical spiral]: an initial moment of *understanding* (a first, naïve encounter with the text), a critical moment of *explanation*, and then a refigured moment of *application* (a 'second naiveté')."[131] Vanhoozer summarizes the "initial encounter" as the "Hermeneutic Philosopher of the 'I Am.'"[132]

This first movement is a philosophical form of anthropology looking to achieve "self-understanding" through "semantics and textual interpretation."[133] Vanhoozer claims, "Ricoeur's fundamental conviction that language discloses human being leads him to engage the so-called 'masters of suspicion' (e.g., Freud, Marx, Nietzsche), who argued that

---

127. Ibid.
128. Thiselton, *Hermeneutics*, 287.
129. Vanhoozer, "Ricoeur, Paul," 692.
130. Ibid.
131. Treier, *Scripture and Communication*, 77.
132. Vanhoozer, *Ricoeur*, 692.
133. Ibid.

language conceals as much if not more than it reveals."¹³⁴ Vanhoozer notes, "Ricoeur similarly incorporates Nietzsche's and Feuerbach's accusation that talk of 'God' is simply a projection of the human will to power."¹³⁵ Finally, Vanhoozer observes, "Ricoeur transcends the historical-critical preoccupation with 'the world behind the text.' He does this by bringing a variety of literary approaches to bear on Scripture's diverse genres ('the world of the text') and by focusing on the way in which the text engages and transforms the situation of the reader ('the world in front of the text')."¹³⁶

Vanhoozer also addresses Ricoeur's second movement titled, "The Second Naïveté: Appropriating the World of the Text."¹³⁷ He notes that,

> Ricoeur describes his position as a 'post-Hegelian Kantianism.' With Kant, Ricoeur carefully respects the limits of reason; with Hegel, he reexplores reason's many forms, both figurative and conceptual (e.g., of history, poetry, culture, and religion). Against Hegel; however, Ricoeur refuses to let conceptual language swallow up figurative language.¹³⁸

Furthermore, Vanhoozer suggests,

> Ricoeur challenges Heidegger's decision to take anxiety as the fundamental 'mood' of human being, arguing that joy and hope have equal claim to be regarded as the basic clue to the meaning of humanity. . . . Like Kant, who claimed to have abolished knowledge in order to make room for faith, Ricoeur abolishes the first naïveté, a faith in what the text literally says. He does this to make room for a second naïveté: 'To smash the idols is also to let the symbols speak.'¹³⁹

Palmer explains the second naïveté, claiming that for Ricoeur, "Hermeneutics is the process of deciphering which goes from manifest content and meaning to latent or hidden meaning. The object of interpretation, i.e., the text in the very broadest sense, may be the symbols in a dream or even the myths and symbols of society or literature."¹⁴⁰ Ricoeur's second

---

134. Ibid.
135. Ibid., 692–693.
136. Ibid., 693.
137. Ibid., 693.
138. Ibid., 694.
139. Ibid., 693.
140. Palmer, *Hermeneutics*, 43.

naïveté makes a distinction between univocal and equivocal symbols focusing on the equivocal meaning of symbols. Palmer explains how Ricoeur views symbols. He writes, "For hermeneutics [according to Ricoeur] has to do with symbolic texts which have multiple meanings; they may constitute a semantic unity which has (as in myths) a fully coherent surface meaning and at the same time a deeper significance."[141]

In summary, according to Ricoeur, hermeneutics seeks to find this "deeper significance" beneath univocal symbols, such as the "literal meaning of the text." Ricoeur's process creates a "hermeneutics of suspicion," for no longer are there any universal canons of interpretation.[142] Thiselton notes, "In effect, he [Ricoeur] recognizes certain insights of postmodern thought, including a hermeneutic of suspicion, but resists evaporating human selfhood into mere semiotic performances."[143] Therefore, the purpose of metaphors and the second naïveté is not to see that which is literally true, but to open up new ways of seeing the "real."[144] Once a person suspends the first naïveté, he is liberated to the new existential possibilities of the second naïveté.[145]

This overview of the history of hermeneutics presents some of the key points to substantiate Palmer's claim that hermeneutics has transitioned from a "Theory of Biblical Exegesis" to a "Philosophical Discipline." Each definition represents a different time period where philosophy affected hermeneutics; however, this overview would be incomplete without allowing Palmer to explain the "hermeneutical problem." Palmer's definition resembles many other standard definitions of the "hermeneutical problem," and for that reason, it will be used to summarize the notion of

---

141. Ibid.

142. Thiselton claims, "A further distinctive of post-Gadamerian hermeneutics emerges from an increasing attention which has been given to psycho-analytic models in formulating what Ricoeur and others term 'a hermeneutic of suspicion'. Neither language nor the human mind is transparent or straightforward. In terms of their world-view, it may be tempting for Christian thinkers to dismiss the works of the three so-called masters of suspicion, Freud, Marx, and Nietzsche, as incompatible with the claims of Christian theology. But their insistence that the human mind can deceive itself in a varieties of ways, often in the interest of individual or of social power, resonates with biblical and theological assertions about the deceitfulness, opaqueness, and duplicity of the human heart." Thiselton, *Hermeneutics*, 13–14.

143. Ibid., 287.

144. Ibid.

145. Vanhoozer, *Ricoeur*, 693.

the "hermeneutical problem" and how it affects present-day theories of hermeneutics as epistemology and methodology.[146]

Palmer's Definition of the Hermeneutical Problem

Palmer begins his discussion on the "hermeneutical problem" suggesting, "The historical development of hermeneutics as an independent field seems to hold within itself two separate foci: one on the theory of understanding in a general sense, and the other on what is involved in the exegesis of linguistic texts, the hermeneutical problem."[147] He does not believe these two foci cancel each other out neither are they absolutely independent; instead, they serve to instruct one another.[148] Palmer goes on to note,

> Hermeneutics is true to its great past in Schleiermacher and Dilthey when it takes its bearing from a general theory of linguistic understanding. It must be willing to think through the nature of understanding and in the broadest possible terms ask: What is understanding? What happens when I say, 'I understand.'[149]

Palmer believes hermeneutics cannot return to naïve pre-critical theories.[150] He insists that interpreters must engage with the developments in philosophical hermeneutics in order to approach all texts in the appropriate manner. Palmer seems to suggests that hermeneutics incorporate a phenomenological approach to interpretation.[151]

Palmer goes on to explain and define the "hermeneutical problem," claiming that,

> ... it [the hermeneutical problem] is a specific instance of the event of understanding: it [the hermeneutical problem] always involves language, the confronting of another human horizon, an act of historical penetration of the text. Hermeneutics needs to go ever more deeply into this complex act of understanding; it must struggle to formulate a theory of linguistic and historical understanding as it functions in text interpretation. Such a

---

146. Gadamer, *Truth and Method*, 376–377.
147. Palmer, *Hermeneutics*, 67.
148. Ibid.
149. Ibid., 68.
150. Ibid.
151. Ibid.

theory must be harmonized with and related to a general phenomenology of understanding; at the same time, it will itself contribute to such a general field.[152]

Palmer notes his definition is a ". . . broad interpretation of the hermeneutical problem."[153] He recognizes that depending on whom one interacts with the "hermeneutical problem" can be more than his definition (e.g., ontological, epistemological, or both); however, Palmer favors his broad definition because he believes it highlights best what philosophers of hermeneutics mean when they communicate the notion of an "event of understanding."[154]

With this overview of Palmer's definitions of hermeneutics in place, the following sections of this chapter will attempt to relate these hermeneutical situations to some of the present-day issues in evangelical hermeneutics by: (1) Investigating some of the ways current dialogues in evangelical hermeneutics have been influenced by the notion of hermeneutics as epistemology; and (2) Note some of the ways hermeneutics as epistemology have affected present-day evangelical hermeneutics.

CURRENT DIALOGUES IN HERMENEUTICS

According to Palmer's overview, it is apparent that reactions to premodern hermeneutics gave way to modern hermeneutics, developing into "general hermeneutics" and varying degrees of philosophical and theological approaches to hermeneutics. In the 19th and 20th centuries, there were dogmatic responses by the Princeton school of interpretation, as represented by A. A. Hodge, Charles Hodge, and B. B. Warfield.[155] Existential or neo-orthodox responses came from individuals such as Karl Barth and Emil Brunner. The existential approach was incorporated into

152. Ibid.
153. Ibid.
154. Palmer opposes E. D. Hirsch's view of the hermeneutical problem because Hirsch seeks to find objective and universal criteria of validation. Palmer suggests, "The view of the hermeneutical problem presented by Hirsch would leave aside the moment of understanding itself and focus on the need to judge among server understandings; hermeneutics then becomes not a phenomenology of understanding but a logic of validation." Ibid.
155. The importance of this comment is that A. A. Hodge, Charles Hodge, and B. B. Warfield are the philosophical and theological precursors of Henry's cognitive-propositionalist approach.

the field of New Testament scholarship, creating the "New Hermeneutic" in the works of Rudolf Bultmann, Ernst Fuchs, and Gerhart Ebling.[156]

The 20th century also had many significant reactions and contributions to the discipline of hermeneutics, offering a plurality of dialogues in current hermeneutics as epistemology and as methodology.[157] Treier lists: Vatican II, the evangelical debates on the inerrancy of Scripture, ideological criticism and globalization, postliberalism, and the theological interpretation of Scripture as examples of the important dialogues in hermeneutics during the 20th century.[158]

The following section will focus on some current dialogues in hermeneutics, in particular: (1) The Yale and Chicago Schools of Interpretation, (2) Postmodern Approaches, (3) Critical-Realist Approaches, and some of the (4) Innovative Hermeneutical Approaches from individuals within evangelicalism such as: (a) Michael Licona, (b) Grant Osborne, and (c) Kevin Vanhoozer.[159]

The Yale and Chicago Schools

David Lauber in his article, "Yale School," claims, "[That while the Yale School] [n]ever intended to describe a unified program and single hermeneutical method, the appellation 'Yale School' usefully designates common themes and related approaches to biblical interpretation among various theologians at Yale University and Yale Divinity School."[160] The three pivotal figures who represent this approach are Hans Frei, George Lindbeck, and David Kelsey.[161]

Lauber explains this school of hermeneutics contributes to that of methodology, not of theological exegesis (with the exception of Brevard

---

156. Thiselton, *Two Horizons*.

157. Treier, *Scripture and Hermeneutics*, 80–95.

158. Ibid.

159. Michael R. Licona does not technically study hermeneutics; however, he interacts with many of the same questions and philosophers of hermeneutics. His approach seeks to offer a new historiographical approach to historical knowledge. In particular, to defend the resurrection of Jesus Christ. That being said, Licona is included because his method only seems to reveal his hermeneutic. Nonetheless, it still is an innovative approach and furthers the conversation in the current dialogues in hermeneutics.

160. Lauber, "Yale School," 859.

161. Ibid.

Childs).¹⁶² He summarizes the contribution of the Yale School, claiming, "Briefly stated, the methodological proposals address three issues: first and foremost, the character of the text of Scripture; second, the role of the church in biblical interpretation; and third, the agency and activity of God in the church's reading and interpretation of the Scripture."¹⁶³ One of the primary texts representing this methodological approach is *The Eclipse of Biblical Narrative* by Hans Frei.¹⁶⁴ Other contributions include, *The Nature of Doctrine* by George Lindbeck, and David Kelsey's book titled, *Proving Doctrine: The Uses of Scripture in Recent Theology*.¹⁶⁵

Frei's contribution to the discussion is his insistence on reading the text of Scripture as a realistic narrative primarily focusing upon Jesus Christ.¹⁶⁶ Frei does not believe it is possible to return to precritical Reformation understandings of Scripture, which view the historical narratives portrayed in the Bible as actual historical facts.¹⁶⁷ Frei recognizes that at the turn of the 18th century, new discoveries in the discipline of philosophy allowed for truth apart from special revelation.¹⁶⁸

According to Lauber, "Frei's preference for the literal sense (the *sensus literalis*) of Scripture, as the consensus form of interpretation in the history of the church, corresponds to his insistence on the inseparability of meaning and truth."¹⁶⁹ Furthermore, "Given the uniqueness of Scripture and the uniqueness of the person to whom they witness, Frei contends that we cannot determine the meaningfulness and truthfulness of Scripture by extra-textual categories and conceptual schemes."¹⁷⁰ In short, there is only one world—that given by the narrative plot of the biblical text—not two. The text portrays a realistic narrative; however, it does not have to correspond with actual historical affairs.

George Lindbeck is the second key figure representing the Yale School and postliberal interpretations of Scripture. Treier claims "Influenced by Frei's focus on biblical narrative, Lindbeck urges Christians

---

162. Ibid.
163. Ibid.
164. Frei, *The Eclipse of Biblical Narrative*, 1–324.
165. Lindbeck, *The Nature of Doctrine*; Kelsey, *Proving Doctrine*.
166. Frei, *The Eclipse of the Biblical Narrative*, 307–324.
167. Ibid.
168. Ibid., 51–63.
169. Lauber, *Yale School*, 859.
170. Ibid.

to have the text's framework determine the cultural-linguistic symbolic lenses through which to view everything else."[171] Treier suggests the reason for this emphasis on the cultural-linguistic aspects of interpretation is Lindbeck's desire to emphasize the community of the church as the *locus* of theological interpretation.[172] Lauber claims,

> For Lindbeck, theological exegesis takes place by the community and in the community, leading to the constitution of the community as the church. By attending to the *sensus fidelium*, the consent of the faithful, the theological exegesis of the church seeks and achieves community-building consensus.[173]

In the end, Lauber believes Lindbeck's method of exegetical validity is a pragmatic approach, since he maintains that the truthfulness of any interpretation of Scripture rests upon whether that particular interpretation edifies the church; not whether it is exegetically or historically accurate.[174] Treier explains the implications of Lindbeck's approach, pointing out that,

> Lindbeck rejected both the conservative tendency to identify doctrine with cognitive propositional content and the liberal tendency to identify doctrine with symbolic expressions of experience (in which the real truth is explained philosophically). According to Lindbeck, doctrine is 'cultural-linguistic,' like the second-order grammatical rules for proper first-order religious speech, such as prayer. Doctrine teaches Christian citizenship in the church.[175]

Lindbeck's view suggests that the proof of any exegesis is not found in systematic theology or philosophical speculation; instead, exegesis is to be practical, functioning to edify the cultural-linguistic community of the church.[176]

The third member of the Yale School offering a theological account of the church's exegesis is David Kelsey. Lauber claims, "Kelsey contributes to the Yale School emphasis on narrative, as seen in his depiction of the Bible as nonfiction narrative that renders the particular identity

---

171. Treier, *Scripture and Hermeneutics*, 91.
172. Lauber, *Yale School*, 860.
173. Ibid.
174. Ibid.
175. Treier, *Scripture and Hermeneutics*, 91.
176. Lauber, *Yale School*, 860.

of Jesus Christ."[177] His approach to exegesis views the text of Scripture according to its functional authority within the church. The purpose of Scripture is to shape and transform the church and its members. Kelsey claims,

> In Part I, we shall try to identify a range of decisions theologians make about how to *construe* the scripture they actually use to help authorize theological proposals. Our thesis in this Part is that there is an actual theological practice no one standard concept 'scripture.' 'Scripture' is not something objective that different theologians simply use differently. In actual practice it is concretely construed in irreducibly different ways.[178]

One of the points Kelsey attempts to make is that the narrative of Scripture, insofar as it transforms the community of the church, does not have to correspond to actual historical affairs.[179] Instead, the functional use of Scripture is what matters most. For that reason, Kelsey spends considerable time describing *how* the Bible is understood as: Doctrine and Concept, Recital and Presence, Event and Expression, Scripture, 'Authority,' and Arguments.[180]

Lauber suggests that another important contribution by Kelsey to the Yale approach is, "Further, though this aspect of his [Kelsey's] work has been overlooked and underdeveloped, Kelsey extends his descriptive ('functional') analysis of *how* Scripture is in fact used by theologians and within the church by offering a constructive proposal for *why* Scripture *ought* to be used in the church."[181] According to Kelsey, the overall purpose of God for Scripture in the church is to create a community of believers and personal identity. The proper role of the Holy Spirit is to foster this type of community through the exegetical tasks of the cultural-linguistic fellowship of the church.

Craig Bartholomew in his article, "Postmodernity and Biblical Interpretation," differentiates the Yale School from the Chicago School of interpretation. Bartholomew claims, "However, the different approaches taken to interpretation and hermeneutics by the Chicago School (Ricoeur; Tracy) as opposed to the Yale School (Frei; Lindbeck) foreground an

---

177. Ibid.
178. Kelsey, *Proving Doctrine*, 2.
179. Ibid., 158–207.
180. Ibid., 14–157.
181. Lauber, *Yale School*, 860.

important issue for theological interpretation: the role of philosophy and general hermeneutics."[182] The Chicago School of interpretation does not focus on the cultural-linguistic and narrative approaches of Scripture. Instead, scholars from the Chicago school believe they can incorporate the discoveries in philosophy and epistemology represented in general hermeneutics into their theories of interpretation. They heavily rely upon and attempt to integrate the discoveries of Heidegger and Gadamer into their approach.

Since many of the principles of interpretation utilized by the Chicago School have already been discussed in Palmer's theses on existential and historically conscious approaches to Scripture, they do not need to be repeated here. For that reason, the next section will focus on Postmodern approaches to Scripture.

Postmodern Approaches

A relatively new phenomenon in the history of ideas is postmodernism. Postmodernists are a group of individuals who loosely follow some aspects of Nietzsche's epistemology. Nietzsche taught there were multiple ways of structuring experience relative to each individual based on non-rational instincts, purely subjective, and void of any absolute value.[183] Many postmodernists believe reality ought to be understood in the ontological categories of idealism, rather than realism. Realism in its contemporary usage is the theory that reality exists independent of our consciousness. It also includes the belief that a metaphysical world exists and it can be known.[184] Idealism is the theory that reality is ultimately mental or consists of the nature of the mind. Idealism characterizes the philosophies of Berkeley and Hegel.[185]

Lawhead claims, "Postmodernists are a loose-knit group of thinkers united around the belief that they are pallbearers of the modern tradition that originated in the Enlightenment."[186] Postmodernism includes philosophers such as Michael Foucault, Jacques Derrida, Richard Rorty, and Jean-Francoisem Lyotard. Some postmodern theologians include Stan-

---

182. Bartholomew, "Postmodernity and Biblical Interpretation," 606.
183. Lawhead, *The Voyage of Discovery*, 418.
184. Ibid., 577.
185. Ibid., 575.
186. Ibid., 559.

ley Grenz, Robert Webber, John Franke, and Brian McLaren. Lawhead continues to say,

> The tradition of modernism they reject includes the following beliefs: (1) there is one true picture of reality, (2) it is possible to obtain universal, objective knowledge, (3) science is a superior form of knowledge, (4) the history of modern thought has been a cumulative progression of increasingly better theories about reality, and (5) the autonomous, knowing subject is the source of all ideas.[187]

Lawhead goes on to suggest that postmodernists believe the dream of finding a metaphysical reality is now over. They no longer claim there are certitudes upon which a person can pin their hopes. Individuals must realize they are products of history, and that history is nothing more than a play of social forces. Stanley Grenz goes on to say,

> Meaning is not inherent in the text itself, they [deconstructionists] argue, but emerges only as the interpreter enters into dialogue with the text. And because the meaning of a text is dependent on the perspective of the one who enters into the dialogue with it, it has as many meanings as it has readers (or readings).[188]

Grenz suggests that postmodernists applied the theories of literary deconstructionists to the whole world. Just as a text can be read differently, so too, can reality be "read" differently. This entails there is no one meaning of the world, no transcendent worldview, nothing to center the whole of reality.[189] Grenz goes on to claim,

> On the basis of ideas such as these [deconstructionism], the French philosopher Jacques Derrida calls for the abandonment of both 'onto-theology' (the attempt to set forth ontological descriptions of reality) and the 'metaphysics of presence' (the idea that something transcendent is present in reality). Because nothing transcendent inheres in reality he argues, all that emerges in the knowing process is the perspective of the self who interprets reality. Michael Foucault adds a moral twist to Derrida's call. Foucault asserts that every interpretation of reality is an assertion of power. Because 'knowledge' is always the result of the

---

187. Ibid.
188. Grenz, *A Primer on Postmodernism*, 6.
189. Ibid.

use of power, to name something is to exercise power and hence to do violence to what is named. Social institutions inevitably engage in violence when they impose their own understanding on the centerless flux of experience, he says. Thus, in contrast to Bacon, who sought knowledge in order to gain power over nature, Foucault claims that every assertion of knowledge is an act of power.[190]

According to Grenz, postmodern thinkers suggest all that is left for humanity is to "deconstruct" the traditional ideals of reason, or else revel in the endless play of interpretations. He believes the postmodern worldview spells the end of the modern worldview, the end of the metanarrative, and the end of science.[191] One might also add that many postmodernists also have called for the death of traditional epistemology, metaphysics, philosophy, and ultimately any hermeneutic offering a valid interpretation of any text, the text of Scripture included.[192]

Two of the most influential postmodern Christian theologians are Stanley J. Grenz and John R. Franke.[193] There are other influential postmodern theologians, such as Brian McLaren and Robert Webber; however, Grenz and Franke have been chosen because they seem to illustrate best the claims of postmodern hermeneutics.

In the first two chapters of their book, *Beyond Foundationalism*, Grenz and Franke attempt to *do* theology in a post-foundationalist culture. They believe the failed project of foundationalist epistemologies led to the fragmentation of modern theology. For that reason they are trying to accurately incorporate theology's sources of (s)cripture, tradition and culture.[194] Grenz and Franke claim, "Two aspects of postmodern ethos are especially important for theological method: the fundamental critique and rejection of modernity, and the attempt to live and think in a realm of chastened rationality characterized by the demise of modern epistemological foundationalism."[195] They incorporate three important aspects into modern hermeneutics.[196]

---

190. Ibid.
191. Ibid., 40–46.
192. Geisler and Roach, *Defending Inerrancy*, 179–192.
193. Grenz and Franke, *Beyond Foundationalism*.
194. Ibid., 3–130. The term "(s)ripture" is used in Grenz and Franke's book.
195. Ibid., 19.
196. Ibid.

First, Grenz and Franke claim, "[W]e suggest that the normative authority for Christian theology, life, and practice is the Spirit speaking through scripture. In this context we argue that the Bible serves as the norming norm in theology in that it functions as the instrumentality of the Spirit."[197] This approach should not be akin to the Protestant principle of *Sola Scriptura*. Instead, they claim,

> The declaration that the Spirit speaking in or through scripture is our final authority means that Christian belief and practice cannot be determined merely by appeal to either the exegesis of scripture carried out apart from the life of the believer and the believing community or to any supposedly private (or corporate) 'word from the Spirit' that stands in contradiction to biblical exegesis. Instead, the reading of the text—and under this rubric we would place all our exegetical efforts—is for the purpose of listening to the voice of Spirit who seeks to speak through scripture to the church in the present.[198]

Grenz and Franke also claim, "As we noted earlier, it is not the Bible as a book that is authoritative, but the Bible as the instrumentality of the Spirit; the biblical message spoken by the Spirit through the text is theology's norming norm. But what is the connection between this 'message' and the text itself?"[199] They conclude the chapter by incorporating a synthesis between Frei's narrative approach and speech-act theory in order to articulate a functional postmodern understanding of Scripture.[200]

In chapter four, titled, "*Tradition: Theology's Hermeneutical Trajectory*," Grenz and Franke address the second aspect on the relationship between tradition and hermeneutics. They survey the role of tradition from the Patristic church until what they consider to be the loss of tradition in Protestant and modern theology.[201] They claim (s)cripture functions in an ongoing dynamic relationship with the Christian tradition, as well as the culture.[202] Emphasizing the role of culture in the hermeneutical trajectory, they claim, "It is simply not possible to step back from the influence of tradition in the act of interpretation or in the ascription of

197. Ibid., 24. The term "norming norm" and its effects on the study of hermeneutics will be explained in Grenz and Franke's own words in a quote below.
198. Ibid., 65.
199. Ibid., 69.
200. Ibid., 69–92.
201. Ibid., 94–112.
202. Ibid., 112.

meaning."²⁰³ For they believe that ". . . tradition provides the hermeneutical trajectory though [sic] which theological construction that is truly Christian emerges."²⁰⁴ Grenz and Franke believe tradition serves theology's hermeneutical trajectory, not by following traditional approaches, but through incorporating an "anti-foundationalist" epistemology.²⁰⁵ Clearly they believe this approach requires a view of (s)cripture understood according to its functional authority.²⁰⁶ Tradition, therefore, provides an essential hermeneutical context and aim for Christian theology. However, as Grenz and Franke suggest, ". . . [T]his performance always occurs in a particular historical-cultural context."²⁰⁷

Like other postmodern theologians, Grenz and Franke's third aspect suggests that culture is the place where theology is properly contextualized. They write,

> In other words, culture consists of 'shared knowledge.' It includes what people need to know so as to behave as functioning members of their society—to act the way they do, to make the things they make, and to interpret their experience in the distinctive way they do. . . . At the heart of the process whereby we construct our world is the imposition of some semblance of a meaningful order on our variegated experiences. For the interpretative framework we employ in this task, we are dependent on the society in which we participate.²⁰⁸

Grenz and Franke believe language is not only the greatest cultural symbol, but a symbolic paradigm in the world-constructing and meaning-creating task.²⁰⁹ For that reason, language is constantly in flux and continually seeking to be contextualized into the appropriate community of faith. The constructive task of theology is to avoid foundationalist approaches that start with a given reality on which they erect complete theological systems.²¹⁰ They claim, "Rather, the constructive task of theology emerges out of the process of give and take, as participants in the

---

203. Ibid.
204. Ibid., 113.
205. Ibid., 113–114.
206. Ibid., 114–115.
207. Ibid., 129.
208. Ibid., 136, 139.
209. Ibid., 143.
210. Ibid., 165.

community converse over their shared cultural meanings as connected to the symbols they hold in common as Christians."[211] This "task" is what Grenz and Franke consider to be hermeneutics.[212]

In the final analysis, the effects individuals like Grenz and Franke have had on the field of hermeneutics are far reaching and more profound than one could ever imagine. They are calling for evangelicals to completely reassess the traditional definitions of hermeneutics. Franke no longer believes hermeneutics ought to be understood as a principle or philological approach to interpretation; neither does he believe language is able to rightly communicate ideas. With that being said, other hermeneutical methods such as critical-realist approaches, have attempted to offer an epistemology based on ontological realism.

Critical-Realist Approaches

The purpose of this next section is to focus on the significant impact critical-realism has made upon hermeneutics and contemporary theological interpretations of Scripture.[213] The *Oxford Dictionary of Philosophy* defines critical-realism as,

> Any doctrine reconciling the real, independent, objective nature of the world (*realism) with a due appreciation of the mind-dependence of the sensory experiences whereby we know about it (hence, critical). In critical, as opposed to naïve, realism the mind knows the world only by means of a medium or vehicle of perception and thought; the problem is to give an account of the relationship between the medium and what it represents.[214]

Roy Bhaskar, Bernard Lonergan (a Roman Catholic), John Polkinghorne, Alister McGrath, and Michael Polyani (even though Polyani never used the term "critical-realism") are advocates of critical-realist approaches.[215]

---

211. Ibid., 166.
212. Ibid.
213. Ibid.
214. Blackburn, *Oxford Dictionary of Philosophy*, 88.
215. Bhaskar, *From East to West*; Collier, *Critical Realism*; Alister E. McGrath, *A Scientific Theology*, 195–244. For an assessment of McGrath's use of Bhaskar, see: Brad Shipway, "The Theological Application of Bhaskar's Stratified Reality," 191–203; Polyani, *Personal Knowledge*; Lonergan, *A Second Collection*; Tekippe, *What is Lonergan Up To in Insight?*.

Alister McGrath claims two of the fundamental principles of critical-realism, "... [i]s to acknowledge that the knower is involved in the process of knowing, and that this involvement must somehow be expressed within a realist perspective of the world."[216] McGrath utilizes Roy Bhaskar's discoveries in critical-realism to explain not only his scientific theology, but his overall natural theology.[217] McGrath suggests, "Bhaskar asserts the primacy of ontology over epistemology, emphasizing that the manner in which things may be known, and the extent of ensuing knowledge, is influenced by how things are in themselves. Bhaskar's critical realism opened up important questions concerning the nature of reality, and the manner in which human reflective agents can represent and interpret what is observed."[218] In brief, critical-realism has been utilized in science, theology, natural theology, and it ought to be used in biblical interpretation.

In the *Dictionary for Theological Interpretation of the Bible*, Thorsten Mortiz describes two reasons why critical-realism is making significant inroads into the discipline of hermeneutics. Mortiz claims,

> There are two main reasons why this development is particularly significant. First, it reflects an increasing willingness among biblical scholars to conceive of their interpretive work as a philosophical enterprise based on epistemological choices and frameworks. Second, critical realism has thrown into question many of the underlying positivistic assumptions of naïve realism, which have underpinned much theological interpretation, but it has done so without selling out to the relativism inherent in idealist, phenomenologist, and even instrumentalist epistemologies. What are the distinctives of critical realism that have propelled it to the forefront of philosophical reflections on theological interpretation? The critical-realist combination of insisting on the external reality of 'the thing known' while acknowledging that human knowledge can be subjective appropriation of reality can hardly be accused of having attained a sheer eccentricity.[219]

---

216. McGrath, *The Open Secret*, 74.

217. Ibid.

218. Ibid., 51.

219. Mortiz, "Critical Realism, " 147; Meyer, *An Evangelical Analysis of Critical Realism and Corollary Hermeneutics of Bernard Lonergan*.

Mortiz suggests there have been three individuals in particular who have synthesized theological method with critical-realism: Bernard Lonergan, Ben Meyer, and N. T. Wright.

Mortiz summarizes the positions of these scholars by claiming that Lonergan's approach to human knowledge involves experience, intelligence, reflection, and deliberation.[220] First, "Experience is the sensing of outer reality and as such is the first step toward knowledge. It generates basic questions about reality such as How? Why? What for? Hypothetical answers are then given."[221] Mortiz explains Lonergan believes that during this process a variety of hypothetical answers are given to those questions. The interpretive process then must progress from hypothetical answers to seeking a true answer (going from a What is it? to Is it?).[222] Mortiz claims, "In other words, there is a progression (by way of 'understanding') from asking questions incapable of being answered affirmatively or negatively to those that require precisely such a judgment by way of answer."[223] This procedure results in an approximation or "virtually unconditioned" type of certainty. The process is refined by continuing to ask questions, ensuring that as much data as possible has been included to form an appropriate judgment.[224]

The consequence of Lonergan's approach is that knowledge claims are judgments of probability. Mortiz claims,

> Moreover, since knowledge is based on experience, it is inconceivable that sound judgment results from looking 'objectively' at the world of experience. Experiential objectivity (i.e., orientation toward experience as an object) as the expression of a crude obsession with sense data (naïve realism or empiricism) is therefore not an option. Cognitive meaning cannot be restricted to what is 'sense perceptible,' for such perception is only preliminary in the acquisition of knowledge. Idealism, on the other hand, is equally deficient in its denial of what is real, for experience is based on precisely what is real, whatever metaphysical realm is reflected by a given reality.[225]

---

220. Mortiz, *Critical Realism*, 148–150. It should be noted that Mortiz does not employ Lonergan's use of "judgment."
221. Ibid.
222. Ibid.
223. Ibid.
224. Ibid.
225. Ibid.

Mortiz explains that for Lonergan these types of approaches affect the interpretation of Scripture in that the "... purification of our subjectivity is a kind of objectivity that transcends experiential and moves toward the absolute, that is, the 'objectivity' that results from judgment."[226] Individuals such as Alister McGrath, John Polkinghorne, and Ben Meyer have utilized the insights of Lonergan's critical-realism to their advantages in hermeneutics and scientific theology in particular.[227]

The third key contributor to a critical-realist approach is N. T. Wright. Wright in his profound work, *The New Testament and the People of God*, addresses in Part II two: (1) Knowledge: Problems and Varieties; and (2) Literature, Story and the Articulation of Worldviews.[228] Wright speaks to the presuppositional aspects of interpretation saying,

> We have seen that the study of the New Testament involves three disciplines in particular: literature, history and theology.... [I]t is therefore inevitable—though some will perhaps feel it regrettable—that we must spend some time at this stage seeing what these large issues look like, and getting some ideas as to what the options are between them. Until we do this, study of Jesus, Paul and the gospels will remain largely the projection of an undiscussed metaphysic: if we do not explore presuppositional matters, we can expect endless and fruitless debate.[229]

Wright notes, "The basic argument I shall advance in this Part of the book is that the problem of knowledge itself, and the three branches of it that form our particular concern, can all be clarified by seeing them in the light of a detailed analysis of the *worldviews* which form the grid through which humans, both individually and in social groups, perceive all of reality."[230] In the subsequent pages, Wright sets forth a critical-realist approach to hermeneutics as epistemology, and spends the rest of this volume and other works attempting to create a consistent hermeneutics as methodology in the field of New Testament scholarship.[231]

Moritz, addressing the significant contribution of Wright in hermeneutics, claims, "... Wright goes significantly beyond a restatement of

---

226. Ibid.
227. Ibid. See also, Meyer, *Critical Realism & The New Testament*, 3–16.
228. Wright, *The New Testament*, 31–77.
229. Ibid., 31.
230. Ibid., 32.
231. Ibid.

Meyer's hermeneutic by developing a 'story'-based approach to biblical interpretation, which leads to more tangible exegetical results and decisions."[232] Furthermore,

> His focus on narrative-historical categories is grounded in the conviction that human transformation and intentionality (as expressed in texts) are most fundamentally affected by the stories that make up human reality and relationality. Our worldviews, and therefore our perception of reality, are most directly affected by the stories we live and encounter.[233]

Mortiz summarizes Wright's position and the importance critical-realism has for biblical interpretation with these four theses:

1. It forces the interpreter to recover both 'story' and 'stories' as major factors in our approach to biblical literature. It is probably no coincidence that the prime genre in the biblical literature is that of storytelling. Far from being intended as vehicles of lightweight doctrinal insights, they have the prime function of drawing the hearer (or reader) into a transformative dialogue in ways that transcend the capabilities of propositionally phrased truth claims.

2. It leads to a recalibration of interpretive priorities. Instead of approaching the task of exegesis from the bottom up (by privileging dictionaries and grammars), the theological interpreter seeks primarily to account for the textually embodied intentionality of the author. . . . Therefore, in contrast to the positivistic objection of knowledge, human intentionality is now seen against the canvas of the storied knowledge of the communicative partners. Knowledge does not exist in a vacuum; neither does intentionality.

3. It follows that the notion of subjectivity in interpretation per se is not an evil to be rejected or lamented; it is to be welcomed as an aspect of human creationality that allows communication to be transformative, that is, 'story-changing." In this sense interpretation has to be subjective to be relevant. Yet critical realism insists that authorial intentionality must be the controlling factor in interpretation. Determinate meaning exists, even if it is not objectively accessible.

4. This is not to deny that the intentionality of empirical or historical authors may be partially or entirely obscured. But insofar as a

232. Mortiz, *Critical Realism*, 149.
233. Ibid.

text (or speech for that matter) conveys authorial presence via the implied author—who is the empirical author's creation—authorial intentionality remains the critical interpretive corrective. The provisionality of an interpretation itself does not imply a value judgment. All interpretations of a given text are provisional, but relative to the others, only one of them will have the strongest claim to accuracy.[234]

In summary, critical-realism distinguishes between external reality and human knowing. Interpreters have a portion of reality that exists objectively even though it is only accessible through a subjective grid. This approach does not entail that all knowledge is relative or purely subjective. Instead, according to Mortiz, both knowledge and biblical interpretation are qualified by the matrix which connects human consciousness and external reality.[235]

Innovative Hermeneutical Approaches

The final section of current dialogues in hermeneutics will investigate innovative hermeneutical approaches.[236] The term "innovative" in this context refers to new methods of appropriating the previous dialogues in hermeneutics. These approaches attempt to synthesize hermeneutics as epistemology and methodology. In particular, each of the following scholars seems to incorporate a form of critical realism in their methodologies. For that reason, they are a subsection of the "Critical-Realist Approaches." While numerous scholars could be included in this list, only three examples are mentioned in this section: (1) Michael Licona, (2) Grant Osborne, and (3) Kevin Vanhoozer.[237]

234. Ibid., 149–150.

235. Ibid., 150.

236. The notion of innovative is found in the way they attempt to synthesize hermeneutics as epistemology and methodology into their hermeneutical approaches. Limiting the selection to these two individuals is not to downplay the influence of numerous other works in the field of hermeneutics. These three were chosen because they are standards in the field and they best illustrate the point that one must intentionally incorporate prolegomena into their methodology. Just as easily one could have incorporated any one of these other works: Pinnock, *Tracking the Maze*; Enns, *Inspiration and Incarnation*; Kenton L. Sparks, *God's Word in Human Hands*; Bruce K. Waltke and Charles Yu, *An Old Testament Theology*.

237. The reference to these scholars' publications will be cited in the sections describing their hermeneutic as epistemology and methodology. Michael Licona is chosen not necessarily because he writes on hermeneutics, but because his method

Michael Licona

The first scholar in the section on innovative approaches is Michael Licona. Licona in his major defense titled, *The Resurrection of Jesus: A New Historiographical Approach*, addresses: "Important Consideration on Historical Inquiry Pertaining to the Truth in Ancient Texts."[238] In chapter one, Licona sets forth a discussion in 1.2 on Theory and in 1.3 Method. In his summary section of *Resurrection of Jesus*, Licona suggests that, "Many scholars do not acknowledge the influence their horizon has on their investigations and appear to proceed unaware that it influences their every step. This is perhaps the main reason for the plurality of historical conclusions in both historical Jesus research as well as historical inquiries unrelated to religious matters."[239]

Licona claims, "Horizon may be defined as one's 'preunderstanding.' It is how historians view things as a result of their knowledge, experience, beliefs, education, cultural conditioning, preferences, presuppositions and worldview."[240] Later he suggests, "Horizons are of great interest to historians since they are responsible more than anything else for the embarrassing diversity among conflicting portraits of the past. How can so many historians with access to the same data arrive at so many different conclusions?"[241] Addressing horizons is important for Licona because, "When the historical Jesus in general and the resurrection in particular are the subjects of inquiry, the horizon of the historian will be in full operation throughout the entire process. Accordingly, it is of no surprise to find similar comments in reference to a history of Jesus and discussions on his resurrection."[242]

Licona believes that theistic bias on the part of the historian can aide in the adjudication of miracle claims in general, and the resurrection in particular.[243] Unlike many historians, Licona believes it is possible to

---

reveals a hermeneutic as epistemology and methodology. Grant Osborne and Kevin Vanhoozer have been chosen because they do write on hermeneutics and because their books and articles are foundational texts in evangelical discussions on biblical interpretation.

238. Licona, *The Resurrection of Jesus*, 29.
239. Ibid., 613.
240. Ibid., 38.
241. Ibid., 39.
242. Ibid., 41.
243. Ibid., 49.

transcend horizons, not by completely eradicating them but by reducing the influence bias has on one's horizon.[244] He proposes six guidelines in order to achieve this end.[245] Licona is quick to add, "The six actions we have just discussed by no means guarantee objectivity. Indeed, complete objectivity is elusive."[246] After surveying the various historiographical and epistemological approaches, Licona appropriates an abductive or argument unto the best explanation model to defend the resurrection of Christ.[247] His model includes these features: (1) Explanatory scope; (2) Explanatory power; (3) Plausibility; (4) Less ad hoc; (5) Illumination.[248] Licona spends the rest of his book appropriating this method to the bodily resurrection of Jesus Christ.

Some of the most important aspects of Licona's book for the present research are the sections on historical method, miracles, and theory, because they reveal his hermeneutic. In his section on theory, Licona offers a definition of history. Licona claims to follow Aviezer Tucker's definition of history and refers to history ". . . as *past events that are the object of study*."[249] Licona distinguishes history from historiography. He defines historiography as,

> . . . the history of the philosophy of history and as writings about the past. Historiography is not historical method but includes it, since method enables one to write about the past. Throughout

---

244. Ibid., 51. Licona explains his theory of truth as a version of both the correspondence and coherence view of truth, arguing for a middle ground between the two. However, he claims to favor the correspondence view more than the coherence. Ibid., 92.

245. Licona's six guidelines are: "1) Method; 2) The historian's horizon and method should be public; 3) Peer pressure; 4) Submitting ideas to unsympathetic experts; 5) Account for the relevant historical bedrock; 6) Detachment from bias is nonnegotiable." Ibid., 52–61.

246. Ibid., 61.

247. Licona explains this abductive method suggesting, "Therefore, when historians say that "x occurred" in the past, they are actually claiming the following: *Given the available data, the best explanation indicates that we are warranted in having a reasonable degree of certainty that x occurred and that it appears more certain at the moment than competing hypotheses. Accordingly we have a rational basis for believing it. However, our conclusion is subject to revision or abandonment, since new data may surface in the future showing things happened differently than presently proposed.* Therefore, preferred hypotheses are like temporary workers waiting to see whether they will one day be awarded a permanent position." Ibid., 68–69.

248. Ibid., 108–111.

249. Ibid., 30.

this volume I will use the term *historiography* to refer to matters in the philosophy of history and historical method. *Philosophy of history* concerns epistemological approaches to gaining a knowledge of the past. It attempts to answer questions such as, What does it mean to *know* something? How do we come to know something? Can we know the past and, if so, to what extent? What does it mean when historians say that a particular event occurred?[250]

Licona suggests that in the act of investigating historical sources, historians must recognize that memories are selective and writers can sometimes embellish on some of the details. Licona reveals he believes the true meaning of an event is found in the author's intention; however, in order to know the authors intention one must know the author's motives. He believes the difficulty in historiography and biblical interpretation arises in the great difficulty to recover the motives of the author and his or her intention. Licona goes on to explain,

> Authorial intent often eludes us, and the motives behind the reports are often difficult to determine. This is a challenge when we consider the four earliest extant biographies of Jesus, known as the canonical Gospels. There is somewhat of a consensus among contemporary scholars that the Gospels belong to the genre of Greco-Roman biography (*bios*). *Bioi* offered the ancient biographer great flexibility for rearranging material and inventing speeches in order to communicate the teachings, philosophy, and political beliefs of the subject, and they often included legend. Because *bios* was a flexible genre, it is often difficult to determine where history ends and legend begins.[251]

Licona claims a historian must know the author's intention in order to know the meaning of the literary work, whether it be a piece from secular or religious history. He suggests a difficulty arises when assessing authorial intention and ancient genre categories.

According to Licona, since many New Testament scholars believe the Gospels are a form of Greco-Roman biography, one of the literary features of this type of literature is the ancient biographer had many liberties in the way he: orders speeches, historical events, and whether or not the events were merely a literary feature or an actual historical event. In brief, due to the literary features of Greco-Roman biography,

---

250. Ibid., 31.
251. Ibid., 34.

it is sometimes difficult to know the author's motives and intentions. He suggests one effect this has on the study of the canonical Gospels is that an interpreter is sometimes unable to distinguish between actual history and legend.[252]

In summary, Licona's hermeneutical approach attempts to develop a method that addresses the present-day theories of historiography, Greco-Roman literature, and how authorial intent can affect the interpretation of Scripture. Licona proposes six guidelines to overcome present-day theories of historiography and synthesizes which he believes are beneficial steps for a proper understanding of authorial intent and the contributions from Greco-Roman literature to the field of biblical studies and the discipline of hermeneutics.

Grant Osborne

The second scholar in the innovative approaches is Grant Osborne. Osborne, in his established work, *The Hermeneutical Spiral: A Comprehensive Introduction to Biblical Interpretation,* sets forth a thorough and fair-minded approach appropriating the hermeneutical spiral to biblical interpretation. Osborne says, "The major premise of this book is that biblical interpretation entails a 'spiral' from text to context, from its original meaning to its contextual or significance for the church today."[253] Furthermore,

> The 'hermeneutical spiral' takes place not only at the level of original intended meaning, as our understanding spirals upward (via the interaction of inductive and deductive research) to the intended meaning of the passage, but also at the level of contextualization, as our application spirals upward (via the movement from biblical to systematic to homiletical theology) to a proper understanding of the significance of the passage for Christian theology today.[254]

Knowing the history of the term "hermeneutical spiral," Osborne attempts to incorporate this concept into a much broader discussion already taking place in the discipline of hermeneutics.[255] In the introduction to the work,

252. Ibid.
253. Osborne, *The Hermeneutical Spiral*, 22.
254. Ibid., 32. See also: 356; 418–419.
255. Thiselton, "Hermeneutical Spiral," 281.

Osborne lays the foundation, which is in keeping with the long history of the concept and the "hermeneutics as epistemology" of the hermeneutical spiral. In the subsequent chapters of his book, Osborne attempts to relate the hermeneutical spiral to "hermeneutics as methodology."[256]

Of the many topics Osborne discusses, one of the most important is the way he understands and defends the notion of "meaning." He suggests that meaning is found in authorial intention. Osborne suggests that evangelical scholarship ought to engage in the discussions on authorial intention because it is foundational to an evangelical view of Scripture. Osborne summarizes the nature of the debate for evangelicals claiming,

> The goal of evangelical hermeneutics is quite simple—to discover the intention of the Author/author (author = inspired human author; Author = God who inspires the text). Modern critics increasingly deny the very possibility of discovering the original or intended meaning of a text. The problem is that while the original authors had a definite meaning in mind when they wrote, that is now lost to us because they are no longer present to clarify and explain what they wrote. The modern reader cannot study the text from the ancient perspective but constantly reads into that passage modern perspectives. Therefore, critics argue, objective interpretation is impossible and the author's intended meaning is forever lost to us. Every community provides traditions to guide the reader in comprehending a text, and these produce the meaning. That 'meaning' differs from community to community, and each is valid for a particular reading perspective or community (so Stanley Fish).[257]

Osborne suggests that "modern" approaches do not allow for an objective interpretation of the text because each reader interprets the text from their own perspective which prevents them from obtaining the author's original intention. In the introduction of his book, Osborne notes that the problem is philosophical in nature; in fact, he labels it as "very real

---

256. The methodological step has given way to Osborne's discussion of: 1) General Hermeneutics, incorporating: Context; Grammar; Semantics; Syntax; Historical and Cultural Backgrounds; 2) Genre Analysis, incorporating: Old Testament Law; Narrative; Poetry; Wisdom; Prophecy; Apocalyptic; Parable; Epistle; The Old Testament in the New Testament; 3) Applied Hermeneutics, incorporating: Biblical Theology; Systematic Theology; Homiletics I: Contextualization; Homiletics II: The Sermon. It concludes with two appendixes on: The Problem of Meaning: The Issues; and The Problem of Meaning: Toward a Solution. Osborne, *Hermeneutical Spiral*, 8–14.

257. Ibid., 24.

and complex" due to the "difficult philosophical issues involved."[258] He explains the outline of his book, suggesting that he will discuss the theoretical aspects of hermeneutics in the appendixes and the practical aspects throughout the entire book.[259] He also notes that the entire book on hermeneutical method is a practical solution to the difficult philosophical problems. While Osborne does not use the terminology, these sections are an open confession that any interpretive approach must address both hermeneutics as epistemology and methodology.

The final section of appendix two titled "A Field Approach to Hermeneutics," provides Osborne's integrative solution to the issues described in appendix one and in the first half of appendix two.[260] This section is important to the current dialogues in hermeneutics because it is there Osborne provides his own answer to the debates in hermeneutics. Osborne has four different points he provides as a solution to the current dialogues in hermeneutics. The first point is, "A close reading of the text cannot be done without a perspective provided by one's preunderstanding as identified by a 'sociology of knowledge' perspective."[261] This point describes Osborne's views of epistemology and hermeneutics. Osborne goes on to explain, suggesting,

> Reflection itself demands mental categories, and these are built on one's presupposed worldview and by the faith or reading community to which one belongs. Since neutral exegesis is impossible, no necessarily 'true' or final interpretation is possible. There will always be differences of opinion in a finite world. However, this does not demand polyvalence. Probability theory allows critical interaction and movement toward the intended meaning, however elusive it may prove at times, so long as the communities are open to critical dialogue. Here I want to stress that preunderstanding is primarily a positive (and only potentially a negative) component of interpretation. Preunderstanding only becomes negative if it degenerates into an a priori grid that determines the meaning of a text before the act of reading begins.[262]

258. Ibid.
259. Ibid.
260. Ibid., 516–521.
261. Ibid., 516.
262. Ibid.

Osborne recognizes the influence of epistemology on biblical interpretation. He affirms that exegesis is never neutral and that a final objective interpretation is impossible. He does not believe it removes critical dialogue and progress, because probability theory allows for critical interaction and progress in the hermeneutical discussions. Osborne opposes those who attempt to "determine" the meaning of a text, prior to the process of the hermeneutical spiral described in his book.[263]

Osborne's second principle is: "I must distinguish *presupposition* from *prejudice*."[264] He claims to follow Paul Ricoeur, who suggests that interpreters place themselves "in front of" rather than "behind" the text, so that the text can have priority."[265] Osborne claims, "This allows us to determine which types of preunderstanding are valid and which are not as the text challenges, reshapes and directs our presuppositions."[266] Osborne believes presuppositions can be external (philosophical or theological) and internal (personality, pressure to publish). He claims they have to be taken into account when studying any text. Osborne notes, "My basic point is that they can be identified."[267] He claims when subconscious prejudices are not addressed they determine the meaning of the text. Osborne desires for a hermeneutic that does not deny the influence of presuppositions; instead, he calls for a hermeneutic where in the process of interpretation the text is allowed to shape or change a presupposed perspective.[268]

Osborne's third principle suggests interpreters must seek controls that enable interpreters to work with presuppositions rather than to be dominated by prejudices.[269] He suggests in his own words that,

> (1) 'We must be open to new possibilities;'[270] (2) 'We must understand the dangers of merely assuming our presuppositions;'[271] (3) 'The interpreter must not only address the text but must allow the text to address him or her (the hermeneutical circle). In exegesis, our presuppositions/preunderstanding must be

263. Ibid.
264. Ibid.
265. Ibid., 516–517.
266. Ibid., 517.
267. Ibid.
268. Ibid.
269. Ibid.
270. Ibid.
271. Ibid.

modified and reshaped by the text. At the same time, the text must address the reader's contemporary *Weltanschauung* ('worldview'). . . . The task of hermeneutics is never finished with original meaning but can only be complete when its significance is realized.'[272] (4) 'Polyvalent interpretations per se are unnecessary, but a pluralistic or polyvalent attitude is crucial. Again, my approach is an 'interpretive realism' that is in constant dialogue with the various communities of faith in order to refine and reformulate theories on the basis of further evidence or more coherent models.'[273] [Furthermore], 'Pure polyvalence lacks this rigorous dialectic because it tends to relativism, that every theory is as good as the next. There is little possibility for the growth of the store of knowledge when rugged individualism is in control of the theoretical process!'[274]

Osborne's third principle indicates he believes there is a strong relationship between epistemology and hermeneutics. In particular, Osborne recognizes the epistemological influences that occur in the interactions between the author, text, and reader.[275]

Osborne's hermeneutic culminates in his fourth principle, "We must allow good hermeneutical principles to shape our exegesis and to control our tendency to read our prejudices into the text."[276] Here he suggests that a good hermeneutic will consider the following: the genre type of the text (which he believes that meaning is genre-dependent),[277] the structural development of the passage, the use of semantic research to discover the sense and reference of a passage, the background information of the text,[278] the implied author and implied reader of the text, and utilize inductive and deductive measures to validate the meaning of the text.[279]

In summary, Osborne's approach attempts to develop a method of interpretation that addresses the author, reader, and text. He recognizes the influence of both epistemology and methodology in hermeneutics.

272. Ibid.
273. Ibid., 517–518.
274. Ibid., 518.
275. Ibid.
276. Ibid.
277. Ibid., 26.
278. Ibid.
279. Ibid., 518–519.

Osborne's solution is that individuals should appropriate the new discoveries in sociology of knowledge approaches into a methodology that helps to validate the meaning of the text, without *a priori* determining the meaning of Scripture.

Kevin Vanhoozer

The third scholar in the innovative approaches is Kevin Vanhoozer. Vanhoozer represents both an innovative and integrative approach to hermeneutics. It is innovative and integrative because he attempts to incorporate elements from both general hermeneutics and the theological interpretation of Scripture. Some of Vanhoozer's primary works include: *The Drama of Doctrine: A Canonical-Linguistic Approach to Christian Theology*; *Is There a Meaning in This Text?*; *Remythologizing Theology: Divine Action, Passion, and Authorship*; and his edited book *Dictionary for Theological Interpretation of the Bible*.[280]

Vanhoozer's innovative hermeneutical approach rests in his ability to blend the best of both the Yale and Chicago Schools. His insistence on the narrative aspects of Scripture reflects the Yale School of interpretation, while his use of philosophical categories in general hermeneutics reflects the Chicago School of interpretation.[281] Vanhoozer is by no means a postmodernist in his approach; neither is he a traditional cognitive-propositionalist.[282] In his work, *Is there a Meaning in This Text?*, Vanhoozer offers a robust systematic defense of the philosophical aspects of hermeneutics.[283] That work should be seen as a type of philosophical prolegomena to his later works. In *Drama of Doctrine*, Vanhoozer offers a special hermeneutic attempting to understand doctrine different from classical cognitive-propositional models in favor of his canonical-linguistic approach to interpretation.

Vanhoozer is well known for his incorporation of J. L. Austin and John Searle's use of speech-act theory into his conception of interpretation.[284]

---

280. Vanhoozer, *The Drama of Doctrine*; Vanhoozer, *Is There a Meaning in This Text?*; Vanhoozer, *Remythologizing Theology*; Vanhoozer, *Dictionary for Theological Interpretation of the Bible*.

281. This comment is derived from reading many of his epistemological and methodological points from the books listed in footnote 287.

282. Vanhoozer, *Lost in Interpretation*, 89–115.

283. Ibid.

284. Austin, *How to Do Things with Words*; Searle, *Speech Acts: An Essay in the*

Austin, and later Searle who built upon his works, observes that not all statements are true or false, or even indicative. For instance, some are warnings, promises, exclamations, and so forth. Later Austin distinguished between three different acts of language: 1) Locutionary act—an utterance with a definite sense and reference; 2) Illocutionary act—an act one may perform in making that utterance; 3) Perlocutionary act—an act one may incite by acting upon the locutionary and illocutionary act.[285]

Applied to the text of Scripture, Vanhoozer in his book, *First Theology* writes, "My proposal, then, is to say both the Bible is the Word of God (in the sense of its illocutionary acts) and to say that the Bible becomes the Word of God (in the sense of achieving its perlocutionary effects)."[286] To focus purely on the text is considered "letterism" or "locutionism" since words do not have meaning in and of themselves apart from their intended purpose.[287] In another place, Vanhoozer writes, "Austin distinguished three components of the total speech act: (a) *the locutionary act* "is roughly equivalent to 'meaning' in the traditional sense," (b) *the illocutionary act* is what we *do* in saying something, and (c) *the perlocutionary act* is 'what we bring about or achieve by saying something, such as conceiving, persuading.'"[288]

Vanhoozer considers his speech-act view a "Trinitarian theology of Holy Scripture." For example, he claims,

> The Father's activity is locution. God the Father is the utterer, the begetter, the sustainer of word.... The Logos corresponds to the speaker's act of illocution, to what one does in saying.... The Spirit's agency consists rather in bringing the illocutionary point home to the reader and so achieving the corresponding perlocutionary effect—whether belief, obedience, praise or some other.[289]

The general task of a speech-act is to appropriate whether any locution holds both to promise and obligation, not necessarily whether or not it actually corresponds to a certain state of affairs. Gregory Alan Thornbury claims,

---

Philosophy of Language.
   285. Ibid.
   286. Vanhoozer, *First Theology.*
   287. Vanhoozer, *Is There a Meaning in This Text?*, 312.
   288. Carson and Woodbridge, eds., *Hermeneutics, Authority, and Canon,* 86.
   289. Vanhoozer, *First Theology,* 154–155.

> The general tack of speech-act theory, then, departs significantly from a cognitive representational account of the truth or falsity of a statement of fact. For the propositionalist view, the accuracy and reliability of such declarations is the main concern. What matters is not just the statement's reception from an intended audience, but whether it corresponds to an objective state of affairs independent of the author-reader enclosure. Consequently, for anyone wishing to depart from the representational view of symbolic meaning, speech-act theory provides an attractive alternative.[290]

It appears Vanhoozer would agree with Thornbury's insightful statement. In his books, Vanhoozer departs from the traditional cognitive-propositonalist model offered by Charles Hodge and Carl F. H. Henry. In *Drama of Doctrine*, he claims,

> Partly in response to the mid-twentieth century tendency to deny the verbal and cognitive dimensions of revelation, Carl F. H. Henry and others argued that God's word should be equated with the revealed propositions of the Bible, objective truth stated in conceptual and verbal form.[291]

Vanhoozer opposes Henry's view, considering himself a "modified propositionalist," stating,

> I recognize all of the cognitive significance not only of statements and propositions but *all* the Bible's figures of speech and literary forms. Yet I resist the temptation to dedramatize—to de-form!—the biblical text in order to abstract revealed truth. My approach to theology—call it "postconservative"—does not deny the importance of cognitive content, but it does resist privileging a single form—the propositional statement—for expressing it.[292]

Some evangelical authors, such as Gregory Alan Thornbury, Paul Helm, Norman Geisler, and myself, believe Vanhoozer not only caricatures the propositionalist model represented by Hodge and Henry, but his use of speech-act theory also undermines an evangelical understanding of Scripture, inerrancy in particular.[293]

290. Thornbury, *Recovering Classic Evangelicalism*, 104–105.
291. Vanhoozer, *The Drama of Doctrine*, 45.
292. Vanhoozer, *Lost in Interpretation*, 107–108.
293. Thornbury, *Recovering Classic Evangelicalism*, 103–115; Geisler and Roach, *Defending Inerrancy*, 132–159; Paul Helm, "Vanhoozer's Remythologizing Theology,"

A second trajectory in Vanhoozer's work is his insistence on a canonical-linguistic approach to Scripture. Vanhoozer claims,

> The cultural-linguistic turn characteristic of postliberal and other types of postmodern theology is a salient reminder that theology exists to serve the life of the church. Yet the turn to church practice seems to have come at the expense of biblical authority. The *canonical*-linguistic approach to be put forward in the present book has much in common with its cultural-linguistic cousin. Both agree that meaning and truth are crucially related to language use; however, the canonical-linguistic approach maintains that the normative use is ultimately not that of ecclesial *culture* but of the biblical *canon*.[294]

Furthermore,

> At the heart of [the] canonical-linguistic approach is the proposal that we come to God by attending to the uses which language of God is put in Scripture itself. Scripture's own use of Scripture is of particular interest, for the cradle of Christian theology is perhaps best located in the interpretative practice of Jesus and the apostles. It was this interpretative practice that enabled them to read the Scriptures of Israel as identifying Jesus as the "Christ." Canonical-linguistic theology therefore takes its primary bearing from the Scriptures themselves, making what we shall call *canonical practices* the norm for the church's speech and thought of God. *Sola scriptura* returns, then, not by positing the Bible as a text-book filled with propositional information but by viewing the Bible as a script that calls for faithful yet creative performance. Scripture is the norm for the Christian way, truth, and life, but only when Scripture is conceived as more than a handbook of propositional truth.[295]

The canonical-linguistic approach is an attempt to deliberate between those who affirm a propositonalist and non-propositionalist approach to Scripture and theology. Vanhoozer claims, "Evangelicals have been quick to decry the influence of modernism on liberal theology but not to see the beam of modern epistemology in their own eye. The present work articulates what an evangelical theology with a postpropositionalist

---

Helm's Deep, entry posted May 1, 2010, http://paulhelmsdeep.blogspot.com/search?.q=Remythologizing+Theology.

294. Vanhoozer, *The Drama of Doctrine*, 16.

295. Ibid., 22.

Scripture principle and an ear cocked to the postmodern condition should look like."[296] Vanhoozer believes evangelical theologians are able to learn from postmodernity without ". . . correlating with or capitulating to it, the most important lesson being to orient theology toward the goal of practical wisdom rather than mere theoretical knowledge."[297] The goal of Vanhoozer's approach is to maintain a Christocentric focus on Scripture while developing an integrative model of interpretation able to interact with both hermeneutics as epistemology and as methodology.

This overview of current dialogues in hermeneutics synthesizes the interactions between contemporary approaches with the epistemological and methodological aspects of hermeneutics and interpretation. There are definitely more individuals and methods that could be added to this section,[298] but what is clear from this chapter is scholarship suggests that any approach to hermeneutics must incorporate and interact with philosophical and theological prolegomena. In particular, evangelical scholarship must address the two aspects of hermeneutics: (1) hermeneutics as epistemology; and (2) hermeneutics as methodology. The reason for this is because each individual's epistemology *per se* is foundational to their hermeneutic as epistemology and as methodology.

CONCLUSION

The overview from this chapter indicates that the definition of hermeneutics in the present context is very unstable. The first section of this chapter presented the development in hermeneutics by discussing Richard Palmer's six definitions of hermeneutics. This chapter also discussed Palmer's definition of the hermeneutical problem and how he opposed Hirsch's view of the hermeneutical problem. The second section of this chapter also discussed the current dialogues in hermeneutics. Four areas were discussed in this second section. The headings of the four sections are: The Yale and Chicago School; Postmodern Approaches; Critical-Realist Approaches; and Innovative Hermeneutical Approaches. In the section on "Innovative Hermeneutical Approaches," it discussed three individuals: Michael Licona, Grant Osborne, and Kevin Vanhoozer. Each of these scholars emphasizes the importance of epistemology in hermeneutics.

296. Ibid., 26.
297. Ibid.
298. Porter and Sovell, *Biblical Hermeneutics*.

The overview from this chapter will be the paradigm in the following chapters to assess critically Carl F. H. Henry's cognitive-propositional model in light of the recent trends in hermeneutics.

2

Carl F. H. Henry's Revelational Epistemology

INTRODUCTION

For most of the twentieth-century, evangelicalism was in the saddle of American Christianity and some of its chief riders were individuals such as Billy Graham, Harold Ockenga, Kenneth Kantzer, Roger Nicole, J. I. Packer, James Montgomery Boice, R. C. Sproul, Norman Geisler, D. A. Carson, Paige Patterson, Francis Schaeffer, and Harold Lindsell.[1] Yet, a list of evangelical forebearers would be incomplete if it did not include one individual whom Timothy George labels as, "Daddy Evangelical."[2] That person is Carl F. H. Henry. George claims, "For many, the first question very well may be, 'Carl who?'"[3] Yet, the rejoinder to that question helps to set the stage for the tone of this chapter. George writes,

> The answer is Carl Henry who invented post–World War II evangelicalism, the evangelicalism we are still largely living with today. If you want to understand the passions of today's evangelicals, you have to understand the passions of Carl Henry. Henry did not invent postwar evangelicalism all by himself, of course.

---

1. This list is only intended to be a partial list of some of evangelicalism's "chief riders." It is beyond the scope of this book to develop an exhaustive list of evangelical scholars in the 20th century.
2. George, *Daddy Evangelical*, 61.
3. Ibid.

> He had lots of help from Harold Ockenga, the strategist; Billy Graham, the evangelist; Bill Bright, the activist; Francis Schaeffer, the apologist; and many others. But Henry, more than anyone else, argued the case and set forth a compelling intellectual apologetic for what was then called the New Evangelicalism.[4]

Henry was able to sustain an apologetic against the barrage of modernist attacks against evangelicalism serving as a professor, author, and lecturer at large. All three of these posts result in the publication of numerous books beginning with *The Uneasy Conscience of Modern Fundamentalism* and the six-volume, *God, Revelation and Authority*. George points out, "The latter is still the most sustained theological epistemology by any American theologian."[5] This chapter is going to explain Henry's epistemology and its relevance for evangelical hermeneutics. It will do this by addressing: (1) Carl F. H. Henry's Importance to Hermeneutics; (2) Epistemology and Theological Method; (3) Henry's Analysis of Epistemological Concerns; and (4) Henry's Epistemology.

CARL F. H. HENRY'S IMPORTANCE TO HERMENEUTICS

The importance of Henry's contribution to hermeneutics is he viewed epistemology as *the* decisive issue for theological method. R. Albert Mohler suggests Henry's overall project in *God, Revelation and Authority*, was to challenge the contemporary philosophy of his day.[6] Henry believed the breakdown of final truth in epistemology and the surety of propositional revelation, was a threat to evangelical orthodoxy. In particular, Mohler claims,

> In *God, Revelation and Authority*, Henry presented a magisterial defense of the Christian truth against the challenges of liberal theology, modern secularism, and contemporary philosophy. He opened the project with a cogent word of warning about the challenge faced by evangelicals in the modern world: 'No fact of contemporary Western life is more evident than its growing distrust of final truth and its implacable questioning of any sure word.'[7]

---

4. Ibid.
5. Ibid.
6. Henry, *GRA*. Mohler makes this claim in the following block quote.
7. R. Albert Mohler, "The Life and Legacy of Carl F. H. Henry." Accessed on 4/17/2013. http://www.albertmohler.com/2003/12/09/the-life-and-

The influence of Henry and the role he played within evangelical theology and philosophy, indicate the importance his views had in the twentieth-century discussions concerning hermeneutics as epistemology and as methodology.[8] Henry's work in publications such as *God, Revelation and Authority*, are considered to be a "magisterial defense of Christian truth," indicating the breadth and precision he brought to the table. Methodologically, according to G. Wright Doyle,

> His [Henry's] decision to focus in *God, Revelation and Authority* on epistemology—the *decisive issue* for modern theology, and for modern thought in general—dealt a body blow to the assumptions with which most twentieth-century theologians worked. Henry amassed mountains of evidence and wielded incisive arguments to demonstrate that the Bible is true, trustworthy, and therefore authoritative as our main source of revelation about God.[9]

In his book, *Recovering Classic Evangelicalism: Applying the Wisdom and Vision of Carl F. H. Henry*, Gregory Alan Thornbury, recognizes the history and legacy of Carl F. H. Henry. Thornbury believes Henry's epistemology offered a valuable insight into the dialogues taking place during his life time, especially those in hermeneutics as epistemology and methodology.[10] Like the individuals listed in chapter one, Henry fulfills the two step process. Volume one of *God, Revelation and Authority*, addresses the issues prevalent in epistemology *per se*, and volumes two through five address (1) hermeneutics as epistemology; and (2) hermeneutics as methodology.

---

legacy-of-carl-f-h-henry-a-rembrance/.

8. When speaking of the stature of Henry in modern theology and the influence he had within evangelicalism, Timothy George states, "Henry's stature within evangelicalism rivals those of Karl Barth in neo-orthodoxy and Karl Rahner in Roman Catholicism. Henry is the only theologian who has served as president of both the Evangelical Thelogical Society (1967–1970) and the American Theological Association (1979–1980). The world evangelical movement owes much to his legacy of personal devotion to Christ, strategic evangelistic thinking, cultural ethical engagement and theological consistency and faithfulness across several generations." George, "Carl Henry," 297–300.

9. Doyle, *Carl Henry*, 37.

10. Thornbury, *Recovering Classic Evangelicalism*, 31; 85–115. Daniel Treier in his article *Scripture and Hermeneutics*, cited above recognizes Henry to be the pivotal figure from his time able to interact with the many theses represented in the current dialogues on epistemology and hermeneutics. See, Treier, *Scripture and Hermeneutics*, 85–88.

Henry's publications interact with nearly fifty years of both evangelical and non-evangelical approaches to epistemology and hermeneutics. The most important contribution he made can be found in his *magnum opus*: *God, Revelation and Authority*. Yet the influence of Henry is not restricted to just that publication or to the mid 1970's and 1980's. He continued to influence the twin issues of hermeneutics as epistemology and as methodology in his numerous articles and other books until his death in 2003. For example, Henry was asked to deliver a message at the closing session of the *Summit II: Hermeneutics Conference* for the *International Council on Biblical Inerrancy* (ICBI). His message was titled, "The Bible and the Conscience of Our Age." The introductory remarks in the book, *Hermeneutics, Inerrancy, & the Bible*, indicate, "It [Henry's paper] is included here because it summarizes the issues of the conference and affirms the role of the Bible in today's world."[11] Furthermore, Thornbury describes this era of evangelicalism represented by the ICBI, as "classic evangelicalism," because individuals from this time period emphasized the role of epistemology in hermeneutics, and the cognitive-propositional aspects of the Bible.[12] Henry represents one of the chief architects of "classic evangelicalism" and its view of Scripture and hermeneutics.

Thornbury suggests Henry's method ought to be reevaluated in light of the recent trends in epistemology and theological method. Summarizing Carl Trueman's comments, Thornbury says,

> Trueman, in typical good form, goes on to liken the work of Henry to the Sistine Chapel, and commends a reappraisal of Henry's insistence on propositional theology as the sine qua non of evangelical authenticity. While Trueman rightly acknowledges that Henry's work must be evaluated in the light of more recent developments in the field of hermeneutics, he points to the crucial issue at hand with which we must deal and to which Henry so directs us: 'Who God is, how he has revealed himself, and how we appropriate that revelation are not really three discrete issues, but three aspects of the one great problem of revelation—and all three aspects must be dealt with in any theology which aspires to the title Christian.'[13]

---

11. Radmacher and Preus, *Hermeneutics, Inerrancy, & the Bible*, 915–921.
12. Thornbury, *Recovering Classic Evangelicalism*, 34–58.
13. Ibid., 31. Also see: Trueman, *Admiring the Sistine Chapel*, 48–58.

Research has shown that recent developments in hermeneutics sometimes downplay or deny Henry's cognitive-propositionalist method.[14] Thornbury confirms this report and elaborates upon it claiming,

> In correspondence with Henry, Marsden claimed that Carl had mistaken Marsden's historical analysis as critique; Marsden went so far as to state that his own theological position was sympathetic with Henry's. While Marsden's criticism of Henry was more oblique, individuals' such as the late Stanley J. Grenz, John Franke, and Kevin Vanhoozer have been more pointed in their cavils of Henry. In sum, they view the epistemology Henry spent the better part of his career cultivating as the philosophical relic of a bygone era.[15]

These types of criticisms raise question such as: What is the role of epistemology in theological method? Does Henry's cognitive-propositionalist model withstand the criticisms of these theologians? Is Henry's epistemology a relic of a bygone era? The following sections will attempt to answer these types of questions about epistemology, hermeneutics, and Henry's method in the current dialogues in hermeneutics.[16]

EPISTEMOLOGY AND THEOLOGICAL METHOD

In his book, *Recovering Classic Evangelicalism*, Thornbury includes a chapter titled, "Epistemology Matters."[17] In that chapter, he notes that a common theme among proponents of classic evangelicalism, such as Bernard Ramm, E. J. Carnell, Kenneth Kantzer, Colin Brown, Donald Bloesch, Gordon Lewis, Bruce Demarest, Norman Geisler, and Millard Erickson, ". . . is that their work was fundamentally philosophical in orientation."[18] Thornbury makes a very keen observation in the next section, noting that, "For various reasons, this philosophical conscience now appears careworn and out of fashion, especially in light of the leading

---

14. Some of these include: Grenz and Olson, *20th Century Theology*; Grenz and Franke, *Beyond Foundationalism*; Franke, *The Character of Theology*; Vanhoozer, *Lost in Interpretation*, 89–114; McGrath, "Engaging the Great Tradition," 150; Wolterstorff, *Divine Discourse*.
15. Thornbury, *Recovering Classic Evangelicalism*, 21.
16. Ibid.
17. Ibid., 34–58.
18. Ibid., 34.

evangelical theologians today."[19] He illustrates this point by referencing the work of Wayne Grudem, who in his systematic theology, did not include a theological prolegomena.[20] Second, Thornbury claims, "Other proposals appeared that confirmed my hypothesis. In *Covenant and Eschatology*, Michael Horton actually argued that, in effect, theology needs to operate confessionally, not epistemologically."[21] Horton's comments raise questions such as: Has evangelicalism come to the point where epistemology does not matter?[22] Can a sustained vision of evangelicalism rest solely on biblical theology, church history, and tradition? Can the Reformed tradition speak coherently to epistemological matters in a modern and postmodern age? Thornbury answers these questions saying, "Ultimately, I [Thornbury] decided that this was not necessarily the case, especially if one considers the work of figures in the tradition such as Bavinck, Ames, Edwards, Turretin, and, arguably, Calvin."[23] Counterexamples to this trajectory of downplaying epistemology in theological method exist.

For example, Norman L. Geisler in his systematic theology, dedicates twelve chapters to prolegomena.[24] Geisler claims in chapter one of a section titled, "The Importance of Preconditions,"

> A precondition makes possible what is based on it. For example, the preconditions for two human beings communicating with each other minimally include: (1) There is a mind capable of sending a message (*encoder*). (2) There is a mind capable of receiving a message (*decoder*). (3) There is a common mode of communication (like language) shared by both persons (*code*). Without these necessary preconditions communication could not take place. Likewise, without the above stated preconditions, evangelical systematic theology is not possible.[25]

---

19. Ibid.

20. Grudem, *Systematic Theology*.

21. Thornbury, *Recovering Classic Evangelicalism*, 35. Horton, *Covenant and Eschatology*.

22. Thornbury raises similar questions in his book *Recovering Classic Evangelicalism*.

23. Ibid., 35.

24. Geisler, *Systematic Theology*. One could also appeal to the work of Alister McGrath, who dedicates large sections of his theological system to prolegomena. See, McGrath, *The Genesis of Doctrine*; McGrath, *The Open Secret*.

25. Geisler, *Systematic Theology*, 14–15.

Geisler's point is well understood. Those advocating for a theological method must take into account the philosophical preconditions that make all theology, including biblical and systematic theology, possible. Geisler believes these philosophical preconditions include epistemology.

In the *Dictionary for Theological Interpretation of the Bible*, Nancey Murphy has an article titled, "Epistemology."[26] The article presents an overview of epistemology from medieval to modern philosophy, the nature of truth and justification, and theories of knowledge after modernity. It includes a section titled, "Significance for Interpretation of Scripture."[27] Murphy claims,

> To a great extent styles of reasoning in theology and biblical studies have followed developments in epistemology. Foundationalism led to revolutions in theology and biblical studies. Theology came to require its own sort of foundations, whether rationalist, experientialist, or biblicist. The requirement for indubitability explains why biblicists would want a doctrine of inerrancy; the demand for truth-certifying construction encourages foundationlists to minimize the gap between text and interpretation. The quest for the objective history behind the text is another manifestation for foundations.[28]

Murphy suggests that epistemology influences hermeneutics because theological and biblical studies have generally followed the developments in epistemology. She uses epistemological foundationalism to illustrate, in her opinion, how epistemology affects the interpretation of Scripture and informs the doctrine of inerrancy. Robert Webber agrees with Murphy petitioning that,

> Many twentieth-century evangelicals continue to teach and defend a form of foundationalism. For them, the inerrancy of the Bible and the commitment to propositional truth as objective statements which can be known and defended by reason is the means of knowing all truth. For them, this literal interpretation of the Bible yields truth not only in matters of faith and practice but also in matters of history and science.[29]

---

26. Murphy, "Epistemology," 191–194.
27. Ibid., 193.
28. Ibid.
29. Webber, *The Younger Evangelicals*.

Carl Henry is Webber's primary example of what he considers to be a "foundationalist" hermeneutic as epistemology. He calls for younger evangelicals to abandon Henry's foundationalism. Thornbury concurs with Webber that Henry's epistemology informs his hermeneutic and theological method; however, he disagrees with Webber claiming that Henry is not a foundationalist, and that modern evangelicals are not incorporating Henry's epistemology into their theories of interpretation. Thornbury claims, "Although I believe discourse on philosophical hermeneutics is essential for theological method in our time, my fundamental concern stems from the fact that those who would in general agree with Henry's approach will not engage the issue [of epistemology]."[30]

So, whereas Webber claims modern evangelicals are incorporating Henry's epistemology, Thornbury suggests many of those same evangelicals are abandoning Henry's "foundationalism," not necessarily because they disagree with it, but because they no longer engage in philosophical hermeneutics. Thornbury summarizes his point noting that,

> What seems to be missing, however, is a substantive milieu—an epistemological backdrop against which the drama of redemption and the work of the church are played out. And if Carl F. H. Henry were still with us, my guess is that he would most likely agree with this assessment.[31]

Henry developed an epistemology to undergird his hermeneutic as epistemology and methodology, so he could engage present-day views of Scripture based upon their epistemological commitments. In like manner, present-day evangelicals ought to follow in the footsteps of Henry by engaging both the claim and philosophical presuppositions of opposing views.

HENRY'S ANALYSIS OF EPISTEMOLOGICAL CONCERNS

G. Wright Doyle in his book, *Carl Henry: Theologian For All Seasons*, writes, "He [Henry] received the PhD in philosophy with a dissertation on Augustus S. Strong's theology, which had been influenced by personal idealism [sic] philosophy. From the beginning, therefore, Henry was critical of theologians who allowed alien philosophical ideas to influence

---

30. Thornbury, *Recovering Classic Evangelicalism*, 37.
31. Ibid., 39.

their interpretation of Scripture."[32] Furthermore Doyle notes, "His [Henry's] rejection of autonomous human reason as the starting point for either theology or apologetics, and his refusal to admit non-biblical categories as norms for theological truth, highlight the prophetic nature of his theological project."[33] Finally, Doyle points out that,

> Modern Western philosophical attacks on biblical revelation receive the most detailed treatment, and come up lacking. Finally, Henry tries to elucidate the superiority of divine revelation as the only valid source and conduit of reliable information about unseen realities, and even of any clarity about the significance of experience (including history and science). In the opening volume, chapter 4, 'Ways of Knowing,' stands out as programmatic for the entire series, and may be one of Henry's major contributions to apologetics and the theory of knowledge in general.[34]

These series of quotes from Doyle are programmatic for understanding Henry's epistemology. First and foremost, Henry insists on a biblical and theistic understanding of epistemology.[35] Second, Henry's epistemology not only stood against, but castigated any approach grounded in non-biblical or alien philosophical categories. Henry endorses the use of philosophy; however, the Bible ought to frame the categories of philosophical discourse. Third, Henry's method shows the incoherence in an opposing position (such as Rationalism or Empiricism), and from that vantage point, offers a robust defense of his Revelational Theistic epistemology. Doyle is correct in claiming that Henry's chapter on, "Ways of Knowing," stands out as programmatic to his theory of knowledge. Doyle points out that, "As a presuppositionalist, Henry begins in volume 1 of *God, Revelation and Authority*, with a sustained examination and critique of a variety of alternative worldviews and truth claims. One by one, he demonstrates their failure to construct a solid case."[36] In volume one,

---

32. Doyle, *Carl Henry*, 6.
33. Ibid., 85.
34. Ibid., 72.
35. Henry, *GRA*, volume one.
36. Doyle, *Carl Henry*, 72. Furthermore, Doyle notes, ". . . Henry tries to elucidate the superiority of divine revelation as the only valid source and conduit of reliable information about unseen realities, and even of any clarity about the significance of experience (including history and science)." Ibid. In brief, Henry employs the presuppositional method, in order to expose the inconsistencies in opposing ways of knowing.

Henry addresses three ways of knowing: (1) Intuition; (2) Experience [*A Posteriori*]; and (3) Reason [*A Priori*].[37] These three categories help to frame Henry's analysis of epistemological concerns.

Intuition

According to Henry, intuition is the notion, "That religious reality is known not by sense observation or by philosophical reasoning but by intuition or immediate apprehension has been asserted by various thinkers who insist that God is to be found in one's own inner experience as an instant awareness of religious Ultimate."[38] Henry offers four theses to explain and critique intuitive ways of knowledge. Only three of them will be explained in this section.[39] The first thesis is, "1. Religious mysticism depicts intuition as a way of knowing that contrasts with both reason and sensation, and therefore also with intelligible divine revelation."[40] Henry explains that, "Since the mystic's immediate union with ultimate reality assertedly supersedes the categories of thought and experience, the religious reality is held to be unverifiable by ordinary ways of knowing applicable to other human relationships."[41] Furthermore, ". . . if what is said about God must be self-contradictory or paradoxical—that is, beyond the criterion of truth and falsehood—then it would appear to critics of this view that we cannot speak intelligibly about the Divine at all."[42] Henry believes mystical approaches affirm contradictory theses. The mystic must use the canons of logic in order to communicate anything about ineffable reality.[43] But this is what they disavow. If this is the case, he upholds, "It simply makes no sense for anyone publicly to claim that he has intuited the inexpressible. The mystic cannot formulate the experience which other men should have, if they would share his belief, since in

---

37. Henry, *GRA*, 1:70–95.

38. Ibid., 1:70.

39. The fourth thesis by Henry states, "4. The proponents of rational intuition, however, include a distinctive group of scholars—foremost among them, Augustine (354–400) and John Calvin (1509–64)—who predicated the case for a priori knowledge on God's preformation of man in his image." Ibid. This view will be explained in the section titled, "Henry's Epistemology."

40. Ibid.

41. Ibid., 1:71.

42. Ibid.

43. Ibid.

the case of an 'inexpressible intuition' nobody could know what anybody else's experience was."[44] In brief, it is contradictory to claim that logic and language are unable to attend to the intuited knowledge of God, then in the next sentence use logic and language to talk about God.

The intuitive approach leaves the mystic no legitimate basis of turning paradoxical and contradictory religious experience into claims about ontological reality. Henry believes that negative theology, which claims God can only be spoken of in negative terms, is an intuitive mystical approach. He also believes Schleiermacher affirms an intuitive approach by claiming that contact with ultimate reality is to be made not intellectually or conceptually, but intuitionally, mystically, and immediately. Henry believes the error of negative theology and Schleiermacher is they are unable to offer any tests of validity for their positions. The incoherence of this intuitive epistemology is it rejects not only validity, but the ability to communicate information about God, the Bible, or reality. If Christianity is not about communicating information but feelings, Henry maintains, "The insistent question remains how one then knows what he intuits or feels, how one is to vindicate as truly objective anything beyond his own interior sentiments."[45] He believes advocates of the intuitive approaches, do not have a coherent epistemological answer because they claim the mind cannot know reality, and language is unable to communicate reality. However, they use language to know reality rationally and communicate about it in a meaningful fashion.

The second intuitive approach Henry discusses is the "rational intuition" position. Advocates of this intuitive approach believe they can have certain knowledge about reality. His second thesis on this type of intuition is,

> 2. Although intuition carries the sense of 'immediate apprehension,' such apprehension may be depicted not only as mystical and superrational but, instead, as rational (so Plato and Descartes, for example; or Augustine and Calvin, on the basis of the divine *imago* in man). Those who espouse rational intuition insist that human beings know certain propositions are immediately to be true, without resort to inference; in other words, that all men possess certain underived a priori truths without any process of inference whereby these truths are derived. Rational

44. Ibid.
45. Ibid., 1:72.

intuition must therefore be clearly distinguished from mystical intuition.[46]

Henry offers a brief overview of Plato's innate idea approach and Aristotle's knowledge through sensation, maintaining both taught that the mind could know first principles, and that intuition is able to grasp these principles.[47] He claims Descartes' epistemology taught that intuition ought to be understood as clear and distinct ideas. From his method, Descartes claimed he could deduce all other truths. This approach to "rational intuition," is also known as foundationalism.[48] Henry offers no critique of this second "rational intuition" approach to knowledge. However, as future research will indicate, that does not entail Henry affirmed a classic foundationalist epistemology.[49]

The third intuitive approach to knowledge Henry addresses is an "empirical" approach. In his third thesis, Henry claims, "3. Modern empiricists, on the other hand, do not derive so-called intuitive knowledge from some innate faculty that provides man with first principles, but ascribes all knowledge to inferences from observation."[50] He surveys the views of David Hume, Friedrich Nietzsche, Emile Durkheim, William James, and John Dewey. Henry critiques what he considers the "logical positivists" approach, claiming, "Logical positivists held that supposed intuitive truths are simply analytic truths derived by following the conventions of logic, although this explanation fails to cope with claims that man has prelinguistic intuitive knowledge, and moreover confuses the acquisition of knowledge with the linguistic ability to express it."[51] Henry claims Immanuel Kant opposed Hume's strong empirical method

---

46. Ibid., 1:74.

47. Ibid.

48. Simon Blackburn in the *Oxford Dictionary of Philosophy*, defines foundationalism as, "The view in epistemology that knowledge must be regarded as a structure raised upon secure, certain foundations. These are found in some combination of experience and reason, with different schools (empiricism, rationalism) emphasizing the role of one over the other. Foundationalism was associated with the ancient Stoics, and in the modern era with Descartes, who discovered his foundations in 'clear and distinct' ideas of reason." Blackburn, *Oxford Dictionary of Philosophy*, 145.

49. See chapter five where the researcher responds to the claim that Henry is a classic foundationalist.

50. Henry, *GRA*, 1:74–75.

51. Ibid., 1:75.

by proposing a critical philosophy, defending "sensuous intuition" rather than an "intellectual intuition."

According to Henry, Kant's approach claims that knowledge does not begin with innate truths, but innate categories of thought and forms of perception, which confer on sensually given objects the status of cognitive knowledge.[52] He attempts to show the connection between Kant's intuitive approach and Hegel's epistemology claiming that,

> Hegel sought to overcome the metaphysical limitations of Kant's views, but his profoundly unbiblical exaggeration of the reason of man into the very mind of God was self-defeating. His theory insisted that we immediately intuit concepts rather than truths. Human reasoning then combines these concepts into propositions, and mediates knowledge. Truth is expressed only in a system, for knowledge is conceptually systematic. But, by equating the Absolute with the reflective self-consciousness of human minds, Hegel obscured any real created existence. For mankind in the image of God he substitutes God externalized as the universe, so that destruction of man and the world would obliterate divine being and life. Hegel made God an inescapable reality by divinizing man, and thereby he caricatured both.[53]

Henry claims both Kant and Hegel's intuitive approaches forfeit the possibility of metaphysical knowledge. He believes their approaches affect metaphysical knowledge by endorsing supra-rational theories unable to overcome skepticism or their theories provide no metaphysical basis for intuitive certainty. Furthermore, followers of Kant and Hegel are unable to agree over which propositions are intuitive or the extent of intuitive knowledge.[54] He claims, "Since not every human being intuited what the various philosophers insisted is a matter of universal intuitive knowledge, the secular theories carried little conviction."[55] For Henry, a sustainable epistemology requires universal and objective criteria. Henry does not endorse an intuitive approach because he believes it lacks universal and objective epistemological criteria.

52. Ibid.
53. Ibid., 1:76.
54. Ibid.
55. Ibid.

Experience–A Posteriori

The second approach to knowledge Henry investigates is experiential or *a posteriori* knowledge. In Bob E. Patterson's book, *Carl F. H. Henry*, he notes for Henry, "Empiricism fails as a way of knowing God because it cannot arrive at truth since it is committed to an unending search. Empirical conclusions are always so tentative that empiricism can never be sure it has found the truth."[56] Henry claims empirical approaches consider sense observation to be the source of all truth and knowledge. He suggests that, "Empiricists do not wholly reject reason, since reason must relate sense perceptions in an orderly way, but all truth is held to be derived from experience."[57]

Moreover, Henry notes that, "The definition of empiricism has been revised frequently throughout the history of philosophy."[58] Mystics claim experiential knowledge must include ineffable experiences, unless philosophers wrongly argue a narrow definition of human experience to only include sense experience. He points out that contemporary empiricists consider perceptual experience the only reliable method of gaining information about the world, and that it is the only verifiable method for sound conclusions.

Henry believes the Aristotelian-Thomistic approach is the "grandfather" of an empirical approach to knowledge.[59] He claims, "Viewed epistemologically, the Protestant Reformation was in some respects a protest against the Thomistic demotion of divine revelation as the controlling axiom; the qualification is required by the fact that many Lutherans carried forward the cosmological argument."[60] In light of Justin Carswell's

---

56. Patterson, *Carl F. H. Henry*, 68.

57. Henry, *GRA*, 1:78.

58. Ibid.

59. Henry was not favorable of Thomistic philosophy. See, 1:203; 2:55; and Henry, *Remaking of the Modern Mind*, 58, 201–307.

60. Ibid., 2:114. Henry elaborates how this affects hermeneutics as epistemology and methodology claiming, "What this development [an empirical method and theistic arguments] attests is that the failure to predicate argumentative theism on intelligible divine revelation as a significant epistemic principle has had costly consequences for both modern theology and modern philosophy. The attempt to concentrate the case for theism upon observations from the not-God, while neglecting the reality of God in his revelation, has led to more than the erosion of the power of God in modern life; it has also betrayed modern philosophy and theology into a time of intellectual sterility." Ibid., 2:119.

excellent dissertation on Henry, which addresses Henry's disavowal of the Thomistic empirical method, the following section will focus on Henry's criticisms of Friedrich Schleiermacher's use of an empirical method.[61] Henry's critiques of Schleiermacher are important, because as chapter one showed, many modern and contemporary philosophers of hermeneutics affirm tenets of Schleiermacher's hermeneutic as epistemology (e.g., various levels of the hermeneutical spiral).[62]

According to Henry, "Schleiermacher boldly identified the empirical method as adequate to deal with religious concerns and decisive for the fortunes of Christianity, yet he sought at the same time to broaden the definition of empiricism so that—contrary to Hume's skeptical analysis of theological claims—an appeal to the religious consciousness could yield a positive and constructive verdict."[63] Schleiermacher considers feeling rather than cognition the locus of religious experience, and as Henry points out, ". . . he [Schleiermacher] applied the empirical method hopefully to the claims of Christian theism. Rejecting the historical evangelical emphasis that the truth of revelation rests on an authority higher than science, Schleiermacher broke with miraculous Christianity and held that all events must conform to empirically verifiable law."[64] Moreover, Henry notes, "Aware that empirical considerations would not yield a fixed definition of ultimate metaphysical reality, Schleiermacher nonetheless believed that experiential considerations can offer tentative and flexible conclusions about God in relation to us."[65]

61. Carswell, *A Comparative Study*, 80–82.

62. Henry makes the observation that, "Although Schleiermacher did not explicitly identify himself as an empiricist (he speaks of the 'religious consciousness' rather than of religious experience as his twentieth-century successors do), yet his method is empirical and his theology empirically grounded. He does indeed criticize the understanding of empiricism regnant in his day for its Kantian limitation of the content of human knowledge to sense percepts. Schleiermacher concedes that we cannot have cognitive knowledge of God as he objectively is, but he insists that the religious consciousness give us knowledge of God-in-relation to us. He also diverges from Kant in holding that religious doctrines are not certain but—conformably to the empirical approach—are tentative explanations, subject to revision by future experience. Absolute truth is excluded in theologically as fully as in all other matters. The finality of any religion is left in doubt, and the Christian religion is shorn of its historic claim for God's transcendent cognitive revelation and of external miraculous attestation." Henry, *GRA*, 1:81.

63. Ibid., 1:80.

64. Ibid.

65. Ibid.

In summary, Henry's primary criticism of Schleiermacher's approach is that by using the empirical method, all concepts (even the concept of God), are tentative, and all definitions are liable to revision in light of human experience.[66] Henry rejects Schleiermacher's empirical approach because he believes it lacks universal, and objective criteria for epistemology. In particular, Schleiermacher's view ought to be rejected because he made feeling rather than cognition the locus of religious experience.

Henry claims the result of Schleiermacher's epistemology is individuals cannot help but offer a variety of confused answers to the questions, "But how then does one know what he feels, and whether we ought to feel concerning God? . . . what firmly grounded cognitive statements about God are to be made solely on the basis of the not-God?"[67] Since Schleiermacher's method does not allow for cognitive knowledge or statements about God, Henry claims his use of the empirical method could never consistently make truthful claims about Christ. Henry addresses the heart of the issue, and its implications for theological method when he claims,

> In this evasion of man's primal cognitive relationship to God, Herzog reflects the mood of recent theological and philosophical traditions influenced by Husserl's phenomenology and Heideggerian existentialism, let alone Schleiermacher's earlier emphasis on precognitive awareness. The fact that the question of man's primal religious experience is so confidently raised in terms of noncognitive factors is doubly significant when one considers the contrary biblical view and also that in the long history of religious philosophy and theology Christianity has frequently been associated with rational apriorism. Evangelical religion discusses man's primal experience only in the context of a universal revelation of God which directly engages man as a carrier of the created image of God in both mind and conscience, and confronts him intelligibly in external nature and history.[68]

Primarily due to Schleiermacher's influence, liberal theologians disdained cognitive-propositional statements about God and Christ, rejecting supernatural beliefs for empirically testable positions based upon

---

66. Ibid., 80–81.
67. Ibid., 82.
68. Ibid., 2:279.

inner experience. For that reason, Schleiermacher has been considered the father of modern theological liberalism.[69]

Henry continues to analyze naturalism, logical positivism, and other empirically oriented approaches to epistemology. He offers similar criticisms of these approaches as he does of Schleiermacher's. Henry also criticizes Bernard Lonergan's theological approach because it is grounded in an empirical method common to all of the other sciences.[70] Carswell explains Henry's criticisms of the empirical method *per se* noting,

> What lies underneath Henry's critique of the empirical theories is the long-standing critique of empiricism. That critique questions the legitimacy of empiricism's appeal to an objective standard outside itself for universal and value judgments. Henry emphasizes that unless there is an objective standard possessed by the human mind apart from experience (but which is used by the human mind in sense perception), the ability of the knower to move from probability to certainty is reduced.[71]

Doyle summarizes Henry's critique and answer to empiricism noting, "He [Henry] describes the weakness of modern empiricism, especially scientific empiricism and logical positivism, and asserts that it can never lead to anything but tentative conclusions. Divine revelation alone can provide certitude."[72] In brief, Henry opposes all empirical approaches to knowledge, because the probabilistic nature of the system provides no universal criteria for justification, and allows for the possibility that the truth claims of divine revelation might be overturned in light of new human experience.

Reason–A Priori

The third approach to knowledge Henry investigates is "reason" or *a priori* knowledge. He begins this section on *a priori* reasoning claiming, "The superiority of reason over all other proposals for gaining information about the ultimately real world has been asserted from antiquity. The rationalistic method of knowing considers human reasoning as the only

---

69. For an explanation of Liberal Protestantism, see: McGrath, *Historical Theology*, 340–334.
70. See Henry, *GRA*, 1:195–196.
71. Carswell, *A Comparative Study*, 80.
72. Doyle, *Carl Henry*, 111–112.

reliable and valid source of knowledge."[73] The "reason" approach insists that truth can never be self-contradictory, and opposes the empiricist claims of tentative knowledge based on sense reality. Henry points out that,

> The underlying assumption of philosophical rationalism is that the mind of man—simply in view of its latent potentialities, or veiled divinity, or the human mind's explicit and direct continuity with the mind of God—possesses an inherent potentiality for solving all intellectual problems. This immanent rational capacity is variously explained by leading philosophers.[74]

Patterson in his book on Henry qualifies Henry's comments on rationalism. He claims Henry agrees with the rationalist that reason is a test for truth. Unlike the rationalists, however, Henry does not believe reason is superior to revelation, or that grandiose theories based on human reason alone are able to explain the interrelationships of all reality.[75] Henry addresses rationalist philosophers such as Plato, Augustine, Anselm, Descartes, Spinoza, Leibniz, and Hegel (even though Henry later claims that Augustine is not a rationalist). He explains four different *a priori* approaches to knowledge using these headings: (1) The Philosophical Transcendent a Priori; (2) The Theological Transcendent a Priori; (3) The Religious Transcendental a Priori; and (4) The Philosophical Transcendent (Critical) a Priori.

The two approaches analyzed in this section are: (a) The Philosophical Transcendent a Priori, focusing on Hegel; and (b) The Philosophical Transcendental (Critical) a Priori, focusing on Kant. Hegel and Kant have been chosen because so much of the literature presents them as two of the key figures influencing hermeneutics as epistemology.[76] In particular, Kant claims that the mind structures all of reality, and Hegel's dialectical method has influenced many theories of knowledge and elements of the hermeneutical spiral. In the order of Henry, which is not the chronological order, Hegel's "Philosophical Transcendent A Priori," will be analyzed first.

---

73. Henry, *GRA*, 1:85.
74. Ibid., 1:86.
75. Patterson, *Carl F. H. Henry*, 69.
76. Grondin, *Introduction to Philosophical Hermeneutics*; Palmer, *Hermeneutics*; Anthony C. Thiselton, *New Horizons in Hermeneutics*.

According to Henry, Hegel champions his theory of knowledge by grounding it in his version of the ontological argument. This allows Hegel to establish the existence of the Absolute. Hegel's view differs from the Christian form of the ontological argument because his advocates for a version of innate ideas according to a pantheistic worldview.[77] Henry notes,

> The existence of an Eternal Reason, an Absolute Thinker, is held to be involved in the very act of thinking. Hegel rules out the a priori and the a posteriori as dual sources of knowledge which are to be contrasted, by tracing the former alone directly to reason. All knowledge issues from reason alone: all is a priori in generation, although its appearance in empirical consciousness might be a posteriori.[78]

Consequently, the logical evolution of the Absolute in Hegel's epistemology is also known as the dialectic. Henry summarizes Hegel's dialectic and its effects on innate ideas suggesting,

> The doctrine of innate ideas is threatened in still another way by Hegel's emphasis on the logical evolution of the Absolute. Finite minds are considered partial and hence as imperfect manifestations of the Absolute. An inner prodding by the Absolute consciousness in which humanity participates brings human minds into conformity with the content of the Absolute mind through the change and transformation of a priori ideas. Here the transition from apriorism to empiricism is almost complete.[79]

Henry proceeds to note that Hegel responds to Kant's critical philosophy, which placed limits on knowledge, by attempting to show that reason is able to take on many forms. In effect, Hegel's dialectic affects epistemology by insisting that reality and our knowledge of reality are in constant flux.

Henry observes that, ". . . whereas the others [Kant and Schleiermacher] denied objective cognitive knowledge of God, Hegel held that religion gains rational significance if one translates its otherwise imaginative

---

77. Henry notes that, "This pantheistic alteration advances the ontological argument by identifying all reality with thought itself, and changes the significance of innatism by assigning an identically innate status to all ideas." Henry, *GRA*, 1:320.

78. Ibid., 1:321.

79. Ibid.

pictorial representations into idealistic metaphysics."[80] Henry elaborates upon the theological implications of idealism. He writes,

> Revelational theology is therefore regarded as a parabolic expression of what the Hegelian philosophy transposes into univocal language and categories of thought. This way is thus prepared for philosophers of religion to hold that theology traffics religious symbols not literally true, while valid assertions about transcendent reality are reserved for philosophy.[81]

Although he lays no claim to objective truth or historical factuality, Hegel's philosophy opens the door for the belief that internal sentiments, symbolic expressions or mythical formulations are the means to connect with ultimate reality[82] Henry rejects Hegel's view because reason is now considered the primary instrument for knowing reality (divine reality included), whereas revelation is downgraded to a secondary status.

The second approach Henry addresses is the Philosophical Transcendental (Critical) a Priori.[83] Henry believes Kant offers a new direction to the classic definition of *a priori* knowledge by advancing a "critical" *a priori* method. Henry distinguishes the two approaches by using the term "transcendental" to refer to Kant's epistemology, and "transcendent" to refer to all other *a priori* theories of knowledge.[84] Henry claims Kant taught that the self is the starting point to knowledge. This starting point is not a novel concept in epistemology, but what Kant claims is that the subjective self is the source of *all* knowledge.[85] Kant's theory was first accepted because it challenged the empiricist approach to knowledge. However, Henry believes the costly implication of Kant's view is it cut

80. Ibid., 1:89.
81. Ibid.
82. Ibid., 1:52.
83. Ibid., 344–363.

84. Ibid., 1:344. Henry claims that Kant attempts to establish a way of knowledge that divorces the a priori from all metaphysics and revelational or rational methods; without coming to the same conclusions as Hume's empirical skepticism. Henry points out that, "Kant has the distinction of projecting the *transcendental* a priori, in contrast to the transcendent aprioristic views that expound metaphysics affirmatively rather than skeptically. The medieval scholastics had used the terms *transcendent* and *transcendental* synonymously, the former being more common. Kant sharply distinguished them; transcendental knowledge is knowledge only of the nature and conditions of human a priori cognition, not a knowledge of objective reality. The transcendental must therefore not be confused with concepts of objectively real things." Ibid., 1:345.

85. Ibid.

individuals off from the possibility of metaphysical knowledge. Like the other empirical approaches to knowledge, Kant criticized innate ideas. Henry writes,

> Kant did not set out by deliberately attacking innate ideas; rather, his Critical Philosophy left no room for them. They fell by the wayside of the Kantian separation of the elements of form and content in knowledge experience. While Kant repudiated any innate knowledge *content*, he insisted nonetheless on the indispensability of innate *forms*.[86]

Evidently Henry believes one of Kant's most significant contributions and innovations to the history of thought was his development of innate categories, not innate ideas.

Ultimately Henry believes Kant's epistemology is self-defeating. Henry goes on to explain the self-defeating nature of Kant's epistemology. He writes,

> Kant himself had not been able to derive the categories from within the epistemological framework by which he proposed to account for all knowledge. For he insisted that there is no knowledge apart from sense content, that sensation furnishes the only content of knowledge. Where then did Kant get his knowledge of the categories? Either he derived them from a source for which his epistemology allows no room—but which the preformation theory would accommodate—or they too are supplied to knowledge through sensation, which was Emile Durkheim's proposal: the categories are simply social contracts. Kant's theory either breaks down in skepticism regarding the categories themselves, that is, his epistemology cannot get itself underway, or he must move to preformation or empiricism to avoid skepticism, and in a time of epistemological trouble a shift to empiricism is of little help.[87]

Kant's theory of knowledge, according to Henry, ". . . cannot escape a skeptical conclusion to the search for trustworthy knowledge."[88] Henry makes an important observation that Kant's theory breaks down into skepticism or empiricism. He claims that Kant's theory might be able to account for certain types of knowledge, but it cannot account for knowledge of the categories of thought. However, Henry also believes

86. Ibid., 1:346.
87. Ibid., 1:361.
88. Ibid., 1:362.

a preformation theory of knowledge is able to overcome the weaknesses in various opposing theories of knowledge (e.g., intuitive, a priori, and empirical approaches)[89] In light of Carl F. H. Henry's critiques of these epistemological systems, the second section of this chapter will explain Henry's "Theological Transcendent a Priori" theory of knowledge.

HENRY'S EPISTEMOLOGY

Henry's epistemology affirms a preformation view of knowledge.[90] Henry points out that a preformation view of knowledge bears noetic implica-

---

89. Henry first explained this theory in his fourth approach to intuitive knowledge. The fourth thesis of Henry is, "4. The proponents of rational intuition, however, include a distinctive group of scholars—foremost among them, Augustine (354–400) and John Calvin (1509–64)—who predicated the case for a priori knowledge on God's performation of man in his image." Ibid., 1:76. Henry maintains that, "They formulated the whole possibility of human knowledge in the context of transcendent divine revelation, and avoided correlating their emphasis on a priori truth with extravagant claims such as those of Descartes, who sought to derive all the content of knowledge from the intuitive certainty of human self-existence." Ibid. Furthermore, "Their position needs to be carefully distinguished from that of secular philosophical rationalists, who depicted human reason as an immanent source of ultimate truth, or that of medieval scholastic Anselm, who considered the human mind independent of divine revelation a source of information not only about God's existence, but also about the Trinity and the incarnation and atonement of Christ." Ibid.

90. The preformation view is not a Christianized form of Kant's epistemology. According to Henry, "Kant strangely thought that if the categories of thought were God-given aptitudes preharmonized with the laws of nature they would not be a priori. He objects to God-given concepts on two groups: (1) one could never in that case determine where such predetermined aptitudes cease to be relevant; (2) the categories would then lose their essential character of necessity. Gordon Clark rightly notes the ambiguity of the first complaint (*Thales to Dewey*, 410). Does Kant here have misgivings that the categories might then be applicable not only to sense experience, but to God and the supernatural?—which is precisely what a theistic epistemology would affirm! Or does he mean that we would not know which category or categories explain any concrete empirical situation?—a difficulty that equally faces Kant's own theory of a priori forms. Kant's second complaint is that, if the categories were implanted at creation, one could not then say, for example, that effects and causes are necessarily connected, but only that 'I am so constituted that I can think this representation as to connect, and not otherwise. Now this is just what the skeptic wants.' But Kant is very wrong in thinking that divinely implanted categories of thought would invalidate their necessary application to reality. The fact is, rather, that Kant's own view—that we cannot think otherwise than we think, alongside which he denies that we can know the objective structure of external reality—ultimately undercuts the necessary relevance of the categories." Ibid., 1:77.

tions that have, "... constrained some of Christianity's profoundest theologians to insist that God is the source of all truth, that the human mind is an instrument for recognizing truth, and that the rational awareness of God is given a priori correlation with man's self-awareness, so that man as a knower stands always in epistemic relationship with his Maker and Judge."[91] Henry uses Augustine and Calvin to explain the classic preformation view of knowledge.[92] He defines the position noting that, "The theory that combines intuitive or a priori knowledge with a Christian view of man (in contrast to an idealistic or rationalistic divinization of reason) is the view of preformation. According to this view, the categories of thought are aptitudes for thought implanted by the Creator and synchronized with the whole of created reality."[93] The way Henry explains the preformation view of knowledge is by advancing what he labels as a "Theological Transcendent a Priori."

Theological Transcendent a Priori

According to Carswell, in the section of his dissertation titled, "Theological Transcendent a Priori," he claims,

> Henry's conception of religious knowledge along the foregoing lines has shown his commitment to the school of theological and philosophical thought which advocates an external object world which can be known by the human mind.... What the a priori interpretation of religious knowledge insists is that God is the source of knowledge and that 'man does not rise to God from the not-God,' but that religious experience is the 'direct apprehension in the inner human spirit.' ... Although Henry objects to the position that it is possible for unaided rationalizing to arrive at truth, he believes that humanity does have a created

---

91. Ibid., 1:78.

92 Henry claims that "Augustine held that on the basis of creation the human mind possess a number of necessary truths. Intellectual intuition conveys the laws of logic, the immediate consciousness of self-existence, the truths of mathematics, and the moral truth that one ought to seek wisdom. Moreover, he held that in knowing immutable and eternal truth we know God, for only God is immutable and eternal. As knowers all men stand in epistemic contact with God. Calvin too held that man's knowledge of self-existence is given in and through a knowledge of God's existence, and that the created *imago Dei* preserves man in ongoing epistemic relationship to God, the world, and other selves." Ibid., 76–77.

93. Ibid., 1:77.

> capacity for knowledge of absolute truth, despite humanity's condition as fallen. . . . Humanity has been created in the image of God, and because God actively preserves his creation (humanity being a part of that creation, even the mind), humanity stands in 'direct knowledge relation' to God, who constantly reveals his existence and attributes through general and special revelation.[94]

Carswell claims both Henry and Plantinga's epistemology demonstrate ". . . the ability of God to communicate with the human mind and the mind's ability to understand what God reveals because God has designed the human mind to function in a way that obtains truth."[95] For that reason, Carswell believes there was a strong affinity between Henry and Plantinga's epistemologies because each view maintains humanity's immediate knowledge of God.[96] In fact, Henry requested that Plantinga's philosophical articles be published in *Christianity Today* and urged for him to receive funding to teach as a leading Protestant scholar in the university system.[97]

In *God, Revelation and Authority*, Henry includes a chapter titled, "The Theological Transcendent a Priori."[98] He argues that the history of Christian theism until Kant allowed for the immediate knowledge of God. Over and against philosophical *a priorism*, which according to Henry, ". . . enthrones the speculative impulse and postulates an aprioristic principle in its question for a rationale of reality, the theological tradition promotes the a priori in the framework of divine revelation."[99] Furthermore, "The Christian view is not content to presuppose Platonic, or Cartesian, or Leibnizian apriorism, any more than it is content with Thomistic empiricism, as natural theology. It not only champions its own metaphysic, but requires a distinctive knowledge theory."[100] Henry summarizes the theological transcendent a priori view and the implications it has upon epistemology, pointing out that,

---

94. Carswell, *A Comparative Study*, 87–88.
95. Ibid., 29.
96. Ibid., 1–30. See also: Hoitenga, *Faith and Reason From Plato to Plantinga*, ix.
97. Henry, *Confessions of a Theologian*, 226, 272.
98. Henry, *GRA*, 1:323–343.
99. Ibid., 1:324.
100. Ibid.

Treated simply as an explanatory theory, the Christian perspective claims to save significance for the whole range of knowledge experience, and to surpass all competitive views in this accomplishment. But the theological transcendent a priori additionally professes a revelational grounding. It comprehends innate knowledge in the context of universal divine revelation and to aprioristic knowledge it assimilates special revelation as well. It affirms that men stand everywhere and always in direct knowledge relation to the living God, in virtue of a specific divine origin and preservation. Whatever it is true to its inner spirit, Christian knowledge theory cannot expound the a priori independently of either general or special revelation. But this does not imply that the a priori argument lacks philosophical force. On the contrary, it best explains the relating of man as a knower to the activity of God and the divine image in creation preferably accounts for all the pertinent data which philosophical apriorism delineates unstably and inadequately.[101]

Henry's "Theological Transcendent a Priori" approach uses Augustine's epistemology to argue for epistemological certainty and objective knowledge of both God and the external world.[102]

Augustinian Epistemology

Carswell approvingly claims, "Henry approaches the question of religious belief within the Augustinian tradition. The Augustinian approach employs the maxim, 'I believe in order to understand.' Henry interprets that maxim as, 'Faith is the minds way of knowing.' In other words, knowledge begins with faith; faith leads one to knowledge."[103] According to Henry, there are two basic sources for knowledge of God, (1) human postulation or (2) divine revelation.[104] Henry claims that Augustine stands, ". . . unrivaled as the brilliant exponent of the Christian thesis that the knowledge of God and of other selves and the world of nature is not merely inferential."[105] Furthermore,

---

101. Ibid.
102. Ibid.
103. Carswell, *A Comparative Study*, 30.
104. Ibid. See Henry, *GRA*, 1:93.
105. Ibid., 1:325.

> Whatever else is contributory to the content of human cognition, this knowledge involves a direct and immediate noesis [sic] because of the unique constitution of the human mind. Knowledge of God is no mere induction from the finite and the nondivine, but is directly and intuitively given in human experience.[106]

Unashamedly, Henry defends humanity's ability to have immediate knowledge of God because he believes knowledge of God is first and foremost, self-evident.[107] Meanwhile, for the sake of this project, since the contemporary concerns of epistemology focus on the relationship between justification and knowledge—and for the reason that hermeneutics seeks to validate knowledge claims about the text—the following section will focus on Henry's use of Augustine's epistemology to justify knowledge claims, and the effects this has upon his hermeneutic as epistemology.[108]

Certainty and Augustinian Epistemology

In his book *Carl F. H. Henry*, Patterson claims, "Augustine hungered for certainty. He was deeply influenced by the philosophical skeptics of his day who taught that neither the five senses nor the mind of man could be trusted to lead to truth."[109] Patterson summarizes Augustine's argument in these terms,

> But how does Augustine get from doubt to certainty? He began where the skeptics began, with universal doubt, but he did not end where they did, in universal skepticism. Doubting, Augustine said, implies a self (a doubter) who can use his mind to think (doubting implies laws of logic, thinking, remembering, judging). 'I doubt, therefore I am.' Doubt implies three things: the reality of the doubter, the reliability of the faculties involved in doubting and the truthfulness of the propositions these

---

106. Ibid.

107. Ibid.

108. Henry does not use the specific epistemological term "Justification." He uses the term "Validation," which closely resembles the term "Justification" in his epistemology.

109. Patterson, *Carl F. H. Henry*, 69.

faculties work with. The doubter possesses truth. The doubting self knows these things with certainty and assurance.[110]

Augustine's theory locates certainty in the self with a thinking mind, rather than outside the self in the world of the five senses. Patterson goes on to note, "... Henry, like Augustine, hungers for certainty, for an objective standard possessed already in the approach to experience."[111] Henry comments about Augustine's epistemology claiming,

> The philosophical foes of Augustine were the skeptics of the New Academy who allowed no knowledge beyond probability, and the sensationalists who professed to derive everything in the intellect from sensation alone. Against both viewpoints, Augustine emphasized that truth is primarily found in the intellect alone. Truth must be located in inner consciousness, where reason operates under its own laws and supplies those thought forms without which sensation and experience would be unintelligible.[112]

By following this epistemology, Augustine believed he could overcome probabilistic claims to knowledge, offering the skeptic at least the plausibility of certain knowledge of the external world.[113] It is this aspect of Augustine's epistemology, along with his concept of Revelational Theism, Henry utilizes to provide at least the plausibility of epistemological certainty *per se*. Both Augustine's view of knowledge, and Revelational Theism, influences Henry's hermeneutic because they thought it allowed for the possibility of objectivity in biblical interpretation.[114]

---

110. Ibid., 70.
111. Ibid., 72.
112. Henry, GRA, 1:325.
113. Matthews, *Thought's Ego In Augustine And Descartes*, 31–37.
114. In the modern world "objectivity" came to connote the epistemological stance that a person is ideally unaffected by prior beliefs or judgments. In some sense "neutral" or viewed apart from any particular "perspective." See, Bowald, "Objectivity," 544. Therefore, universal validity is impossible because there are no Archimedean points upon which objectivity is based. Henry advocates for a different view of objectivity. He opposes the idea that "objectivity" connotes epistemological neutrality or freedom from perspectives. Henry claims that presuppositions affect knowledge; however, the subjective elements of the knowing process do not usurp the possibility for principles of universal validity, or there are no means of adjudicating between interpretations. For a better explanation of this form of objectivity, see: Thomas Howe, *Objectivity in Biblical Interpretation*; Thomas, *Evangelical Hermeneutics*.

Revelational Theism and Augustinian Epistemology

According to Henry, Augustine's epistemology allows for the possibility of sure knowledge about the external world.[115] Henry believes Augustine endorses a "theistic epistemology."[116] Augustine's view of knowledge claims God created the world and humanity in order for them to relate with each other.[117] God created the human mind and senses in order to properly function in the external world. Henry explains *how* Augustine uses a theistic epistemology to substantiate the notion that humanity can have certain knowledge of the external world. He writes,

> Augustine regards the human soul as uniquely fashioned by creation and divinely maintained for an existence in a dual environment. The senses link man to an objective world of sense perception, while the intellect links man to an objective world of intellection. The certitude of consciousness involves at the same time certitude of the external world. The Creator's determination constantly maintains man in this joint relationship to the rational and phenomenal worlds, and to the Creator himself as decisive for all. The soul, like the sense world in which man is placed, has in God its constant support and direction.[118]

For both Augustine and Henry, God as Creator fashioned the world and humanity to harmoniously interact with each other. God as providential Sustainer determines and sustains man's ability to relate and know the objective, rational, and phenomenal world with certainty.

Henry addresses the issue of epistemological subjectivity. His first criticism of both Christian and non-Christian forms of epistemological subjectivity is they downplay or deny Revelational Theism. Henry critiques "Subjectivism Idealism," claiming, "Subjective idealism, with its notion of the subjectivity of the phenomenal world, could therefore be no live option for Augustine. Man's sensations relate him to an objectively real world."[119] He claims that some scholars believe Augustine is a

---

115. Henry, *GRA*, 1:325.
116. Ibid.
117. Ibid.
118. Ibid.
119. Ibid., 1:325–326. Henry believes this includes both pantheistic and Stoic forms of idealism because ". . . [t]he phenomenal world is no mere creation of the human spirit viewed as part of the divine Spirit; man creates neither the intelligible world nor the sense world. In relation to neither is the human mind sovereignly creative; in both cases the mind is in some respects passive." Ibid., 1:326. This quote shows that

precursor to Cartesian rationalism and foundationalism, or his views are a form of Hegelian idealism, where the Absolute regulates the extension of knowledge in the external world. Henry responds to these criticisms noting that, "Later idealism retained Augustine's emphasis that truth must not be sought exclusively outside man, but modified it beyond recognition. To consider the great Christian philosopher a forerunner of Descartes and Hegel is as false as to label him as a product of Plato."[120] He believes it is a category mistake to compare Augustine's Revelational Theism to later Cartesian or Hegelian rationalism.[121] Henry claims Augustine taught that due to God's creative decree, divine revelation is the source of all knowledge. This knowledge is mediated by the Logos through the image of God in humanity. The Logos and the *imago Dei* serve to connect the rationale of humanity to both God and the external world.[122] He believes Augustine's view differs significantly from Descartes and Hegel's because they taught that truth and epistemological certainty were primarily found within humanity (not in divine revelation).[123] In brief, for Henry, the fact that knowledge is based on God's revelation; instead, of human reason alone, distinguishes Augustine's view from later rationalistic theories of knowledge.[124]

According to Henry, "All knowledge experience, whether sensible or rational, he [Augustine] views as God-given. That man has valid knowledge at all is explained by Augustine on the ground of his creation-link to the supernatural world."[125] The implication of Augustine's epistemology is that, "Never is human knowledge adequately described as an achievement of human factors operating wholly in isolation from a divine activity. Man's search for knowledge is 'a consultation of God'; fulfillment of this question comes as a 'divine imprinting' of truth upon the soul."[126] Augustine taught that God is the source and determiner of

---

Henry believes that ancient views erred because they added a creative element to the human intellect, instead of being a passive recipient. Henry does not claim that the mind is unable to extend knowledge; rather, he denies that the mind is the creative source of *all* knowledge.

120. Ibid.
121. Ibid.
122. Ibid.
123. Ibid.
124. Ibid.
125. Ibid.
126. Ibid.

all knowledge. God decrees the categories and limits of knowledge, not human postulations or alien philosophies. Henry claims that the divine initiative to knowledge has been taught since the ancient world.[127] However, ". . . Augustine's exposition is rooted in Revelational Theism, and it runs counter both to the pantheizing philosophy of the ancients and to the deistic tendency of the later period."[128]

Henry responds to the claim that Augustine's theory of knowledge is a modified form of Plato's doctrine of recollection or imitation. Instead, for Augustine, divine activity is the key to man's knowledge and relationship to the objective world of intellection. All knowledge is grounded in the broader theological sense of general revelation, offering knowledge both truth and assurance.[129] Henry claims because God is the author of humanity's rational faculties, he must also be the ground of man's certitude, and the validity of knowledge.[130] He notes, "Even before the fall, man's attainment of truth involved this creation-dependence upon God, since all truth is a reflection of God's truth into the soul."[131] For Henry, Augustine's theory of the "divine initiative" allows for the possibility of true and certain knowledge of God and the external world (especially the text of Scripture, God's main form of revelation).

According to Henry, another benefit of Augustine's theory of knowledge is it provides a way for humanity to overcome the noetic effects of sin, and the moral results of the fall. For Augustine, the noetic effects of sin have epistemological implications throughout an individual's life. The longer a person lives sin continues to plague the mind. Henry notes that for Augustine, the noetic effects of the fall entail, ". . . that human faculties become so impaired by sin that the natural man is precluded from the ascertainment of truth. The soul is plagued by an obstacle to knowledge which it cannot itself overcome."[132] He claims Augustine believes the answer provided by Christian theism is that regeneration is able to overcome the noetic effects of sin and the moral results of the fall. For Henry, Augustine's insistence on the role of regeneration provides a

---

127. Ibid.
128. Ibid.
129. Ibid. See also: Patterson, *Carl F. H. Henry*, 71.
130. Ibid.
131. Henry, *GRA*, 1:328.
132. Ibid., 1:329.

consistent answer to overcome the *moral* gulf separating humanity from genuine knowledge of God and the external world.[133]

In brief, Henry believes evangelical epistemologists should incorporate Augustine's theory that humanity was created to know God and the external world. For Henry, Augustine's epistemology provides a consistent way to account for knowledge of the external world and epistemological certitude. Furthermore, it accounts for human error by tracing the problem of flawed human knowledge back to the fall. Through regeneration, God overcomes the noetic effects of sin by transforming the mind of believers and by changing their hearts to overcome the moral results of the fall.[134] The next section will discuss *how* Augustine influenced the presuppositional method and *how* Henry incorporates presuppositionalism into his epistemology.

Presuppositional Method

Patterson explains that the presuppositional method finds its roots in Augustine, noting, "Long ago Augustine saw that all thought depends on original assumptions—we must believe something before we can know anything. These absolutistic assumptions are seldom expressed, sometimes unrecognized, and most often unprovable."[135] Moreover, since Henry's epistemology is within the Augustinian tradition, Patterson points out that for Henry,

> Basic assumptions are most significant because they determine the method and goal of thought: axioms determine theorems. Once assumed, an ultimate principle becomes the foundation for all other patterns of thought. In the strictest sense, ultimate principles cannot be proven, but they can be indirectly verified. Some assumptions are more probably true than others, and all assumptions are subject to consistent investigation by reasonable minds. One's faith assumption (or hypothesis) at the beginning of an investigation should be a reasonable one and give a coherent picture of the world. If one's original faith assumption is false, then its falsity will become evident if it is pursued far enough. A scientist, for example, tests his hypothesis by various experiments; if the hypothesis is consistent with the

---

133. Ibid.
134. Ibid.
135. Patterson, *Carl F. H. Henry*, 61.

experiments, then it is assumed that the hypothesis is verified (or 'workably true').[136]

Methodologically, Henry believes all claims to absolute epistemological neutrality are impossible because there is no such thing as a "presuppositionless methodology."[137] Carswell points out, "For Henry, what justifies the use of presuppositions is the relevance of the presupposition to the particular subject under study. By relevance Henry means whether or not one's presuppositions are applied with objectivity, consistency and with a recognition that the presuppositions themselves have limits."[138] But, if a basic assumption leads to a true worldview, and if a worldview reflects the reliability of one's basic assumptions or presuppositions, then how can someone *actually* offer a valid test for a true worldview?[139] This approach seems to affirm a form of circular reasoning.

Henry's offers a series of axioms and sub-axioms to overcome the charge that presuppositionalism is a form of circular reasoning by explaining his particular theological method and epistemology.[140] Henry's method affirms two fundamental presuppositional axioms: (1) The ontological axiom, which states that God exists, and (2) The epistemological axiom, which states that God reveals himself.[141] Carswell explains these two axioms and their significance noting,

> These two presuppositions meet Henry's requirements for presupppositions in that they are not, in themselves, what he is trying to prove; rather, they are the proper starting point for a Christian epistemology, in that they presuppose two crucial doctrines vital to Christian belief and therefore vital to Henry's approach to Christian epistemology.[142]

For Henry, the ontological axiom is the ground of all being and knowledge. The epistemological axiom is the means by which God freely

---

136. Ibid.

137. Carswell, *A Comparative Study*, 43. Justin Carswell addresses this same point and quotes Henry, who says, "Whatever method of investigation is employed, we must of course abandon all claims to absolute neutrality, since a presuppositionless methodology is an absurdity and, in fact, an impossibility . . . No method is without underlying axioms and assumptions or aims and goals." Ibid. See Henry, *GRA*, 4:388.

138. Carswell, *A Comparative Study*, 43.

139. Patterson, *Carl F. H. Henry*, 62.

140. Frame, "Presuppositional Apologetics," 576.

141. Carswell, *A Comparative Study*, 47.

142. Ibid.

communicates knowledge of himself to humanity. Both of these axioms are considered to be self-justifying. Henry believes this is not a form of circular reasoning because all disciplines of inquiry start with unproven first principles in order to justify their hypotheses.[143] Furthermore, instead of trying to prove the existence of God, he is using God to explain the relevant data.

Henry's ontological axiom affirms that a basic characteristic of humanity being made in the image of God is an innate "God-relatedness." Carswell explains the epistemological significance this has for Henry suggesting that, "Henry further describes this 'God-relatedness' as 'basic to [every] human noetic structure,' explicitly claiming that the knowledge of God's existence, or having in some sense an awareness of God's existence, is a universal aspect of knowledge."[144] It is this aspect of Henry's epistemology that mirrors the *sensus divinitatis* in other epistemological approaches, for all of humanity is created to know God innately. This innate knowledge is not something that can be proven; instead, it is a necessary axiom for all thought and required in order to adequately address the concerns of epistemology.

Henry's second axiom is his epistemological axiom. For Henry, this axiom flows from the Augustinian belief that in order for God to be known by humanity, God must reveal himself.[145] Carswell explains the significance of this axiom for Henry's overall method suggesting, "Henry develops this axiom in the traditional pattern of voluntaristic general and special revelation that is common among evangelical theology and philosophy."[146] Furthermore, "Henry's [epistemological] axiom seeks to show that Christian epistemology does not attempt to be creative but descriptive of the realities of God's design and purpose for creation; the theologian and philosopher must depend upon God for his information about God."[147] This aspect of Henry's epistemology reveals the dependent character of Christian philosophy and theology. Humanity must begin with the God who reveals, and who sets the categories and means in

---

143. Patterson, *Carl F. H. Henry*, 61.

144. Carswell, *A Comparative Study*, 48.

145. It is important to the overall project to note that Henry opposes natural theology. He believes that it is an empirical approach to knowledge, not derived from the Scriptures. In volumes five and six of *GRA*, Henry discusses what he considers to be the weakness of natural theology.

146. Ibid., 49.

147. Ibid.

which he can be known. It is by an act of God's grace, not human ingenuity, that allows for the person and will of God to be known.

Henry offers six principles about his epistemology and method of validation (which is very similar to justification in Henry's epistemology), to better understand the nature of justification and epistemological axioms.[148] Before Henry explains the details of his approach, he summarizes it with this well-known quote,

> Divine revelation is the source of all truth, the truth of Christianity included; reason is the instrument for recognizing it; Scripture is its verifying principle; logical consistency is a negative test for truth and coherence a subordinate test. The task of Christian theology is to exhibit the content of biblical revelation as an orderly whole.[149]

Henry's six principles are: (1) God in his revelation is the first principle of Christian theology, from which all truths of revealed religion are derived; (2) Human reason is a divinely fashioned instrument for recognizing truth; it is not a creative source for truth; (3) The Bible is the Christian's principle of verification; (4) Logical consistency is a negative test of truth and coherence a subordinate test; (5) The proper task of theology is to exposit and elucidate the content of Scripture in an orderly way; (6) The theology of revelation requires the apologetic confrontation of speculative theories of reality and life.[150]

The first four principles pertain to Henry's epistemology, and the fifth and sixth principles pertain to his hermeneutic and apologetic method. This section will focus on the first four of Henry's epistemological principles.[151]

Principle One

Henry lays out his first epistemological principle. It states, "God in his revelation is the first principle of Christian theology, from which all truths of

---

148. Pojman, *What Can We Know?*, 14–15.
149. Henry, *GRA*, 1:215.
150. Ibid.
151. Chapter four will focus on Henry's hermeneutic and will address Henry's fifth principle. Chapter six will explain Henry's sixth principle by suggesting that his method confront speculative theories of hermeneutics as epistemology and methodology.

revealed religion are derived."¹⁵² The importance of this first principle for Henry's method is it seeks to show the superiority of God and his revelation. He opposes epistemologies which entertain the idea that knowledge is merely a structural *gestalt* or an epistemic social construction.¹⁵³

In his book titled, *What Is Truth?*, James Emery White explains, and evaluates Henry's view of truth and epistemology.¹⁵⁴ White addresses Henry's first principle claiming it flows from his theological method, which is deductive, rather than inductive. Henry believes a deductive method grounds metaphysical truth in God, not autonomous human postulations.¹⁵⁵ Henry's epistemological axiom explains his ontological axiom in greater detail.¹⁵⁶ In particular, that he grounds his theory in Trinitarian theism, not a generic theism derived from philosophy.¹⁵⁷ For Henry, divine revelation is to be understood as the foundational epistemological axiom "from which all other truths are deduced."¹⁵⁸ Within his method, since divine revelation is a foundational epistemological axiom, then epistemology rests on a fully orbed Trinitarian theism,¹⁵⁹ instead of a "God of the philosophers" or "general theism."¹⁶⁰ Thus, Trinitarian theism is a necessary prerequisite in order to have a fully orbed Christian epistemology.

Henry's epistemology appeals to the Bible as a transcendental theological revelational authority, to ground the meaning and significance of empirical events such as the resurrection.¹⁶¹ White claims that, for Henry, "Henry rejects beginning with 'particulars and them moving to universals'; rather he advocates postulating a universal explanatory principle

---

152. Henry, *GRA*, 1:215.

153 Ibid., 2:224; 1:219; 2:220.

154. White, *What Is Truth?* As the title of the book indicates, White also discusses Cornelius Van Til, Francis Schaeffer, Donald Bloesch, and Millard Erickson's views of truth and epistemology too.

155. Ibid., 92.

156. Henry lists four ways this epistemological axiom has been questioned and responds to each. See, Henry, *GRA*, 1:216.

157. White, *What Is Truth?*, 93.

158. Ibid., 92.

159. Trinitarin theism is a term used to explain a specific Christian understanding of a theistic God that affirms God is a tri-unity, meaning there are there persons in one essence.

160. In order to better understand the notion of "general theism" or "God of the philosophers," see, Kenny, *The God of The Philosophers*.

161. White, *What is Truth?*, 92.

which is subject to verification."[162] If White is correct (which the research indicates that he is), then Henry's theological transcendental approach finds in Scripture the authorized summary of all God's revelation. For Henry, the Bible presents in objectively intelligible statements, and in a divinely inspired form, *the* correct explanation of the origin of the universe, redemptive history, and the life of Jesus of Nazareth.[163] The result of giving Scripture epistemological logical priority over general revelation (including scientific and historiographical theories), according to Henry, is that "Scripture as an inspired literary document 'republishes the content of general revelation objectively, over against sinful man's reductive dilutions and misconstructions of it.'"[164] With this first principle in place, Henry's second principle relates divine revelation and human reason.[165]

Principle Two

Henry's second epistemological principle is that "Human reason is a divinely fashioned instrument for recognizing truth; it is not a creative source for truth."[166] Henry believes Christianity must insist on the rationality of the faith. Henry claims, "The Christian faith emphasizes that one has nothing to gain and everything to lose by opposing or downgrading rationality."[167] He suggests that by insisting on the legitimate use of reason in syllogisms and other valid forms of thought, Christianity is not falling prey to a form of rationalistic philosophy.[168] Henry opposes Søren Kierkegaard's method because he believes it errs by emphasizing an irrational and contradictory epistemology.[169] Instead, Henry desires for an epistemology that seeks to find truth, not to be the creative source of truth. For Henry, "creative approaches to knowledge," contradict the divinely fashioned purpose of reason in humanity. Henry believes they overstep the role of reason beyond its created limits by elevating reason to be the source of all truth, instead of God (who is the source of all

162. Ibid., 93.
163. Ibid.
164. Ibid., 93–94.
165. Ibid.
166. Henry, *GRA*, 2.225.
167. Ibid., 2:225.
168. Ibid., 2:226.
169. Ibid.

truth). In brief, one of the key tenets of the presuppositional method is that God is the source of all truth, revealed and general truth included.

In his book, *Confessions of a Theologian*, Henry recounts his studies under Gordon Clark. He claims, "Philosophy we learned from one of the most brilliant faculty members [at Wheaton], Gordon Haddon Clark, whom Buswell had persuaded to come from the University of Pennsylvania."[170] Henry learned the presuppositional method from Clark. Clark's presuppositionalism is described as a *deductive* presuppositionalism, whereas Van Til's is best characterized as a *transcendental* presuppositionalism.[171] That being said, Henry opposes Van Til's presuppositional method. Boa and Bowman in their book, *Faith Has Its Reasons*, offer the following chart between Van Til and Clark to compare the two types of presuppositionalism.[172]

VAN TIL	CLARK
Transcendental argument	Deductive argument
Scripture provides rational basis for scientific and historical knowledge	Scripture provides only rational source of knowledge; science and history are not valid sources of truth
Logic must be defined and understood on the basis of God's revelation in Scripture	Logic is the method by which we derive truth from God's revelation in Scripture
External consistency *with* Scripture as the test for truth	Internal consistency *of* Scripture as the tests of *its* truth
Believers and unbelievers do not share a common reason	Believers and unbelievers share reason in common

White suggests there are three specific differences between Henry and Van Til's presuppositionalism. In White's estimation,

> Henry feels his presuppositionalism withstands the concerns against presuppositionalist theology, that presuppositionalist

---

170. Henry, *Confessions of a Theologian*, 66.
171. Boa and Bowman, *Faith Has Its Reasons*, 270.
172. Ibid., 272.

theology (1) exaggerates the noetic consequences of the fall of humanity; (2) denies the existence of any 'common ground' between believers and unbelievers; and (3) bows to the demand of a coherence theory of truth. For Henry, the fall of humanity does not mean that human beings cannot comprehend God's special revelation prior to the regenerative work of the Holy Spirit. Instead, it is humanity's will, as opposed to reason, that affected most pervasively.[173]

For Henry, the categories of human thinking are to be understood as valid and invalid, not regenerate and unregenerate.[174] Henry believes revelation is able to overcome the limits of human finitude and the noetic effects of sin. However, this does not entail he believes the mind is unaffected by sin. Instead, like other presuppositionalists, Henry believes the regenerate mind allows for the possibility of humanity to overcome the clouding effects of sin.[175] He claims that due to the image of God in humanity, the unregenerate mind is still able to utilize the laws of logic, and that the fall did not eradicate man's ability to know both God and truth.[176]

Principle Three

Henry's third epistemological principle is, "The Bible is the Christian's principle of verification."[177] He defines this principle claiming, "The inspired Scriptures are the proximate and universally accessible form of authoritative divine revelation."[178] For Henry, the Bible is a form of revelation that can be verified because its truth is intelligibly expressed in valid propositions, and therefore, universally communicable.[179] Because of the cognitive and propositional nature of special revelation, it [special revelation] is able to be communicated and verified cross-culturally. The Bible's meaning and significance are not restricted to a particular community or sociological group.[180]

173. White, *What Is Truth?*, 97.
174. Ibid., 98.
175. Ibid.
176. Ibid.
177. Henry, GRA, 1.229.
178. Ibid.
179. Ibid.
180. Ibid. For Henry, propositional revelation entails that revelation is able to be contained in sentences, propositions, and judgments. A proposition is a logically

According to White, Henry infers from this third principle that the Bible is able to serve as a universally valid criterion of meaning and truth.[181] For example, Henry claims, "The Bible is not a textbook on science or on history. But attention to the Bible's statements bearing on the physical sciences and history and on politics and sociology will enable its readers to avoid many misconceptions to which empirical inquiry remains ongoingly vulnerable."[182] The significance of propositional revelation for Henry is it allows for the divinely inspired and inerrant Bible to serve as the principle of verification for science, history, and all theological matters.[183] Not human reason or speculative philosophies.

Principle Four

Henry's fourth epistemological principle is, "Logical consistency is a negative test of truth and coherence a subordinate test."[184] For Henry, one of the main tests for truth is logical consistency. If a proposition or theory is logically inconsistent it is *de jure* incoherent and a false position. The test for truth is the law of non-contradiction. Henry believes, "Without noncontradiction and logical consistency, no knowledge whatever is possible."[185] He goes so far as to say, "The fact is that whatever violates the law of contradiction cannot be considered revelation."[186] Furthermore, Henry claims, "Consistency is a negative test of truth; what is logically contradictory cannot be true. A denial of the law of contradiction would make truth and error equivalent; hence in effect it destroys truth."[187]

---

formed statement that is either true or false (see White, *What Is Truth?*, 99). Propositionalism does not entail that meaning is only contained in concepts, isolated words, or that sentences merely point to meaning (see Henry, *GRA*, 4:429; see White, *What Is Truth?*, 99). According to Henry, the various genres in Scripture do not diminish its propositional nature. Regardless of the genre type, Scripture contains universally valid truth in propositional form communicating the mind of God to humanity (see White, *What Is Truth?*, 100.

181. White, *What Is Truth?*, 100.
182. Henry, *GRA*, 1:232.
183. Ibid.
184. Ibid., 1:232.
185. Ibid.
186. Ibid., 1:233.
187. Ibid.

Logical consistency is able to adjudicate whether a worldview is true and worthy of one's commitment.

For Henry, logical consistency is not a positive test for truth; instead, it is a negative test. If it were a positive test, any view that is logically consistent would be true.[188] Statements like this by Henry seem to imply that he affirms a coherence theory of truth. Henry critiques Clark Pinnock's view of correspondence, claiming, "When Pinnock urges us to subscribe to a correspondence theory of truth, which finds truth not in internally consistent propositions but in conformity to external facts, the problems of knowledge-theory multiply."[189] For Henry the problems of the correspondence theory of truth are,

> If the human mind cannot know reality itself, but only what corresponds to it, the consequence would seem to be skepticism. If we cannot know reality, then what allegedly corresponds to it will not help us much; unless we can know reality itself, reality is unknowable. And if we can know reality, there is no need to know something else that merely corresponds to it. Such considerations should reinforce the view that truth is a consistent system, and that all facets of it (including all facts) have meaning as part of that system.[190]

However, Henry asserts that Christianity has nothing to gain if someone advocates solely for a coherence theory of truth. He claims, "To contend that assertions are true if they hang together is inadequate, particularly when all that so hang together may ultimately prove to be less than logical."[191] This comment by Henry seems to imply that he does not hold to a coherence theory of truth. So, which theory of truth does Henry affirm? According to White,

> What Henry ultimately offers is a modification of the correspondence theory of truth.... Henry holds to a correspondence understanding of truth in terms of divine revelation, which gives us reality in true correspondence ... Favorably quoting Clark, Henry points out that if no proposition 'means to man what it means to God, so that God's knowledge and man's knowledge

---

188. Ibid., 1:235.
189. Ibid., 1:237.
190. Ibid.
191. Ibid.

do not coincide at any single point, it follows by rigorous necessity that man can have no truth at all."[192]

These two statements seem to indicate that Henry affirmed a form of the correspondence theory of truth (where correspondence takes priority over coherence, yet coherence is a sub-test for truth). He also claims that without a univocal set of concepts man is unable to have knowledge of truth. Henry believes divine revelation is the means by which humanity obtains these univocal concepts, not empirical data. In brief, for Henry, revelation is to explain the empirical data, not *vice versa*.[193]

For Henry, Revelational Theism is able to address the issues of truth and epistemology because, "The Christian faith offers not mathematical or speculative certainty, but rather spiritual assurance. Divine authority eliminates the rational gap between probability and certainty."[194] Christianity provides assurance not in empirical probability but in a supernatural witness by the Holy Spirit validated by propositional revelation. For Henry, "The Spirit uses truth as an instrument of persuasion, truth attested by Scripture and testable for logical consistency."[195] Methodologically, by combining revelation and reason, he is able to affirm the core tenets of a presuppositional method and Revelational Theism. In order to better explain Henry's Revelational Theism, and how it affects his epistemology, two sub-axioms must be explained: the Logos doctrine and the role of the image of God.[196]

Sub-Axioms of Revelational Theism

Henry's epistemology attempts to answer the questions: (1) How does divine revelation get to humanity? and (2) How does humanity know they have received that revelation? Henry answers these questions by positing a series of axioms and sub-axioms. For Henry, an axiom is something that cannot be proven; instead, it is posited in order to provide a coherent

192. White, *What Is Truth?* 104.

193. Henry, *GRA*, 2:238.

194. Henry, *Toward a Recovery*, 59. This quote should not be taken to mean that Henry denied epistemological certainty. He clearly affirmed certainty. Instead, Henry bases his epistemological certainty on the categories of Revelational Theism, not speculative alien theories of knowledge.

195. Ibid.

196. A definition and exposition of these doctrines will be given in the section below titled, "Sub-Axioms of Revelational Theism."

explanation of the data.[197] The term "sub-axiom" is not used in Henry's epistemology. Instead, it is introduced here to explain more of the particular Christian aspects of Henry's epistemology.[198] They are "axiom-like," in that according to Henry's presuppositional method, they are posited in order to show the superiority of Revelational Theism. They cannot be proven from non-Christian or alien categories, and for that reason, they are considered "sub-axioms" because they are derived from Henry's two primary axioms (e.g., the ontological axiom, which states that God exists; and the epistemological axiom, which states that God reveals himself).

The Logos Doctrine

The first sub-axiom in Henry's epistemology is the Logos doctrine.[199] In the introduction section of volume two, Henry summarizes each of his fifteen theses.[200] Thesis nine is titled, *"The mediating agent in all divine revelation is the Eternal Logos—preexistent, incarnate, and now glorified."*[201] Carswell helps to clarify the epistemological significance of the ninth thesis claiming,

> This confrontation [of primal religious experience or the divine confrontation of the existence of God] is described by Henry as an innate *a priori* knowledge of God's existence that God reveals to the mind of each human, created in God's image to know truth. These two axioms are tied together through the Logos doctrine in which revelation is mediated through the Logos.[202]

The first thing to note is the Logos serves as the mediator between God, the mind of humanity, and the image of God in humanity. Second, Carswell explains the epistemological significance of the Logos, noting, "Thus, in the Logos doctrine the ontological and the epistemological axioms come

---

197. Henry does not consider this to be a futile approach since other disciplines, especially those within the scientific community, affirm unproven axioms in order to explain their various hypotheses.

198. The justification for introducing the term "sub-axiom" is because Justin Carswell introduces a similar term in order to explain Henry's epistemology.

199. Henry, GRA, 2:11–12; 3:164–247; 4:58, 226, 272, 288, 371, 476, 493, 601.

200. Ibid., 2:7–16.

201. Ibid., 2:11. This section is important because here, Henry summarizes the ninth thesis concerning the Logos as the divine Agent in creation.

202. Carswell, *A Comparative Study*, 50.

together in the biblical λόγος."²⁰³ For Henry, the Logos fulfills two important mediating roles. The first is a salvific mediating role; whereby, the Word of God made flesh mediates salvation between God the Father and humanity. The second is an epistemological mediating role; whereby, the Word of God, serving as the agent of revelation, mediates between the mind of God and the mind of humanity.²⁰⁴

Henry defends the epistemological function of the Logos in volume three of *God, Revelation and Authority*, chapters ten through fifteen.²⁰⁵ The chapter titles are: (10) The Intelligibility of the Logos of God; (11) The Biblically Attested Logos; (12) The Living Logos and Defunct Counterfeits; (13) The Logos as Mediating Agent of Divine Revelation; (14) The Logos and Human Logic; (15) The Logic of Religious Language. In order to understand the epistemological role of the Logos, chapters ten and fourteen will be explained.²⁰⁶

The *Intelligibility of the Logos of God*. In chapter ten titled, "The Intelligibility of the Logos of God," Henry attempts to develop a view of the Logos against what he considers neo-Protestant theologians.²⁰⁷ For Henry, in order to develop a hermeneutic as epistemology, revelation must be cognitive. If it is non-cognitive, then developing any hermeneutic that stresses the cognitive aspects of revelation becomes a moot-point. Henry follows Gordon Clark, insisting on a Logos that is logical.²⁰⁸ The term "logical Logos" means that the Logos adheres to the canons of logic, (e.g., law of identity: A is A, law of excluded middle: Either A or non-A, and law of non-contradiction: A is not non-A).²⁰⁹ By emphasizing a logical Logos, Henry opposes the view advocated by Karl Barth who declared that divine disclosure is "inherently dialectical or paradoxical [non-rational or intelligible]."²¹⁰ He also opposes Emil Brunner who stressed that the revelation of the Word is personal, denying the "objective rationality

---

203. Ibid., 50–51; 62; Henry, *GRA*, 1:322.

204. Patterson, *Carl F. H. Henry*, 97.

205. Henry, *GRA*, 3:164–230.

206. Chapter fifteen on, "The Logic of Religious Language," will be explained in the third chapter of this research titled, "Carl F. H. Henry's Analysis of Language and Hermeneutics."

207. Henry, *GRA*, 3:164. For Henry, neo-Protestant theologians were typically neo-orthodox theologians such as Karl Barth or Emil Brunner.

208. Ibid.

209. These are the three standard laws of logic.

210. Ibid.

of divine disclosure."[211] Finally, Henry criticizes Rudolf Bultmann's existential hermeneutic, that demeans the incarnation as a "myth."[212] Last but not least, he critiques Bultmann's hermeneutic because,

> His [Bultmann's] emphasis that God confronts man as language is akin to Martin Heidegger's stress on the linguistic character of Being as it presents itself to man; he speculatively applies Heidegger's emphasis on the call of conscience to the New Testament Word (cf. Richard E. Palmer, *Hermeneutics*, p. 50), and further insists that the kerygma—as Word within words—speaks to existential self-understanding.[213]

In this quote, Henry indicates that epistemology affects hermeneutics, because hermeneutics is a form of epistemology. Second, he also notices that epistemology affects the way theologians view the Logos or Word of God. The denial or downplaying of rational divine revelation affects the neo-Protestant theologians understanding of the Logos by accommodating it to dialectical and existential metaphysics and epistemological categories.

The epistemological considerations of non-cognitive approaches have far reaching effects for a person's understanding of propositional revelation. Henry points out that,

> The prevalent tendency of recent anti-intellectual theologies is to reduce the Christian message to the one affirmation that *the Word became flesh*, and on that basis to demean and disown the propositional teaching of the Bible as Word of God. If propositions as such are not to be considered as carriers of truth, neither can the Johannine proposition that asserts the enfleshment of the Logos.[214]

Henry suggests that the prevalent issue of "anti-intellectual theologies," is they deny the rational and cognitive elements of divine revelation. In doing so, they reduce the Logos to a non-cognitive category. The epistemological implication of anti-intellectual views is the Logos is no longer able to act as a rational mediator between the mind of God and humanity; instead, the Logos must be understood in non-rational and personal

211. Ibid.
212. Ibid.
213. Ibid.
214. Ibid., 3:165.

categories.²¹⁵ However, if the Logos is rational, it can serve as the epistemological mediator between the mind of God and the mind of humanity.

Henry is aware of criticisms raised by philosophers and theologians against the idea of a rational Logos who mediates between the mind of God and humanity. These critics claim the rational Logos arose from Greek philosophy, not from the Bible or Christian theology. Henry spent ample time in *God, Revelation and Authority*, responding to these kinds of criticisms. Contrary to the critics, Henry taught that the Logos arose from the Old Testament.²¹⁶ Carswell, in his section on Henry's use of the "Logos doctrine," explains the many ways Henry taught that the New Testament writers parted ways with the Greek uses of the Logos. First, Carswell points out that Heraclitus defines the Logos as a universal reason or a universal law immanent in all things. It served to unify the constantly changing universe. However, Carswell notes, "This universal law or reason was not a personal God; rather, Heraclitus was a pantheist as were most of his Greek counterparts."²¹⁷ Second, the Stoics taught that the Logos was an impersonal cosmic reason. In this system, the Logos is viewed as an impersonal cosmic reason.²¹⁸ Third, Philo of Alexandria taught that the Logos is a faculty of reason and a spoken word proceeding from the faculty of reason. It is always subordinate to God, serving as God's instrument.²¹⁹

Henry claims the early church recognized that in both Jewish and Greek thought, the idea of the "Logos," played an epistemological role by relating (and mediating) the divine and human minds. Beyond the basic epistemological role, much of the early church opposed the Greek view. The exception to this might be Justin Martyr. Carswell claims Martyr affirmed that the "universal reason" or the Logos enabled men such as Socrates to understand features of reality that agree with the Christian

---

215. Ibid. Henry believes when neo-Protestants downplay the rational Logos it affects their understanding of the Bible as the Word of God. Ibid., 3:165–66.

216. Ibid., 3:173–191. Henry also denies the Logos is borrowed or derived from Greek language, since it is not derived from secular categories of thought and language. Henry taught the gospel writers derived their view of the Logos from the Scriptures and deliberately parted ways with the Greek use of the term, along with its religious overtones. Ibid., 2:11.

217. Carswell, *A Comparative Study*, 57.

218. Ibid., 58.

219. Ibid., 58–59; Henry, *GRA*, 3:187; 3:194

worldview.[220] However, this does not entail that he incorporated the whole Greek pantheistic and impersonal aspects into his Logos doctrine. Instead, Martyr identifies the epistemological role of the Logos, and demonstrates his biblical understanding of the term by recognizing the personal aspect of universal reason in his theory of knowledge.

The second criticism Henry faces is what he considers to be the loss of the Logos of God in Western philosophy.[221] The main issue for Henry in this section is the denial of objectivity in favor of epistemological subjectivity. He considers this turn towards subjectivity to be a "counterfeit logos."[222] Henry believes Auguste Comte and Ludwig Wittgenstein illustrate this trend away from the Logos doctrine by modern and contemporary philosophers.[223] He also claims that contemporary science has bought into the drift of denying the Logos. Henry suggests the neglect or rejection of the Logos is the reason scientists have ". . . abandoned the traditional emphasis of classical physics on objectivity."[224] The motive Henry gives for the turn towards subjectivity is that modern thought stems from their downplaying of the Logos of God. He claims the only way for evangelicals to overcome epistemological subjectivity is to recover a robust biblical view of the Logos doctrine.

Henry believes one of the many results of abandoning the Logos of God in modern epistemology is the insistence on the creative activity of the mind. For Henry, the Logos grounds objective knowledge. The error of modern views is they "idolize the human mind" and they are insistent on the "knower's autonomous creativity."[225] Henry recognizes that some

220. Carswell, *A Comparative Study*, 60–61.

221. Henry, GRA, 3:167.

222. Henry claims, "The counterfeit logos of secular thought—whether ancient or modern—could not long sustain either a distinctive view of human knowledge or a rationally compelling view of externally reality." Ibid.

223. In particular Henry addresses Wittgenstein's attack on objective reasoning, claiming "The modern attack on objective reason and meaning, and the secular denial that cognitive thinking can carry us beyond immediate experience to a foundational unity of meaning, sounded a death-rattle for metaphysical inquiry. The contention of Ludwig Wittgenstein (*Tractatus Logico-Philosoophicus*, 4.1 f., 4.12 f.), that, whatever reference and relationship theological statements have to a reality beyond, we cannot represent in language the relation of language to the external world, was finally seen to be in principle not only destructive of theology but equally destructive of the empirical sciences." Ibid., 3:168.

224. Ibid. Henry also addresses the relationship between objectivity and modern science. See, 3:168–169.

225. Ibid., 3:169.

modern approaches to science attempt to penetrate behind the subjective variables of the observer by mathematical approaches.[226] However, for Henry, even these attempts are futile apart from the Logos of God and represent the trend of abandoning the Logos of God.

Henry's main concern with epistemological subjectivity is it is grounded in non-Logos approaches to knowledge. He warns, "The present mood gives evidence of a rising curiosity about objective meaning which, if not captured for and by the Logos of Scripture, will merely ripen into encroachment by one or another phantom logos."[227] The correction Henry offers to these approaches is a return to the divinely revealed Word as ". . . an intellectual possibility to the awareness of the meaning of God as the revelationally given reality that certifies the rational coherency of created reality."[228] For Henry, the Logos is the epistemological mediator between both God and man, and between man and the external world.[229] He argues that the only way to overcome epistemological subjectivity and/or irrationality is to return to the objectively intelligible reality of the Logos.[230] In brief, for Henry, the rational Logos of Revelational Theism allows for there to be a valid, trans-cultural approach to knowledge, able to overcome personal and cultural epistemological subjectivity.

The Logos and Human Logic. In chapter fourteen titled, "The Logos and Human Logic," Henry interacts with Thomas F. Torrance's book *Theological Science*.[231] Henry opens this chapter with these words, "The knowledge of God confronts us, Thomas F. Torrance notes, 'not only with the problem of the ontologic, but the problem of the *theologic*: How are we to relate the *logos* of man to the Logos of God, formal logic to the Logic of God?' (*Theological Science*, p. 205)."[232] Torrance believes there are different logics between God and humanity. Henry believes there is no such thing as a "human logic" and a "divine logic." For Henry, there is only one logic between God and man, the Logos, Christ Jesus. Henry attempts to correct the devaluation of the cognitive Logos by defending

226. Ibid., 3:169–170.
227. Ibid., 3:170.
228. Ibid.
229. Ibid., 3:170–172.
230. Ibid., 3:170.
231. Torrance, *Theological Science*.
232. Henry, *GRA*, 3:216.

a rational Logos and the claim there is only one type of logic which corresponds in both the mind of God and in the mind of humanity.

Torrance claims that due to the fall, humanity is twisted in untruth and resistant to truth.[233] Furthermore, because of the fall, humanity is unable to have rational knowledge of God and the Logos. Henry claims Torrance's views indicate a complete disregard for the law of contradiction.[234] By rejecting the law of contradiction, Torrance thinks that nonsense can be regarded as divine truth. Torrance attempts to create a new view of "dialogical truth." This view claims that religious messages (include the Bible's message) must be received in personal relationship to the Truth. Torrance believes his view opposes dialectical and existential views of truth. "Yet," according to Henry, "the 'dialogical objectivity' of revelational truth (p. 42) espoused by Torrance nonetheless erodes the universal validity of theological truth."[235] For Henry, theological truth is bound to God's revelation and sovereign will to disclose information concerning himself. Therefore, personal decisions do not determine the status of truth.[236]

Henry does not believe Torrance carries his distinction between truth and being "truthfully related to Jesus Christ" far enough.[237] For Henry, Kierkegaard is consistent in his approach, even though Henry considers Kierkegaard's method to be incoherent because revealed truth seems to "breach logic."[238] Henry goes on to say, "Now if it be the fact that revealed truth breaches logic and turns strategically on inner decision, not only might sin and holiness be convertible, but God and the devil as well."[239] However, Henry believes, if the truth of revelation cannot be known apart from personal decision, then humanity cannot be held accountable for rejecting the light of revelation. The result of this view,

233. Ibid., 3:218.
234. Ibid. Henry says.
235. Ibid., 3:219.
236. Ibid., 3:220.
237. Ibid.
238. Henry notes, "The truth of the eternal revealed in time cannot be known in terms of fixed categories, he [Torrance] tells us, but requires a fundamental role for movement, as Kierkegaard realized in seeking to go 'beyond logical connections . . . to develop . . . a mode of thinking that is itself a free movement inseparable from real becoming' (p. 153). 'Thinking of this kind takes place in the medium of the historical and involves *decision*,' for which traditional logic has no room. It 'moves across a 'breach' in the process of logic' (p. 153)." Ibid.
239. Ibid.

according to Henry, is that humanity would be immune to revelation and there would be no definite way to validate revelational knowledge.[240]

Henry responds to Torrance and Kierkegaard-like views claiming man could have, ". . . objectively valid knowledge of God on the basis of divine disclosure, without in any way denying the omniscience of God."[241] He thinks this is possible because the image of God in humanity offers man categories of thought and forms of logic which are able to know God, and the external world.[242] Henry believes the implications of this are that scholars should not make claims to a "higher logic."[243] He expounds on this idea suggesting, "Whoever calls for a higher logic must preserve the existing laws of Logic to escape pleading the cause of illogical nonsense."[244] For Henry, if Torrance and Kierkegaard's views are correct, then God's revelation is no longer permanent and universally valid. Instead, whenever revelation reaches a new people group, it must be constantly updated simply because sporadic up-dating would be essential to historical revelation. Henry believes this "updating" would be a form of situational theology. In contrast, his Revelational Theistic epistemology affirms revelation must be a mental act of rational cognitive disclosure. Humanity has been created in the image of God to receive rational revelation.[245] Revelation, is then both rational (in that it can be understood), and personal (in that it calls for a response or faith).[246] However, it does not fall prey to situational theology or require updating. Instead, revela-

240. Ibid. Henry claims, "If, however, man cannot, apart from inner decision, know the truth of revelation, then he cannot be held accountable for personal rejection of the light of revelation; in fact, he would be wholly immune to revelation. Even an unpredictable 'divine' lightening stroke of which man has not the slightest intimation could be so correlated with an intense subjective leap of faith that there would be no surety of objective revelational knowledge." Ibid.

241. Ibid., 3:222.

242. Ibid.

243. Ibid.

244. Ibid., 3:229.

245. Ibid., 3:248–303. Henry claims, "We are therefore back to the emphasis that the laws of logic belong to the *imago Dei*, and have ontological import." Ibid., 3:229. Henry claims that without the ontological objectivity of certain human conceptions and the mediating Logos, epistemology is doomed to skepticism.

246. Justin Carswell explains this aspect of Henry's use of the Logos noting, "The ability to have justified or warranted beliefs about God is important if salvation is the ultimate goal of the revelation of the λόγος. Revelation, then, is both rational (in that it can be understood) and personal (in that it calls for a response, or faith)." Carswell, *A Comparative Study*, 67.

tion serves to confront and correct speculative thought and vain knowledge of God. This is important to hermeneutics as epistemology because according to Henry's view, revelation sets the parameters of valid and sound knowledge; not existentialism, phenomenology, two-horizons, or *Dasein*.

The following section will explain how Henry utilizes the rational structures of thought and the image of God in humanity to discuss *how* man was designed to know the special revelation of God, through the agency of the mediating Logos.[247]

The Image of God

Henry believes many of the errors in contemporary philosophy and theology are due to a false view of the image of God in humanity. The difficulty many have when it comes to the image of God is coming to a mutual agreement about the definition and scope of the *imago Dei*. Thornbury explains this difficulty, noting,

> Although he [Henry] allows that the Bible does not define the precise content of the *imago Dei*, he does not believe that the doctrine itself is vague. Especially in the Western tradition, the *imago Dei* has been understood as coextensive with humanity's rational and moral faculties. Other options have been the human capacity for self-transcendence, the human exercise of the will, immortality, and gender distinction.[248]

Henry affirms a view which equates the image of God in humanity with man's rational and moral faculties. The rational elements entail that at creation every human-being has an ineradicable awareness of God's existence, the existence of other human beings, and that the external world subsists.[249] They also are able to distinguish between the God and non-God, good and evil, truth and falsehood.[250]

According to Henry, there are formal and informal aspects of the image of God. The formal aspects of the image of God are the rational, moral, and faith aspects.[251] Henry claims, "Only if man is logically

247. Patterson, *Carl F. H. Henry*, 98–99.
248. Thornbury, *Recovering Classic Evangelicalism*, 74; Henry, *GRA*, 2:125–126.
249. Henry, *Toward a Recovery*, 57.
250. Ibid.
251. Henry, *GRA*, 2:126.

lighted, and not simply morally or spiritually involved independent of intelligence, can he be meaningfully aware of responsible relationships to God and other selves and to the cosmos."[252] Furthermore, "If man made any sense of his own experience, the laws of logic must intrinsically have qualified the *imago Dei*. From the first, man as man possessed reasoning capacities and rational discernment on the basis of creation."[253] In particular, Henry proposes the image of God requires that humanity knows and functions according to the laws of logic.[254] Reason is what illuminates divine revelation by providing the concepts for truth and error about man, nature, and God. It helps humanity to discern between good and evil, God from false gods, revelation from pseudo-revelation, and true from false religion.[255] Henry does not teach that the laws of logic exist independent of God; instead, the Logos of God is his mind, his way of thinking and the divine pattern that issued the spoken order in creation. Human reasoning merely reflects the divine mind by mirroring the logical Logos of God in his rational capacities.[256]

The second feature of the image of God in humanity is the material aspect of the image of God. For Henry, the material aspect of the image of God in man has epistemological implications. Henry believes these material aspects are all known by divine revelation; however, they also validate his claims concerning the formal aspects of the image of God. First, it recognizes and affirms the Bible claims that man can know something about God.[257] This is a divine record of God's declaration about the knowledge creation has of himself. Second, it implies that God is the source of all true thought and knowledge about himself and the world. The reason humanity has any knowledge of God is because God graciously and freely chose to reveal himself.[258] Third, it recognizes that humanity is the creation and God is the Creator.[259] Finally, it teaches that humanity knows a great deal about God, humanity, and life because of the intrinsic nature of the image of God.[260]

252. Ibid.
253. Ibid.
254. Ibid.
255. Ibid.
256. Ibid., 2:133.
257. Ibid., 2:128.
258. Ibid., 2:133.
259. Ibid., 2:134.
260. Ibid.

The next thing Henry addresses is the effects of the fall on the image of God in humanity. Henry recognizes that the fall was a catastrophic event disrupting man's worship and contemplation of God.[261] However, the noetic effects of the fall do not invalidate man's rationality. Doyle discusses the noetic effects of sin in Henry's theology claiming,

> Although the fall affected every department of the human personality, it 'affects the functions of the reason and the will in different ways.' Henry agrees with Gordon Clark that the will is so totally corrupted that no act can be without sin; that the content of our thinking, including our philosophical premises, is likewise darkened; but that sin does not 'affect the laws of valid inference. True propositions are universally true now, as they were before the fall and as they always will be.'[262]

Doyle rightly notes that Henry did not claim the fall invalidated the laws of logic in humanity. Doyle believes this distinguishes Henry from medieval philosophers because he claims Aquinas taught that reason was unaffected by the fall. Instead, it places Henry in the tradition of the Reformers who insisted on the noetic effects of sin, but they did not claim that the fall eradicated the image of God in humanity. Henry's view must also be distinguished from Cornelius Van Til, who insists that the fall negates humanity's ability to use reason and the laws of logic.[263] For Henry, Van Til's position entails that the image of God in humanity was eradicated at the fall. Finally, Henry believes his view distances himself from neo-Protestant theologians who downplay the rational aspects of the image of God by emphasizing the plaguing effects of the fall.

The implications of the image of God in Henry's epistemology, is it shows that humanity was divinely fashioned to know God through revelation. Like Augustine, Henry claims the image of God in humanity enables them to receive revelation directly from God. This knowledge of God is innate or *a priori*, rational, and coherent. Since each individual bears the image of God, all of humanity has the ability to use the canons

---

261. Ibid. G. Wright Doyle claims, "Against Thomas Aquinas and even Vatican II Roman Catholic thought, Henry agrees with Calvin and the Reformers that 'the fall of man was a catastrophic personality shock,' and that the so-called noetic effects of sin make impossible 'any knowledge of God except . . . that God exists and that he executes moral judgment.'" Doyle, *Carl Henry*, 57; Henry, *GRA*, 2:135.

262. Doyle, *Carl Henry*, 58–59.

263. Van Til, *Christian Apologetics*, 83–122.

of logic. Henry believes Kant's epistemology is the greatest epistemological hurdle for Revelational Theism. He criticizes Kant's view, claiming,

> Immanuel Kant had validated the universal validity of human thought on the basis only of innate forms of thought. But because he arbitrarily ruled out the divine preforming of these innate categories, he sacrificed the metaphysical objectivity of man's knowledge and forfeited transcendent divine revelation that conveys cognitive knowledge of the supernatural world. Precisely because Kant did not recognize the formal aspects of human knowing to be elements of the divinely created *imago*, he correlated the categories not with metaphysical reality but only with sense perceptions.... But God's existence or nonexistence then remain for Kant intellectually problematical in view of the nonconnectibility of the categories with the supersensuous and metaphysical. Kant consequently assumed the autonomy of the human mind, and compromised the objectivity of human knowledge in respect to God and the supernatural order yet other important respects.[264]

For Henry, Kant's method errs by presupposing that God is not the source of man's innate categories of thought which function by structuring all knowledge. Henry claims, "He [Kant] ignores the transcendent Logos as the indispensable ground of universally valid knowledge. Yet for all that, he violates his epistemic theory by attributing human knowledge some relation to an objective world."[265] In contrast to Kant's view of knowledge, Henry maintains that the innate image of God in all of humanity necessitates a preformative understanding of knowledge. The philosophical implications of this view for Henry is that Revelational Theism allows for humanity to have justified true beliefs about God, the Logos, humanity, and externally perceived reality.[266]

CONCLUSION

From this chapter, it is apparent Henry believes prolegomena is essential to theological method and hermeneutics. In order to address the concerns of prolegomena—theological method and hermeneutics included—Henry believes theologians must be able to interact with both

264. Henry, *GRA*, 2:130–131.
265. Ibid., 2:131.
266. Henry, *Toward a Recovery*, 35–96.

metaphysics and epistemology. Having presented a review of Henry's epistemology, chapter three will relate his epistemology to his view of language, and chapter four his view of hermeneutics as epistemology and methodology. On the whole, this chapter argues that Henry's approach offers a paradigm for overcoming epistemological subjectivity and recovers the proper role of validating principles, the role of the image of God, and a proper understanding of the image of God. This chapter's analysis of Henry's epistemology is important to the overall project because he believes Revelational Theism is able to overcome the dominant subjectivist epistemologists in present-day theories of hermeneutics.

3

Carl F. H. Henry's Revelational Epistemology and Language

INTRODUCTION

CARL F. H. HENRY's method has been labeled as a "cognitive-propositionalist" approach.[1] Within Henry's literature, "cognitive-propositionalism" is used to signify the relationship between revelational epistemology and propositional language. By defining Henry's method in such terms, it raises questions such as: What does it mean to affirm a "cognitive-propositionalist" view of revelation? What is the relationship between logic and religious language? How does propositional revelation relate to the various genres of the Bible? In chapter two, Henry's view of "cognitive" revelation was explained. This chapter will explain how Henry's understanding of cognitive revelation relates to propositional language and its impact on hermeneutics. Chapter four will explain Henry's analysis of hermeneutics as epistemology and methodology.

---

1. Vanhoozer, *Lost in Interpretation*, 89–114; Vanhoozer, *The Drama of Doctrine*. In Vanhoozer's book, *The Drama of Doctrine*, he writes, "Partly in response to the mid-twentieth-century tendency to deny the verbal and cognitive dimensions of revelation, Carl F. H. Henry and others argued that God's word should be equated with the revealed propositions of the Bible, objective truths stated in conceptual and verbal form." Vanhoozer, *Drama of Doctrine*, 45.

EPISTEMOLOGY AND LANGUAGE

Perhaps one of Henry's most significant contributions to hermeneutics is his insistence that epistemology informs language. Some critics of Henry's approach are Stanley Grenz, Roger Olsen, John Franke, Robert Webber, Nicholas Wolterstorff, Alister McGrath, and Kevin Vanhoozer.[2] From this select group of critics, Vanhoozer's canonical-linguistic approach offers the most thorough critique of Henry's method, and has the most potential to affect future evangelical views of hermeneutics and philosophies of language.[3] Furthermore, Vanhoozer's approach offers one of the most appealing models in contemporary hermeneutics to replace Henry's cognitive-propositionalism.

Thornbury discusses the effects of Vanhoozer's new method in the section of his book titled, "Henry verses Vanhoozer? Looking Ahead." Thornbury makes this bold statement, "Perhaps no other figure looms so large over the possible reception of Henry's view of revelation as Kevin Vanhoozer, whose prolific output, scholarly reception, and mastery of current philosophical and theological hermeneutics distinguishes him as the leading academic theologian of the evangelical movement today."[4] Furthermore, "His [Vanhoozer's] theological method differs markedly from that of Henry because he seeks to develop doctrinal categories out of a deep appreciation for the Bible's rich mixture of genres." Thornbury's comments indicate there are two competing hermeneutical methods within recent paradigms of evangelicalism. Both views reject postmodernism and seek to uphold a high view of Scripture. However, as Thornbury comments,

> In *Drama*, he [Vanhoozer] sought to conceive of doctrine differently than did Henry's classical verbal-propositional motif. Instead, he pointed his readers towards thinking about God by way of theo-poetic drama, following the cues of the history of

---

2. Some of these include: Grenz and Olson, *20th Century Theology*; Grenz and Franke, *Beyond Foundationalism*; Franke, *The Character of Theology*; Vanhoozer, *Lost in Interpretation*, 89–114; Frame, "Presuppositional Apologetics," 576. 150; Wolterstorff, *Divine Discourse*; Webber, *The Younger Evangelicals*, 83–93.

3. It should also be noted that Norman L. Geisler and William Roach offer similar critiques of Vanhoozer's method. See, Geisler and Roach, *Defending Inerrancy*, 140–144.

4. Thornbury, *Recovering Classic Evangelicalism*, 105.

redemption in its canonical linguistic form. This new path was both an arrival and a departure for evangelicalism.[5]

These two views, while bearing many similarities, also have many irreconcilable differences. Vanhoozer's approach attempts to use canonical-linguistic theology in order to protect evangelicalism from the perceived reductionism of propositional theology, or what he labels as "epic classicism."[6] Whereas, according to Thornbury, Henry uses a "cognitive-propositionalist" method to defend what he labels as "classic evangelicalism." In thesis ten of *God, Revelation and Authority*, Henry claims, "*God's revelation is rational communication conveyed in intelligible ideas and meaningful words, that is, in conceptual-verbal form.*"[7] Thornbury suggests that the debate between classic evangelicalism and Vanhoozer's approach center on hermeneutics and the nature of propositional revelation.[8]

These statements by Thornbury raise the question:[9] What does it mean to affirm a "cognitive-propositionalist" view of revelation?[10] This next section will answer this question by articulating Henry's cognitive-propositionalism according to the following six sections: (1) The Logic of Religious Language; (2) The Origin of Language; (3) Meaning and Religious Language; (4) A Theistic View of Language; (5) Linguistic Analysis and Propositional Truth; and (6) The Bible as Propositional Revelation.

The Logic of Religious Language

Henry insists on the relationship between logic and religious language. For Henry, the "logic" of religious language is a way of stressing the influence epistemology has on language. He claims, "Some writers affirm that the language of religion involves a peculiar thought-structure that distinguishes it from other discourse; more particularly, some say, the language of the biblical or Hebrew revelation has a thought-structure and language

---

5. Ibid., 105–106.
6. Vanhoozer, *The Drama of Doctrine*, 83, 267–268.
7. Henry, *GRA*, 2:12–13; 4:248–488.
8. Thornbury, *Recovering Classic Evangelicalism*, 105–115.
9. Ibid.
10. Paul Helm specifically critiques Vanhoozer's assessment of A. A. Hodge. This can be found on his website: Paul Helm, "Vanhoozer's Remythologizing Theology," Helm's Deep, entry posted May 1, 2010, http://paulhelmsdeep.blogspot.com/search?.q=Remythologizing+Theology. Helm, *Faith, Form, and Fashion*.

structure different from that of Hindu or other religious discourse."[11] These individuals do not deny that religious ideas and vocabulary differ in their concepts and terms, or that they differ from one another according to their claims. "Rather," as Henry notes, "[T]he *logic* of religious belief, or of redemptive revelation, is said to be wholly peculiar in nature."[12] By this comment, Henry is noting that some philosophers of language downplay or deny that the rational structures of human cognition inform language. Henry labels these approaches as "non-cognitive." He illustrates his point by critiquing three non-cognitive views of religious language.

The first view Henry critiques is one that claims it is problematic to ground religious language in Western thinking or logic. Henry illustrates his point using Thomas J. Alitzer. Henry quotes Alitzer, who claims ". . . that all authentic forms of religious language, that is, all language which is the product of a uniquely religious vision, are grounded by one means or another in a dialectical logic, that is, a mode of understanding which assumes the *necessity of contradiction*."[13] The implication of Alitzer's approach is that all religious books, which by their very nature contain religious language, *necessarily* communicate contradictory information. In particular, the Bible by its very nature, *necessarily* communicates a contradictory message. Furthermore, because books or commentaries on the Bible (or any other religious book for that matter) use religious language to convey their ideas, in the elliptical sense, *necessarily* they too convey dialectical or contradictory information (including Thomas Alitzer's).

For Henry, these types of claims demonstrate the intricate relationship between epistemology and language. He notes, "On his [Alitzer's] premise that religious language is exempt from the logical laws of identity and excluded middle, no discussion of any religion would be intelligible, and religious language would forfeit clear meaning. Those who write on religion would seem to have no sound way of knowing what they mean when they discuss religious themes."[14] However, individuals such as Alitzer are inconsistent in their approach. They write books on religion and use religious language to convey intelligible information; meanwhile, in the very act of writing books and expecting others to read and understand those books, they are contradicting their claims on the

---

11. Henry, *GRA*, 3:230.
12. Ibid.
13. Ibid., emphasis added.
14. Ibid., 3:231.

unintelligibility of religious language: oriental and occidental logic and language included.

Henry believes the only way for Alitzer to remain consistent with his method, would be to maintain a "discreet silence" about "religious reality."[15] Altizer attempts to respond to criticisms such as Henry's by claiming there are two types of religious logic and language. Alitzer believes his view is grounded in Oriental religions, which affirm the dialectical nature of logic. Whereas, views like Henry's are grounded in western, Aristotelian logic. Henry questions Alitezer's premise, claiming that the history of religion provides a different answer.[16] Henry suggests it is wrong to apply a dialectical view of religious language upon the Bible. He believes this view of logic and religious language is not rooted in good history or exegesis; instead, it reflects the philosophical spirit of the age. Henry claims,

> In modern times, to be sure, Hegel propounded his dialectical logic in the interest of a rational ontology. Hegelianism may in some ways have stimulated, as a reaction, the dialectical theology of Kierkegaard and the early Barth and other theologians of sporadic confrontation whose surrender of the conceptual nature of divine revelation finally blurred the very reality of God. But in the Hegelian dialectic there were intermediate syntheses, and an ultimate synthesis also; Hegel's dialectic involved more an emphasis on conceptual inadequacy and on necessary movement than on a contradiction in formal logic.[17]

Henry's point is that Altizer may claim he is following eastern religion, when in fact he derives his views from Hegel.[18] However, Alitzer has gone beyond Hegel by affirming not just a *dialectic*, but an actual contradiction. Henry notes that some religions such as Buddhism represent ultimate-reality as an "intuitive experience," not as an object of rational knowledge. The Buddhist conception is a non-cognitive view of ultimate reality, which forbids formulating ultimate reality into rational and linguistic forms. He believes if a person is to take non-cognitive views seriously and actually believe that words are not able to grasp and convey reality, then approaches like Alitzer's should be dismissed as irrational.[19] Henry

15. Ibid.
16. Ibid.
17. Ibid., 3:232.
18. Ibid.
19. Ibid.

claims, "Either the assertions made about ultimate reality are factually informative, and hence not reducible to contradictory propositions, or one ought not to affirm anything about what is adduced as ultimate reality—not even that it is ultimate or real—as valid truth."[20] In brief, for Henry, reality can be known cognitively, which entails that the laws of logic and structures of reality influence the logic of religious language. Furthermore, since epistemology directly influences language, any view of language that fails to uphold the law of non-contradiction ought to be rejected as irrational.

The second non-cognitive view of language Henry critiques is conventionalism. He believes conventionalism denies the influence of logic on religious language. One of the reasons Henry labels conventionalism as non-cognitive is because conventionalists understand language according to its various *uses*, not by its cognitive information.[21] Henry insists a conventionalist view of language entails that the laws of logic are exempt from language and theological method.[22] Henry is not the only classic evangelical to make such strong claims about conventionalism. The *International Council on Biblical Inerrancy*, claimed, that a conventionalist theory of meaning is incompatible with the doctrine of inerrancy, because it denies the rational structures of thought and the cognitive nature of propositional revelation.[23]

Henry agrees with the ICBI's criticism of conventionalism because he believes the conventionalist insistence on the non-cognitive aspects of language downplay or deny the rational and cognitive structures that ground the propositional nature of the Bible as divine revelation. Henry critiques a conventionalist theory of meaning, claiming, "The many human languages have a basis in the logic of human thought; all languages express fundamentally the same modes of thought. Language is

20. Ibid.

21. Henry claims, "The recent modern trends regard logic not as a set of conditions necessary for thinking, but as a mere system of rules stipulating language uses. Religious experience, thought, and language are alike said not to fall under the exclusiveness that governs other realms of interest. Religious concerns are exonerated from answerability to the logical principles of identity, non-contradiction, and the excluded middle. But unless thought is, in principle, all-illusive, it comprehends nothing universally valid. Nor does the validity of religious experience depend on a limitation if its concerns, far less a limitation to the non-logical. If religious thought concerns only an undifferentiated totality, it distinguishes nothing." Ibid., 3:234.

22. Ibid.

23. Feinberg, "Non-Cognitivism: Wittgenstein," 163–201.

a necessary tool of communication, but it cannot effectively serve this purpose unless it defers to the laws of logic."[24] Furthermore,

> Logic is concerned not with the origin of ideas or with the origin of language, but with the formal validity of implications or inferences and not with the truth of their conceptual content. Human language must from the first have been connected with reason and logic. All significant speech presupposes a regard for the law of contradiction; the admission of contrary meanings to the same word at the same time and in the same sense would turn conversation into a madhouse. Not even one who opposes a theistic view of language, and who thinks that logic has no ontological or linguistic import, can hope to communicate his notions to others unless speech presupposes the law of contradiction. Without language human culture seems impossible and without logic as an activity of human reasoning implicit in language the structure of civilization could not have emerged. The same logical distinctions are common to the mental nature of all men.[25]

In short, language cannot be conventional because reason and logic are not conventional. Reason and logic reside in all of humanity regardless of their nationality or geographical location. All of humanity bears the image of God, which implies they all have the universal canons of logic that are used to convey meaningful concepts through language.

Another interesting point about Henry's evaluation of conventionalism is his claim that all language, including religious language, has its basis in reason, therefore meaning is not conventional. However, he also believes the implication of a cognitive verses non-cognitive basis to language is that someone cannot claim there is any such thing as a "Hebrew mind" verses a "Greek mind." Instead there is only one "mind" found in all of humanity, each having the capacity for rational thought that is able to communicate cross-culturally due to the cross-cultural nature of the laws of logic.[26]

The third trend Henry evaluates is what he labels as "a new logic."[27] He points out that, "[Robert] Blaikie calls for a 'new logic that can some-

24. Henry, GRA, 3:235; 3:384–385.

25. Ibid., 3:235–236; 3:384.

26. It should be noted that more of Henry's criticism of conventionalism will be addressed in the section, "Linguistic Analysis and Propositional Truth."

27. Ibid., 3:244.

how accommodate the dynamic 'doing' aspect for verbs' as an alternative to 'a static logic.'"[28] Henry claims,

> 'There are, in connection with action,' he writes, 'linguistic problems which seem insoluble in terms of formal and relational logics; and within the totality of our knowledge of reality there are 'boundaries of logic' or of discursive linguistic thinking, boundaries beyond or beneath which we must acknowledge another type of direct or intuitional *knowledge* which includes the knowledge, through action, of reality as one (without subject/object division), of freedom, of other persons, and of God' ('*Secular Christianity*' *and God Who Acts*, pp. 107–81). But how can subject-object (subject-predicate?) be annihilated? Plotinus sought to transcend this duality in the *One*. Do these scholars propose a revival of neoplatonism?[29]

Henry believes Blaikie has embraced the ideas of Thorlief Boman. Henry claims, "Blaikie's strictures against the static logic of the Greeks as inadequate to deal with personal activity reflects Thorlief Boman's misleading contrast of the Hebrew and Greek mentalities."[30] He quotes from William Albright, who responds to Boman's thesis that the differences in language were characteristics of different ways of thinking.[31] Henry remarks, "The supposed differences turned for Boman on a contrast of the Greek 'to be' (*eimi*) with the Hebrew 'to be' (*hayah*) in the sense of 'coming to be' (*hayoh*). But, as Albright notes, the Greeks too have a word for 'to become' (*gignomai*) [too]."[32] Evidently, as Henry notes, it is false to claim that different kinds of verbs indicate different ways of thinking. For such a claim not only confuses the relationship between epistemology and language, but it also fails to account for the way different languages actually use verbs.

Henry continues to interact with Blaikie, who criticizes Francis Schaeffer for tracing the modern intellectual predicament to the influence of the Hegelian dialectic.[33] Blaikie critiques Schaeffer for claiming the dialectic has caused people to alter the logical process of modern thinking so that the categories of truth and error and right as well as

28. Ibid.
29. Ibid.
30. Ibid.
31. Ibid.
32. Ibid., 3:244–245.
33. Ibid., 3:245.

wrong are no longer viewed as "irreducible claims."[34] Henry responds to Blaikie's argument by denying that Schaeffer actually taught modern man has a new way of thinking. If this were the case, it would be counterproductive to Schaeffer's entire apologetic efforts, and all apologetic efforts for that matter. Namely, as Henry says, "Were it the case that dialectical thinking has actually changed the thought-process of twentieth-century humanity, no apologetic could any longer serve to persuade modern man of a logical alternative."[35] As an alternative, Schaeffer is trying to communicate the notion that modern secular man "relativizes" all claims of truth and morality and views all of religion and philosophy to be culture-bound.[36] He claims, "I do not understand Schaeffer to hold that the impact of dialectical logic has changed the actual thought-process of humanity, ontologically reconstituting and inherently determining modern man to think with a dialectical 'triangular' logic."[37] Henry believes modern society is prone to relativistic patterns of thought because they look for truth beyond divine revelation. This tendency, according to Henry,

> . . . reflects a deepening revolt against the fixed truth/error distinction of which revealed theology. Despite the chronic lapse from rationality and logical consistency, and the growing disposition to regard truth and error as not always nor completely antithetical, the forms of morality and of valid thought nonetheless remain forever unchanged.[38]

It is fairly clear, in retrospect, to note that Henry believed this collapse of truth/error was not a result of Hegel's dialectic, but a reflection of the fact modern society was prepared to receive the dialectic because they already misconstrued the rational Logos of God.[39] If anything, modern society's denial of the rational aspects of language is a result of denying the Logos in epistemology. For, as Henry insists, if there is no rational epistemological Logos, there can be no rational cognitive-verbal Logos either.

34. Ibid.
35. Ibid.
36. Ibid. Henry explains this comment and defends Schaeffer by noting Schaeffer did not believer humans were able to think apart from or contrary to the laws of logic. Instead, the mood of the day ventures man to relativize truth and create a "new way of thinking."
37. Ibid.
38. Ibid.
39. Ibid., 3:245–246.

The Origin of Language

Henry opens his chapter on "The Origin of Language" with these words, "Wherever human beings are found they possess the faculty of speech and communicate by language."[40] Henry pens those words in order to affirm his belief that human language is unique. He favorably quotes Edward Sapir, Noam Chomsky, and Mortimer Adler, who also affirm language is unique to human beings. In particular, Henry agrees with Adler that the possession of language by humanity makes a difference of kind versus a difference of degree, between humanity and animals.[41] For example, if a mathematician compares a smaller circle with a larger circle, the essential difference is one of degree. However, if that same mathematician compares a circle with a square, the essential difference is one of kind. Regardless of how many sides you add to the square, it will only *approach* and not actually *become* a circle. In a similar fashion, while humans and animals might have many common properties, the essential difference that distinguishes the two is the property of human language. For these scholars, humanity is uniquely fashioned for communicative speech because of the mind's ability to have rational and abstract thought.[42]

Most philosophers of language agree with the proposition, "Humanity has the ability or the faculty of communicative language." Not all philosophers agree with the statement, "Humanity *alone* has the ability or faculty of communicative language." Neither do they agree with the origin of humanity's ability of communicative language. For example, Henry addresses two types of theories concerning the origin of language. The first is an empirical or naturalist theory of language. He claims, "During the past three centuries empirical philosophers have contended, as did John Locke and David Hume, that all human knowledge, linguistic knowledge included, arises from sense experience."[43] For these empirical thinkers, the human mind is a *tabula rasa* on which nature writes, and by doing so, conditions what the mind sees, hears, and feels.[44] Henry explains that for empiricists, "Language emerges from his [humanity's] adjustment to nature, and by children imitating their parents' speech

---

40. Ibid., 3:235.
41. Ibid. See, Adler, *The Difference of Man and the Difference It Makes*.
42. Henry, *GRA*, 3:235.
43. Ibid.
44. Ibid., 3:325–326.

habits."[45] Henry believes naturalistic accounts of language were highly influential upon various expressions in logical positivism and linguistic analysis or logical analysis.

The second account of language is an evolutionary theory. Like naturalistic theorists, evolutionary models believe human and animal "language" only differs by degree. Because of that belief, Henry claims,

> Evolutionary theory nonetheless considers human speech to be a complex development of animal cries, and graces its essential element to the fact that man possesses vocal organs. Human language is identified in terms of 'instinctual sound-making powers' of a merely quantitatively different sort than those of other species. Edmund Leach grants on the one hand that human speech is 'a message bearing and information storing device of a quite different kind from that possessed by any other animal,' and refers to man's creative thought and verbal communication as a 'god-like activity,' the locus of man's divine inventiveness and creative transformation of reality. He insists on the other hand, however, as must every humanist in view of his denial of the supernatural, that the difference between man and the lower animals, and machines as well, is merely one of degree (*A Runaway World?*, pp. 21, 88–89).[46]

Typically people understand naturalistic accounts to include some type of connection between higher and lower animals. However, some evolutionary theories affirm there is only a difference of degree between humanity and machines. Henry believes the problem with naturalistic and evolutionary accounts is their explanations fall prey to reductionism. Following Donald MacKay, whom Henry labels as "one of the world's foremost brain researchers," he claims ". . . that nothing in biblical teaching requires that the brain be exempted from normal physical principles, the lower animals need not therefore be considered capable of all human functions."[47] Instead, Henry thinks the logic of the debate seems to indicate that humanity has a genetically unique and cognitively distinct capacity for language.[48]

For Henry, the unique and distinct aspect of human language is its cognitive dimension. Henry claims, "What distinguishes human speech

---

45. Ibid., 3:326.
46. Ibid., 3:327.
47. Ibid., 3:328.
48. Ibid; 3:329–330.

and langue [sic] is the objective meaning that man attaches to symbols or words, and his logical ordering of the units of linguistic communication. Human beings correlate language with abstract thought, and they combine sounds as units to convey complex ideas and information."[49] Henry goes on to explain,

> Parrots and myna birds can be taught to repeat two sentences—perhaps even a major and minor premise of a simple syllogism—but they will never logically formulate the conclusion. There is a structural characteristic of an empirical nature that separates animal communication from human language, viz., syntax and semantic arbitrariness. Language is a system of linguistic units having an orderly representation and arrangement. These units of language are conventional; no particular identity prevails between them and what they publicly symbolize. The same referent can be depicted by the English term *horse*, the German *Pferd*, or the French *cheval*. In human language the relation sound to meaning is not necessary either semantically or syntactically.[50]

These types of comments by Henry reveal he affirms a conventionalist theory of symbols, but a realist theory of meaning. Language is able to be objective because of the cognitive aspects of language. The logical categories of thought prevalent in all of humanity structure the cognitive aspects of language. Therefore, according to Henry, regardless of the geographical origin, social or historical conditioning, or mechanical advancements; the ontological aspects of human thought allows for an objective origin and transmission of language.[51]

Does this mean Henry completely dismisses the discoveries of empirical data? No. Instead, Henry believes the error of naturalistic theories is not found in the empirical data but in their naturalistic presuppositions. In fact, Henry goes on to say, "Christian theism can in fact take the empirical data available in linguistics and view this data through a more comprehensive and yet simple model of language."[52] In this statement, Henry utilizes his presuppositional method in order to show how naturalistic accounts are unable to offer as compelling of a comprehensive

---

49. Ibid., 3:330–331.
50. Ibid., 3:331.
51. Ibid., 3:331–334.
52. Ibid., 3:333.

explanation as Christian theism because their presuppositions and the data available do not coincide.

Before Henry offers a defense of a theistic view of language, he explains and attempts to refute the claim that language is an innate ability of humanity. In his chapter on the origin of language, Henry interacts with a variety of views, but the most pressing is a structuralist view of language. He uses Lévi-Strauss to explain this view. According to Henry,

> A leading exponent of structuralism, which emphasizes the human mind's organizing and interpretative role in relation to the perceptual world, Lévi-Strauss insists that man's cultural behavior conveys information that can be deciphered into a kind of sematic algebra. Human experience is what transmutes elementary spatiotemporal communities into segments that man designates as specific classes and separate events. This distinctively segmented apprehension of nature and events man then imitates in his own construction of artifacts, writing of history, and achievements of culture. The relationships as man apprehends them to exist in nature then generate cultural effects that reflect these relations as he understands them. As Lévi-Strauss sees it, man's distinction from the animals corresponds to this confrontation of culture/nature in the manner that man relates himself to nature and in the way that culture separates nature. The specifically human distinctive is that man uses language; it is language that accomplishes the transition from nature to culture.[53]

From this comment, Henry goes on to say that while a person does not need to accept all of the conclusions of structuralist thinkers such as Lévi-Strauss, J. B. Foncault, and Louis Althusser; they should at least appreciate the fact that structuralists understand that human beings have "... an unparalleled capacity for category information."[54] This "category information" is a universal aspect of humanity that allows humanity to communicate and enter into social relationships.[55] It is a basic element in thinking and humanity. According to Henry, the significance of this for a structuralist view of language is that sounds, meanings, combinations of words, etc. "... for verbal categories supply the means by which universal structural features of the human mind are transformed into universal

---

53. Ibid., 3:338.
54. Ibid.
55. Ibid.

structural features of human culture."⁵⁶ Therefore, Henry suggests, "Although born without any full-blown innate language, the human infant has an innate capacity to make meaningful utterances and to decode the meaningful utterances of others."⁵⁷ He favors aspects of the structuralist approach because it insists on the cognitive aspects of language; however, that does not entail he affirms each aspect of the structuralism.

Henry views structuralism as rivaling his theistic view of language. Structuralism offers innate cognitive categories to undergird a particular philosophy of language. He disagrees with structuralism because it is not a theistic view of language, and Henry disagrees with the idea that the reason for the difference between humans and primates lies in a basic binary structure of opposites found in all human language. Henry remarks, "[T]he binary structure of opposites that he [Lévi-Strauss] finds in all human language is not as basic as are the laws of logic; indeed, the notion of a variety of logics implied by Lévi-Strauss's contrast of system of notation is itself highly debatable."⁵⁸ Because logic is more basic and fundamental to humanity, it holds precedence over the supposed binary-like structures.

In addition to what has already been said, Henry also disagrees with structuralism because of Lévi-Strauss's close epistemological proximity to the Hegelian and Fichtean dialectic.⁵⁹ Furthermore, because reality is only understood by these imposed innate language structures, ". . . do we therefore (recalling Kant) distort the world beyond? Rather than unveiling reality . . . language and its categories are windows into it."⁶⁰ In brief, Henry critiques structuralism for its use of innate language to mirror the epistemological aspects of Kantian epistemology.⁶¹ Since he has already found Kant's epistemology to be incoherent, he also views the similar cognitive aspects in structuralist views of language to be incoherent too.⁶²

56. Ibid.
57. Ibid.
58. Ibid., 3:340.
59. Henry remarks, "Lévi-Strauss's generalizations—from a basic scheme of binary oppositions that uses mediating middle-terms, reminiscent of the Hegelian and Fichtean dialectic of thesis-antithesis-synthesis—became too dogmatic an assertion about the universal categorical characteristics of the unconscious process of human thinking." Ibid.
60. Ibid., 3:345.
61. Ibid.
62. At this point, it is apparent that Henry's presuppositional method undergirds

Meaning and Religious Language

In his chapter titled, "Is Religious Language Meaningful?," Henry discusses the relationship between epistemology and religious language.[63] There, Henry attempts to defend a view of objective religious meaning and the literal truth of language. Two in particular are logical positivism and analytic philosophy. This following section considers how Henry critiques logical positivism and analytic philosophy.

Henry opposes some aspects of analytic philosophy because he thinks it fails to properly relate epistemology and language. He claims, "Evangelicalism exhibits little enthusiasm for certain analytic philosophers of a positivistic strain who contend that religious language has only non-cognitive uses and who consequently conform their inquiries into the meaning of theological statements to this underlying prejudice."[64] Henry also opposes David Hume's logical positivism, who affirms only analytic and empirically verifiable statements. He believes logical positivism rests upon a faulty commitment to an empirical method and the

---

his linguistic methodology and philosophy. According to the presuppositional method, an apologist ought to first show the incoherence of opposing positions before they offer a more coherent explanation of the data and the Christian position. At this point, Henry has already offered passing remarks about the superiority of a Christian theistic view of language, but he has not offered an explanation or defense of the position. Instead, he spends multiple chapters offering critique after critique of opposing positions, before offering an explanation and defense of a theistic view of language in chapters twenty-two and twenty-three.

63. Ibid., 3:347–361. Henry also has a chapter titled, "The Meaning of Religious Language." In this chapter he discusses nine different approaches to religious language: (1) Analogical Predication; (2) Pragmatic; (3) Use-Principle of Language; (4) Pictorial Revelation; (5) Inner-Word-Event; (6) Doxological; (7) Political; (8) Phenomenology; (9) Kerygmatic. Ibid., 3:363–379. This section is not included in the present research because in this chapter Henry only critiques opposing theories of language. Besides the actual critiques, no new information on Henry's cognitive-propositional view of language is included in this chapter. However, it ought to be noted that Henry opposes Bernard Longergan's view of language for what he considers its similarities to a phenomenological approach to language. Henry claims, "To establish the possibility of God-knowledge on a metaphysical basis, Gilkey affirms, we must show that 'ordinary experience includes legitimate uses of cognitive thought beyond immediate experience.' so too, B. J. F. Lonergan would begin with the secular experience of knowing to assert a basis for cognitive metaphysical knowledge (*Insight*, 1958). 'The revelationist must ask,' says Gilkey, 'what elements of general experience point to, give meaning to, and help to validate what he wishes to say about man or God on the basis of . . . revelation through the proclaimed Word' (*Naming the Whirlwind*, p. 228)." Ibid., 3:371.

64. Ibid., 3:361.

so-called "verifiability principle," which is self-defeating because according to its method one could not empirically verify the verifiability principle.[65]

Henry addresses two types of linguistic philosophy that affect evangelical theology. The first view he addresses is logical positivism. Henry claims, "Taking a cue from David Hume, logical positivists asserted that only two kinds of propositions have literal meaning: (1) analytic statements, and (2) empirically verifiable statements."[66] Hume used this method to deny the legitimate knowledge and verifiability of metaphysical statements, including knowledge of God. Three more influential logical positivists Henry interacts with are: John Wisdom, Rudolf Carnap, and A. J. Ayer.[67] Logical positivists use the verifiability method to label as nonsense all affirmations except statements about mathematics, logic, analytic, or those that are empirically verifiable.[68] Henry notes that for logical positivists,

> Abstract reasoning, e.g., mathematics, is logically necessary but factually empty; matters of fact are empirically verifiable, say the positivists, or they are simply nonsense. Metaphysics thus becomes an effort to converse about entities inaccessible to any possible experience. Assertions about alleged matters of fact that transcend sense experience—theological and ethical statements, for example—are declared meaningless. The verification principle, positivists felt, relieved them of any obligation to provide a detailed refutation of metaphysical theories, since they summarily dismissed metaphysics as nonsense on the ground that it deals with supposed realities inaccessible corroboration by observation and experience. The term *God*, statements about divine being, agency, purpose, redemption and judgment are therefore stripped of all intelligible content.[69]

The implications of logical positivism are that all metaphysical and theological statements are considered to be nonsense. In particular, a positivist approach opposes Henry's notion that the Bible conveys cognitive information about God. This view in turn, opposes Henry's idea of the "Logic of Religious Language."

65. Ibid., 3:347, 351.
66. Ibid., 3:347.
67. Ibid., 3: 348–351.
68. Ibid., 3:347–348.
69. Ibid., 3:348.

Henry responds to this "paradigm of meaningful statements," claiming that it [logical positivism] ". . . overlooked other statements that also are meaningful, at least in some sense."[70] He uses the presuppositional method in order to locate what he considers to be the inherent logical contradiction within logical positivism. Henry believes the principle of verification is self-defeating. He claims, "A basic error of the verificationist in respect to significance was their conflation of the ideas of meaning and truth. To say that only statements which are empirically verifiable are true is a meaningful claim, even though it is unverifiable and false."[71] Furthermore, the contradiction lies in this fact, "That a sentence is empirically verifiable or falsifiable qualifies it as a sentence that presumably deals with empirically verifiable referents; such verifiability or falsifiability is not the basis of its meaningfulness, however."[72] In summary, it is fallacious for logical positivists to claim that the verification principle proves the nonsense of religious language, when by their very own principle, they cannot establish the validity of a logical positivist theory of meaning.

The second view of language Henry critiques is analytic philosophy because he believes it has the potential to negatively influence evangelical theology.[73] Analytic philosophy traces its origins in what has been considered the "linguistic turn."[74] William F. Lawhead claims, "In the early part of the twentieth century and continuing on today, a group of philosophers united around the conviction that clarifying language is the most pressing, if not the sole, task of philosophy. This movement is known as analytic philosophy or linguistic philosophy."[75] Lawhead goes on to explain, "These labels signify the fact that, in spite of their diversity, the philosophers within this movement believe that analysis is the correct approach to philosophy and that language is its primary subject matter."[76] Lawhead offers two reasons for the "linguistic turn,"

> First, these philosophers felt science had taken over much of the territory formerly occupied by philosophy. . . . If the mission of

---

70. Ibid., 3:350.
71. Ibid., 3:351.
72. Ibid.
73. Allen and Springsted, *Philosophy for Understanding Theology*, 211–212.
74. Ibid.
75. Lawhead, *The Voyage of Discovery*, 499.
76. Ibid.

acquiring knowledge about our world has been taken over by science, then the only task that remained for philosophy was to clarify linguistic meaning. Second, new and more powerful methods of logic had been developed in the twentieth century that promised to shed new light on some of the old, philosophical stalemates. With these logical techniques, expressions that appeared to be meaningful propositions, but that were actually vague, equivocal, misleading, or non-sensical, could be exposed and eliminated by careful analysis.[77]

Lawhead lists whom he considers some of the most influential philosophers of the "linguistic turn." They are: Bertrand Russell (1872–1970); G. E. Moore (1873–1958); A. J. Ayer 1910–1989); Ludwig Wittgenstein (1889–1951); Gilbert Ryle (1900–1976); and John Austin (1911–1960).[78]

Henry seems to have mixed feelings about analytic philosophy.[79] On the one hand, he says, "Analytical philosophy at best only clarifies the theological language and concepts. Yet this proper role of clarification of the language of faith and of religious concepts should not be demeaned. In order to determine if a statement is true or false, we must first know its meaning and use; only then can it be assessed in terms of relevant evidence."[80] On the other hand,

> The analysis of language makes no pretense of justifying the truth or falsity of factual statements but simply asks how particular statements can be verified or falsified. Analytic philosophy remains neutral regarding truth-claims. It cannot be expected to support or confirm theological assertions. In it the Christian will find no direct philosophical contribution to the content of the theology of revelation. In principle, analytical philosophy has no tools for investigating a superscientific realm and therefore abandons metaphysics. Nor can it make value judgments concerning competitive views.[81]

Henry has positive feelings about analytic philosophy because he considers it a useful method for clarifying thought and furthering communication. Analytic philosophy rightly seeks to discern the various uses of language, which according to Henry, ". . . logical positivists condemned

77. Ibid.
78. Ibid., 499–526
79. Ibid.
80. Henry, *GRA*, 3:351–352.
81. Ibid., 3:352.

to simply emotive or volitional nonsense."[82] Theologians can benefit from this method because it is important to clarify all statements, including theological statements.[83] In particular, it requires theologians to seek the precise sense and use of language.[84]

Henry's positive/negative feelings toward analytic philosophy seem to arise because the new method it has created for *doing* theology. Henry claims,

> Analytic philosophers thus shaped a new method of doing theology—not an orderly wresting of first-order questions, crowned by a case for the existence of God and the exhibition of his will, but a discussion of the legitimacy of God-language not narrowly framed in terms of what *empirical* tests might be implied by any theological assertion. Religious language, as we know, is often scandalously loose and notoriously obscure; what now emerged, with analytic philosophy, was the clarification of meaning—especially a preoccupation with what is sometimes called metatheology, that is, the cognitive significance of God-sentences. The abiding value of analytic philosophy, or linguistic analysis, lay in its demand for eliminating vagueness and promoting clear and definable meaning.[85]

Henry's statements on analytic method clearly affirm that ". . . . Christianity has every cause to welcome the demand for clarity of meaning by linguistic analysts, since clear expression and logical thought commend Christian theology and apologetics and are serviceable to the life of the faith."[86] However, he claims, if someone traces the history of doctrine, it is evident that theologians from all eras took careful precautions to clarify and clearly define their terms. Those same theologians also required their opponents to define their terms too. In that sense, Henry suggests that requiring scholars to define their terms is not a novel concept for Christian theology.

Henry's negative feelings towards analytic philosophy, beyond its inability to determine the truthfulness or falsity of a statement, are its commitment to a non-Christian method of philosophy.[87] He remarks,

82. Ibid., 3:353.
83. Ibid.
84. Ibid.
85. Ibid., 3:354.
86. Ibid., 3:355.
87. Ibid.

> And it is hardly the role of philosophy, secular or otherwise, to define the scope of meaningfulness in advance by sponsoring preconceptions that exclude certain statements simply because they do not meet an arbitrary test. Verificational analysts arbitrarily oversimplified the meaning of meaning by simperimposing a priori definitions of significance on sentences.[88]

Furthermore, Henry follows in the trajectory of F. H. Cleobury and E. O. Mascall, who take a dim view of analytic philosophy due to its ". . . premature marriage to logical positivism, which discarded theological language as nonsense."[89] Moreover, Henry claims,

> Anyone who looks to analytical philosophy to expound a schematic metaphysics or to provide a philosophical basis for theology expects from analytic philosophy what it is powerless to provide unless tendentious premises are arbitrarily appended to it . . . But we must be sure to distinguish the verificatory method of logical positivism from linguistic analysis, even though some philosophers combine them. The fact that some linguistic analysts are hostile to supernatural theism is no reason for shunning the task of clarifying concepts; their hostility proves only that the rejection of revelational theism is not confined to nonphilosophers, and that even the results of analytic philosophy need further clarification when they are wedded to a questionable knowledge-theory.[90]

It is not by accident Henry has three types of feelings towards analytic philosophy. This can be seen in the following comments about Henry's analysis of analytic philosophy.

First, Henry praises analytic philosophy's ability to require clear concepts for both philosophy and theology. The importance of this comment is it helps to foster clear and precise dialogue amongst various scholars. Second, Henry has mixed feelings leaning towards negative feelings because of its method for *doing* theology. Due to his presuppositional method, he cautions theologians from wedding any theological pronouncement with philosophical methodology. In particular, because Henry believes analytic philosophy is only able to declare if a statement is meaningful or logically coherent, not if it is true or false; he cautions

---

88. Ibid.
89. Ibid., 3:353.
90. Ibid.

evangelicals from completely embracing the system.[91] For Henry, Christian theology must go beyond logical consistency into the realm of truth. If a theological method is not able to combine both the logical and truth conditions, it is an inadequate method. His final criticism of analytic philosophy stems from his belief that God is the sole determiner of revelation, including the concepts and principles for truth and meaningful language, not an abstract man made philosophical method. This final point is a logical extension of his Revelational Theistic epistemology and indicates Henry believes synthesizing analytic philosophy with an evangelical theological method has the potential to undermine an evangelical epistemology and hermeneutic.

Furthermore, Henry recognizes that since the dawn of the twentieth century, numerous scholars have affirmed not only an analytic understanding of language, but a variety of ways in which religious language is said to "function."[92] He raises a few important questions: "Does theological language serve only to express wonder? Or simply to facilitate worship? Or to 'witness' to transcendent reality? Or does theological language fill some other role in respect to the knowledge of God?"[93] Henry discerns that many of the recent proposals of religious language are obscure about the relation of religious "meaning" to the functions concerning language and logic.[94] He says,

> Some scholars even claim that religious language possesses a special logic; others suggest that a variety of logics attaches to religious discourse. . . . Elsewhere we consider whether there are indeed a variety of logics—whether the logical considerations governing religious truth and language differ from the logical criteria determinative for other realms of thought—and whether the logic of religious meaning in fact has multiple forms. We shall concentrate here on representative views of the supposed non-literal meaning of religious affirmations, and evaluate the theory that theology has a unique language and meaning.[95]

Henry argues for a literal meaning of religious statements, one might even consider his approach a univocal view of religious meaning. Henry

91. Ibid., 3:362.
92. Ibid., 3:362.
93. Ibid.
94. Ibid., 3:363.
95. Ibid.

defends his theory of religious language in his chapter titled, "A Theistic View of Language."

A Theistic View of Language

Similar to his view of epistemology, Henry appeals to the Bible in order to ground his knowable concepts of God and the world, and also for the language it uses about them.[96] One debated topic amongst linguists pertains to the origin of language.[97] Following the trajectory of Gordon Clark, Henry believes because the Bible does not offer a definitive account on the origin of language that a theory of linguistic origins is speculative in nature.[98] For Henry, the implications of this are as he says, "The notion that human language originated in sense experience—as many evolutionists claim—not only lacks scientific confirmation but also cannot explain the nature and function of language, nor does it account for the origin of the idea of God."[99] Henry like Clark, taunts theistic evolutionists who accept some form of Adamic creation yet tend to explain language as an evolutionary development.[100]

Like both Augustine and Clark, Henry's explanation of verbal communication is that a rational theistic God stands behind humanity in time and is the ground for all thought behind language.[101] This does not mean God created all words; however, he did create some words.[102] Instead, as Henry claims, "In the theistic view, language is possible because of man's God-given endowment of rationality, of *a priori* categories and of innate ideas, all of which precondition his ability to think and speak. Since every mind is lighted by the Logos or Reason of God, thought stands behind language."[103] Furthermore, he adds, "The gift of human speech and language, in brief, presupposes the *imago Dei*, particularly rationality. Logic is indispensable to human thought and to human speech. Without the law of contradiction no significant speech is possible; even

---

96. Ibid., 3:386.
97. Ibid.
98. Ibid.
99. Ibid., 3:387.
100. Ibid., 3:389–390.
101. Ibid., 3:388.
102. Ibid.
103. Ibid., 3:389.

attempts to refute the law of contradiction would have to be formulated in intelligible language that presupposes it."[104] These two comments by Henry indicate according to a theistic view of language, due to the *imago Dei*, humanity was fashioned in such a way so that human beings could speak from the moment of creation, and there is an internal connection between thought, language, and the Logos of God.[105]

In order to explain a theistic view of language, Henry develops twenty one different statements. These are not, however, to be taken as precise declarations like his fifteen theses. Instead, they consist of some very short pronouncements, while others are much more elaborate. Operationally, at this point, Henry begins to utilize the second step of his presuppositional method. The first step consists of critiquing opposing views by showing them to be inconsistent or contradictory. The second step is to demonstrate the superiority of the Christian worldview's ability to account for the relevant data under consideration. This subsection seeks to establish Henry's position by accomplishing two tasks: First, due to the importance of this subsection for Henry's method each statement will be listed. Second, these statements will be explained in order to better understand Henry's view of language and how it affects his cognitive-propositionalist method of hermeneutics.

> 1. *God appears in the Bible from the very beginning not simply as the sovereign God who acts but as the living God who speaks, and who declares his purpose before he acts (Gen. 1:3–29; 1:26). Even the conversation within the Godhead at the creation is depicted in linguistic propositional form: 'Let us make man in our image.'*[106]

The importance of this first statement is its insistence on the "living God who speaks." The next phrase "who declares his purpose before he acts" sets Henry apart from event-oriented approaches to theology. It shows God is able to communicate in words that are separate from the events they record. Furthermore, it shows Henry's commitment to the classical theist's insistence on God's omniscience.[107] Since God knows all things,

---

104. Ibid., 3:390.

105. This comment is justified by Henry's remark, 'The theistic claim that, in view of his divine image, man 'could think and speak from his first moment' maintains, as Clark says, an inner connection between thought, language and the Logos of God' (*Religion, Reason and Revelation*, 135)." Ibid., 3:390.

106. Ibid., 3:390.

107. Ibid.

he can make definite verbal pronouncements about those acts before they take place. Finally, from the very beginning God spoke about the created universe in propositional form, especially declaring the importance of the image of God for humanity.

> 2. *God's word in the creation of the cosmos is not cryptic, paradoxical or super-rational, but takes the form of intelligible, orderly sentences, e.g. (cf. Gen. 1:3, 6, 9, 11, 14, 20, 24).*[108]

Henry goes on to quote Karl Barth who agrees that in the creation account the Bible makes some declarations about epistemology and the nature of the intellect. Henry includes this statement to insist on the cognitive aspects of revelation, including propositional revelation. He also endeavors to stand against neo-orthodox theologians and phenomenologist's who consider the Bible to be non-cognitive, paradoxical, and event-oriented. These theologians reject the evangelical insistence on the Bible as cognitive and propositional revelation.

> 3. *The use of words as symbols has divine precedent: 'And God called the light Day, and the darkness he called Night' (Gen. 1:5; KJV; cf. 1:8, 10).*[109]

The key phrase from this short statement is, "The use of words as symbols." The *Oxford Dictionary* defines the word "precedent" in this way, "Previous case or legal decision, etc., taken as a guide for subsequent cases or as a justification."[110] Within the legal field, if something takes "precedence," it typically is understood that a previous legal case is the guide for a later legal decision. Henry's use of "precedent" in this section is quoted from the Genesis account in which God uses actual words to communicate symbols. God does not use non-cognitive, non-linguistic, or evocative, modes of expression. In the present day, many theologians maintain the symbolic nature of the Genesis account.[111] Henry would remind them that from the very beginning, God used words when he could have used symbols in the Genesis account. For Henry, due to the nature

---

108. Ibid., 390–391.
109. Ibid., 3:391.
110. Jewell, *The Oxford*, 648.
111. Enns, *Inspiration and Incarnation*; Enns, *The Evolution of Adam*; Walton, *Ancient Near Eastern Thought and the Old Testament*; Walton, *The Lost World of Genesis One*; Falk, *Coming to Peace with Science*; Tremper Longman, III, *How to Read Genesis*; Sparks, *God's Word in Human Words*.

of a theistic God and the way he relates to humanity through cognitive revelation, God from the very beginning used words as a precedent for the rest of his special revelation.

4. *The valuational use of language also has divine precedent: 'And God saw that it was good' (Gen. 1:22, 28; cf. 1:10, 12, 18, 21, 25, 31).*[112]

Henry offers no further comment on this statement. The only insight gleaned from it for the present research purposes is Henry taught God valued propositional language and set as a precedent that it was a noble way to communicate about the good creation.

5. *God's address to man does not differ in kind from the Word of God spoken in humanly intelligible statements in the creation of the universe (cf. Gen. 1:28–30). Man is divinely addressed as hearer and doer of the understandable word of God.*[113]

A difference of kind insists that inherent between two beings is at least one property that distinguishes them. For example, the property of speech is what distinguishes the cognitive abilities of humanity from animals. In this instance, Henry claims there is no difference of kind between God's use of language to address Adam in the Garden and from the rational Word of God spoken to humanity. The purpose of this declaration is two-fold. First, it emphasizes that man is both a hearer and a doer of the Word of God.[114] Second, Henry claims, "This continuity between God's word spoken in the formation of the cosmos and of man, and his comprehensible instruction of man, reflects the larger biblical emphasis that the universe was created in anticipation of God's coming in human flesh and that the redemptive sacrifice of Christ was decreed in eternity (cf. Rev. 13:8)."[115] The key word from this quote is "continuity." Henry does not want to divide the Word of Truth wrongly. Instead, he affirms there is a necessary continuity of kind between the propositional and personal Word of God.

6. *Already in Eden and prior to the fall, God addressed special revelation to Adam both in the form of explicit moral commandments*

---

112. Henry, GRA, 3:391.
113. Ibid.
114. Ibid.
115. Ibid.

> *(Gen. 2:16–17) and in the expression of his intention concerning human marriage (Gen. 2:18, 21–24).*[116]

Henry elaborates on this statement saying, "Even on the basis of the original creation, therefore, God addressed Adam not solely by general divine revelation given through nature and conscience, but also in special revelatory disclosure of his purpose, verbally articulated."[117] The important concept is "verbally articulated." From the very beginning, prior to the fall, the Bible records that God spoke to Adam not through mystical paradox or through unintelligible events, but through cognitive, verbal-propositional revelation.

> 7. *Adam was divinely enlisted to name the animals (Gen. 2:19) over which the Creator had given his dominion (Gen. 1:26, 28), and this naming of the living creatures was accomplished in the presence of God. Adam understood that names are designated referents symbolizing nature and purpose.*[118]

According to Henry, in the Garden metaphysics influenced the meaning of language.[119] This is evident by the fact that Adam named animals according to their "nature." Within classical realist philosophy, the term "nature" refers to the "whatness" of a thing. Daniel J. Sullivan notes that, "Still a third name, *nature*, is used to designate what we mean by essence; nature is essence considered as the principle, the source, of the operations or activities which the thing (*nata*, born) to produce."[120] Henry elaborates on the functional aspect of essences claiming, "This is indicated by his [God's] remarks about the naming of Eve: 'She shall be called Woman, because she was taken out of Man' (Gen. 2:23, KJV), 'And Adam called his wife's name Eve; because she was the mother of all the living' (Gen. 3:20, KJV)."[121] These types of comments indicate Henry believes there is such a thing as "human nature" that contains both men and women.[122] There is not just an *ad hoc* idea framed by individuals to say, "There are just men and women, but there is no such thing as metaphysics or human

---

116. Ibid.
117. Ibid.
118. Ibid.
119. Ibid.
120. Sullivan, *An Introduction to Philosophy*, 218.
121. Henry, *GRA*, 3:391.
122. Ibid.

nature." Moreover, it indicates that Henry believes ontology informs both epistemology and language, the language of the Bible included.

8. *As Satan's mouthpiece, the serpent uses human speech to cast doubt on God's verbal disclosure of his purpose and will: 'Yea, hath God said, Yea shall not eat of every fruit of the garden?' (Gen. 3:1, KJV).*[123]

Henry retorts to a theological position in order to explain the breakdown of language. According to Henry, "This maneuver is doubly confusing, since it extends the prohibition to 'every fruit' of the garden and puts in doubt the divine prohibition and the actuality of divine speech."[124] In this section, Henry quotes Satan and Eve, who both exhibit disobedience and moral rebellion towards the command(s) of God. He summarizes this statement with his theological response claiming, "The pattern of moral doubt and revolt here outlined as its parallel throughout fallen human history, and notably involves a distortion of language."[125] Evidently, for Henry, the breakdown of human language is a result of human rebellion towards the clear verbal commands of God.[126] By logical extension, he believes the distortion of language in the Garden is a sign of moral rebellion. Henry also considers the breakdown of language by philosophers of language and hermeneutics to be a result not of pristine academic theories, but of human rebellion to the God administered gift of human language given to communicate divine propositional truth.[127]

9. *After the fall, God's address to man overtaken in moral disobedience (Gen. 3:8-9) is heard fearfully by Adam because of his sin and a bad conscience (3:10-12).*[128]

The important phrase is, "After the fall, God's address to man . . . is heard fearfully by Adam. . . ." Henry's philosophy of language claims that sin affects communication from God to humanity. Due to his interpretation of the Genesis account, Henry believes sin does not completely destroy humanity's ability to receive and respond to divine revelation in

123. Ibid.
124. Ibid.
125. Ibid., 3:391–392.
126. Ibid.
127. Ibid.
128. Ibid., 3:392.

propositional form. The fall may have corrupted human language, however, it did not destroy human language.

> 10. *God's expanding revelation of his name and will, including his redemptive purpose, is divinely shaped in written form—from 'the book of the generations of Adam' (Gen. 5:1, KJV).*[129]

Henry includes this statement in order to affirm the superiority of written revelation to oral traditions. Henry claims, "The inspired writings authoritatively summarize the content of God's general revelation and expound his special revelation; merely oral tradition would have been more vulnerable to the accretions of legend and myth."[130] Furthermore, he adds, "The written revelation captures in objectively permanent manner the disinstinctives [sic] of God's verbal disclosure from the beginning. It prevents God's special once-for-all revelation from being submerged into ongoing history and from being absorbed into general or universal revelation."[131] These comments together summarize Henry's insistence upon three important tenets: First, divine revelation is incompatible with the concepts of myth or legend.[132] Second, God's revelation consists in the written propositional revelation of the Word of God, not oral forms or source documents that influenced the Scriptures. Third, there is a distinction between special revelation and general revelation.

> 11. *The Bible indicates that the diversification of human tongues took place at a point later than man's beginnings. It indicates that human beings at the beginning had a universally intelligible language, and that the subsequent confusion of tongues was associated with the promotion to priority status of humanistic and materialistic concerns (Gen. 11).*[133]

This statement by Henry indicates he believes the text of Scripture teaches there is one type of logic underlying human language, not a plurality of logics. The reason for a plurality of languages stem from human rebellion, not social diversification or the conventional nature of language.[134]

---

129. Ibid.
130. Ibid.
131. Ibid.
132. Ibid., 1:44–69.
133. Ibid., 3:392.
134. Ibid.

Furthermore, Henry goes on to describe the necessity for literal truth and the factuality of the historical biblical data. He remarks,

> It is clear that neither the biblical writers nor the central biblical characters viewed the biblical drama as unrelated to spiritual truth and human history. Some modern secularists view the Bible as an impressive literary work shaped by a series of writers, and not intended, any more than the Homeric poems are, to give factual information or literal truth. Some would add that the Bible is a sublime myth providing the categories and forms for Christian self-understanding. The biblical writers would have deplored recent notions that their statements are in no sense factual but only emotive, or that they present only 'convictional' language that reflects merely an inner perspective not necessarily related to external and transcendent realities. Biblical faith depends on the historical reality of certain persons and the historical factuality of certain events and a specific interpretation of their meaning.[135]

This quote by Henry is a reminder of his insistence on the necessity of literal truth and the Bible's historical factuality. He also distances himself from any type of existential notions of the biblical text revealing "self-understanding" or evocative convictional language. Henry addresses the importance of a biblical hermeneutic when he uses the phrase, "and a specific interpretation of their meaning," to communicate the idea that there is only one true meaning of the events recorded in Scripture (which is the divine interpretation of those events). For example, when Christ died on the cross, there arose many interpretations of the event from the Jews, Romans, disciples, and unbelievers. However, the only true interpretation of the event is the one recorded in the canonical Gospels.

12. *God's personal address and verbal call to the inspired prophets often involved a vision and at times even physical shock (cf. Dan. 10:8–9; Ezek. 3:15), but there was no loss of self-consciousness or absorption into the Godhead.*[136]

Henry discusses the authors of Scripture in this statement, in particular, that God addresses the prophets in meaningful language, which they understood and communicated to the nation of Israel.[137] He claims, "Almost

---

135. Ibid.
136. Ibid.
137. Ibid.

without exception the prophets heard and received divine revelation in words; visions were not complete until there was a word from God (cf. Isa. 6:8). . . . It is not too much to say that the prophets understood Yahweh's revelations and word-revelations. Divine word-revelation is presupposed by prophetic proclamation and supplies its themes and content."[138] Henry does not deny the revelational aspect of visions or encounters with God; however, according to his interpretation of Scripture, a theistic view of language insists on the superiority and necessity of verbal propositional revelation above experiential and event oriented approaches to revelation.

> 13. *The prophetic call gives rise to a new literary form, notes von Rad, namely, the account of an exclusive call in the first-person singular (ibid., pp. 33-34; cf. Amos 7-9; Isa. 6; 40:3-8; Jer. 1; Ezek. 1-3; Zech. 1:7-6:15; 1 Kings 19:19-21).*[139]

For Henry, the biblical writers were not restricted to the literary forms of their day. These literary forms were definitely utilized, however, they should not be considered shackles that bind the authors of Scripture to a particular use of that genre, or from creating a new type of literary form such as the "first-person singular."[140] The importance of this statement is the biblical writers are not required to follow the writing styles of Jewish Apocalyptic literature or Greco-Roman biography because through the prophetic activity of God during the inspiring act of Scripture, the act of inspiration allows for the authors of Scripture to develop and utilize new literary forms. In addition, even if the writers of Scripture happen to utilize a particular literary form, such as Greco-Roman biography, the divine activity from the prophetic call protects the text of Scripture from factual or historical error regardless of the flexibility of a particular genre.

> 14. *When the writer of Hebrews declares that God 'has spoken' (1:2), he does not employ a high-sounding metaphor to designate a phenomenon wholly other than verbal communication.*[141]

Henry explains this statement by claiming, "As the epistle [Hebrews] as a whole elucidates, the writer believes completely in God who speaks and conveys information and gives instruction. In contrast with false gods; which are lifeless and wordless, the God of the Bible is a personal agent

---

138. Ibid., 3:392-393.
139. Ibid., 3:393.
140. Ibid.
141. Ibid.

who rules, acts, speaks and enters into mind-to-mind relationships."[142] For Henry, a theistic view of language insists upon the cognitive and propositional nature of divine revelation.[143] In fact, to deny this aspect of divine revelation is to equate the text of Scripture with the "lifeless and wordless" false gods. He claims, "In both the Old Testament and the New, Yahweh is the speaking God who initiates conversation with his human creation, who since and despite the fall has gone to astounding lengths to renew the conversation interrupted by sin."[144] God could overcome sin through amazing acts or astonishing events, but, as Henry remarks, ". . . [God] has chosen the instrumentality of a human tongue to convey his redemptive message."[145]

15. *The Bible is the authoritative narrative of God's verbal message to mankind. It is not a written record of all that God has spoken.*[146]

Henry does not believe Scripture contains all God has spoken. However, divine inspiration has recorded what is permanently true for the community of faith.[147] The purpose of the inspired text of Scripture is as Henry claims, to ". . . set forth the content of general revelation in objective form and do so alongside the good news of God's special grace proffered to repentant sinners."[148] Richard Palmer claims silent reading is a modern phenomenon and the purpose of the Bible was to be read aloud as the oral word in contrast to the written Scriptures. Henry responds to Palmer by pointing out that having a written record of the Bible preserves what God has spoken; hence, Scripture can be proclaimed and the value of hearing the written Word experienced. Furthermore, even Jesus and the apostles appealed to the written text of the Old Testament in their oral proclamations. These appeals never hindered but heightened the power of their proclamations.[149] Henry comments that, "Palmer, in other words, is promoting a special theory of revelation and hermeneutics."[150]

142. Ibid.
143. Ibid.
144. Ibid.
145. Ibid.
146. Ibid.
147. Ibid., 3:394.
148. Ibid.
149. Ibid.
150. Ibid.

He believes Palmer's view of hermeneutics downplays the cognitive and written form of Scripture. Henry responds to Palmer's view claiming,

> But how can the Bible appeal to the whole man if it does not appeal also to the rational faculty? Why cannot biblical language communicate conceptual information? That, precisely, is what it indeed claims to do and does do. If valid, Palmer's premises would drain Scripture of most of the values it has historically held for Judeo-Christian religion, and would do so on the basis of an arbitrary theory of hermeneutics. To identify the language of the Bible as a call to a reality to which the speaker and hearer creatively contribute, as an event-shaping power that modifies existence, and not as a statement about the real nature of things or the communication of objectively valid information, reflects the influence of modern existentialism.[151]

In his response, Henry insists on the superiority of a theistic view of language to proclaim objectively the Bible as God's authoritative message to mankind. He taught that appeals to non-cognitive revelation drain the Judeo-Christian Scriptures of truth value in order to uphold an "arbitrary" view of hermeneutics. Henry believes twentieth-century word-theology represents this type of hermeneutical method. Their emphasis on dialectical-existential revelation and its repudiation of conceptual verbal and historical revelation differentiates it from historic evangelical orthodoxy.[152]

Henry appeals to James Barr to discuss those who depreciate the authoritative narrative of the written text by allegorical interpretations, thus canceling the evangelical insistence on the cognitive and verbal status of the Bible. Barr opposes those who quote 2 Corinthians 3:6 talking about

---

151. Ibid., 3:394–395.

152. Note, the use of the word "conceptual" in this context does not mean that Henry affirms a form of conceptual inspiration. He clearly believes more than the concepts of Scripture were inspired. In fact, the totality of his project in *GRA*, indicates he believes in plenary verbal inspiration. Henry says, "Twentieth-century word-theology took a variety of forms. But what specially differentiated this word-theology from historic evangelical orthodoxy were its association with dialectical-existential emphases, and its repudiation of conceptual-verbal and historical revelation. This modern theology of 'the Word,' as it presumed to call itself, espoused a "Word-revelation" alleged to be personal and internal. Carl Braaten describes the many recent views that revelation is God's direct address to man as 'an avalanche of rhetoric'; Barth's 'Word of God,' Brunner's 'personal encounter,' Gogarten's 'I-thou relationship,' Bultmann's 'kerygma' are but some of the formulations that neglected historical (and we would add, cognitive) concerns in their summons to faith and truth (*History of Hermeneutics*, 25)." Ibid.

how the letter kills and the Spirit gives life in order to justify spiritualizing interpretations of Scripture. Barr remarks that 2 Corinthians 3:6 addresses the operation of the Jewish law as opposed to the Spirit, not a form of allegorical interpretation.[153] Henry quotes Barr in order to state,

> The Bible's linguistic form does not cancel real meaning; it is simply the means by which its meaning is conveyed. 'The verbal form of the Bible does not stand in contrast with its meaning,' Barr adds, 'but is the indicator of that meaning.' While Barr does not accept the doctrine of verbal revelation, he concedes that 'it is therefore not unreasonable that the older theologians spoke about inspiration as 'verbal" (p. 178).[154]

From this quote, it is evident Henry's use of Barr serves to illustrate that historically, evangelicals have affirmed special revelation is both cognitive and verbal, and all who deviate from that position are turning away from classic evangelical Bibliology.

> 16. *The fact that the Bible is completed in more than one language evidences that the confusion of tongues does not frustrate the verbal promulgation of God's word.*[155]

Following his opening address, Henry goes on to argue two points about language and the plurality of languages.[156] First, he uses the actual text of Scripture to defend the cognitive aspects of the Bible.[157] Those theologians who argue for a plurality of logics based upon a diversity of cultures have to deal with the fact that the Bible is written in both Greek and Hebrew, yet it provides a single type of logic in propositional form.[158] Second, Henry argues it was by sovereign choice that Hebrew and Greek were the languages God chose to make the "literary deposit of his revelation."[159] He goes on to say, "[T]his choice was not made, however, by either the Hebrews or the Greeks; the gospel is in fact 'a stumbling block to Jews and folly to Greeks' (1 Cor. 1:23, NEB)."[160] Henry quotes Kenneth Kantzer

153. Ibid.
154. Ibid.
155. Ibid., 3:395.
156. Ibid.
157. Ibid.
158. Ibid.
159. Ibid.
160. Ibid.

to contend that God chose to use both human language and specific languages (e.g., Greek, Hebrew, and Aramaic) to communicate the gospel. However, in the final analysis, the Bible is written in the common forms of these languages to communicate the gospel to the common man.[161]

> 17. *Yet the language of Eden had served as an instrument of revelation long before the prophets wrote in Hebrew.*[162]

Henry's seventeenth statement is written to discuss two issues. First, he attempts to communicate the fact that languages come into and out of existence. Typically, whenever a language is no longer spoken, it is labeled as a "dead language." Henry remarks that language is a diverse phenomenon because there are not only a "thousand tongues" but various other forms of communication and symbols like sign language, phonetic language, diplomatic language, journalistic jargon, just to name a few. One could also add emails, text messaging, and twitter. However, Henry asks, "The only question that must ever confront the task of translation is this: do the words truly express and serve the truth of divine revelation?"[163] Henry answers his question by transitioning to his second issue. Henry notes that numerous heresies have arisen because the church has failed or lagged to translate the Bible. He claims this was the case with both the Nestorians in the early church and Roman Catholicism during the Middle Ages and the Reformation.[164] Henry addresses the need for respectable Bible translations and notes that not all translations are of equal value. Henry points out that, "Every translation is a reduction; something of the original is inescapably lost, though a good translation will actually preserve the original meaning."[165] He believes having a mastery of the biblical languages is a necessary pre-requisite in order to have a faithful translation of the Bible (in particular, one that captures both the biblical content and idioms). Henry points out that not all translators agree about methodology, however, he suggests,

> Biblical translators are divided into champions either of what Eugene Nida calls 'formal equivalence' (literal rendering) or 'dynamic equivalence' idiomatic translation (*Toward a Science of Translating*, p. 159). The current passion for contemporaneity

161. Ibid., 3:396.
162. Ibid.
163. Ibid., 3:397.
164. Ibid.
165. Ibid.

reflected by some paraphrases tends to raise needless questions about the propriety of idiomatic translation but, as Beekman emphasizes, the fact that the New Testament was written in koine Greek supplies the highest precedent for remembering that the language of revelation and translation is to be the language of the common people. The reading of Scripture ought to be anything but drudgery.[166]

One could only wish that Henry made stronger declarations at this point about the relationship between theistic language and Bible translations; however, he did not. It seems like he favored some type of middle position, one that is faithful to the biblical text, yet is also able to include the idiomatic aspects of language and is easily accessible to the common reader. Nevertheless, Henry believes a faithful translation of the Bible is one that rightly conveys the cognitive status of the Scriptures as divine revelation and preserves the truth value of the autographic text.

> 18. *Jesus Christ stands at the center of biblical language not only as the Word or Logos of God to whom the inspired writings bear witness, but as the Redeemer and Judge to whom human beings are answerable for their speech and communication.*[167]

Henry paints Jesus Christ as the "Lord of language" in this section. He quotes Jesus who promises to judge each person for their careless words (Matt. 12:36–37; 16: 13, 14). Henry remarks that, "Jesus' words bear on all our words, verbal and written, and on everything to which they testify."[168] For Henry, theology deals with the visible and invisible, the sacred and the sinful, the judgment of sinners and the bliss of heaven. He comments that ". . . nowhere in human history have these and their related themes been addressed with greater verbal power than by the incarnate Word."[169]

In effect, Henry attempts to relate one's view of the propositional Word of God to the personal Word of God. If a person is going to downplay or disregard the propositional text of Scripture, he is by logical extension making those same pronouncements upon the Word of God made flesh. However, Christ the Word, judges men for their words about both the propositional and personal Word of God. In the elliptical sense, this affects Henry's hermeneutic because he believes those who downplay or

---

166. Ibid.
167. Ibid., 3:396–397.
168. Ibid., 3:398.
169. Ibid.

diminish the propositional Word of God are in effect, making the same pronouncements upon the Word of God made flesh.

19. *In the twentieth century, ancient Hebrew and Greek ways of thinking have been depicted as radically different from each other, and from this contrast scholars have drawn striking theological implications.*[170]

Henry responds to what he labels as the recent "biblical theology" movement in America.[171] He criticizes it for believing there is a Hebrew and Greek way of "thinking." Henry claims, "These contrasting views were traced to a basically different approach to reality, and beyond that to a different mind-set and conception of truth. The Greeks, we are told, considered truth to be objective, discursive and rational; the Hebrews, on the other hand, regarded truth not as cognized nor to be reflected upon but as personally experienced."[172] This distinction is defended by claiming there are two different types of language.[173] For example, Henry notes, "These distinctions were variously supported. One approach contrasted the nature of the two languages: whereas Greek is essentially substantival and adjectival, it is said, Hebrew (i.e. biblical) language is verbally based."[174] However, doubts of this view have arisen due to scholarly research.[175] Henry believes John Robinson's work failed to document the Greek thought from the primary sources.[176] He also claims,

> James Barr's *The Semantics of Biblical Language* contended that the 'biblical theology' spokesmen were tendential in their selection of evidence and that the radical contrast of semantic

---

170. Ibid., 3:398.
171. Ibid.
172. Ibid.
173. Ibid.
174. Ibid. Henry notes, "Thorlief Boman's book *Hebrew Thought Compared with Greek* expounded the dichotomy, and doctrinal research such as H. Wheeler Robinson's *Corporate Personality in Ancient Israel* and John A. T. Robinson's *The Body: A Study in Pauline Theology* were thought to provide supportive evidence. Those who propounded this contrast championed the Hebrew way of thinking; to express the biblical thought forms in Greek categories, it was said, would inevitably distort them. One result of this differentiation was to call into question the entire enterprise of dogmatic or systematic theology, since it seemed to be based upon rational reflection of the 'Greek' type." Ibid.
175. Ibid.
176. Ibid., 3:399.

characterizations of the two languages could not really be sustained. Barr's linguistic research and exegetical study of pertinent biblical passages, both in the Old and New Testaments, noted the failure of such theologians to do justice to the biblical representations of the nature of man and the character of truth.[177]

To further substantiate his claim and in order to add evidence to enlist a denial of the distinction between Hebrew and Greek ways of thinking, Henry quotes from William F. Albright and Bervard Childs (two prominent scholars on the topic).[178] This trend amongst those who affirm two different minds is seen by Henry as a denial of the unified logical structure of human rationale. This is important to Henry's hermeneutic because he believes that due to the *imago Dei* there is a single logical structure in humanity. In addition, since all of humanity is created in the image of God, and since the image of God entails a universal character to the rational faculties, then there is no actual distinction between Hebrew and Greek thinking.[179] There is only one kind of mind, rationale, and logic.

> 20. *The interpreter must ask not only if and how the New Testament writers were influenced by the Septuagint (the Old Testament and Apocrypha in Greek) but also whether the New Testament koine conveys nuances not found in classical Greek and carries new and decisively Christian meanings.*[180]

In this passage, Henry is not trying to relate the New Testament's use of the Old Testament.[181] Instead, he investigates the notion that new meanings of words have arisen due to their specific Christian use. He quotes C. F. Evans to substantiate the idea that biblical words have a subtle deflection from their ordinary meaning.[182] Henry proceeds to focus on Gerhard Kittel's, *Theological Dictionary of the New Testament*.[183] He disagrees with Bruce Metzger, who favors the idea that Christianity almost regenerates the nature and use of words, and favors James Barr and Stephen Neill's assessment of Kittel.[184] Henry offers these words of instruction, claiming,

177. Ibid.
178. Ibid.
179. Ibid.
180. Ibid., 3:399.
181. Ibid.
182. Ibid., 3:399–400.
183. Ibid., 3:3:400.
184. Ibid.

> Such comments on the regeneration of language have been criticized ... as a transference to linguistics of the soteric effects that Christianity imported to human life. Neill (p. 333–34) approves Barr's criticism that Kittel's impressive effort has a tendency to introduce theological presuppositions into linguistic studies and consequently to read too much into isolated units of language. It must not be forgotten that words, whether inside or outside the Bible, gain their precise meaning from their propositional context, and that the meaning that words carry as isolated terms is conventional or customary rather than derived from the nature of words.[185]

This quote summarizes a few key aspects of Henry's view of language. First, he opposes the idea that Christianity somehow "saves" or "regenerates" language. Language has a specific nature, regardless of whether or not it is used in the text of Scripture. Second, Henry affirms a realist understanding of meaning, and a conventionalist view of signs. A theistic view of language opposes Wittgenstein's conventionalist view of both meaning and signs. Third, he affirms that isolated words do not have meaning, nor do they just point to meaning. Instead, words find their meaning within propositional sentences. Another way of putting it is to say that words have *potential* meaning, whereas sentences have *actual* meaning.[186]

> 21. *The question whether other words may serve to transmit God's special revelation can be answered both yes and no: yes, if they have the same meaning, irrespective of the language in which they occur—that is, if they faithfully translate the biblical words; no, if they are words from another world of thought, with no cognitive basis in revelational theism; and no, even when as human words they are formally or outwardly the same but are framed in a universe of discourse and meaning alien to God's Word and hence hostile to biblical revelation.*[187]

This is Henry's final statement on the nature of theistic language. In this comment, Henry affirms that words are capable of transmitting the revelation of God. He argues that all languages can transmit the revelation of God, insofar as they faithfully translate the original biblical words.

---

185. Ibid.
186. Ibid.
187. Ibid., 3:400.

This entails different languages communicate the same propositional truth value. However, the translation fails if it communicates a truth value other than the cognitive truth value in the original propositions of Scripture. The reason is because some thought patterns are alien and hostile to biblical revelation. For Henry, if a translation of Scripture communicates a hostile meaning, it also communicates a meaning hostile to the cognitive status of divine revelation.[188] For that reason, Henry spent so much time discussing the relationship between linguistic analysis and propositional truth.

Linguistic Analysis and Propositional Truth

Henry evaluates linguistic positions that deny or devalue the cognitive significance of propositional statements about God. In the early section of volume three, chapter twenty-six, Henry interacts with logical positivism, neo-orthodoxy, and kerygmatic theologies.[189] While the present research has already discussed some of Henry's criticisms of these three approaches, this section will only focus on his criticisms of language defined according to its "use."[190] This view of language has traditionally been known as Ludwig Wittgenstein's "conventionalist" theory of meaning.[191] The reason for this narrow analysis is two-fold.

First, if the amount of time a scholar discusses a topic suggests how much importance he or she places on a topic, then Henry must view conventionalism as an important topic for hermeneutics. This is evidenced by the fact he spends more time in chapter twenty-six discussing conventionalism (or language understood according to its "use") than any other position. Second, a growing number of philosophers of language, and evangelical approaches to hermeneutics incorporate the discoveries of conventionalism into hermeneutics as epistemology and methodology.[192]

---

188. Ibid., 3:401–402.

189. Ibid., 3:441.

190. This chapter has already discussed conventionalism; however, due to the wide acceptance of this theory amongst evangelicals, that makes Henry's assessment of it important and worthy of more elaboration.

191. Norman L. Geisler in the *Baker Encyclopedia of Christian Apologetics*, defines conventionalism as ". . . the theory that all meaning is relative. Since all truth claims are meaningful statements, this would mean that all truth is relative." Geisler, *Baker Encyclopedia of Christian Apologetics*, 158.

192. Vanhoozer, *Is There Meaning in This Text?*; Vanhoozer, *The Drama of Doctrine*;

For that reason, having a greater understanding of Henry's critiques of conventionalism allows for better interaction on the implications of his hermeneutic in light of the current dialogues in hermeneutics.

The various theories arising from linguistic analysis, such as conventionalism, rightly attempt to understand the various meanings of words. However, Henry claims that "... [r]efuting the confusion of the question of meaning and trust mainly with such linguistic considerations, Brand Blanshard warned that 'the discussion of words and their uses is either irrelevant in philosophy, or should take at most an ancillary part' (*Reason and Analysis*, p. 363)."[193] Henry and Blanshard are not saying the analysis of words and their varying uses is irrelevant. He claims works from antiquity such as Plato's *Cratylus* and Aristotle's *Metaphysics*, have discussed the nature and use of language. So, in that sense, it is not like studying the use of words is anything new. Instead, Henry criticizes certain elements of conventionalism, claiming,

> But Blanchard emphasizes that 'the discussion of words in philosophy is prefatory and preparatory only. How expressions are used is not a philosophical problem. How they ought to be used *is* a philosophical problem, but not primarily one about words at all, but about the character and relations of the objects talked about' (*Reason and Analysis*, p. 364).... While Blanshard credits linguistic philosophers with illuminating many curious details in the philosophers' use of words, he observes that at the end they nonetheless leave us 'strangely unilluminated. ... Words give the philosopher no compass. The interest in usage is trifugal and dispersive. ... When philosophers in the past asked themselves What is the nature of knowledge? instead of What, are the uses of the verb 'to know'? they usually did so with a conviction, having nothing to do with language, that some types of knowledge, or some claims to it, were of central importance'— including, Blanshard notes, the mathematician's insights, the scientific grasp of natural law, and the claims of authoritarian religion (*Reason and Analysis*, pp. 380–81).[194]

Although some conventionalists believe they are engaging in philosophical dialogue, Henry critiques the "use" theories of language for not actually asking philosophical questions. He claims traditional philosophy

---

Duvall and Hays, *Grasping God's Word*; Fee and Stuart, *How to Read the Bible for All Its Worth*; Osborne, *The Hermeneutical Spiral*.

193. Henry, GRA, 3:443–444.

194. Ibid.

concerned itself with metaphysics and epistemology, not just the "preparatory" role of clarifying language. Henry believes linguistic analysts are not engaging in actual philosophical dialogue because they are only discussing pre-philosophical issues of defining and understanding the use of words, not validating the claims made by the words or suggesting how they ought to be used.

Henry continues by analyzing Wittgenstein's notion of "language games."[195] Wittgenstein's approach attempts to find the various "uses" of language. However, Henry thinks there is an error in this approach pointing out that,

> He [Wittgenstein] therefore warned against assuming what the cognitive meaning of a word is, or even that they intended a cognitive meaning. Consequently, his followers operated on the dictum 'don't look for the meaning, look for the use' and concentrated on the use of words rather than on traditional sources of meaning, and considered them human instruments that take on the meaning with which people invest them. And extremely important work in this area was John L. Austin's *How to Do Things with Words*.[196]

Henry's primary issue with Wittgenstein's theory is it downplays, if not outright dismisses, the cognitive status of language. He believes conventionalists wrongly assume that all philosophical analysis must be subsumed under the philosophy of language.[197] Henry believes the error of conventionalism is it detaches meaning from the locus of thought and correlates meaning to "sentence-factors" or "linguistic units" that presume to refer to concrete experience from sense perception. He claims conventionalists are no longer searching for the truth-value of sentences, but search for new possibilities of meaning in the governing context of sensuous experience.[198]

Henry thinks that the signs and symbols of words are instrumentally useful and necessary to communicate "meaning." However, he comments, "While words or marks are instrumentally useful and necessary to communicate meaning, they become fully intelligible only if they express thought,

---

195. Ibid., 3:445.
196. Ibid.
197. Ibid.
198. Ibid., 3:445–446.

ideas, beliefs—in short, propositions."[199] Furthermore, Henry claims, "Words are ultimately useful instruments only if they convey meaning; merely as isolated sounds or marks they fall short of this. Words without meanings are actually not words at all; words become intelligible through their meanings."[200] Apparently for Henry, words obtain meaning by their cognitive status and propositional nature, not according to their use.

Following E. D. Hirsch, Henry reasons that sentences have universal meaning independent of any particular language in which they might occur.[201] He believes, "This is confirmed many times over when logicians, who are not grinding metaphysical or epistemological axes, speak of sentences in the grammar of several different languages as containing the same logical content or, better, as expressing the same proposition (cf. Peter Manicas and Arthur Krugar, *Logic: the Essentials*, pp. 40, 51–52)."[202] Henry uses the law of non-contradiction to respond to conventionalist theories of meaning. He believes conventionalist actions (speaking in sentences of grammar in several languages as containing the same logical content or position) are self-defeating. For example, many conventionalists claim language is conventional and diminish or deny the cognitive status of propositional language; however, when they are not *doing* philosophy (e.g., lecturing and writing), they uphold the cognitive and propositional status of language.

Henry resumes his critique of conventionalism by appealing to the ancient philosopher Aristotle, who in his book, *Metaphysics*, criticized a similar approach advanced by the Athenian Academy, which attempted to downplay or diminish the cognitive status of language.[203] He cites this case in order to note that historically philosophy has done more than "unmask" the supposed absurdities of language. Henry claims, "[P]hilosophy never restricted itself to describing the use of words, but extended its task to matters signified by words."[204] Philosophers have never been uninterested in language; however, he notes, "[T]hey considered philosophy to be engaged in searching out the comprehension of the nature

---

199. Ibid., 3:446.
200. Ibid.
201. Ibid.
202. Ibid.
203. Ibid.
204. Ibid., 3:447.

of knowledge and reality."[205] The disciplines in philosophy that study the nature of knowledge and reality are epistemology and metaphysics. However, with the rise of linguistic analysis, philosophers of language, according to Henry have ". . . forfeited the pursuit of ontological reality [Metaphysics]."[206] Conventionalists have also stopped pursuing the discipline of epistemology because they downplay the necessity of knowledge, specifically metaphysical knowledge. For Henry, conventionalism should be viewed as a departure from the concerns of western philosophy because conventionalists are no longer primarily concerned with metaphysics and epistemology. Henry believes conventionalists are,

> Pledging sole allegiance to the cause of metaphilosophcial concerns (i.e., meaning and justification), [however] linguistic analysts tapered all warranted knowledge-claims to an elucidation of the structures of language; we know nothing else with certainty, in science, in history, in philosophy or religion, it follows, but linguistic conventions.[207]

For Henry, this type of philosophical discourse leads to relativism. The reason he makes these claims is because if the only basis of human knowledge is language, then language is no longer based on the structures of reality, but upon human agreement.[208] Since human agreements can change for a variety of reasons, conventionalists allows for the possibility of epistemological relativism.[209] In summary, since Henry opposes all forms of epistemological relativism because they are unable to offer objective criteria of validation, he also opposes any form of relativistic approach to language too.

In the final analysis, for Henry, truth must be checked by epistemology, instead of linguistic conventions and sense perceptions.[210] According to Henry, conventionalism is self-defeating because ". . . [t]he claim that we can know only conventions of language is itself, of course, a philosophical dogma that presumes to know much more than linguistic units."[211] Henry also says, "The notion that truth is a feature

205. Ibid.
206. Ibid., 3:448.
207. Ibid.
208. Ibid; 3:451.
209. Ibid.
210. Ibid., 3:449.
211. Ibid., 3:448.

156   HERMENEUTICS AS EPISTEMOLOGY

only of language determined solely by grammatical rules actually presupposes that there is no reality beyond language itself, or that if there is we cannot know it. This arbitrary restriction of philosophy to detecting literary confusions conceals a presuppositional flight into just another metaphysic."[212] The self-defeating nature of their claim is they are offering knowledge of reality, while claiming that reality cannot actually be cognitively known. Furthermore, Henry claims, "The attempt of some linguistic analysts to correlate the discussion of category mistakes only with the use of words is itself a grandiose category mistake, since all mistaken or erroneous uses attach actually and solely to the realm of thought and belief."[213] If anything, while conventionalists are committed to non-metaphysical theories and the non-cognitive status of language, their theory of language has developed a very conjectural metaphysic and speculative epistemology.[214]

Henry believes the problem of defining language according to its "use," and denying the propositional nature of language, is individuals are practically committed to a form of linguistic solipsism because they are unable to make claims about extra mental reality.[215] In the final analysis, Henry believes the view that the truth of a particular language is defined by its "use" has proven to be indefensible. For Henry, the correct use of words decides the words meaningfulness in a particular context, not their truth value. The following quote is a summary in Henry's own words, giving his view of propositional language. Henry maintains that cognitive propositional language is required in order to govern the truth value of a sentence. He writes,

> Truth must ultimately be checked by intellection, not by linguistic convention or sense perception. It attaches not to words per se, but to words used together to express mental judgments—i.e., propositions. What is either true or false is the meaning of words used in logical relationships. Absurdity and falsity pertain not to isolated words and their use, but to their meaning in sentences; truth is a property of sentences. A judgment constitutes the minimal unit of logical meaning and of objective

212. Ibid., 3:448–449.
213. Ibid., 3:449.
214. Ibid.
215. Henry claims, "But this new linguistic approach seemed to promise nothing better than linguistic solipsism on the one hand, or semantic atheism on the other." Ibid., 3:452.

truth; while a judgment is mentally affirmed, a proposition affirmed extra-mentally either in speech or writing. Propositions or judgments are composed of cognitive elements, but no array of cognitive elements will in and of themselves constitute meaningful communication unless conveyed or conveyable in propositional form. Naturally, propositions may be about all the various domains of reality, language, cosmos, God or values, and intellection must undertake the pursuit of the truth of propositions in any of these areas. But to reduce all search for truth to empirical verification and fail, and then to reduce the search further to linguistic investigation and trivialize, is in large part the story of analytic philosophy. Unless propositions are rehabilitated to speak not merely of grammatical elements, but of categories of truth, reality, and fact, that is, unless there is some implied commitment to the deeper task of philosophy as an avenue to reality, the inevitable consequences—as in the case of linguistic philosophy—are the absurdity of all expression and the demotion of communication to noises emitted by a human mynabird.[216]

This section on "Linguistic Analysis and Propositional Truth" is programmatic for understanding Henry's cognitive-propositional hermeneutic for the following reasons.

First, in this quote, he affirms that propositions express "mental judgments." For Henry, a proposition is a mental judgment that can either be true or false. Truth value is a property of a sentence, not an isolated word or its particular use in a body of literature.[217]

Second, a judgment or a proposition is the basic or minimal unit of logical meaning. This statement affirms the cognitive status of propositions. These propositions also have objective truth value, because they are "mentally affirmed" and based on "extra-mental reality."

Third, the only meaningful way to discuss "cognitive elements" is through propositions. Henry notes they are either already meaningfully "conveyed" in propositional form, or they are "conveyable" (e.g., they can be reduced to propositional form, since propositions are the minimal unit of logical meaning).

Fourth, propositions are able to communicate meaningfully about a variety of different types of beings (e.g., God, reality, morality, and language itself) because propositions address categories of truth and reality.

216. Ibid., 3:449.
217. Ibid., 3:452.

Since God, reality, morality, and language have cognitive truth value; propositions can address meaningfully each type of being.

Fifth, unless philosophy of language insists upon the cognitive aspects of language, it will not be able to affirm or deny categories of truth and falsity. The consequence of denying the cognitive aspects of language is the discipline reduces to epistemological skepticism and meaningless chatter.[218]

Sixth, Henry believes a conventionalist theory of meaning is contrary to the historic Christian view of language and divine revelation. He claims, "The historic Christian view is that divine revelation takes the form of propositionally given truths set down in the linguistic form of inspired *verba*. The locus of meaning and language is to be found . . . in the Bible as an inspired literary deposit of divinely revealed truths."[219] Furthermore, "If God reveals himself intelligibly and truly, then that revelation takes propositional form."[220]

Seventh, Henry addresses the various genres of Scripture and propositional revelation. He writes,

> Regardless of the parables, allegories, emotive phrases and rhetorical questions used by these writers, their literary devices have a logical point which can be propositionally formulated and is objectively true or false. It is manifestly the case that Jesus of Nazareth—even though his teaching involved mastery of the varied languages *uses*—was not minimizing but effectively communicating the *truth* of God.[221]

Make no mistake about it, Henry opposes any view that diminishes the cognitive propositional status of the Scriptures due to the Bible's various genres of literature.[222] Henry believes each genre of Scripture contains truth value or it can be reduced to meaningful propositions that contain objective true or false statements.[223] This influences his hermeneutic because Henry believes one of the tasks of hermeneutics is to approach each genre of Scripture to obtain the objective truth value of the text. However,

---

218. Ibid., 3:448–449.

219. Ibid., 3:452. Henry notes, "By the Word of God, the Judeo-Christian prophets and apostles mean not some strange solitary sound or commanding linguistic unit, nor even a sequence of exotic hieroglyphics written in the sky; they mean, rather, logically formed sentences which the inspired writers identify as the very utterances of man's supernatural Creator and Lord." Ibid., 3:452–453.

220. Ibid., 3:453.

221. Ibid.

222. Ibid.

223. Ibid.

as will be seen below, Henry does not fall prey to the charge of the heresy of "propositional paraphrase."

The Bible as Propositional Revelation

Henry defends the propositional nature of divine revelation. He claims, "The controversy between Protestant orthodoxy and neoorthodoxy focused with special intensity on the issue of the propositional or non-propositional character of divine disclosure, that is, on whether God's revelation is rational and objectively true, or whether God's revelation is noncognitively life-transforming."[224] In a book titled, *The Word of God and the Mind of Man*, Ronald Nash defends the propositional nature of divine revelation too.[225] Nash surveys the cognitive aspects of propositional language and revelation.[226] In particular, he addresses the claims of David Hume, Immanuel Kant, Friedrich Schleiermacher, and Albrecht Ritschl.[227] He also surveys the "assaults on propositional revelation" from Karl Barth, Paul Tillich, and H. Richard Niebuhr.[228]

In chapter four, titled, "A Defense of Propositional Revelation," Nash uses Aristotle's Square of Opposition in order to frame the discussion of the propositional nature of divine revelation.[229] He writes,

> Applying Aristotle's Square of opposition to the four possible positions on the issue of cognitive revelation, we get the following:
>
> (A) ALL REVELATION IS PROPOSITIONAL
>
> (E) NO REVELATION IS PROPOSITIONAL
>
> (I) SOME REVELATION IS PROPOSITIONAL
>
> (O) SOME REVELATION IS NOT PROPOSITIONAL

---

224. Ibid., 3:455.
225. Nash, *The Word of God and the Mind of Man*.
226. Ibid.
227. Ibid., 17–34.
228. Ibid., 35–41.

229. Nash notes, "For convenience, Aristotle named the four kinds of propositions the A, E, I, and O propositions. He also had names for the logical entailments that can exist among propositions. For our purposes, the only relationship we need to consider is that of contradiction, the relationship that exists between A and O, and between the E and I propositions. When two propositions are contradictory, it follows that if one is true, the other is necessarily false; and if one is false; the other is necessarily true." Ibid., 43.

> For the purposes of our discussion, the view stated by the O proposition is unimportant and will be ignored. The three positions we have to consider are those represented by the A, E, and I Types.[230]

From the previous chapters of his book, Nash claims that ". . . the view expressed by the E proposition (No revelation is propositional) express the dominant theory of revelation in contemporary nonevangelical Protestant theology. It is the form in which the skeptical legacy of Hume and Kant appears among their present-day theological heirs."[231] Nash also notes it is clear some aspects of divine revelation assume forms that are not propositional.[232] For example, God is revealed in divine acts such as the Exodus and the Resurrection. Nash makes this claim to distinguish between a revelatory event (which cannot be a proposition) and an accompanying interpretation (which is able to be put in propositional form).[233]

Nash goes on to claim that position (A) All revelation is propositional, is not the evangelical position. He makes an important observation, claiming,

> The evangelical doctrine of propositional revelation should be understood then as a contradictory of the neo-orthodoxy thesis that no revelation is propositional. The contradictory of this E proposition is the I [proposition], namely, *some* revelation is propositional, some revelation conveys cognitive information. Basic to the evangelical position is the claim that we *can* have cognitive information about God. Since a proposition is the minimal vehicle of truth, the information about God is contained, in this view, in divinely revealed propositions. Note again that this position *does not* claim that *all* revelation must be cognitive or reducible to human language. It asserts only that some revelation is cognitive and has been expressed in human language. That some revelation is personal and noncognitive and that some revelation (such as God's revelation through His mighty acts in history) is compatible with the evangelical position.[234]

---

230. Ibid., 44.
231. Ibid.
232. Ibid.
233. Ibid., 44–45.
234. Ibid., 45–46.

Nash claims the classic evangelical position is: (I) Some revelation is propositional.[235] He insists that evangelicals must communicate their belief in both the personal and cognitive aspects of revelation. Nash does not want people to believe the object of revelation is just some truth about God. Instead, it is God himself, revealed in both personal and propositional forms.[236] However, the evangelical view of inspired special revelation in the text of Scripture is always cognitive and propositional.[237]

Henry agrees with each of these points listed by Nash.[238] This can be seen in the following quote, where Henry claims, "In stressing propositional revelation, evangelical theologians of the recent past have emphasized the intelligible nature of divine disclosure."[239] Henry opposes those who limit the value of propositions to moral judgments alone. In order to limit propositions they would have to undervalue or devalue the clear propositions of Christianity's core beliefs. This act of limiting propositions would include the series of propositions in 1 Corinthians 15 on the death, burial, and resurrection of Christ.[240] Henry goes on to make an important comment about the propositional nature of divine revelation, suggesting,

> When we speak of propositional revelation we are not, however, referring to the obvious fact that the Bible, like other literature, is written in sentences or logically formed statements. The Bible depicts God's very revelation as meaningful, objectively

---

235. The cross-roads between Carl Henry and Kevin Vanhoozer seem to meet at this point. In the introductory comments of this section, Thornbury pitted Henry against Vanhoozer because of their different views of propositional revelation. Geisler and I also critique Vanhoozer at this point because his view of propositional revelation. It seems like the essential difference between the two positions arises because both Henry and Vanhoozer affirm proposition (I). However, they depart from one another at that point. Vanhoozer does not deny that the Bible contains propositional revelation. Vanhoozer lists his departure in these words, "Henry comes close to what literary critics call the "heresy of propositional paraphrase" when he suggests that the truth expressed in literary forms such as poetry and parable may be expressed in "declarative propositions" (*GRA*, 3.463). Even speech acts such as promising and commanding can be "translated into propositions" (p. 477). Such paraphrases and translations are necessary for Henry because "the primary concern of revelation is the communication of truth" (p. 477)." Vanhoozer, *Lost in Interpretation*, fn. 21.

236. Nash, *The Word of God and the Mind of Man*, 46.

237. Ibid., 49–50.

238. Henry, *GRA*, 3:455–488.

239. Ibid., 3:455.

240. Ibid., 3:456.

> intelligible disclosure. We mean by propositional revelation that God supernaturally communicated his revelation to chosen spokesmen in the express form of cognitive truths, and that the inspired prophetic-apostolic proclamation reliably articulates these truths in sentences that are not internally contradictory.... The inspired Scriptures contain a body of divinely given information actually expressed or capable of being expressed in propositions. In brief, the Bible is a propositional revelation of the unchanging truth of God.[241]

This passage corresponds with Nash's claims on the propositional nature of special revelation. Henry agrees with Nash by emphasizing that God has revealed himself in ways other than the text of Scripture (e.g., historical events and the mighty acts of God).[242] For Henry, revelation is able to be communicated to fallen sinners. In fact, it is necessary for fallen sinners to have knowledge of revealed truths to receive salvation.[243] However, to deny or diminish the cognitive and propositional status of divine revelation hinders an evangelical proclamation of the gospel.

Henry spends a considerable amount of time discussing the claims by neo-orthodox theologians such as Karl Barth, Paul Tillich, and Shubert Ogden, who affirm the non-cognitive "aspects" of revelation. These aspects have already been considered in the present research. So a more narrow discussion of Henry's view will better allow for it to interact with the contemporary dialogues in hermeneutics. This narrow discussion will focus on the relationship of cognitive-propositional revelation to words and the various genres of Scripture.[244] Henry's position is summarized in the following quote. He writes,

241. Ibid., 3:456–457.
242. Ibid.
243. Ibid., 3:460.

244. Vanhoozer claims, "Carl Henry was absolutely right to stress the cognitive content of Scripture and doctrine over against those who sought to make revelation a noncognitive experience. Is it possible, however, that in so focusing on biblical *content* he, and other conservative evangelicals, have overlooked the significance of biblical literary *form*? We shall return to this point below. The immediate point is this: of all theological traditions, evangelicals must respect the nature of the biblical books they interpret. It is no service to the Bible to make a literary-category mistake. At least on this point, I agree with James Barr: "Genre mistakes cause the *wrong kind of truth values* to be attached to the biblical sentences." The dialogue between conservative and emergent evangelicals could be helped by a recognition of the cognitive significance of Scripture's literary forms. To interpret the Bible truly, then, we must do more than string together individual propositions like beads on a string. This takes us only as far

By its emphasis that divine revelation is propositional, Christian theology in no way denies that the Bible conveys its message in many literary forms such as letters, poetry and parable, prophecy and history. What it stresses, rather, is that the truth conveyed by God through these various forms has conceptual adequacy, and that in all cases the literary teaching is part of a divinely inspired message that conveys the truth of divine revelation. Propositional disclosure is not limited to nor does it require only one particular literary genre. And of course the expression of truth in other forms than the customary prose does not preclude expressing that truth in declarative propositions.[245]

For Henry, genre declarations do not determine the truth value of the text of Scripture. Kevin Vanhoozer, however, disagrees with Henry's view of propositional revelation. Gregory Alan Thornbury explains Vanhoozer's critique, claiming,

Vanhoozer wants to move theology away from a 'cognitive-propositional' method and toward a genre-informed approach, it is still hard to see how one escapes the inevitable return to the sentences that describe a state of affairs in which some thing or attribute is predicated of a subject, linked by the verbal form 'to be.'[246]

Vanhoozer departs from Henry's view by labeling himself as a "modified propositionalist."[247] In a subsection of an article with the heading titled, "The cognitive contribution of literary forms: the literal sense is the literary sense," Vanhoozer claims, "The form of what Scripture says is not merely incidental to its truth. I am thus a modified propositionalist. I recognize the cognitive significance not only of statements and propositions but of *all* the Bible's figures of speech and literary forms."[248] He goes

---

as fortune cookie theology, to a practice of breaking open Scripture in order to find the message contained within. What gets *lost* in propositionalist interpretation are the circumstances of the statement, its poetic and affective elements, and even, then, a dimension of its truth. We do less than justice to Scripture if we preach and teach only its propositional content. Information alone is insufficient for spiritual formation. We need to get beyond "cheap inerrancy," beyond ascribing accolades to the Bible to understanding what the Bible is actually saying, beyond professing biblical truth to *practicing* it." Vanhoozer, *Lost in Interpretation*, 100. Thornbury confirms these comments in his book. See, Thornbury, *Recovering Classic Evangelicalism*, 106–109.

245. Ibid., 3:463.
246. Thornbury, *Recovering Classic Evangelicalism*, 108.
247. Vanhoozer, *Lost in Interpretation*, 107.
248. Ibid., 107–108.

on to note, "Yet I [Vanhoozer] resist the temptation to dedramatize—to de-form!—the biblical text in order to abstract a revealed truth. My approach to theology—call it "postconservative"—does not deny the importance of cognitive content, but it does resist privileging a single form—the propositional statement—for expressing it."[249]

From these quotes, it seems like the distinction between Vanhoozer and Henry is in their view of the relationship between truth statements and the various genres of Scripture.[250] Henry affirms truth is objective and that the various genres of Scripture do not diminish the truth value of propositional revelation.[251] Vanhoozer claims Henry's view diminishes the richness of the canonical form of Scripture.[252] However, it seems like Vanhoozer's "modified propositionalism" and use of speech-act theory modifies not only the propositional status of divine revelation, but the plenary cognitive status of Scripture too. It does this by downplaying a correspondence view of truth and diminishing the relationship between logic and propositional revelation.[253]

In the third volume of *God, Revelation and Authority*, Henry identifies John L. Austin's book, *How to Do Things with Words* (which is a primary text used by speech-act theorists, such as Vanhoozer), as a conventionalist theory of language.[254] Speaking of Wittgenstein (who is a pivotal conventionalist philosopher of language), Henry claims,

> He [Wittgenstein] therefore warned against assuming what the cognitive meaning of words is, or even that they intend a cognitive meaning. Consequently, his followers operated on the dictum 'don't look for meaning, look for the use' and concentrated on the use of words rather than on the traditional sources of meaning, and considered them human instruments that take on

249. Ibid., 108.
250. Ibid.
251. Ibid.
252. Thornbury, *Recovering Classic Evangelicalism*, 114.
253. Geisler and Roach, *Defending Inerrancy*, 140–144.
254. Henry, *GRA*, 3:445. Thornbury raises the question, "Can Speech-Act Theory Be Deployed in Service to Religious Epistemology?" Thornbury, *Recovering Classic Evangelicalism*, 103–104. Thornbury does not believe speech-act theory can be reconciled with classic cognitive propositionalism. He also believes Vanhoozer's speech-act method undermines classic cognitive propositionalism. Paul Helm agrees with Thornbury at this point, citing the numerous ways Vanhoozer's method incorporates the axioms of post-modernism: Helm, *Faith, Form, and Fashion*, 71–262.

the meaning and with which people invest them. And extremely important work in this area was John L. Austin's *How to Do Things with Words*.[255]

Henry finds it commendable on the part of these philosophers of language they desire to clarify the sense in which words are used.[256] He believes, however, these philosophers err in their insistence that the basic philosophical task is linguistic analysis. Henry warns that the error of Wittgenstein and Austin-like approaches is found in the fact that some of them detach meaning from the locus of thought and correlate it with sense-factors or linguistic units.[257] In effect, every element of any proposition must be searched for "possibilities of meaning" in the "governing context of sense experience."[258] In fact, it is at this level Henry criticizes speech-act theory for its foundation in a non-cognitive view of language.[259]

Henry correlates Nicholas Wolterstorff's proposals of metaphysical God-talk and propositional revelation to speech-act theory.[260] Henry explicitly addresses Wolterstroff's rules for distinguishing legitimate and illegitimate accounts of God's figurative speech in the Bible.[261] He suggests,

> Wolterstorff contends that God produced meaningful sounds not by uttering words, that is, by performing a language-act, but by a 'speech-act' which need not involve the use of words as we know them (ibid., p. 11). When the biblical writers 'talked of God's speaking, what they were talking of is God's performing of various speech-acts (not language-acts)' and 'when they talked of God's Word, what they were talking of is not the speech-objects of God's speech.' Such divine speech-acts need not have involved any language-acts at all, he says, although they may in some cases have involved God's 'producing' some verbal sounds.[262]

---

255. Henry, *GRA*, 3:445.
256. Ibid.
257. Ibid., 3:446.
258. Ibid.
259. Ibid; Thornbury, *Recovering Classic Evangelicalism*, 104–105.
260. Henry, *GRA*, 3:446.
261. Ibid., 3:409.
262. Ibid., 3:410.

Henry claims Wolterstoff makes these types of comments in order to safeguard the Bible from dictation theories of inspiration.[263] He notes that evangelicals are left with the difficult question of sorting out what God actually was and is saying, from what belongs to the writer's manners of expressing what God is saying.[264] Wolterstorff believes the answer is found in the distinction between the divine speech-act and the human language-act. Henry notes, "One, he [Wolterstorff] observes that deputized spokesmen often employ words not actually communicated by their superiors when they speak authoritatively for those who commission them. Second, he emphasizes that what really counts in virtually all speech is the speech-act achieved through the utterance of the words."[265] Henry addresses both of Wolterstoff's points.[266]

Henry speaks to the first point noting that Deuteronomy 18 correlates the prophets' task as more than a divinely commissioned spokesman. The Bible does in fact charge the prophet to speak the very words of God. Henry recognizes that references to the "mouth of God" are anthropomorphic, however, the real debate is whether what the prophet says coincides with God's actual words.[267] Henry notes, "By his emphasis on divine speech-acts in distinction from word-acts, Wolterstorff does not intend to imply the noncognitive significance of such speech-acts."[268] Henry summarizes Wolterstorff's view, claiming,

> He [Wolterstorff] emphasizes that what we really care about in all speech, whether human or divine, is the content of the speech-act except in cases where for aesthetic reasons we care about the very words. Our concern in communication is not with the mode or manner in which an assertion is made or a command given, but rather with what is asserted or commanded. Wolterstoff contends, moreover, that just as human beings can perform speech-acts (by using gestures, works of art, etc.) without using language at all, so on many occasions God too may perform speech-acts without performing any language act at all. The question arises, are not such representations of divine communication less appropriately applicable to the content of

---

263. Ibid., 3:411.
264. Ibid.
265. Ibid.
266. Ibid.
267. Ibid., 3:412.
268. Ibid., 3:413.

the scriptural revelation, and even to the universal disclosure of God to the mind and conscience of mankind, than to the universal divine revelation in nature contemplated as a work of cosmic beauty and activity of God? Yet even here Scripture after all focuses on the mental or cognitive penetration of revelation (Rom. 1:20). Would a divine 'speech-act' in Wolterstorff's sense adequately inform us of justification by faith?[269]

So, how does Henry respond to Wolterstoff's claim that the Bible does not always express God's Word? Henry believes Wolterstoff's emphasis on "internal structural considerations" is a nebulous criterion offering no objective principle for distinguishing where the sacred writers do and do not say precisely what God says. Consequently, there is no way to ensure the divine truth of Scripture.[270] Henry claims, "It seems artificial to insert any contrast between God's utterance and Scripture if all of Scripture is identified as his outbreathing (even if the divine initiative does not frustrate the freedom, vocabulary range or stylistic peculiarities of the human writers)."[271] In another place he writes,

> The pedantic distinction between divine speech-act and divine language-act is not particularly significant for Christian theology because the Word of God is normatively given only in its inspired form. . . . The New Testament discloses no governing principle for distinguishing the voice or speech of God from divinely conveyed truths linguistically expressed.[272]

In brief, Henry maintains that the biblical doctrine of inspiration involves a concursus in which God's speech and human language express the very Words of God in the words of man, thus achieving an identity between what the prophet says and what God says.[273]

Furthermore, Henry critiques Wolterstoff's second distinction between speech-acts and language-acts. He rejects Wolterstoff's claim that evangelicals should not insist on revelation in propositional form because God's communication includes various commands and expressions of consolation, and hence, more than propositions.[274] It is worth

269. Ibid., 3:413–414.
270. Ibid.
271. Ibid., 3:424.
272. Ibid., 3:423–424.
273. Ibid.
274. Ibid., 3:416; 3:477.

168   HERMENEUTICS AS EPISTEMOLOGY

offering Henry's full response to Wolterstoff because Wolterstorff's claim is similar to Vanhoozer's. Henry claims,

> In common philosophical parlance today, a proposition and a command (imperative) are no doubt viewed as two entirely different things. Commands are not said to be true or false and are often treated today simply as noncognitive uses of language. But the commands and promises of Scripture are only a subsidiary problem; in no way do they undermine the essential claim that the primary concern of revelation is the communication of truth. Even though commands are not expressed in valid propositional form, they nonetheless yield cognitive inferences: 'Thou shall not kill!' implies at very least that to murder is wrong. Moreover, while imperatives are neither true nor false, they can be translated into propositions. 'Rise and eat,' for example, can be expressed as 'God said to Peter, 'Rise and eat.'' As for aesthetic or other experience, it, too, can be expressed propositionally insofar as it has objective cognitive content or includes moral obligation. Even if, as it sometimes happens, meaning is conveyed in abbreviated exclamations or by bodily motions, or even in shorthand of some kind or other, these symbols can be transcribed quite easily into everyday sentences.[275]

Therefore, Henry claims speech-acts can be translated into propositions because the concern of revelation is the communication of truth.[276]

Nash and Henry claim the evangelical position is "Some revelation is propositional." Henry also notes that by propositional revelation evangelicals insist that God expressed himself in the form of cognitive truths. In that sense, Henry claims all of Scripture is cognitive. Applying Aristotle's square of opposition to possible positions on the cognitive status of Scripture, there are four positions:

(A) ALL SCRIPTURE IS COGNITIVE.	(E) NO SCRIPTURE IS COGNITIVE.
(I) SOME SCRIPTURE IS COGNITIVE.	(O) SOME SCRIPTURE IS NOT COGNITIVE.

275. Ibid., 3:478–479.
276. For Henry, there is only one kind of truth. For that reason, the various genres of Scripture do not present different types of truth. However, it seems like Vanhoozer is claiming there are various kinds of truth and that the plurality of literary genres present the various kinds of truth.

In principle, Henry claims the evangelical position is (A)" All Scripture is Cognitive. According to Henry, speech-act theorist's claim, "Commands are not said to be true or false and are often treated today simply as noncognitive uses of language."[277] Henry is charging speech-act theorist's with denying the plenary cognitive status of Scripture by affirming position (O): Some Scripture is not Cognitive. He believes that while not all commands or imperatives are in propositional form, they nonetheless yield cognitive inferences.

Does this mean that Henry falls prey to Vanhoozer's charge that he commits the "heresy of propositional paraphrase"?[278] In one sense, it seems to be yes, and in another sense, no. Clearly, Henry claims speech-acts can be translated into propositions because the concern of revelation is the communication of truth. However, since he believes all of God's propositional revelation is cognitive—in that it conveys rational information—Henry is merely translating one form of cognitive linguistic information into another cognitive (propositional) form. It seems like Vanhoozer is falsely charging Henry with a category mistake for translating the non-cognitive forms of language into a cognitive form, when in fact Henry insists he is translating one form of cognitive revelation into another form of cognitive revelation. Henry does not believe the various types of claims in Scripture, such as commanding and promising, undermine the fact that the primary concern of revelation is to communicate truth. The way the Bible expresses truth may not be expressed in valid propositions; however, those statements yield the possibility of cognitive inferences and valid propositions.

CONCLUSION

The purpose of this chapter was to answer the question: What does it mean for Henry to affirm a "cognitive-propositionalist" view of revelation? For Henry to affirm a "cognitive-propositionalist" view of revelation means,

---

277. Ibid.

278. Vanhoozer claims in the corresponding footnote, "Henry comes close to what literary critics call the 'heresy of propositional paraphrase' when he suggests that the truth expressed in literary forms such as poetry and parable may be expressed in 'declarative propositions' (GRA, 3.463). Even speech acts such as promising and commanding can be 'translated into propositions' (p. 477). Such paraphrases and translations are necessary because 'the primary concern of revelation is the communication of truth' (p. 477)." Vanhoozer, *Lost in Interpretation*, 95, fn. 21.

as he claims, "That divine disclosure is cognitive and intelligible—hence a mental activity—is intrinsic to Judeo-Christian revelation."[279] Furthermore, "If God reveals himself intelligibly and truly, then that revelation takes propositional form."[280] This aspect of Henry's view was explained in the six sections titled: (1) The Logic of Religious Language; (2) The Origin of Language; (3) Meaning and Religious Language; (4) A Theistic View of Language; (5) Linguistic Analysis and Propositional Truth; and (6) The Bible as Propositional Revelation. There are a few things to note from this discussion.

First, it is evident Henry's view of language is informed by his epistemology. Henry opposes not only empirical and mystical approaches to knowledge, but similar approaches to language.[281] Furthermore, Henry affirms a view of truth and language that allows for: a) the actual possibility of truthful statements; b) literal knowledge of God and reality; c) the truthfulness of language apart from personal decision and existential response.

Second, Henry's view of divine revelation has important bearings on his view of cognitive-propositionalism. He defends the notion that language is able to speak meaningfully and truthfully about God, creation, morality, and language itself. For Henry, because the purpose of language is to communicate cognitive information, then the purpose of propositional revelation is to communicate actual information. This entails Scripture communicates statements that can be objectively verified as either true or false. For Henry, the inspiration of the Bible guarantees the errorlessness, complete truthfulness, or inerrancy of Scripture.[282] Furthermore, the truthfulness of Scripture is mind independent and not based on existential response. This view of Scripture distinguishes Henry from existentialism and neo-orthodoxy.

Lastly, Henry believes his approach is able to affirm the propositional nature of revelation regardless of the various types of literature or genres of Scripture. For Henry, like many other propositionalists, Scripture is either already in clear propositional form (e.g., God is love) or it can be reduced to propositional form (its minimal unit of meaning).[283] The task

279. Henry, *GRA*, 3:481.
280. Ibid., 3:453.
281. Ibid.
282. Ibid., 4:129–295.
283. Geisler and I offer a counter example to Vanhoozer's approach similar to this point: See, Geisler and Roach, *Defending Inerrancy*, 141–142.

of the following chapter will bring chapters two and three together in order to explain Henry's analysis of hermeneutics as epistemology and methodology.

4

Carl F. H. Henry's Revelational Hermeneutic as Epistemology and Methodology

INTRODUCTION

THERE IS NO QUESTION new developments in epistemology will present a continuing challenge to evangelical hermeneutics.[1] Given the grow-

---

1. The term "evangelical" is debated amongst contemporary scholars. For example, the book *Four Views On: The Spectrum of Evangelicalism*, presents as the titled indicates, four varying views on evangelicalism. The contributors are Kevin T. Bauder, R. Albert Mohler, John G. Stack House., Jr, and Roger E. Olsen. See, Naselli and Hansen, *The Spectrums of Evangelicalism*. George Marsden notes that Carl F. H. Henry challenged the fundamentalist positions; however, he remained faithful to conservative theology and confessional standards. See, George M. Marsden, *Fundamentalism and American Culture*, 231–260. If Henry were alive today and remained consistent with his publications, he would mostly likely endorse the "Confessional Evangelicalism" represented by R. Albert Mohler. Henry's publications challenged the fundamentalist positions and he opposes the epistemology and Bibliology of "Generic Evangelicalism" and "Post Conservative Evangelicalism" of Stackhouse and Olsen. Mohler suggests that a confessional evangelical affirms: (1) Both a center and definably theological boundaries; (2) An affirmation of theological triage (aka., a scale which determines the urgency of a specific doctrine entailing there are first order doctrines such as the Trinity and incarnation, second order doctrines such as baptism, and third order doctrines like matters of eschatology; (3) The necessity of *sola fide* in opposition to movements such as ECT; (4) Classical theism; (5) Substitutionary atonement; (6) Exclusivity of the gospel; and (7) The inspiration, infallibility, and inerrancy of Scripture. Ibid., 68–96. However, this quote should be temptered with Henry's notion that inerrancy is a test

ing attention within theological circles on the nature of hermeneutics, this chapter will present Carl F. H. Henry's revelational hermeneutic as epistemology and methodology. The following sections will attempt to answer questions such as: How does Henry address the so-called "hermeneutical problem"? Are interpreters left to *Existenzverstandis* or narrative theology?[2] Can historical-criticism be reconciled with Henry's hermeneutic and view of Scripture? Are evangelical interpreters still able to affirm propositional theology and proclaim: *Gottes Wort bleibt ewig* (God's Word stands forever)?

HERMENEUTICS AS EPISTEMOLOGY

The overview of modern and contemporary hermeneutics presented in chapter one indicates an unstable definition of hermeneutics. Varying philosophical and theological contributions have influenced the discipline, offering a plurality of definitions to the term, "hermeneutics." In his book titled, *Frontiers in Modern Theology*, Henry discusses the contributions of philosophy, especially epistemology on the discipline of hermeneutics; in particular, how hermeneutics as epistemology affects views of reason and divine revelation.[3] He writes,

> Contributing to this novel reformulation of revelation were numerous speculative trends. *Kant* emphasized that the concepts of human reason cannot grasp metaphysical realities and maintained that affirmations about the spiritual order therefore lack universal validity. *Schleiermacher* insisted that God communicates himself but not truths about himself. *Lessing* believed that no historical event can communicate absolute meaning. *Darwin* taught that reflective reason is a relatively late emergent in the evolutionary process. *Kierkegaard* stressed the disjunction of the temporal and eternal as being so radical that only a leap of naked

---

for evangelical consistency, not evangelical identity. See, Lindsell, *The Bible In The Balance*, 31–36.

2. Henry defines the German term *"Existenzverstandnis"* noting that it means, "Self-understanding in terms of *existenz* (q.v.), or the unique individuality of the self. Although Bultmann emphasized existential self-understanding to forestall a scientific reduction of man to impersonal categories, his appeal to volitional, emotional and subconscious elements of human experience bypassed the significance of conceptual reasoning in relation to transcendent reality." Henry, *Frontiers In Modern Theology*, 65.

3. See chapter one in order to understand how the term "hermeneutics as epistemology" is being used in the context of this book.

faith can bridge it. *Bergson* declared that conceptual reasoning imposes an artificial structure upon reality, whose rationally incomprehensible dimensions must be grasped intuitively. There was also *Ebner's* emphasis that God confronts persons only as Subject, never as Object. And *Heidegger* held that reality must be existentially experienced rather than conceptually grasped. In one way or another, these currents undermined confidence in the ontological significance of reason, in the rationality and objectivity of divine revelation, and in the role of cognition in religious experience.[4]

Each of these philosophers different philosophical and theological ideas frame the epistemological conversation to discuss Henry's analysis of hermeneutics as epistemology. Henry opens his main chapter on hermeneutics titled, "Are We Doomed To Hermeneutical Nihilism?" noting,

For two generations Western Christianity has echoed with reverberations of the 'hermeneutical problem.' Contemporary theologians formulate this problem in various ways that reflect the disagreements of modern theology and require a prejudicial solution. As a consequence, the problem itself worsened rather than overcome [the problems of interpretation]."[5]

As will be seen later in this chapter, Henry suggests that the worsening of the "hermeneutical problem" is a result of the speculative trends in epistemology.[6] Some Christians developed a posture of accommodating to the epistemological preconditions of modernity and late modernity. Henry resists these philosophical preconditions. In particular, he opposes in theory the "hermeneutical problem" and varying other "hermeneutics of suspicion" that developed in the eighteenth through the twentieth centuries due to shifts in epistemology.[7]

In order to discuss Henry's analysis of hermeneutics as epistemology the following section will consider six topics: (1) The Hermeneutical Problem; (2) Hermeneutical Spiral; (3) Authorial Intent; (4) Fallibility of the Exegete; (5) The Role of Reason; and (6) The Holy Spirit and Interpretation.

4. Henry, *Frontiers in Modern Theology.*, 81–82, emphasis added.
5. Henry, GRA, 4:296.
6. See chapter one in order to understand the different scholars and philosophical views that converge to create what is known as the "hermeneutical problem."
7. Anthony Thiselton defines "a hermeneutic of suspicion." Thiselton, *New Horizons in Hermeneutics*, 13–14.

The Hermeneutical Problem

Since chapter one discusses and defines the hermeneutical problem, this section will briefly summarize some of the key points and scholars that makeup the hermeneutical problem.[8] In Richard Palmer's book titled, *Hermeneutics*, he discusses the hermeneutical problem claiming, ". . . a specific instance of the event of understanding: it always involves language, the confronting of another human horizon, an act of historical penetration of the text."[9] In other words, as chapter one argues, the hermeneutical problem is a term used to discuss a theory of understanding in a general sense and how metaphysics, epistemology, language, and historical situatedness affect the process of interpretation.

Palmer calls for a hermeneutic that "dives deep" into the complex act(s) of understanding, which involve comprehending how linguistic and historical situatedness affect interpretation.[10] Due to the scope of the hermeneutical problem, Palmer limits his treatment of the subject to four pivotal scholars whom he believes signify the breadth and complexity of the hermeneutical problem. These four philosophers are Friedrich Schleiermacher, Wilhelm Dilthey, Martin Heidegger, and Hans Georg Gadamer.[11] In like manner, in one way or another, Henry addresses the way three of these four scholars shape and define the discipline of hermeneutics.[12] Henry's analysis of Schleiermacher appeared in chapter two of this book. For that reason, Henry's analysis will not be restated. Furthermore, since Henry believes Heidegger and Gadamer present evangelicals with the most pressing objections,[13] labeling their positions as "herme-

---

8. See chapter one under the section titled "hermeneutical problem" for a better understanding of the exact arguments and influential philosophers that make up what is known as the "hermeneutical problem."

9. Palmer, *Hermeneutics*, 68; Thornbury, *Recovering Classical Evangelicalism*, 144.

10. Ibid., 144–147.

11. Palmer, *Hermeneutics*, 75–194.

12. The one individual Henry does not discuss at length is Wilhelm Dilthey. He does discuss Dilthey in *GRA*; however, for the purpose of hermeneutics as epistemology, only Heidegger and Gadamer will be discussed. See chapter two for Henry's analysis of Schleiermacher.

13. In *GRA* Henry focuses on Gadamer more than Heidegger. He does not indicate why he considers the one more important than the other, other than he believes that Gadamer's views are more influential in the contemporary dialogues in philosophy of hermeneutics. For that reason, this section is going to discuss Henry's analysis of Heidegger and Gadamer. It should be noted that of the four pivotal philosophers of hermeneutics, Henry spends most of his time critiquing Schleiermacher, Heidegger,

neutical nihilism,"[14] the following section will consider Henry's analysis of Heidegger and Gadamer.

Martin Heidegger

Henry's main criticism of Heidegger's approach is it offers no binding paradigm for the continuity of meaning from one culture to another.[15] He links Heidegger to Schleiermacher's method, believing both consider hermeneutics to be an explanation of the philosophical character and preconditions of all understanding.[16] Henry notes, "The speculative theory of the historicity of understanding shaped by Heidegger exaggerates the obvious fact of basic differences between past and present cultures into a denial of any identity and continuity of meaning."[17] He claims that Heidegger, due to the nature of time, presents the past as *ontologically* distant from the present and claims past meaning cannot be *understood* in the present.[18] This "ontological distance," creates a necessary gap between the past and the present.

Consequently, in response to Heidegger's "ontological distance," Henry raises two questions. He writes, ". . . [I]f different periods of time imply a discontinuity of meaning, why then does not the passing of a single moment also involve ontological alienation? And if it does not, why must the passing of many moments involve this?"[19] Henry points out that proponents of Heidegger's theory, must extradite any written communication between livings persons, speaking in the "same" time period and language, from the consequences of Heidegger's "alien" ontology of time.[20] However, Henry believes in order for Heidegerrians to remain consistent with their philosophy, they must recognize their own forms

---

and Gadamer. Since chapter two already addressed Henry's criticisms of Schleiermacher, the research in this section will lay out his criticisms of Heidegger and Gadamer.

14. Henry, *GRA*, 4:312. For a better explanation, see: Geisler, *Systematic Theology*, 236–260; Geisler, *Inerrancy*, 307–336.

15. Allen and Springsted, *Philosophy for Understanding Theology*, 206.

16. Henry, *GRA*, 4:299.

17. Ibid. Henry also remarks, "Gadamer extends the Heideggerian approach by asserting the linguistic nature of human reality: 'Being that can understand is language.' (*Warnheit und Methode* [*Truth and Method*])." Ibid.

18. Ibid.

19. Ibid., 4:300.

20. Ibid., 4:304.

of communication and relationship to periods of time are affected by the consequences of Heidegger's ontology and epistemology too. In that sense, Henry relativizes Heidegger's position showing how it is a self-defeating theory.

On the one hand, Henry believes it is obvious human-beings differ from one another by time (e.g., person X lived in the first century and person Y lived in the tenth century), even within the same age. On the other hand, Henry points out, ". . . [I]f this [ontological] difference bars people from comprehending each other's meanings, then nothing whatever [including Heidegger's theory] can bridge the ontological gap between them."[21] In fact, if true, not even Heidegger's theory can uphold the standards of its own philosophical criteria. Henry explains the nature of his critique against Heidegger. He writes,

> The theory of the historicity of understanding cannot in fact be true unless it is false, else nobody could communicate it intelligibly to anyone else. If words can serve as a meaningful medium to convey even this colossal fiction of ontological alienation, then words can communicate identifiable meaning to men in all ages and cultures. The alternative to fixed meaning is not some subtle theory of significance predicated on internal response or human creativity, but the deintellectualization and dehumanization of mankind.[22]

Consequently, Henry believes if time erodes fixed meaning, then radical historicists should stop writing books or giving speeches, and pray (non-verbally at that) for a generation of "mind readers," or people accept the theory is a futile approach.[23] He offers no more criticisms of Heidegger's method; instead, Henry proceeds to discuss Gadamer, whom he believes is the more pivotal philosopher affecting hermeneutics as epistemology.

Hans-Georg Gadamer

Henry describes Gadamer's book, *Truth and Method*, as the "*summa*" of the "new hermeneutic."[24] Gregory Alan Thornbury discussing the

---

21. Ibid.
22. Ibid.
23. Ibid.
24. Ibid., 4:304. The "new hermeneutic" in this context referring to the scope of New Testament scholarship represented by Bultmann, Ebeling, Fuch, etc; however, it

relationship between Henry and Gadamer, claims, "Henry rejects both the Heideggarian and Gadamerian systems because they regard the interpreter as the source of meaning itself, rather than merely an agent of interpretation and translation."[25] Thornbury goes on to note that the stakes are very high for Henry, since Henry claims, "This theory [Gadamer's] repudiates, as a by-product of fallacious subject-object thinking and as a correlate of a futile quest for objective meaning, the traditional view of language as an instrument or system of symbols for communicating 'meaning.'"[26] Thornbury claims Henry is over reading Gadamer, and that much of Henry and Gadamer's theories can be reconciled with each other.[27] The two places of reconciliation being their emphasis on the "inescapability of presuppositional interpretation" and the "fallibility of the exegete."[28]

While Thornbury's comments are not the main topic of this book, he does seem to rightly recognize Henry's method allows for fallibility; however, just because both of them affirm the role of presuppositions and fallibility is not enough to claim they can be reconciled with each other. As chapters one, two, and three argue, Henry and Gadamer affirm different views of metaphysics (e.g., Realist vs. Existential), epistemology (e.g., Augustinian vs. Existential or Phenomenological), and language (e.g., Realism vs. Conventionalism and the importance of propositionalism); hence, there cannot be any meaningful or logical reconciliation of the two.

In *God, Revelation and Authority*, Henry discusses Gadamer's theory. He notes, "H. G. Gadamer (*Truth and Method*) claims that the cultural differences between eras are so radical and absolute that even the most painstaking historical study cannot recapture the meaning of the past documents."[29] Henry suggests Gadamer's view on the historicity of humanity's *being* renders futile any attempt to recover the original conditions of a text. He claims, "Gadamer rejects the idea of recognition of the author's meaning on the ground that every cognition of the text is new and different; in view of the historicity of understanding, no truth can

also represents a key text for those who advocate *new* hermeneutical approaches that deny the objectivity of interpretation.

25. Thornbury, *Recovering Classical Evangelicalism*, 146.
26. Henry, *GRA*, 4:300.
27. Thornbury, *Recovering Classic Evangelicalism*, 146.
28. Ibid.
29. Ibid., 4:463.

transcend the interpreters own historicity."[30] By emphasizing meaning is not located solely in the author's intention, Gadamer insists that meaning is in the "subject matter" shared by both the author and the reader.[31] In order to not lapse into pure relativism, Gadamer develops three norming concepts of interpretation: tradition, repetition, and fusion of horizons.[32] Henry rejects all three principles; however, for the purposes of understanding Henry's hermeneutic as epistemology, the reasons he rejects the "fusion of horizons," is of the most importance.[33]

Henry addresses the concept of "fusion of horizons," by criticizing the way Gadamer uses the word "fusion" in his writings.[34] Gadamer claims, "In the process of understanding, a real fusion of horizon occurs—which means that as the historical horizon is projected, it is

30. Ibid, 4:304. Henry also notes, "The historicity of our being, he insists, renders futile any attempted recovery of the original conditions of a text; all philological aspirations for objectivity is to be dismissed therefore as naïve." Ibid.

31. Ibid. Henry does not define or qualify precisely what he means by "subject matter."

32. Ibid., 4:305.

33. The first principle claims that tradition is a way to carry the hidden past into the present. Henry says, "By this, Gadamer seems to mean (objectively?) that the cultural phenomena through which a text passes determine its supposedly changing content, and that this wider significance of the text is comprehended in turn by each existing and succeeding culture." Ibid. Henry rejects Gadamer's first principle because the "traditional sense" seems to affirm that tradition ought to be equated with the commonly accepted interpretation. Henry reasons that Gadamer's theory cannot account for the rise of new traditions of interpretation. Furthermore, he claims, "But its weakest feature [of Gadamer's hermeneutic] is that it lacks a normative criterion of interpretation; in the absence of an objective textual meaning, no valid choice is possible between two or more conflicting interpretations." Ibid. The second principle Henry critiques is the repeatable aspects of historical events. He claims, "Yet one can hardly derive this from his insistence that the understanding of a text is 'not repetition of something past, but participation in a present meaning.'" Ibid. Henry illustrates this by saying people engage in historical repetition by understanding a text in his or her own words; but, this does not imply that in order to truly understand a text a person must formulate it in his or her own way, with a private meaning. He notes, "The notion that every man's historicity results in a necessarily different meaning erodes valid meaning; indeed, such a notion implies that he alone can understand a text who misunderstands it himself." Ibid. Henry seems to believe this aspect of repeatable historical events is self-defeating. For only the individuals advocating the view can communicate valid meaning. Each reader of these scholars texts are expected to understand their works, whereas other works cannot be understood. His epistemology suggests that if there is valid meaning for one, then there can be valid meaning for all. And if there is no valid meaning for all, then there can be no valid meaning for anyone.

34. Ibid.

simultaneously superseded. To bring about this fusion in a regulated way is the task of what we called historically effected consciousness."[35] Henry discusses Gadamer's notion of "historically effected consciousness" and the "fusion of horizons," remarking,

> Gadamer contends, moreover, that the historical situation of the interpreter always 'codetermines' the text's real meaning, a meaning which is established by a *Horizontverschmelzung* or a fusion between the original perspective and that of the interpreter. But how can one identify an original perspective if it is never knowable as an original perspective? And if the primal sense of a text is beyond an interpreters grasp, how can valid interpretation be identified? One the one hand, Gadamer implies that the interpreter is shackled by his own historicity. He ought therefore to abandon any talk about fusion with the original meaning and about norm-concepts. On the other hand, Gadamer reaches for fusion with the original meaning in a quest of a norm-concept, and ought therefore to forego unnecessary concessions to the historicity of meaning and the requirement of creative understanding.[36]

Henry believes he catches Gadamer in what seems to be "double talk." In one arena, Gadamer claims historical conditioning renders any fusion with the original meaning of the text impossible. In another arena, he develops norming-concepts to achieve a fusion with the original meaning of the text. The latter, in Henry's opinion, is a concession by Gadamer to the interpreter's ability to break free from their historical-situatedness. He believes if an individual is able to break out of his or her own perspective, whether large or small, then the premise that "one's place in history renders objectivity futile" is no longer valid.[37]

Henry refers to Gadamer's "norming-concepts," claiming they are incompatible with his claim that "fusion: with the original meaning" is

---

35. Gadamer, *Truth and Method*, 307.

36. Henry, *GRA*, 4:305.

37. Henry also says, "E. D. Hirsch Jr., is surely right when he says: 'Once it is admitted that the interpreter can adopt a fused perspective different from his own contemporary one, then it is admitted in principle that he *can* break out of his own perspective. If that is possible, the primary assumption of the theory is shattered' (*Validity in Interpretation*, 254)." Ibid. In Hirsch's judgment, "*Meaning* is that which is represented by a text; it is what the author meant by his use of particular sign sequence; it is what the signs represent. *Significance*, on the other hand, names a relationship between that meaning and a person, or a conceptual or a situation." Hirsch, *Validity in Interpretation*, 8.

"naïve" and "impossible."[38] In order to overcome Gadamer's unnecessary "sacrifice of true meaning on the altar of present significance," Henry uses E. D. Hirsch's distinction between meaning and significance.[39] Hirsch claims, "*Meaning* is that which is represented by a text; it is what the author meant by his use of particular sign sequence; it is what the signs represent. *Significance*, on the other hand, names a relationship between that meaning and a person, or a conceptual or a situation."[40] Ultimately then, the research indicates Henry endorses Hirsch's claim that the meaning of a text remains the same; however, the significance of a text can change in light of the reader's present context.

According to Henry, Gadamer's theory is self-defeating because not only is the interpreter the source of meaning, he or she must also use "norming-concepts" to transcend their historical situatedness. This "transcending" is exactly what Gadamer's theory claims the interpreter is unable to do.[41] If Gadamer is going to attribute prejudice in interpretation due to the ontological part of the interpreter, then he must recognize the self-defeating nature of his claim.[42] Gadamer claims individuals cannot transcend their own historicity and make objective pronouncements across different cultures and periods of time. Yet, in the very act of making that pronouncement (e.g., that individuals cannot make transcultural pronouncements), Henry believes Gadamer renders his own theory futile. Gadamer must transcend his own historical situation and make an objective declaration on the nature of historical conditioning, in order to claim individuals cannot transcend their historical situation and make objective pronouncements. But this is precisely what Gadamer claims individuals are unable to do (except Gadamer and his followers of course!).

The Hermeneutical Spiral

One of the terms used to discuss the relationship between metaphysical, epistemological, and historical conditions affecting hermeneutics is the hermeneutical spiral (sometimes synonymous with the hermeneutical circle). The various meanings and uses of the hermeneutical spiral were

---

38. Ibid.
39. Ibid., 4:304–305.
40. Hirsch, *Validity*, 8.
41. Henry, *GRA*, 4:305.
42. Ibid., 4:305–306.

discussed in chapter one.⁴³ The first question to ask about the subject of Henry's analysis of the hermeneutical spiral is: How does Henry interact with the hermeneutical spiral? The answer to this question, in the eyes of some scholars, will probably reveal the greatest weakness of his analysis of hermeneutics as epistemology. In fact, there is no explicit treatment by Henry on the term "hermeneutical spiral" (or hermeneutical circle) in any of his primary literature.⁴⁴ However, just because Henry does not include a chapter on or use the term "hermeneutical spiral," does not entail he carelessly neglects to interact with the concept of the "hermeneutical spiral."⁴⁵ In fact, the case will be made that Henry addresses the concept by interacting with dialectical theories of knowledge and addressing the proper role of presuppositions in the act of interpretation.

One can only speculate for possible reasons why Henry did not explicitly interact with the term "hermeneutical spiral."⁴⁶ One possible

43. Thiselton, "Hermeneutical Circle," 281.

44. The researcher has searched through volumes of Henry's major published literature and cannot cite a single reference to his interactions with the hermeneutical spiral. In fact, it seems like he might have only used the term once or twice in all of his literature, however, the term cannot be located. A topic for future studies would be to place all of Henry's works into a digital format in order to search for the term. Even then, it would be surprising to see him utilize the term "hermeneutical spiral."

45. This point stresses the fact that just because someone does not utilize a theological or philosophical term, does not entail that they do not understand and interact with the concept. For example, in the early church all orthodox believers affirmed the deity and the humanity of Christ; yet, not all of them affirmed the language of the Nicene and Chalcedonian councils. Instead, they affirmed the concepts that each of these councils taught. See, Behr, *Formation of Christian Theology*. In a similar respect, Henry responded to the concept of the hermeneutical spiral by critiquing Schleiermacher, Heidegger, and Gadamer. Grant Osborne claims, "The major premise of this book [Hermeneutical Spiral] is that biblical interpretation entails a 'spiral' from text to context, from its original meaning to its contextual or significance for the church today." Osborne, *The Hermeneutical Spiral*, 22. Thiselton describes the view as a type of "progressive dialectic," and "parallel dialectic between the two poles of a 'preliminary' understanding or (reflecting the German) of *preunderstanding* (*Vorverständnis*), and a fuller understanding (*Verstehen*)." Thiselton, "Hermeneutical Spiral," 281. Thiselton goes onto say, "The fuller (or more accurate) understanding 'speaks back' to the preunderstanding to correct and reshape it. This revision contributes to a better understanding. Hence, to reread a 'difficult' book, or even to undertake successive readings, may bring about a deeper understanding of it." Ibid.

46. First, it is not because the view was not prevalent during his life time. In fact, the first edition of Grant Osborne's book on the hermeneutical spiral was published in 1991. Henry died in 2003. In many respects, he interacted with the ideas of evangelical scholarship until the time of his death, so ignorance or lack of awareness of the topic does not seem to be a good answer. Furthermore, both Henry and Osborne taught at

hypothesis is Henry believes he has already critiqued the major epistemological premises of the hermeneutical spiral by addressing the views of Schleiermacher, Heidegger, and Gadamer.[47] In the context of *God, Revelation and Authority*, it appears Henry interacts with a similar view he labels as "Hermeneutical Nihilism." Henry conceptually relates the "hermeneutical spiral" and "hermeneutical nihilism" because he believes both do not have criterion(s) of validity. That being said, the following section will attempt to explain better Henry's notion of hermeneutical nihilism in order to show how it conceptually relates to the hermeneutical spiral, and offer some reasons why he rejects the concept of the hermeneutical spiral.[48]

Henry defines hermeneutical nihilism in these terms, "Without a criterion of validity we are doomed to hermeneutical nihilism."[49] In other words, the first thing to notice is Henry alludes to the idea that it is either "criterion of validity" or "interpreters are doomed to hermeneutical nihilism." His approach to hermeneutics is to develop an epistemology and methodology which provides the appropriate conditions for universal and objective epistemological validity. In order to explain these hermeneutical conditions, Henry develops the term "validity." This term "validity" is used by Henry and Hirsch to discuss legitimate interpretive norms to justify an interpretation of any text, not the philosophical status of a syllogism.[50]

The second thing to notice is his choice of words. Henry uses the term "hermeneutical nihilism" and the first time he uses it is after a long discussion of Heidegger and Gadamer. The context of Henry's writing indicate he was referring to these two scholars when he used the term "hermeneutical nihilism."[51] He seems to suggest that without a method

---

Trinity Evangelical Divinity School. So, it would seem to be a far stretch to claim that Henry was unaware of at least Osborne's view of the hermeneutical spiral.

47. Each of these scholars affirms tenets such as: (1) The epistemological notions of original context meaning to present context and significance; (2) A dialectical method arising from "preunderstanding" to "understanding," resulting in a "fuller understanding." (3) The reshaping of understanding or the more correct rereading of a text. (4) This process results in a deeper understanding of the text and/or author.

48. Ibid.

49. Henry, *GRA*, 4:307.

50. Henry discusses how new definitions of validity arose due to the prominence of Critical philosophy. Ibid., 1:378.

51. The *Oxford Dictionary of Philosophy* defines Nihilism as, "A theory promoting the state of believing in nothing, or of having no allegiances and no purposes. The

of universal validity, interpreters are placed in the epistemological state of not being able to know anything. Their ontological and epistemological commitments prohibit them from offering their allegiance to any theological doctrine or interpretation of Scripture,[52] because all exegetical conclusions are tentative and able to be revised in light of new hermeneutical theories.

Henry responds to philosophers of hermeneutics who reject in theory the possibility of universal and objective validity.[53] He claims, "If we are to escape hermeneutical nihilism we must deliberately disown the whole series of exegetical compromises that have brought biblical interpretation to its present sorry state."[54] Henry suggests modernism prepared the way for the "present sorry state" by affirming dialectical and existential theologies, despite its effort to escape the rationalistic philosophies that deny the biblical concept of revelation. In fact, Henry believes dialectical and existential philosophy "worsened rather than solved the [hermeneutical] problem," because they introduced new epistemological criterion of validity. For example, he believes Schleiermacher's moral projection of Christianity, apart from the cognitive and doctrinal aspects of the Bible, ". . . detached the definition of God from biblically revealed propositions, and suspended it upon revisable experiential considerations."[55] Henry goes on to connect Schleiermacher with Barth, noting,

> Barth did disservice to biblical exegesis, however, by rejecting the propositional-verbal nature of revelation and by correlating the truth of revelation instead with a superconceptual inner response; he thereby forfeited the universal intelligibility and validity of the content of divine disclosure. Going a step further, Bultmann and his followers invoked Heidegger's theory of understanding [which is a non-cognitive approach] to undergird a phenomenological approach to literary interpretation.[56]

term is incorrectly used to characterize all persons not sharing some particular faith or particular set of absolutes." Blackburn, *Oxford Dictionary of Philosophy*, 263.

52. Henry, GRA, 4:312.

53. Ibid.

54. Ibid.

55. Ibid. Henry notes, "According to Henry, Schleiermacher went only part of the distance of these scholars because he affirms that the enduring significance of Christian revelation is not found in the theological, historical, and scientific context of the Bible; instead it is to be found in the ". . . harmonious selfhood assertedly experienced in emulating Jesus' obedient sonship to God." Ibid.

56. Ibid.

Henry later claims, "If we are to avoid hermeneutical nihilism, we must avoid mistakes to which many twentieth century exegetes are prone. Besides acknowledging the inescapability of presuppositional interpretation, we must affirm the indispensable importance of valid exegetical assumptions."[57] His main criticism of dialectical and existential approaches to hermeneutics is their epistemology rejects the cognitive status of revelation and the concept of universal principles to validate interpretation.[58] Consequently, if he remains consistent with his previous comments, Henry would also reject the existential aspects of the hermeneutical spiral because it lacks universal criteria of validity and denies the cognitive-propositional status of the Bible as divine revelation (even though he does not explicitly interact with the term "hermeneutical spiral").[59]

Throughout *God, Revelation and Authority*, Henry makes it clear he rejects both Heidegger and Gadamer's theories. In this present chapter it is apparent Henry labels their (e.g., Heidegger and Gadamer's) approaches as "hermeneutical nihilism." He also rejects Schleiermacher's epistemology because of its similarities with intuitive and empirical approaches to knowledge.[60] In the *Dictionary for Theological Interpretation*, there is an article by Anthony Thiselton titled, *Hermeneutical Spiral*.[61] Thiselton discusses different versions of the hermeneutical circle, which is sometimes synonymous with hermeneutical spiral, noting that the leading proponents are Schleiermacher, Heidegger, and Gadamer.[62]

---

57. Ibid., 4:314.

58. Henry claims, "Hence a wholesome reaction is now underway against associating hermeneutics with the subjective process of understanding, or with the present relevance of the text to an interpreter. The primary task of hermeneutics lies in umpiring competitive meaning-possibilities and identifying the author's intention. The determination of the verbal meaning of the biblical or any other text does not depend upon twentieth-century historical understanding shaped by Heideggarian ontology, phenomenology, and contemporary language-theory. Evangelical scholarship should deplore the confusion that results from the hermeneutical tendency of identifying verbal meaning with personal significance. There is no better rule for interpreting the Bible or any other literary work than to find out what the author meant." Ibid., 4:308; 4:308–10.

59. Ibid.

60. Ibid., 1:70–85.

61. Thiselton, "Hermeneutical Circle," 281–282.

62. Ibid.

As chapter one argued, generally understood, Schleiermacher, Heidegger, and Gadamer's versions of the hermeneutical spiral affirm tenets such as (this section is not intended to offer an exhaustive list):

1. A dialectical method arising from "preunderstanding" to "understanding," resulting in a "fuller understanding."
2. The reshaping of "understanding" results in a more correct rereading of the text.
3. This "spiraling process" results in a "deeper understanding" of the text and/or author.[63]
4. The influence of either *Existenzverstandnis* metaphysics, epistemology, or historical conditioning upon both the text and the interpreter.[64]

Considering the works of these three scholars and the tenets of the hermeneutical circle, the characteristics of the hermeneutical circle seem to be very similar to what Henry labels "hermeneutical nihilism" and "*Existenzverstandnis*." This correlation is made because both the hermeneutical circle and hermeneutical nihilism affirm the same core philosophers, tenets, and *Existenzverstandnis* principles of interpretation. In the final analysis, the research indicates that while Henry never interacted with the term "hermeneutical circle (or spiral)," he rejects it for the same reasons he rejects the concept he labels "hermeneutical nihilism." Once again, Henry not only rejects the epistemology of the hermeneutical problem, he also rejects the *Existenzverstandnis* aspects of the hermeneutical spiral.

Authorial Intent

The next issue important to hermeneutics is the matter of authorial intention. Following E. D. Hirsch, who attempts to bring hermeneutical concerns under general principles of validity (e.g., legitimate interpretive norms), Henry poses the question: "What conditions make possible a valid interpretation of verbal texts?"[65] He answers,

---

63. Ibid.
64. Henry, *Frontiers In Modern Theology*, 65.
65. Henry, *GRA*, 4:313.

> Hirsch's *Validity in Interpretation* so far poses the most formidable challenge to the recent hermeneutical trend. He shows that the loss in the authors meaning exposes textual criticism to relativism and subjectivism, however much the critics may dignify their interpretative endeavors as being seriously academic. Although biblical literature is not his special interest, his analysis of trends in the broad realm of literary criticism helpfully illumines recent developments in the field of Scripture commentary. Especially timely is his insistent demand for relevant supportive evidence to validate textual interpretation.[66]

Remarks like this by Henry, offer justification to the claim: Henry's principle of validity is similar to that of Hirsch.[67] Henry believes the interpreter can know the author's intention by knowing the grammatical meaning of the text. He also distances himself from those who claim meaning is found above or behind the text. He emphatically claims, "I agree also that the meaning of Scripture is found not above or behind the text but in it."[68] Henry utilizes Hirsch's view of authorial intention to distance himself from those whom he believes "naïvely" assume that literary works exist as "autonomous aesthetic" entities independent of all minds.[69] Finally, Henry claims if this "naïve autonomous aesthetic," is what radical phenomenological views aim to challenge, then he is ready to join their protest against naïve autonomy. However, Henry is not willing to join phenomenologists and existentialists in their protest that textual meaning should be correlated with the creative ingenuity of the perceiving interpreter.[70]

Henry opposes the view of some literary critics and biblical interpreters who attempt to establish meaning apart from the author's own cognitive intention. He criticizes Richard Palmer, who denies that a piece of literature is an "object" to be understood by conceptualizing it or analyzing it in a scientific fashion (because a work of literature is not a "scientific object").[71] The following quote by Henry illustrates *how* he responds to those who separate validity from authorial intention.[72] He writes,

66. Ibid., 4:312.
67. Ibid.
68. Henry, *gods of this age or . . . God of The Ages?*, 247.
69. Henry, GRA, 4:313.
70. Ibid.
71. Ibid.
72. Ibid.

> It is imperative to rescue the field of hermeneutics from those literary critics who in establishing the meaning of any text reject the importance of an author's own cognitive intention. An author's meaning is now widely abandoned as the normative ideal of exegesis; any objective foundation for textual criticism in an earnest philological pursuit of authorial meaning is disowned. But through this 'banishment of the author,' as Hirsch characterizes it, the meaning of a text is readily altered. The modern emphasis on the semantic autonomy of language and the critical delight in a meaning independent of the literary source rest upon a curious evasion of the simple confidence that textual meaning is not a creative invention of the reader but is properly supplied by the writer. Hirsch insists, and rightly so, that valid interpretation and authorial meaning stand or fall together. . . . Once textual critics ruthlessly banish the author as the primary determiner of textual meaning, no principle remains to establish interpretational validity. . . . When a literary critic detaches meaning from authorial intention and emphasizes significance, then, as Hirsch warns us, 'the shortest and most banal text' can be 'related to all conceivable states of affairs—historical, linguistic, psychological, physical, metaphysical, personal, familial, national' and can even 'be related at different times to changing conditions in all conceivable states of affairs . . . There are innumerable varieties of significance beyond these, and plenty of breathing space for all conceivable exercises of criticism' (p. 63).[73]

This quote is axiomatic to illustrate the way Henry establishes hermeneutical validity. Like Hirsch, Henry believes once a person abandons the author's meaning of a text, then the meaning of the text can be altered. If authorial intention no longer stabilizes the text—then anyone can reread that text according to their emotional, psychological, historical—conditions, presuppositions, and biases. However, if the meaning of a text is not the creative invention of a reader, but the purposeful product of an author, then the meaning of a text cannot be readily altered. The author and the text hang or fall together; to abandon the author's intention is to abandon the possibility of an objective meaning for any text.

During the second summit meeting of the *International Council on Biblical Inerrancy* (ICBI), Henry addresses an evangelical "use and abuse" of authorial intention. In order to capture the force of his argument, Henry must be quoted at length. He writes,

---

73. Ibid., 4:313–314.

Little did I realize that I was not the first to steal the Bible. The medieval church had kept the Book from the masses for whom it was intended and we evangelicals kept it from nurturing our own lives. But in recent years a different type of theft has emerged as some fellow evangelicals, along with non-evangelicals, wrest from the Bible segments they derogate as no longer the Word of God. Some now even introduce authorial intention or cultural context of language as specious rationalizations for this crime against the Bible, much as some rapist might assure me that he is assaulting my wife for my own or for her good. They misuse Scripture in order to champion as biblically true what in fact does violence to Scripture. It is one of the ironies of church history that even some professed evangelicals now speak concessively of divine revelation itself as culture-conditioned, and do so at the precise moment in Western history when the secular dogma of the cultural relativity of all truth and morality and religious beliefs need fervent challenging.[74]

Abuses of authorial intention are not new to the scene. In fact, in the 1980's Henry cautioned the ICBI to not use authorial intention in such a way so as to dismiss the clear propositional statements of Scripture. However, many present-day evangelicals have failed to heed Henry's warning.

One can find many contemporary examples to illustrate Henry's concern for abuses of authorial intention in present-day scholarship. The first is an example from Michael R. Licona's dehistoricizing of the raising of the saints in Matthew's Gospel.[75] Licona responds to his critics in a paper delivered to the Evangelical Philosophical Society, claiming, "I hope that it has become clear in this paper that my intent was not to dehistoricize a text Matthew intended as historical. If I had, that would be to deny the inerrancy of the text. Instead, what I have done is to question whether Matthew intended for the raised saints to be understood historically."[76] This is precisely what Henry cautioned the ICBI to avoid

74. Radmacher and Preus, *Hermeneutics, Inerrancy, & the Bible*, 917, Emphasis added.

75. Geisler and Roach, *A Response to Methodological Unorthodoxy*, 61–87; Quarles, *Review of Michael R. Licona: The Resurrection of Jesus*, 839–44; Mohler, "The Devil Is In the Details: Biblical Inerrancy and the Licona Controversy." Accessed at: http://www.albertmohler.com/2011/09/14/the-devil-is-in-the-details-biblical-inerrancy-and-the-licona-controversy.

76. http://www.risenjesus.com/images/stories/pdfs/2011%20eps%20saints%20paper.pdf., Emphasis Added.

as an abuse of authorial intention. For in doing so, interpreters such as Licona invalidate the clear meaning of Scripture and use "authorial intention" to assault the clear propositions of the Bible.[77]

The second illustration is the *way* Kevin Vanhoozer argues for authorial intention. In Thornbury's book, *Recovering Classic Evangelicalism*, he discusses the influence Henry might have in this debate on authorial intention. In the section titled, "Henry Verses Vanhoozer," Thornbury remarks that one of Vanhoozer's primary complaints against Henry is that,

> ... authorial intent vis á vis inerrancy, implying that Henry had little appreciation of genre and discourse. Vanhoozer refers to Henry's discussion in volume 4 of *GRA* in which Henry openly worries that a narrow focus on authorial-intent interpretation can tempt commentators to sidestep the matter of the reliability and historicity of texts.[78]

Thornbury openly chastises Vanhoozer's reading of Henry, claiming he is reading him in the "worst possible light."[79] He claims, ". . . if one makes the author's intent supreme, and if one says the authors intention was a genre other than historical and scientific accuracy, we have opened Pandora's box. Once you make this move, Henry warns, you can take any problematic or disputed text as a matter of genre confusion."[80] Thornbury continues to say,

> As we will discuss later in this volume, this is precisely the interpretive move behind crucial abandonments of inerrancy in

---

77. Henry says, "Emphasis on the inspired writers intention as the key to the meaning of Scripture has become highly important in recent decades when post-Bultmannians have emphasized, instead, the interpreter's creative contribution to meaning. But this stress on the importance of the author's intention can be misapplied. For one thing, it is now often assumed, in the interest of a prejudiced hermeneutic, that the scriptural writers did not intend or could not tell the truth, e.g., state historical facts or convey permanently valid revelational teaching. For another, even where this intention to the tell the truth is granted, it must not be assumed—since the Holy Spirit is the primary communicator of Scripture—that the human author necessarily is aware of the full meaning of his message. The exegete is indeed bound to the text that expresses the mind of God and the writer's purpose; he has no other access to this purpose except the text taken in its literary and historical context." Henry, *GRA*, 4:281, Emphasis added.

78. Thornbury, *Recovering Classic Evangelicalism*, 106.

79. Ibid., 106–107. Thornbury does not criticize Vanhoozer for raising questions against Henry's view; yet, he believes that Vanhoozer is reading Henry out of context.

80. Ibid., 107.

contemporary evangelicalism. So, for example, if you are uncomfortable saying that Genesis 1 literally reveals the way God created the universe, don't worry. Simply say that the author's purpose was literary, poetic, or allegorical, and your problem is solved. This was Carl Henry's fear, and he was right to be concerned—if not with Vanhoozer, then with others who do not possess the better angels of Kevin's theological nature.[81]

Thornbury does not shy away from naming the names of those who use authorial intent to deny the inerrancy of the Bible. In the chapter of his book titled "Inerrancy Matters," Thornbury lists Peter Enns, John Schneider, Daniel Harlow, and Mike Licona as examples of individuals who have utilized this "authorial intention" argument, and have been fired from their posts over charges of violating the inerrancy of Scripture.[82] In any event, the point is that in his address at the ICBI, Henry almost prophetically foresaw many of the evangelical uses and abuses of authorial intention and the negative effects a poor use of authorial intention could have upon the doctrine of inerrancy and evangelicalism.

At this point, it is instructive to note Henry affirms that reason is operant for establishing the truth value of any text, ensuring the author's intention corresponds with the grammatical meaning of the sentence. Henry's hermeneutic as epistemology opposes all views that attempt to use a supposed "author's intent" to alter, deny or contradict the grammatical meaning of the Bible.[83] Henry also insists that an interpreter can know the author's intent only by using the grammatical-historical method of interpretation, and that the author's intention corresponds with the grammatical meaning of the text. He rejects all theories that bifurcate

81. Ibid.
82. Ibid., 122.
83. Henry would oppose the notion that in order to properly understand a text, one must "read it the way they would have read it." For, according to Henry, either the original readers would have read it according to its historical, logical, grammatical meaning, or they would have not. If they do not read it according to its historical, logical, and grammatical meaning; Henry would claim they are abusing authorial intent. For Henry, there are two types of reader responses. Either the present day reader can change the meaning of the text or the present day reader can change the meaning of the text by claiming the original author did not "intend" his audience to read it that way. However, according to Henry, there is only one type of logic, and due to the image of God in humanity, there is only one kind of mind. In brief, as was seen in the quote by Henry at the ICBI, any attempt to interpreters of Scripture to use "authorial intention" to override the grammatical aspects of the text, is considered a misguided approach and abusive to the Bible as the Word of God.

authorial intent and the grammatical meaning of the Bible (e.g., theories that look for meaning behind, in front of, or beneath the text). In other words, Henry believes interpreters must uphold the motto made famous by Walter Kaiser: "keep your finger *on* the text!"

Fallibility of the Exegete

Henry's epistemology also clashes with relativism and subjectivity in favor of epistemological objectivity. Henry seems to use the terms "relativism" and "subjectivity" interchangeably. He addresses the topics of hermeneutical subjectivity and/or relativity in volume four, chapter fourteen of *God, Revelation and Authority*, titled, "The Fallibility of the Exegete."[84] His opening statement in this chapter is, "Alongside the inerrancy of the inspired autographs and the infallibility of the copies, evangelical theology must stress also the fallibility of the exegete, whether evangelical or non-evangelical."[85] Henry believes exegetes can make mistakes in their interpretations of infallible Scripture. His epistemology accounts for objectivity, but it does not presume to guarantee objectivity in every instance.

In order to illustrate his point, Henry spends most of chapter fourteen of volume four addressing what he considers to be the "exegetical errors of higher-criticism" as reflected in the hermeneutical views of James Barr. In his book, *Carl Henry: Theologian for All Seasons*, G. Wright Doyle offers a concise summary of Henry's chapter on the fallibility of the exegete, noting,

> In the past two centuries biblical critics have claimed to find errors and contradictions in the Scriptures, and they have posited a variety of theories concerning the origin and composition of the various books of the Bible. These theories, often stemming from naturalistic and even evolutionary presuppositions, have been proven wrong time and again. Historical criticism may and must be used by the careful exegete, but not in such a way as to

---

84. Henry, *GRA*, 4:316–352.

85. Ibid., 4:316. Some of the higher-critical issues Henry addresses are: 1) Conflicts over Documentary-Source Theory; 2) Ancient Near Eastern Studies; 3) Literary-Critical Studies; 4) Controversies over the book of Daniel; 5) Authorship and dating of the Pentateuch and book of Isaiah; 6) Source criticism and the synoptic problem; 7) The Nature of Biblical Truth; 8) Non-Evangelical Presuppositions; 9) Miracles; 10) Historiography; 11) Commentaries; and 12) Tradition. Ibid., 4:316–352.

deny the authenticity of the canonical writings or the truth of their contents. Henry is aware of problem passages in the Bible, and spends an entire chapter discussing some of the more difficult ones. Though he believes that most problems can be resolved by careful study, he admits that some apparent errors and contradictions remain, awaiting further knowledge or perhaps even the return of Christ to solve. In fact, 'the enormity in the range of error involved in the fallacies of higher critics in contrast to the scope supposedly attaching to Scripture is striking.'[86]

Doyle insists that Henry recognizes the effects of epistemology upon hermeneutical methodology. For Henry, the reason higher critics err is because their non-evangelical presuppositions negatively affect their exegesis of Scripture. Henry attempts to overcome the epistemological errors of higher-critics by positing biblically based categories of thought and providing logical principles of verification to overcome the fallibility of the exegete.

It seems like the vast majority of contemporary evangelical and non-evangelical scholars would agree with the claim "presuppositions affect interpretation."[87] These same scholars also believe the presence of presuppositions negate the possibility of objectivity in biblical interpretation. For example, Grant Osborne says, "The primary barrier to a valid interpretation is, as already stated, one's preunderstanding."[88] Osborne believes objectivity is impossible because no one neutrally approaches the text of Scripture. On the one hand, Henry agrees with Osborne that neutral exegesis is impossible. On the other hand, he opposes the claim that the presence of presuppositions necessarily eliminate the possibility of an objective interpretation of the Bible (or any text for that matter).[89]

86. Doyle, *Carl Henry*, 63, emphasis added.

87. Silva and Kaiser, *An Introduction to Biblical Hermeneutics*; Klein, Blomberg, and Hubbard, *Introduction to Biblical Interpretation*; Fee and Stuart, *How to Read the Bible for All Its Worth*.

88. Osborne, *The Hermeneutical Spiral*, 404. Osborne continues to say, "I must distinguish 'presupposition' from 'prejudice.' The key is to follow Ricoeur's suggestion and place ourselves 'in front of' rather than 'behind' the text, so that the text can have priority. This allows us to determine which types of preunderstanding are valid and which are not, as the text challenges, reshapes and directs our presuppositions." Ibid., 412.

89. Henry claims, "Harnack deplored Barth's delimitation of the capability of historical science because it is not only disparaged critical and scientific historical scholarship, but also attacked the historical and scientific nature of theology. Against this Barth replied, and rightly so, that the interpreter's own presuppositions exclude the

In the section on how to avoid hermeneutical nihilism, Henry maintains that exegetes cannot escape the presence of presuppositions. He balances his claim, however, by insisting on the indispensable importance of valid exegetical assumptions. For example, Henry claims, "Foremost among these is the recovery of divine revelation as a mental concept rather than as a paradoxical or extra mental event inaccessible to reason; revelation involves cognitive knowing."[90] In this quote, Henry reveals one of his presuppositions (aka., that theologians should recover the cognitive aspects of divine revelation).[91] He believes Revelational Theism's emphasis upon cognitive revelation is superior to other approaches because it insists on the rational Logos and *imago Dei* to ground objectivity.[92] Henry believes both of these concepts are derived from the Bible, not alien concepts (e.g., non-biblical) or phantom-logos.

Because of Henry's use of what he believes are biblical presuppositions (e.g., the Logos and *imago Dei*), he denies the claim that presuppositions remove in theory the possibility of a correct interpretation of Scripture; instead, the presence of alien presuppositions remove the possibility of objectivity by maligning the text of Scripture contrary to the author's intention. For example, Henry claims, "[Higher] Criticism may imply a new theology [according to anti-supernatural presuppositions], but it can hardly imply a new logic except at the cost of destroying both old and new theology and the very criticism on which the new theology presumes to rest."[93]

For Henry, these new "critical theories" are not offering just a new theology, but a new type of epistemology (or as he is using it here "logic") to undergird their study of Scripture. Both his epistemology *per se* and hermeneutics as epistemology, deny the claim there are any new forms of logic. Henry also believes the image of God found in all of humanity, allows from an Augustinian worldview, for the possibility of a singular and trans-cultural logic found in all people. The point being, Revelational Theism provides the framework to discuss properly the relationship

---

possibility of neutral exegesis; moreover, rationalistic projection of a nonsupernatural historical Jesus does not cancel out a reliable alternative that survives responsible New Testament criticism and in which the crucified and reason Jesus is the center of divine revelation." Henry, *GRA*, 4:298.

90. Ibid., 4:314.
91. Ibid.
92. Ibid.
93. Ibid., 4:330.

between presuppositions and objective principles required for hermeneutical validity.

Henry offers the following comments about critical presuppositions and exegesis. He writes,

> It makes a great difference whether the Bible's message and meaning derive from authoritatively inspired prophets and apostles or from postbiblical commentators and/or twentieth-century Montanists. Critical scholars often elevate to preferred status whatever theology is congenial to their own presuppositions, and do this in correlation with literary criticism of the Bible; a case in point of the modernists sponsoring of the supposedly non-supernatural Jesus of Q rather than the supernatural Christ of the New Testament.... Barr grants that critical methods were worked out in the context of modern theological and philosophical presuppositions.... Barr thus assigns critical consensus evident priority over a concern for authentically biblical presuppositions, and even over critically shared governing assumptions.... [Henry concludes] Christians have reason to fear lest critical interpreters pursue a rationalistically oriented 'biblical research' which deigns to comment itself as objective scholarship.[94]

It is apparent Henry does not oppose the influence of presuppositions in hermeneutics. Instead, he opposes what might be considered "alien" or "false presuppositions." Henry goes on to say, "Furthermore, they [most evangelical interpreters] would locate the difference over governing assumptions not in evangelical freedom from presuppositions but in the legitimacy or illegitimacy of the particular interpretive principles that differing scholars employ."[95] He continues to say,

> Moreover, their disagreement with nonevangelicals is not at all wholly reducible to contrary presuppositions, for the question of which presupposition most consistently explain the so-called data remains indispensably important. There are, to be sure, no independently existing neutral 'data,' since the very assertion requires intellectual interpretation. Since truth is systematic, and theorems can only be deduced from axioms, disagreements are in a sense 'reduced' to the choice of axioms. Otherwise much would remain *outside* the system and apart from all

---

94. Ibid., 4: 324–325, 333, 335.
95. Ibid., 4:337.

presuppositions, and frequently does, make mistakes of all sorts. But that is psychology, not apologetics.[96]

Henry suggests both evangelical and non-evangelical exegetes operate according to a set of presuppositions.[97] For him, the presence of presuppositions remove any concept of a neutral "data," "interpretation," or "scientific research," etc. because many of the theorems advanced by scientists are the logical extension of systems of truth (e.g. presuppositions) and their governing axioms. He believes any approach to knowledge that does not consider presuppositions "governing axioms" should not be considered a valid approach to apologetics, theology, or hermeneutics. Instead, they become systems of psychological analysis; rather than biblical axioms that could be used alongside reason to demonstrate the superiority of a Christian worldview or an interpretation of Scripture.

The following quote by Henry helps to answer the question: How does fallibility and presuppositions affect Henry's notion of objectivity in biblical interpretation? He claims,

> At stake, however, is whether this fallibility relativizes all of our knowledge of absolutes and condemns us to hermeneutical skepticism. Are we constrained to say, as some would have it, that while we defend transcendent absolutes on the basis of divine disclosure, we must admit that—since fallibility clouds our knowledge of revelation—we therefore know the content of revelation only in a distorted way?[98]

Henry responds to the relativist by questioning the statement that "fallibility necessarily entails a distorted knowledge of revelation" (e.g., revelation being the objective disclosure of truth and inspiration being the means by which the revelation became an objective disclosure). In fact, he suggests this type of argument would seem counter-intuitive to the purposes of God who reveals himself to fallible human beings (e.g., the God who speaks). Henry claims, "Such a position could only erode the significance of revelation by relativizing it, much as one may seek to avoid

---

96. Ibid. Henry comments, "Now all this is highly interesting, but it blurs the central point. The reading of texts and the selection of evidence inescapably involves presuppositions, whether pursued by evangelicals or alternatively by Wellhausen, Oesterley and Robinson, or Barr." Ibid., 4:338.

97. Ibid.

98. Ibid., 4:350.

doctrinal relativity."⁹⁹ At this point, he strategically employs a presuppositional method in order to show the contradiction in the claim that "fallibility removes absolute hermeneutical objectivity." The following quote by Henry captures his most thorough response to hermeneutical subjectivity, epistemological relativism, and the fallibility of the exegete. He writes,

> It is self-defeating to say that there are absolutes, but that we can only know them relatively. If we know assuredly that there are absolutes, then the limits of relativity are breached; but if we consistently apply the relativity principle then we must disallow any confident affirmation of absolutes. In respect to general revelation, man as a knower does indeed relativize divine revelation, although that revelation continually penetrates to his conscious self and renders his rebellion culpable. But special revelation objectively publishes and supplements the content of general revelation in perspicuous scripture form. Neither man's finitude nor his sinfulness can therefore completely relativize transcendent revelation. Judeo-Christian religion sets the exegetes fallibility in a revelatory framework that brackets the epistemic consequences of human revolt, even if finite and sinful man can and does in some respects cloud the content of revelation.¹⁰⁰

As a Christian philosopher, it is evident Henry believes Revelational Theism provides a superior framework than secular theories to define and discuss the proper role of presuppositions and hermeneutics. This relates to his "cognitive-propositional" hermeneutic because human limitations are unable to undermine the claims of divine revelation (e.g., because in Revelational Theism the Logos and the *imago Dei* serve to ground the fixed nature of meaning), so too, alien theories of knowledge (e.g., non-biblical views) and false presuppositions or new hermeneutical approaches cannot override the fixed nature of meaning and the absolute nature of truth.¹⁰¹

---

99. Ibid. Henry says, "Nor will an appeal even to the church, or to its teaching hierarchy, or to biblical critics specially enlightened by modern gnosis, escape that verdict. If Protestants for two centuries after the Reformation claimed that Rome irremediably diluted the Bible by boldly superimposing tradition and legend, then it can just as properly be said that neo-Protestant churchmen import myth and legend into modern Christianity on a scale unrivaled by Romanism." Ibid.

100. Ibid., 4:350–351.

101. Henry, *gods of this Age or . . . God of the Ages?*, 251.

The Role of Reason

Given his view of the fallibility of the exegete and the power of revelation, Henry moves to a discussion on the role of reason. In chapter fourteen of volume four of *God, Revelation and Authority*, titled, "The Method and Criteria of Theology (II): The Role of Reason, Scripture, Consistency and Coherence," Henry discusses his fifth principle of validity. This fifth principle states, "*The proper task of theology is to exposit and elucidate the content of Scripture in an orderly way.*"[102] This fifth principle helps readers to understand Henry's *use* of reason in respect to theology and hermeneutics (e.g., to *exposit* and *elucidate* Scripture in and *orderly* way).[103] Henry claims, "The province of theology is to concentrate on the intelligible content and logical relationships of the scripturally given revelation, and to present its teachings as a comprehensive whole."[104] In this quote, Henry responds to the claim that not all of Scripture's truth-content is explicitly known; hence, it either cannot or should not be systematized.[105] On the contrary, while Henry recognizes the various genres of Scripture do not always have explicit propositions, he does not believe that entails they do not contain truth-content and cannot be systematized. The very fact that all of Scripture is a rational and intelligible revelation suggests they contain truth-value. Moreover, as chapter three argued, the implicit passages can be reduced to their propositional form and from that standpoint, they can be systematized.

---

102. Henry, GRA, 1:238. In chapter two, it was claimed that the fifth principle would be discussed and how it relates to his hermeneutic as epistemology. Henry's six principles listed from this quote, which are: (1) God in his revelation is the first principle of Christian theology, from which all truths of revealed religion are derived; (2) Human reason is a divinely fashioned instrument for recognizing truth; it is not a creative source for truth; (3) The Bible is the Christian's principle of verification; (4) Logical consistency is a negative test of truth and coherence a subordinate test; (5) The proper task of theology is to exposit and elucidate the content of Scripture in an orderly way; (6) The theology of revelation requires the apologetic confrontation of speculative theories of reality and life.

103. The *Oxford Dictionary* relates the word "exposit" to the term "exposition." It defines exposition as an "explanatory account," or "commentary." Jewell, *The Oxford*, 279. It defines the term "elucidate" as a verb to "throw light on" or the synonym "clarify." Ibid., 255. Henry claims, "Christian theology is the systematization of the truth-content explicit and implicit in the inspired writings. It consists essentially in the repetition, combination, and systematization of the truth of revelation in its propositionally given biblical form." Henry, GRA, 1:238.

104. Ibid., 1:238–239.

105. Ibid.

Henry explains what he considers to be the "ideal procedure" to systematize the text of Scripture. He grounds his "ideal procedure" in the governing axioms of Revelational Theism. Henry suggests,

> The ideal procedure would be to arrange all of the truths of Christianity logically by summarizing and systematizing the texts and teachings of Scripture and supplying an exposition of the logical content and implications of the Bible on its own premises. Pinnock is right in insisting: 'The exegesis of Scripture . . . has absolute priority over all systems. . . . Scripture is capable of disciplining her theologians and correcting their work' (*Biblical Revelation*, p. 135). But Scripture is itself implicitly systematic. No one who contends that the Bible as a literary document is a canon of divinely inspired truths can hold otherwise without reflecting adversely on the mind of God.[106]

Henry claims divine revelation originates from the mind of God. In the paradigm of his Revelational Theistic metaphysic and epistemology, reason is that which unites the rational mind of God with the rational mind of humanity, through the mediating Logos contained in the propositional revelation of the Bible. Consequently, for Henry, reason is the unifying factor for his theological method. Within Henry's version of Revelational Theism, humanity can properly order the text of Scripture because God's revelation is implicitly systematic, and the role of the interpreter is to *recognize* and *order* the *intelligible* and *rational* structures of special revelation.[107]

---

106. Ibid., 1:239.

107. Ibid., 1:239. Henry suggests that the ideal method is systematic theology, opposed to the biblical theology movement. Henry notes, "The point is not that Christian scholars can attain infallibility in this life. Too often the distinction is forgotten between the canonical content of revelation and systems derived from it for which absolute claims are made. Yet the content of revelation does indeed lend itself to systematic exposition, and the more orderly and logical that exposition is, the nearer the expositor will be to the mind of God in his revelation. Montgomery stresses that the gaps in revelational data have resulted in the emergence of different systems of Christian theology. We do not indeed as yet have a theology of glory. Even the apostles had to confess their knowledge to be only 'in part,' and even this knowledge includes elements that, while not beyond human understanding, await profounder clarification. Not only Calvin and Luther in Reformation times, but even in modern times revelationally presupposed theologians like Gordon Clark, Herman Dooyeweerd and Cornelius Van Til mount theistic schemas on somewhat different premises. The danger confronts us continually of formulating models on hypotheses not really required by revelation, and forcing into these assumptions and deductions what is merely surmised to follow, and of disowning as unauthentically biblical anyone who questions

In light of what has been said, the following section will analyze Henry's response to objections raised against his rational systematic approach to theology.[108] The first objection Henry responds to is the claim that a rational explanation of theology was borrowed by modern science and philosophers who emphasize an empirical method.[109] He notes that, "... its [the rational systematic approach] are far deeper in the nature of man as a reflective being and in sustained constructive thought, and beyond that in the fact that man as a distinctive creature of God stands continually in touch with revelation."[110] First of all, Henry praises modern scientists by agreeing with their aim to find a systematic unity and regulative understanding of general revelation contained in the universe. However, he insists that humanity's rational approach to the universe finds its origin, not in modern philosophy of science, but in the divinely endowed faculties of reason given by God to humanity since they have been made in the image of God.[111]

Henry responds to a second objection that his view is too closely aligned with Spinoza's geometrical rationalism. He writes, "But axiomitization is simply the best means of demonstrating the logical consistency of a given system of thought, and showing that all logically dependent theorems flow from the basic axioms."[112] He goes on to explain, suggesting,

> If God is himself the Truth and the origin and substance of all truth is to be found in him, if revelation is its source and truth is a unity as Christianity contends, then such axiomization would be the model way to overcome the notion that Christianity is deduced from first principles held in common with other religions or world views; it would also avoid an inconsistent adoption or unwitting espousal of alien beliefs. Such theological arrangement of propositions into a system or axioms and theorems has never been achieved. In the past, orthodox theologians strove valiantly towards this goal.[113]

From this first quote, it is evident Henry argues for a deductive hermeneutical method. He claims that since God is the source of all truth, all other

---

the propriety of doing this." Ibid., 1:240–241.

108. Ibid.
109. Ibid., 1:239.
110. Ibid.
111. Ibid.
112. Ibid.
113. Ibid., 1:239–240.

truth statements must be deduced from the axioms of God's existence and the Bible as God's revelation, in an orderly and systematic fashion. Henry suggests that by applying the laws of logic, Christian theologians can demonstrate the internal inconsistencies of other approaches, while at the same time exhibiting the internal consistency and superiority of Christian axioms. This is a presuppositional approach to hermeneutics, where the law of non-contradiction is utilized to show rational order and internal validity (or invalidity).[114] In the final analysis, for Henry, an "orderly exegesis of revelational truth" means the exegete is ". . . bound to the text that expresses the mind of God and the writers purpose; he has no other access to this purpose except the text taken in its literary and historical context."[115] As will be shown, Henry believes an exegete can only validly know the truth-content of Scripture according to the grammatical-historical method of interpretation and it is the role of reason to systematically order the content of Scripture.[116] Therefore, given the debate between present-day biblical and systematic theologians, Henry's view of reason locates him clearly within the systematic theology camp.

The Holy Spirit and Interpretation

While arguing for an orderly and systematic approach to Scripture, Henry also incorporates a Reformed view of the Holy Spirit's ministry into his hermeneutic as epistemology.[117] According to Henry, the primary purpose of the Holy Spirit is to reveal the truths of God to humanity.[118] The Spirit also empowers humanity to receive and appropriate the Scriptures in order to develop a robust theology and transformed life.[119] There are two steps necessary to achieve this end. First, the church should recognize it was the Spirit who first breathed into humans the breath of life, and the same Spirit, who breathed out the prophetic-apostolic Scriptures.

---

114. Ibid., 1:241.

115. Ibid., 1:241; 4:281.

116. Aspects of Henry's use of the grammatical-historical method will be discussed in the section titled, "Hermeneutics as Methodology."

117. Ibid., 4:278–279.

118. Henry claims, "The Bible does not use the specific term *illumination*; it does, however, refer to that special activity of the Holy Spirit by which man can recognize that what Scripture teaches is true, and can accept and appropriate its teachings." Ibid., 4:282.

119. Ibid., 4:273.

This first step serves as a reminder that it is the Holy Spirit's ministry to give life to humanity and inspire the text of Scripture.[120] Henry explains the Holy Spirits ministry, claiming,

> The Holy Spirit brings God's Word to us not first and foremost in illumination—although as a matter of psychological case history the experience of the new birth may indeed appear to rank first; in actuality the Holy Spirit has already engaged antecedently in revelation and inspiration. Moreover, God's special revelation to the biblical prophet's and the Spirit's inspiration of their proclamation hold logical priority.[121]

The second step is the church ought to recognize that the Holy Spirit enables believers to understand God's revealed Word. He explains this second step, claiming,

> The revelation we share comes to us ultimately from no other source than the Spirit of God, who inspires, illuminates and interprets the prophetic-apostolic disclosure. Yet this fact implies no basis for holding that the depths of God are disclosed to us directly as they were to prophets and apostles, and apart from dependence on them.[122]

In brief, for Henry, the Holy Spirit is the source of inspiration and revelation, as well as the agent who aides exegetes interpret and apply the Bible through the instrumentality of illumination.[123]

Henry proceeds to discuss *how* the Holy Spirit operates through the act of illumination. He believes one of the purposes of illumination is to help believers set forth the "grammatical-literal sense" of Scripture.[124] Though Henry does not offer an extended conversation on the particular details or procedures of the Spirits ministry, he does offer a helpful word of caution to his readers, claiming,

---

120. Ibid., 4:275.

121. Ibid. Henry comments on these ideas later claiming, "Paul, moreover, in this passage [1 Cor. 2:10] employs the first person plural ('we') more frequently than the second person ('you'). Charles Hodge interprets the text 'God hath revealed (them) unto us by his Spirit' (1 Cor. 2:10, KJV) as meaning that what human reason was unable to discover, God revealed by his Spirit to the holy apostles and prophets (cf. Eph. 3:5)." Ibid., 4:276.

122. Ibid.

123. Ibid.

124. Ibid., 4:280.

> If we ask how the Holy Spirit illumines us, we must readily acknowledge that Scripture does not supply much data about the *how* of inspiration or illumination, any more than the *how* of divine incarnation in Jesus Christ. Yet the ministry of the Spirit of God, distinct in each operation, is as essential and unique in enlivening God's revelation in the lives of his people as it is in the phenomena of divine incarnation and divine inspiration.[125]

Henry believes an evangelical interpreter ought to recognize that while humanity might only have a finite knowledge of the Holy Spirits ministry, however, that does not entail they have a false knowledge of the Spirits ministry. A finite amount of knowledge does not equal false knowledge, for finite knowledge can still be true knowledge (even if it is only partial knowledge). If one had to have exhaustive knowledge in order to have true knowledge, then no one except God could have true knowledge. Moreover, foreseeing the argument, Henry responds to the claim that "veiled knowledge" is a result of sinful resistance to the revelation of God. Henry's response clearly reflects his theological conviction that it is the task of the Spirit to remove this "veil" by persuading individuals (e.g., regeneration, sanctification, and illumination) of the veracity of the God who speaks in propositional form through the agency of special revelation.[126]

In this first section on Henry's analysis of hermeneutics as epistemology, it is apparent Henry endeavors to provide a way for evangelical exegetes to still affirm the Protestant principles of interpretation, while engaging in philosophical hermeneutics. He rejects the so-called "hermeneutical problem" and the "hermeneutical spiral." Henry attempts to ground the meaning of Scripture in authorial intention; however, he argues for a correspondence between authorial intent and the grammatical meaning of the text. He believes the role of reason is to search the text of Scripture for its truth claims and to systematize them in a consistent and orderly fashion. Finally, through the act of regeneration and illumination, the Holy Spirit is able to overcome the noetic effects of sin and humanity's moral rebellion against God's revelation.

---

125. Ibid., 4:277.
126. Ibid., 4:277–288.

HERMENEUTICS AS METHODOLOGY

The purpose of the following section is to explain the *way* Henry interacts with two different methods of interpretation: (1) The Historical-Critical Method; and (2) Narrative Theology. These two have been chosen by the researcher because Henry discusses both methods at length and interacts with what he considers to be the valid and invalid aspects of each approach.[127] The final portion of this section will discuss aspects of Henry's *use* of the grammatical-historical method and a literal interpretation of Scripture.

As has been mentioned, Henry believes there is a connection between epistemology and hermeneutical methodology. According to Henry, prior to modernism, "The sense of the revelation was to be found by grammatico-historical exegesis that aimed to recover as accurately as possible the intention of the inspired prophetic-apostolic writers."[128] Henry suggests that due to the plurality of different epistemologies and hermeneutical methods, which seem to oppose each other in a variety of ways, some scholars desire to shun the use of the term "hermeneutics."[129] He responds to this claim pointing out,

> But whether we shun the term *hermeneutics* or not, theologians dare not shun the question of the methodological principles to be employed in biblical interpretation and explanation. The issues at stake are foundational to all literary understanding in general and to the validity of scriptural meaning in particular. The crucial issue today is whether, in the face of rival theories of textual interpretation, any universal canons of exegesis remain to be affirmed. If biblical language is not to be regarded as conveying objectively valid information, but is simply the medium through which God confronts man internally with the possibility of new self-understanding, then the significance of Scripture lies no longer in its shared cognitive message but only in private internal response.[130]

---

127. Henry, *gods of this Age or . . . God of the Ages?*, 245–255; 257–276; Henry, *GRA*, 4:385–404.

128. Ibid., 257–258.

129. For Henry, the plurality of different views would be: Heidegarrian and Bultmannian exegesis or Marxist exegesis. It could also include feminist exegesis or neo-orthodox exegesis. Contemporary evangelicalism has a plurality of different models too. See, Gundry and Meadors, *Moving Beyond The Bible To Theology*.

130. Henry, *GRA*, 311–312.

Apparently for Henry, the so-called "hermeneutical problem," affects all literary works, including the Bible. In particular, he believes innovative approaches to epistemology affect methodology *per se* (e.g., scientific methodology and hermeneutical methodology included), which in turn gave way to new methods contrary to the grammatical-historical and literal interpretation of Scripture.[131] In keeping with Henry's model for evaluating opposing theories of knowledge and language, this section will first discuss Henry's analysis of the historical-critical method and narrative theology before explaining his analysis of the grammatical-historical method of interpretation.

Historical-Critical Method

The question to be answered about Henry and historical criticism is: Can historical-critical methods be reconciled with Henry's hermeneutic and view of Scripture? The answer to the question is "yes and no." On the one hand, it is yes, because Henry does not believe evangelical scholars must oppose the historical-critical method *per se*; instead, they must reject many of the alien presuppositions (e.g., non-biblical) of the historical-critical method. On the other hand, it is no, because Henry believes some of the alien presuppositions of critical scholarship have been utilized to undermine the classic evangelical view of Scripture. In particular, the evangelical insistence upon the Bible being divine revelation, that is both historically accurate and without error (i.e., inerrant). That being said, the following section is going to further discuss Henry's analysis of the philosophical presuppositions of historical-critical methodology and the concepts of revelation and myth.[132]

In *God, Revelation and Authority*, Henry has a chapter titled, "The Uses and Abuses of Historical Criticism."[133] He discusses topics in historical criticism ranging from literary and redaction criticism to the authorship of the books of Isaiah and Daniel. Henry proposes ten guidelines for evangelicals to assess historical-criticism. He claims evangelicals can properly affirm:

---

131. Mueller-Vollmer, *The Hermeneutics Reader*; Mueller, *The Study of Theology*; John Franke, *The Character of Theology*; Wolterstorff, *Divine Discourse*.

132. Ibid., 4:386.

133. Ibid., 385–404.

1. Historical criticism is not inappropriate to, but bears relevantly on, Christian concerns.
2. Historical criticism is never philosophically or theologically neutral.
3. Historical criticism is unable to deal with questions concerning the supernatural and miraculous.
4. Historical criticism is as relevant to miracles, insofar as they are historical, as to nonmiraculous historical events.
5. Historical criticism cannot demonstrably prove or disprove the factuality of either a biblical or a nonbiblical historical event.
6. To assume the unreliability of biblical historical testimony—or of Xenophon's *Anabasis* Thucydides's *History of the Peloponnesian War*—in order to believe only what is independently or externally confirmed, unjustifiably discounts the primary sources.
7. Discrimination of biblical events as either historically probable or improbable is not unrelated to the metaphysical assumptions with which a historian approaches the data.
8. A historian's subjective reversal of judgment concerning the probability or improbability of an event's occurrence does not alter the objective factuality or nonfactuality of the event.
9. Although the historian properly stresses historical method, he is not as a person exempt from claims concerning supernatural revelation and miraculous redemptive history, for the historical method is not man's only source of truth.
10. Biblical events acquire their meaning from the divinely inspired Scriptures; since there could be no meaning of events without the events, the inspired record carries its own intrinsic testimony to the factuality of those events.[134]

At the center of Henry's analysis of historical-criticism in these ten guidelines is the second guideline that: historical-criticism is never philosophically or theologically neutral. Henry believes philosophical

---

134. Ibid., 4:403. Henry further addresses the historian by saying, "If the historian begins with the assumption that the most qualified or concerned witnesses are likely to be unreliable, even where they lay down their lives in full confidence of the truth of their cause, not only does the recovery of history become an impossible task, but historical criticism then renders no greater service than the aesthetic self-entertainment of the historiographer himself." Ibid., 4:403–404.

presuppositions affect the governing axioms of the historical critical method and critical scholarship. For example, guideline seven suggests that some historical critics discriminate against the historical probability of biblical events because of their "metaphysical assumptions." Furthermore, guideline eight suggests the historical method has been influenced by an empirical approach to epistemology because of its "subjective reversal of judgment" and the probabilistic nature of its judgments about the "objective factuality" of an historical event. From these guidelines, it is apparent Henry believes there is a connection between epistemology and historical-critical methodology.

Epistemology and Methodology

The following quote by Henry is one of his pivotal comments on the topic of epistemology and methodology. He explicitly discusses in both positive and negative terms, the relationship between hermeneutics as epistemology and methodology. Henry claims,

> Every methodology has its presuppositions, and no interpreter is wholly—nor is he ideally so—free of presuppositions. No method is without underlying axioms and assumptions or aims and goals. Reliance on any given methodology involves a certain preunderstanding about the nature of the subject being investigated. The use of method presupposes that the matter studied can be handled adequately by that method. Thus behaviorism started as a neutral method of examining mind, and resulted in defining mind as the *behavior* examined. The only legitimate questions about method therefore are whether its relevance to the subject matter is conclusive, whether its limitations are recognized or arbitrarily ignored, whether the interpreter in practice employs the method in the service of restrictive assumptions or with academic objectivity, and whether the method is consistently or inconsistently applied.[135]

Henry suggests that whenever an exegete approaches the text of Scripture, underlying axioms and assumptions govern the aims of his or her study. For example, one of the abuses of the historical-critical method by some critical scholars is they employ an anti-supernaturalist bias to the miraculous passages of the Bible in order to discredit the historical

---

135. Ibid, 4:388.

reliability of the Scriptures.[136] Henry argues that certain presuppositions can negatively affect ones view of Scripture evident in the way some historical critics deny its verbal-rational nature. In another respect, Henry believes if coupled with the right presuppositions (namely, those of Revelational Theism), historical-criticism can be utilized by evangelicals to explain and defend an evangelical view of the Bible.[137]

In light of this claim, Henry analyzes some of the major discussions amongst evangelical proponents of the historical-critical method. These include the use of an empirical method, the influence of Ancient Near Eastern sources, and the role of dogmatic theology and philosophy. He records that during the 1960's and 1970's some members of the Evangelical Theological Society, attempted to employ a form of the historical-critical method by removing some of its alien presuppositions in order to reconcile it with an evangelical view of Scripture.[138] He believes this is a good task by evangelical scholars, only if they can free the method from non-biblical presuppositions and replace them with biblical presuppositions (e.g., in particular, Revelational Theism). Nevertheless, Henry continues to question whether or not evangelicals should embrace the historical-critical method.[139]

In the following quote, Henry raises some serious questions about the historical-critical method. He asks,

> But does acceptance of the historical-critical method—if its limitations and goals are properly defined—necessarily create doubts about the supernatural and miraculous? Does its acceptance require the forfeiture of personal confidence in the inerrancy of Scripture and free the interpreter to interpret a passage contrary to the writer's intention, instead of engaging in exegesis in order to expound the writer's meaning? Does historical-critical methodology mean that the hermeneutical framework of the analogy of Scripture must give way in interpretation to a philosophically conceived analogy of history? Must the research scholar assume not merely the supposedly inspired biblical writer may have been wrong, but that he could not under any circumstances been invariably right? Does the method of historical criticism require us not simply to reject in advance the appeal to inspiration as guaranteeing trustworthiness, but to

136. Ibid., 4:390.
137. Ibid., 4:393.
138. Ibid., 4:387–402.
139. Ibid.

reject biblical authority and reliability per se? And if so, what assured results, what trustworthy conclusions, can the historical-critical method arrive at? Can it arrive at anything?[140]

Henry answers these questions suggesting one of the common commitments of historical-critical methodology (especially as it relates to new methods of historiography), is "In its approach to the Bible, historical criticism professes to treat the scriptural documents like all other writings, without special deference to their claims to divine inspiration and authority."[141] Obviously from what has already been said about Henry's views, this approach is a capitulation by supposed evangelical scholars to non-evangelical presuppositions and alien categories of thought.

Consequently, Henry opposes the downplaying of the inspiration of the Bible by some evangelical historical critics, and the denial of inspiration by others. He believes an affirmation of the inspiration and authority of Scripture does not negate historical investigation; instead, historical critics undermine the authority of the Bible because their alien presuppositions bias them against the historical reliability of the biblical text.

For example, contemporary historical critic, Peter Enns, denies much of the miraculous details in the Bible and the inerrancy of Scripture.[142] Enns approaches the Bible with the presupposition that it is merely a reflection of a primitive culture bearing all of its literary features, including non-historical genres and mythological categories. If Henry were still alive he would most likely respond to Enns claiming Revelational Theism provides evangelicals with a much a better way to substantiate the Bible as an inspired literary document that is both historically accurate and free from myth.[143] Because according to Revelational Theism and classic evangelicalism, when God speaks in propositional form he speaks truthfully, not in fictional and mythological categories. The point being that epistemology, whether good or bad, has a functional role in the way evangelicals approach hermeneutics, historical criticism included.

140. Ibid., 4:401–402.
141. Ibid., 4:402.
142. Enns, *Inspiration and Incarnation*.
143. Henry, *GRA*, 1:44–69.

210 HERMENEUTICS AS EPISTEMOLOGY

Revelation and Myth

In his book titled, *The Evolution of Adam*, Enns attempts to use historical-critical methodologies to reconcile the Bible with modern day scientific theories of human origins and ancient Near Eastern concepts of myth. In the first section of *The Evolution of Adam*, Enns offers his readers an overview of the book of Genesis and the challenges facing it claiming he believes biblical criticism and archaeology discredit the truthfulness of a literal historical Adam.[144] Enns goes on to explain the hermeneutical implications of his project in *The Evolution of Adam*, claiming,

> My own thinking reflected above [on Paul's understanding of Adam] is focused solely on hermeneutical issues—the purpose of the book—and so I make no claim to answer the many intellectual issues that the Christianity/evolution discussion raises. But the fact that the 'why' question remains does not dismiss the hermeneutical observations; failure to provide at once an adequate counterproposal to a historical Adam for 'why' does not mean that the scientific data that raised the problem in the first place can be set to the side. The hermeneutical factors discussed concerning Genesis and Paul are here to stay, and they bring to the front and center the tremendously important work of Christian philosophers and theologians sorting out the implications of hermeneutics.[145]

In *The Evolution of Adam*, Enns is reflecting the same hermeneutical method found in his book, *Inspiration and Incarnation*.[146] In both of these books, he attempts to use the parallels between ancient Near Eastern mythology and the book of Genesis, to undermine a literal interpretation of the text in favor of a socially conditioned mythological understanding of Scripture.[147]

In his book, *Inspiration and Incarnation*, Enns claims, "It is important to understand, however, that not all historians of the ancient Near East use the word *myth* simply as shorthand for 'untrue,' 'made up,' 'storybook.' It may include these ideas for some, but many who use the

144. Enns, *The Evolution of Adam*, xviii–xix.
145. Ibid., 126–127.
146. This comment is made because the same methods are utilized in both books in order to arrive at the same conclusions on matters pertaining to myth, ANE parallels, and so forth.
147. Ibid., 137–138.

term are trying to get at something deeper."[148] How does Enns define this "something deeper"? He answers, "A more generous way of defining myth is that it is *an ancient, premodern, prescientific way of addressing questions of ultimate origins and meaning in the form of stories: Who are we? Where did we come from?*"[149] While Enns suggests not all scholars believe the category of myth communicates a non-historical view of revelation, however, Enns confesses he denies a literal interpretation of Scripture concluding the book of Genesis is both mythological and non-historical.[150]

Enns is not the first scholar to address the concepts of revelation and myth.[151] In the first volume of *God, Revelation and Authority*, Henry includes a chapter titled, *Revelation and Myth*.[152] Henry claims, "The most critical question in the history of thought is whether all the convictional frameworks through which different peoples arrive at the meaning and worth of human life are by nature mythical, or whether perhaps at least one of these perspectives stems from divine revelation and has objective cognitive validity."[153] He goes on to note,

> Many modern theologians set aside any emphasis on intelligible divine revelation (that is, the view that God communicates to mankind the literal truth about his nature and purposes); they affirm, instead, that God uses myth as a literary genre to convey revelation in the Bible and perhaps elsewhere as well. To them the biblical accounts of creation and redemption are written mythological representations of transcendent realities that defy formulation in conceptual thought patterns.[154]

Henry raises the question, "Could the God of the Bible have used myth as a literary device? Surely we must allow the sovereign God of Scripture complete freedom among the various possible means of expression. But whether God has in fact used myth as a revelatory means is quite another question."[155] Henry's answer is: no, God did not use myth as a literary

---

148. Enns, *Inspiration and Incarnation*, 40.
149. Ibid.
150. Enns, *The Evolution of Adam*, 138.
151. Henry lists numerous scholars throughout *GRA* that utilize the categories of myth.
152. Henry, *GRA*, 1:44–69.
153. Ibid., 1:44.
154. Ibid.
155. Ibid.

device because the concept of myth cannot be reconciled with the concept of the Bible as true cognitive revelation.

After a long survey of the various views of myth, Henry claims he is most concerned with neo-Protestants who create a new special literary category, "... one where theological realities are considered neither literally true nor false nor historically fact nor fable."[156] Henry offers three reasons why myth cannot be reconciled with biblical revelation. First, the biblical writers were aware of the concept of myth and rejected it.[157] The apostle Peter claims the human writers of Scripture did not follow "cleverly devised myths" (2 Pet. 1:16) and the apostle Paul commands believers to not devote themselves to "Jewish myths" (Titus 1:14).

Second, Henry believes any hermeneutical theory that must appeal to sociological conditioning to understand the nature of biblical revelation are undermining his first thesis on divine revelation which states: "*Revelation is a divinely initiated activity, God's free communication by which he alone turns his personal privacy into a deliberate disclosure of his reality.*"[158] Henry discusses the implications of his first thesis claiming,

> While concerns of critical investigation have their rightful role, they are not by subtle intrusion to be allowed to cancel in advance even the possibility that God alone in his sovereign initiative determines the actuality, direction, nature, content and diversity of his self-disclosure. When contemporary conjectural theories so penetrate the discussion of the theology of revelation that the living God cannot be conceived as revealing himself in nature because either the inner continuity or pervasive chaos of cosmic reality, or in history because of the supposed finiteness or interdependence of events, or in conscience because of its answerability to culture, or in human concepts and words because of the supposed relativity of truth or empirical origin of words, then it should be clear that the matter of God's initiative in revelation is being avoided on demerit ... In this case human beings and not God are decisive for the 'varieties of revelation.'[159]

Evidently Henry believes when scholars claim revelation is a category of myth they are undermining the fact that God is the source-criterion for revelation, not ancient Near Eastern theories or pagan accounts of

---

156. Ibid., 1:66.
157. Ibid., 1:45.
158. Ibid., 2:8.
159. Ibid., 2:78,

religion. Furthermore, when those same scholars deny the historical factuality and truthfulness of the Scriptures by appealing to pagan parallels they are allowing paganism to be the spokesman and determiner of Scripture, not the God of the Bible.[160] Finally, when critics claim the Hebrews did not have a distinct worldview and Scripture a distinct message, they can only substantiate their claim by arguing that pagan views of religion were the guide and determiner of divine revelation, not the God of the Bible.

Henry's third response to individuals who conflate revelation and myth is they must convert cognitive propositional revelation into a form of non-cognitive revelation. However, Henry claims,

> To insinuate any objective intellectual import into a symbolic or mythical view involves a confusion of categories and ignores either myth or logic. To be told that 'the mythical' concerns a realm of reality that is cognitively inaccessible and therefore not logically falsifiable, and in the next breath to be informed what its alleged meaning is, so that myth becomes intellectually explanatory, intrudes conceptual content into an arena that prior restriction has declared off limits to reason and is gross inconsistency. What makes a myth 'Christian—if there be any such thing—can hardly be its literal truth or historical factuality.[161]

Later on in *God, Revelation and Authority*, Henry writes,

> In whatever mode God speaks, his divine revelation is a mental act, for it seeks to convey to the mind of man the truth about the Creator and Lord of life, and to write upon the spirit of man God's intelligible holy will. Every mediating alternative not only sacrifices the cognitive significance of divine revelation, but also dissolves revelation itself into a vaporous and insignificant concept.[162]

Henry believes critical theses, like those postulated by Enns on revelation and myth, fail because it is logically impossible to translate the cognitive truth value of Scripture into a non-cognitive type of literature containing no historical or factual truth value. Myth can be translated from one myth to another; however, it is a category mistake to claim Scripture can go from myth (non-cognitive) to revelation (cognitive). Consequently,

---

160. Ibid., 2:25.
161. Ibid., 1:65.
162. Ibid., 4:271.

the concept of "true myth" is a misnomer and contradiction in terms because it is impossible to synthesize the cognitive and the non-cognitive into the same kind of proposition.[163]

Returning to the question: Can historical-critical methods be reconciled with Henry's hermeneutic as epistemology and methodology? Henry believes historical criticism can be reconciled with his hermeneutic, *only* if it is freed of its unbiblical philosophical presuppositions. He opposes the belief that historical-criticism is philosophically or theologically neutral. In fact, Henry seems to indicate philosophical and theological presuppositions create governing axioms that directly affect methodology and determine the goals of interpretation and how historical-criticism operates.[164] In summary, Henry denies many aspects of historical-criticism; however, he believes historical method *per se* is able to provide valuable insights into historical events, not that it is the most appropriate or only legitimate method of inquiry.

Narrative Theology

On November 12th, 1985, Henry was invited to Yale Divinity School to discuss Narrative Theology with Professor Hans Frei. He presented a paper titled, "Narrative Theology: An Evangelical Appraisal." Henry opens his address with these questions, "Does the approach to Scripture merely as narrative really do justice to the evangelical orthodox view of the Bible as an authoritative, divinely inspired book? Does its notion of textual authority require or accommodate divine authority and inspiration in the

---

163. Ibid.

164. Henry does not want to so limit an evangelical use of historical criticism or historiography to discredit the methods ability to validate biblical miracles. For him, the real benefit of historical research for an evangelical scholar is it provides a way to validate historical events recorded in the Bible. Henry places limits on the historical method. It is (a) unable to *demonstrably* prove or disprove a historical event; (b) can only offer a probable or improbable declaration of the historicity of a historical event; (c) the historicity of an historical event is usually tempered by the subjective biases of the particular historian, and just as easily as the historical reality of an event can be affirmed, it can also be denied; (d) the historical method can only tell *that* an event has not occurred, not *why* an event occurred. For Henry, the historical method does not offer a valid interpretation of the meaning or significance of a historical event. Instead, one must appeal to the divinely revealed text of Scripture to arrive at the only sure interpretation and significance of a historical event.

historical evangelical sense?"[165] His answer is no, narrative theology does not do justice to an evangelical view of the Bible and it compromises biblical authority. The following section will: (1) Explain a few irreconcilable differences between narrative theology and Henry's cognitive-propositionalism; and (2) Explain Henry's four objections to narrative theology.

Thornbury explains one aspect of narrative theology claiming, "Central to Frei's concern, as we shall see, is that there is no meaning behind the text, and thus no special historical or metaphysical hermeneutical tools are needed for interpretation, just the narrative."[166] According to Henry, Frei criticizes pre-critical theories for being seduced by the Bible's "history-likeness."[167] Henry claims,

> Frei's thesis is that 'a realistic or history-like (though not necessarily historical) element is a feature . . . of many of the biblical narratives that went into the making of Christian belief.' In realistic narrative Frei emphasizes, 'characters and individual persons in their internal depth or subjectivity as well in their capacity as doers and sufferers of actions and events, are firmly and significantly set in the context of the external environment, natural but more particularly social.'[168]

Henry notes Frei does not consider all of the narrative content of Scripture to be historical.[169] Furthermore, Thornbury points out,

> For Frei, arguing for the historical reliability of miracles and for a meaning that refers to the author's original intention compromises interpretation. Such an approach, for Frei, is a categorical mistake. Frei considers it unfortunate that the conservatives, in his opinion, replaced biblical narrative with dogmatic propositions that they felt replaced objective reality. He argues that meaning is bound to the narrative sequence itself. He would be extremely uncomfortable with saying that propositional

---

165. Henry, *gods of this Age or . . . God of the Ages*, 257.
166. Thornbury, *Recovering Classic Evangelicalism*, 86.
167. Ibid. Henry comments, "In some respects this representation glosses nuances that distinguish evangelicals from modernist critics. Evangelicals consider the Gospels not as mere historical chronicle but as a distinct genre that combines history and interpretation; moreover, they lean on inspired Scripture more than on historical research for assurance of past salvific acts. They insist, however, on the historical factuality of the divine redemptive acts, and they are confident that historical research will not disprove the factuality of redemptive history." Ibid.
168. Henry, *gods of this Age or . . . God of the Ages*, 260–261.
169. Ibid.

statements or doctrinal affirmations derive their legitimacy in any way from the mind of God.[170]

Henry continues to note that not all narrative theologians agree on the single meaning of the text (e.g., *sensus unum*), and some assert that the meaning of Scripture is unaffected by the interpreters presuppositions and perspectives.[171] The second point Henry makes about narrative theology is found in his appeal to David Kelsey, who utilizes a narrative approach in order to affirm the *functional* authority of the Bible. Kelsey primarily appeals to the narrative approaches ability to illustrate the Bible's life-transforming function for the life of the church.[172] Henry believes Kelsey's theory of functional authority undermines biblical authority by reducing the Bible's historical accuracy to a secondary category.[173]

Thornbury notes that according to narrative theologians, interpreters should not be concerned with supposed "objective" truth outside of the narrative of Scripture.[174] With this overview in place, the following section will discuss the way Henry analyzes some of the "difficulties of narrative theology" even in its most "conservative forms."[175] Henry offers four objections to narrative theology by championing the battle cry: "Evangelicals dare not ignore the biblical narrative—nor deny its narrative form—but they cannot seek refuge in narrative theology."[176]

Objection 1

Henry's first objection to narrative theology contains two criticisms.[177] His first criticism of narrative theology is that by only affirming the literary phenomena of the Bible, it offers no rational basis to affirm the plurality of genres and historical accuracy of Scripture. Henry asks two poignant questions,

> On what rational basis does narrative theology insist that the biblical narrative reflects a unified theme and orderly

---

170. Thornbury, *Recovering Classic Evangelicalism*, 89.
171. Henry, *gods of this Age or . . . God of the Ages*, 263.
172. Ibid., 264.
173. Ibid.
174. Thornbury, *Recovering Classic Evangelicalism*, 90.
175. Henry, *gods of this Age or . . . God of the Ages*, 264.
176. Ibid., 276.
177. Ibid.

> content? . . . Does narrative theology offer a credible alternative to classic Protestantism's emphasis on intelligible, divine revelation and God's cognitive inspiration of chosen prophets, an emphasis that narrative theologians dilute or subordinate?[178]

Henry claims if all of the Bible must be understood as narrative, then narrative theology cannot account for the non-narrative portions of Scripture. For that reason, narrative theology is unable to reflect a unified theme and order the Bible's genres and non-narrative content. For Henry, any theory unable to account for the unity of the various genres of Scripture, cannot account for the unity of the Bible. Henry distinguishes the classic evangelical position from narrative theology, alluding to the fact that, "Evangelicals insist that authorial intention and grammatico-historical interpretation do not exclude a single divine Author or a single sense that permeates the diverse genres and constitutes an undergirding and overarching unity. They do so, however, on the premise that the Bible is a singularly inspired book."[179] Henry believes the mind of God is the evangelical's rational basis for affirming the unity and diversity of the Scriptures, not the mere presence of narrative.[180]

Henry's second criticism of narrative theology addresses the use of redaction criticism by some narrative theologians. According to Henry, some narrative theologians affirm the validity of historical criticism and redaction criticism, whereas others reject it. Henry appeals to a critique by D. A. Carson in order to show the flaws of accommodating narrative theology to redaction criticism. He claims,

> Donald A. Carson surfaces the flaw in such accommodation. The historical reconstruction of earlier sources is supported on the ground of a literary analysis of biblical documents that supposedly requires diverse contributory sources, whereas the narrative approaches assumes the integrity of the scriptural story. To neglect the later in contending for the former is circular. In Carson's words, 'Any approach that takes the text as a *finished literary product* and analyzes it on that basis calls in question the legitimacy of the claim that layers of tradition can be peeled off the gospel in order to lay bare the history of the community.' In short, if the text is judged to be a comprehensive unity, 'what

---

178. Ibid., 265.
179. Ibid., 266.
180. Ibid.

right do we have to say the same evidences testifies to *dis*unity, seams, disparate sources and the likely?'[181]

Henry believes the way some narrative theologians use redaction criticism to affirm the unity and disunity of the narrative sections and source documents of Scripture, is a form of circular reasoning. This is because at one point in their exegesis narrative theologians appeal to historical sources as events, whereas at other points, they claim these sources and events are irrelevant to theological method. Apparently, Henry believes if he is able to find a logical flaw in an opposing method (e.g., circular reasoning), that epistemological flaw, in turn, discredits the validity of that hermeneutical theory and the theory should no longer be utilized as a valid approach to exegesis. Here is an example *how* Henry uses epistemology to invalidate an incoherent hermeneutical theory and exegetical position.

Objection 2

Henry's second objection to narrative theology is it wrongfully divides faith and reason by claiming biblical history is of a different category of history than actual and factual history (e.g., type of history contemporary historians write). Henry writes,

> The notion that the narrative simply as narrative adequately nurtures faith independently of all objective historical concerns sponsors a split in the relationship to faith and reason and to history that would in principle encourage skepticism and cloud historical referents in obscurity.[182]

According to Henry, narrative theologians wrongly categorize the Scriptural narrative as "realistic-narrative," that has a loose and unsure connection with actual history.[183] Henry believes the error of this "realistic-narrative" approach is some narrative theologians claim the biblical narrative portrays accurate historical data, however, ". . . such data is said to be in no way relevant to a proper understanding of the text."[184]

---

181. Ibid.
182. Ibid., 267.
183. Ibid.
184. Ibid., 269.

In Henry's opinion, one of the consequences of narrative theology is by making a loose connection between the text and the texts original historical referent, narrative theologians subtly undermine the truthfulness of Scripture under the misimpression they are best promoting the authority of the Bible's "final form."[185] In turn, by encouraging this epistemic split between the "realistic-narrative" and factual history, narrative theologians ultimately dilute the factual accuracy of the Bible and reduce inerrancy to a secondary category under the mask of "biblical authority."[186]

In the final analysis, Henry believes narrative theology contradicts Luke's expressed concern to write a historically reliable gospel and Paul's affirmation that the Christian faith is in vain, unless Christ rose factually and historically from the dead. Unsurprisingly, Henry believes narrative theology undermines the Bible's self-testimony to historical accuracy and renders itself vulnerable to the salvific implications of denying certain historical events (e.g., Paul's admonition, "If Christ has not been raised, your faith is futile and you are still in yours sins." 1 Cor. 15:17).

Objection 3

Henry's third objection to narrative theology is it undermines the Bible's transcendent and divine authority. He suggests, "Narrative hermeneutics removes from the interpretive process any text-transcendent referent and clouds the narrative's relationship to a divine reality not exhausted by literary presence."[187] For Henry, narrative theology contradicts Calvin's approach to Scripture, who claims the Bible is distinct not because of its literary aspects, but by the fact that the transcendent God is found speaking to humanity through his revealed propositional Word.[188] In that sense, Henry believes narrative theology runs contrary to the long standing tradition in Protestantism which affirms the transcendent and divine authority of the Scriptures.

Furthermore, Henry claims narrative exegesis is misguided because its primary test for truth, places the literary affirmation of the narrative

---

185. Ibid.
186. Ibid.
187. Ibid., 269.
188. Ibid.

document over and above, any appeal to the divinely revealed propositions found in the Scriptures.[189] He goes on to say,

> Without an Archimedean lever that lifts us above the narrative, one may bask day and night in the literary affirmation of an incarnation that had eyewitnesses and insist that John the beloved would have argued even to a historian that the tomb was empty; yet simply on that basis one would not necessarily rise above the dramatic literary depiction.[190]

Henry claims Rudolf Bultmann illustrates best the effects of this narrative only approach over factual history, who endorses the literary presentation of Christ as a semantic myth; however, he opposes the notion that world history or revelation is able to demonstrate Christ actually rose from the dead. He claims, "It takes more than strenuous assertion to establish the historical factuality and objective truth. Literary concentration on the risen Jesus by itself does not logically entail belief that He is alive and risen, nor does it preclude an identification of the risen Lord as mythical."[191] Consequently, Henry argues that a mere literary approach to Scripture undermines the transcendent divine authority of the text by separating the literary narrative from factual history.

Objection 4

Henry's final objection, while closely resembling his third objection, is narrative theology does not do justice to the inspiration and inerrancy of the Bible.[192] He suggests, "For narrative theology the Scriptures function infallibly in the Christian language game; they are inerrant in the sense that Scripture is received by the Christian community with all confidence that it can never deceive the community or lead it away from the gospel and truth."[193] He goes on to say,

> Narrative theologians reduce biblical historicity and inerrancy to second-order questions; historical reliability is not a basic exegetical premise, nor is biblical inerrancy. Since narrative hermeneutics focus upon the received text, question of what

189. Ibid.
190. Ibid., 270.
191. Ibid.
192. Ibid.
193. Ibid.

lies behind the text—such as its authorship and its historical referentiality—are bracketed. These questions, it is said, are not forefront concerns for the believer living in the biblical world.[194]

Henry believes the *way* narrative theologians' view "inerrancy" does not capture what evangelicals mean when they claim the Scriptures are "inspired by God" and therefore "inerrant in the original autographs." He illustrates his point by elaborating on two errors of the narrative approach or narrative-like approaches. Henry writes,

> If we speak of inerrant verbal inspiration simply in the literary context of narrative theology, we should be aware that Bultmannian scholars can assess the narrative as an 'inerrant' myth whose meaning is anthropological-existential rather than theological.... Robert H. Gundry sponsors the notion that the Gospel of Matthew is inerrantly inspired, yet catalogs much of its content under the literary genre of midrash. The notion that history is not the main biblical interest need not promote a clarification of theological motifs, but it can become a pretext for escaping lucid discussion on the relationship between literary form and historical fact, between genre and historical setting.[195]

Henry concludes that narrative theology offers a hermeneutical theory which affirms the comprehensive authority of Scripture; yet, it does so by ". . . suspending the question of its ontological truth and historical factuality."[196]

Henry's problem with narrative approaches to Scripture is they offer no objective criterion for distinguishing truth from error, fact from fiction, and myth from history.[197] Moreover, they allow for no way to adjudicate between two rivaling schools of narrative exegesis.[198] Each of them presents a viable narrative; but, from the narrative alone, there are no objective criterion to declare one narrative true and the other false. In effect, according to Henry, narrative theology,

> ... eclipses transcendent divine authority and revelatory truth that initially spurred immense interest in scriptural exegesis.... The unresolved dilemma facing narrative theology is

---

194. Ibid., 271.
195. Ibid.
196. Ibid., 275.
197. Ibid.
198. Ibid.

how the method itself, given its divorce from a truly authoritative text, can escape the divergent and contradictory theological claims that its practitioners advance.[199]

His answer is narrative theology cannot escape contradictory claims offered by narrative theologians. At this point, Henry's answer to the question, "Are interpreters of Scripture left to narrative theology?" is—No. Instead, Henry believes the grammatical-historical method of interpretation is superior because it offers evangelicals a way to affirm the full authority of Scripture and present the Bible as *both* a true narrative *and* an historically accurate book.

The Grammatical-Historical Method of Interpretation

Henry is not hesitant or shy to declare, "In brief, evangelical Christianity espouses grammatical-historical interpretation rather than alternatives that attach to the Bible passages exotic meanings that depend upon reader decision."[200] In his chapter titled, "Are We Doomed to Hermeneutical Nihilism?" Henry offers a definition of the grammatical-historical method. He claims,

> In the eighteenth century, however, classical philology refined the techniques of grammatical analysis and through an interest in the biblical past and attention to historical context shed a great deal of light on the biblical narratives. Champions of the historical-critical method in theology and the grammatical-historical method in interpretation emphasized that the verbal sense of the Bible must be ascertained in the same as that of any other book and not by alternative techniques.[201]

Henry notes a proper understanding of the grammatical-historical method of interpretation: (1) Pays special interest to the historical context of the biblical narratives; and (2) Emphasizes the verbal sense of the text by utilizing the techniques of grammatical analysis.[202]

---

199. Ibid.

200. Henry, *GRA*, 4:104. Henry also notes, "The Protestant Reformers strenuously resisted allegorical exegesis that encourages looking beyond the *sensus litteralis* to some obscure meaning to which the text is supposed to point or witness." Ibid., 104–105.

201. Ibid., 4:296.

202. Henry claims, "We must insist that ideally the interpreter shares the objective

Henry's explanation of the grammatical-historical method can be found in volume four of *God, Revelation and Authority*.[203] In his chapter titled, "The Meaning of Inerrancy," Henry has a "Supplementary Note: The Chicago Statement on Biblical Inerrancy."[204] There he endorses the manner in which, *The Chicago Statement on Biblical Inerrancy*, defines and defends the grammatical-historical method of interpretation.[205] Henry offered the closing address at the Summit II Meeting on Hermeneutics, where the purpose of the conference was to explain and defend the grammatical-historical method of interpretation.[206] Not once did Henry critique or renounce the ICBI's definition and use of the grammatical-historical method.[207] Instead, he defended it throughout the totality of his ministry, and his *magnum opus* stands as a six volume testimony to the legitimacy and coherence of the ICBI's definition of the grammatical-historical method of interpretation. Since Henry does not include a section in any of his major works with specific reasons why he believes interpreters should subscribe to the grammatical-historical method, the following section will illustrate and derive some specific reasons why he preferred the grammatical-historical method over other hermeneutical approaches.[208]

The best way to understand Henry's use of the grammatical-historical method is to see *how* he employs the method. After an inductive study of Henry's *use* of the grammatical-historical method, some probable reasons why he preferred the method will be discussed after each section. This section is going to offer three examples of Henry's use of the grammatical-historical method.

The first example is seen in the way he opposes Robert Gundry's use of midrash to undermine the historical factuality of the Gospel of

---

meaning of the inspired biblical writers as expressed in conceptual-verbal form; we must repudiate recent notions of the historicity of understanding as destructive not only of the normativity of any and all communication but as self-destructive." Ibid.

203. Ibid., 4:129, 162, 201, 243. In particular the four chapters titled, "The Meaning of Inspiration," "The Inerrancy of Scripture," "The Meaning of Inerrancy," and "The Meaning of Infallibility."

204. Ibid., 4:211–219.

205. Sproul, *Explaining Inerrancy*, 53.

206. Radmacher and Preus, *Hermeneutics, Inerrancy, & the Bible*, 881–921.

207. The ICBI wrote an official commentary on the Chicago Statement on Biblical Inerrancy. They specifically discussed and defined the grammatico-historical method. See, Sproul, *Explaining Inerrancy*, 53–54.

208. Ibid.

Matthew. Henry warns about Gundry-like approaches in his address at the ICBI Summit II meeting on hermeneutics, suggesting, "We are emerging into an age in which critical scholars increasingly claim the inspiration of the Spirit for their own production of novel critical theories. . . . The Holy Spirit is alleged to inspire scriptural commentary also not only midrash, but even commentaries by modern publishers."[209] Henry opposes the midrash approaches to interpretation because he believes they undermine the literal grammatical sense of Scripture by presenting the book of Matthew as a non-historical narrative.

Henry prefers the grammatical-historical method to Gundry-like approaches because it is able to accept the grammatical sense of Scripture and the factual history of the Bible contrary to Jewish methods of interpretation. With that being said, if remaining consistent with his method, Henry would also reject the popular incorporation by present-day interpreters to include supposed ancient Near Eastern influences on the Scriptures and Semitic interpretations of the Bible (e.g., midrash and pesher). He would also reject the hermeneutical approaches by some biblical scholars who undermine the factual history of the Bible by correlating the genres of Scripture to the non-historical and flexible genres of Greco-Roman literature.[210]

A second example of Henry's use of the grammatical-historical method is seen in his speech at Yale Divinity School titled, "The Doing and Undoing of Theology."[211] Henry opens his address with the statement that, "The proper task of theology is to exposit and elucidate the content of Scripture in an orderly way, and by presenting its teaching as an orderly whole to command and reinforce the worship and service of God."[212] For Henry, the proper means for obtaining the rational and orderly content of Scripture is the grammatical-historical method. He claims any exegesis opposed to the canons of logic or the literal sense of Scripture, necessarily invalidates itself as an appropriate interpretation of the Bible. He believes approaches, such as narrative or neo-orthodox ap-

---

209. Radmacher and Preus, *Hermeneutics, Inerrancy, & the Bible*, 918.

210. Geisler and Roach, *A Response to Methodological Unorthodoxy*, 61–87; Quarles, *Review of Michael R. Licona: The Resurrection of Jesus*, 839–44; Mohler, "The Devil Is In the Details: Biblical Inerrancy and the Licona Controversy." Accessed at: http://www.albertmohler.com/2011/09/14/the-devil-is-in-the-details-biblical-inerrancy-and-the-licona-controversy.

211. Henry, *The Doing and Undoing of Theology*, 245–255.

212. Ibid., 245.

proaches undermine either the rational or propositional aspects of Scripture, by allowing paradoxical and internally contradictory exegetical conclusions.[213] Henry believes these exegetes are in effect, denying the rational structure of the Bible as divine revelation because they are in theory, denying the grammatical-historical method of interpretation.

A third example of Henry's use of the grammatical-historical method is seen in the way he describes the literal sense of Scripture. He responds to the caricatures against evangelical Protestants as "literalists of unimaginative mentality."[214] Henry approvingly states, "As Bernard Ramm writes: 'The 'literal' meaning of a word is the *basic, customary, social designation of that word*. . . . to interpret literally (in the sense) is nothing more or less than to interpret in terms of *normal, usual designation*' (*Protestant Biblical Interpretation*, pp. 90–91)."[215] Henry goes onto claim it is an evangelical rule to follow the natural meaning of Scripture. The proper means to arrive at the natural meaning of a text is the grammatical-historical method of interpretation.[216] He suggests,

> Berkouwer notes that a hidden apologetic motivation is what often underlies declaring the literal text to be offensive and what proffers a fanciful 'deeper' meaning to resolve supposed contradictions and conflicts. . . . Neo-Protestant writers who deplore evangelical literalism often champion a sophisticated kind of allegorical interpretation.[217]

Henry claims some critics of a literal approach to Scripture undermine a literal interpretation by appealing to the conventional nature of language. He does not oppose the conventional use of symbols; although, he opposes a conventionalist theory of meaning.[218] For Henry, ". . . if so-called nonliteralists hold that, *because* of their conventional or symbolic nature, words can convey no literal truth, then their thesis is self-refuting, since if no literal truth can be conveyed because words are symbolic, it is impossible to communicate even *this* literal truth about the nature of truth."[219] Henry illustrates his point appealing to those who use the Bible as a form

---

213. Ibid., 251.
214. Henry, *GRA*, 4:103.
215. Ibid., 4:104.
216. Ibid.
217. Ibid., 4:105.
218. Ibid.
219. Ibid., 4:105–106.

of mythological literature.[220] Some mythologists appeal to Jesus' use of parables to justify a non-literal interpretation of Jonah or the Gospels.[221] Finally, because humanity cannot speak literally about God, Henry believes many non-literalists portray much of the Bible as a collection of metaphors.[222]

As seen in the section discussing Henry's analysis of revelation and myth, he believes mythological (e.g., non-cognitive and non-literal) approaches undermine the clear teaching of Scripture and abuse biblical truths about God. In contradistinction, Henry affirms that theological truth is true in the same sense as all other truth (e.g., true truth); however, contrary to what some of them might claim, evangelicals do not ignore the various literary genres of Scripture.[223] He goes on to note,

> To imply that evangelicals are wooden-headed literalists who cannot distinguish between literary types is a resort to ridicule rather than to reason. No evangelical takes literally what biblical writers explicitly declare to be figurative (cf. Rev. 11:8) or what they portray metaphorically as, for example, the Isaian statement that 'the trees of the field shall clap their hands' (55:12, KJV). In no way does the claim for the literal truth of the biblical revelation mean that prose is the only vehicle of truth or, on the other hand, that truth cannot be conveyed by poetry. That Scripture contains metaphors, similes, parables and verbal techniques such as hyperbole in no way excludes the truth of what the Bible teaches.[224]

Henry opposes individuals he labels as "neo-Protestants," who attempt to reject the literal truth of Scripture on the ground that religious language is by nature, only metaphorical or figurative. He insists evangelicalism has always recognized the presence of figurative language in the Bible.[225] Henry suggests, "Figurative language provides no basis for ignoring the ontological question. Without a literally true ingredient, allegorical language cannot insist on a rationally identifiable object referent. Otherwise symbols would collapse into emotive referents, and this would raise the

---

220. Ibid., 4:106.
221. Ibid.
222. Ibid., 4:107.
223. Ibid., 4:109.
224. Ibid.
225. Ibid., 4:120.

specter of illusions."²²⁶ In brief, for Henry, unless statements about God are literally true, in the sense that they rightly depict what the figurative language is communicating, then it begs the question whether or not God can be known at all.²²⁷

Henry illustrates his point by appealing to the works of James Barr, who opposes classic evangelicals (e.g., like Henry, Geisler, Boice, Schaeffer, Sproul, and so forth) for insisting on the literal interpretation and inerrancy of Scripture. Barr attempts to evade the literal meaning of Scripture claiming the authors of the Bible did not intend a literal meaning. Henry notes that, "Barr alters only the last prong of this argument [about the authors intending a literal meaning]; he insists that the biblical writers usually intend to be taken literally. Yet he holds that when they do thus convey literal meaning they often do not tell the literal truth."²²⁸ However, Henry believes Barr insists evangelicals affirm the literal sense of Scripture, only to preserve the notion of biblical inerrancy.²²⁹ Barr also critiques evangelicals such as Bernard Ramm, who argues for a local instead of a worldwide flood, for being inconsistent with the literal method of interpretation. In Barr's opinion, Ramm affirms a local flood in order to accommodate the Bible to modern scientific research, not from a clear exegesis of the text.

Henry responds to Barr's arguments by suggesting, "Barr's point is nonetheless hermeneutically important, even if it is more appropriately discussed not under the rubric of literalness but under the fallibility of the interpreter."²³⁰ Henry recognizes some evangelicals might be inconsistent with the literal method; however, that is not an argument against the method *per se*, but the *use* or *abuse* of the method. He also notes it was not evangelicalism that first subverted a literal interpretation to modernism, but neo-Protestantism by labeling the miracle claims of Scripture

---

226. Ibid., 4:121.

227. Ibid. Henry claims, "All man needs in order to know God as he truly is, is God's intelligible disclosure and rational concepts that qualify man—on the basis of the *imago Dei*—to comprehend the content of God's logically ordered revelation. Unless mankind has epistemological means adequate for factual truth about God as he truly is, the inevitable outcome of the quest for religious knowledge is equivocation and skepticism." Ibid., 4:119.

228. Ibid.

229. Ibid., 4:122.

230. Ibid.

as legend and myth.[231] Henry suggests the best way to know whether the author intends for the text to be taken literally or figuratively is from the context of the passage. He warns his readers noting,

> Evaluation of an author's intention can, of course, be manipulated by critical presuppositions. . . . Surely writers who use sayings or events for apologetic purposes need not require or presuppose the nonfactuality of those sayings or events. Yet Barr proposes that we take 'very seriously' what is nonfactual, and dignifies this approach as literal interpretation.[232]

Henry believes individuals like Barr attempt to escape the literal method by examining the authors supposed intention, when in reality they repudiate the literal interpretation of the Bible and use authorial intention to gut the Scriptures of their literal meaning.[233] He concludes this new "literal method" used by these neo-evangelicals (e.g., individuals going beyond the tenets of historic or classical evangelicalism), is a result of their disdain for the inspiration of the Scriptures. Furthermore, when they do make use of a "literal" interpretation, they do so upon the premise that the Bible is not historically and factually accurate.

In summary, Henry suggests the real reason those who claim the title "evangelical" deny the grammatical-historical method of interpretation is because a literal interpretation of the Bible is inconsistent with their hermeneutic as epistemology. Henry favors the grammatical-historical method because he believes it upholds the grammatical meaning of the Scripture and the factual accuracy of the Bible.

CONCLUSION

In the final analysis, if Henry were asked the following question: Can evangelical interpreters still affirm propositional theology and proclaim: *Gottes Wort bleibt ewig* (God's Word stands forever)? The research from chapters two through four indicate his answer would be: *ja, natürlich!* (yes, of course!). According to Henry, by understanding the Bible as cognitive-propositional revelation interpreted according to its grammatical-historical sense, Scripture is able to stand forever. This is because God serves as the ontological axiom of all revelation that guarantees the

---

231. Ibid.
232. Ibid., 4:127–128.
233. Ibid., 4:128.

everlastingness of the Scriptural message. Furthermore, due to the objective nature of truth and because the Scriptures contain objective propositional truth, the Bible is able to evade epistemological and hermeneutical nihilism and the so-called "hermeneutical problems," which seem to dominant present-day theories of hermeneutics.

The research from this chapter on Henry's hermeneutics as epistemology indicate he rejects the prevailing concepts and controlling ideas of the so-called hermeneutical problem and spiral. He also affirms a modified form of authorial intention, whereby, the author's intent corresponds to the text, and is known when the grammatical meaning of the text is known. Henry believes presuppositions affect interpretation; however, he does not believe objectivity should be defined as a "presuppositionless methodology." His epistemology accounts for objectivity, but it does not presume to guarantee objectivity in every instance. Objectivity is possible because the mind has direct contact with the world, and the fact that any truth claim may be subject to analysis in terms of first principles of metaphysics and logic. Indeed, the denial of objectivity is self-defeating because it ultimately reduces to a violation of the law of non-contradiction. The possibility of objectivity assures the possibility of adjudicating between truth claims and even between perspectives and worldviews. Finally, according to Henry, the task of the Holy Spirit is to regenerate and illumine the mind, heart, and will of the believer to know and accept God's revelation.

The second section of this chapter focused on Henry's hermeneutics as methodology and analyzed his ten guidelines for historical-critical scholarship. He rejects many of the unbiblical epistemological presuppositions of higher-critics believing their presuppositions create methodological axioms, when consistently applied to Scripture, undermine the historical factuality and inerrancy of Scripture. Henry also rejects the claim that myth, even "truth myth," is a concept that can be reconciled with the classic evangelical doctrine of Scripture. This is because according to Henry, myth is by definition a non-cognitive approach to language and Scripture, whereas the classic evangelical view of Scripture affirms the cognitive status of special revelation. Henry also rejects narrative theology because he believes its emphasis on the "history-likeness" of Scripture undermines the classic evangelical insistence on the factual accuracy and inerrancy of the Bible. Finally, Henry argues for the grammatical-historical method of interpretation because he believes it accounts best for: (a) the historical setting of Scripture; (b) the literal grammatical meaning of the text; (c) the various genres of Scripture; and (d) it does not attempt to reconcile the text of Scripture with Jewish, Greco-Roman, and neo-Protestant methods of hermeneutics that undermine the classic evangelical view of the Bible.

5

Negative Responses to Carl F. H. Henry's Cognitive-Propositional Hermeneutic[1]

INTRODUCTION

HAVING PRESENTED AN OVERVIEW of Henry's analysis of epistemology, language, and hermeneutics; the following chapter will focus on two negative responses to Carl F. H. Henry's "cognitive-propositionalist" hermeneutic.[2] In particular, it will investigate and respond to claims made by Stanley Grenz, John Franke, and Alister McGrath, that Henry's epistemology *per se* is a form of rationalism or foundationalism.[3] All three of these

---

1. In chapter four, the researcher claimed that Henry follows the two fold method of (1) Hermeneutics as epistemology and (2) Hermeneutics as methodology. Henry's cognitive-propositionalism is an example of his hermeneutic as epistemology, whereas the grammatical-historical method is an example of his hermeneutic as methodology. The cognitive-propositional hermeneutic describes Henry's view of epistemology *per se* and the relationship between epistemology and language.

2. This chapter is only going to discuss Henry's hermeneutic as epistemology. The reason it will only discuss Henry's hermeneutic is because the purpose of this book is to explore Henry's epistemology *per se* and his hermeneutic as epistemology. It also discusses his hermeneutics as methodology; however, it is assumed that if Henry's hermeneutics as epistemology is flawed, then his hermeneutic as methodology is flawed too. Second, it is because most of the criticisms are leveled against Henry's cognitive-propositionalism, not his use of the grammatical-historical method.

3. These scholars like Robert Webber use the terms "rationalism" and "foundationalism" interchangeably. In his book, *The Younger Evangelicals*, Webber traces the

scholars critique Henry's view of propositional revelation too. However, Kevin Vanhoozer offers a new critique of Henry's view of cognitive-propositional revelation, and for that reason, his criticisms will be explained in the section titled "cognitive-propositionalism."[4] This chapter will: (1) Present Grenz, Franke, McGrath, and Vanhoozer's charges against Henry's epistemology and cognitive-propositionalism; and (2) It will attempt to analyze and refute the charges that Henry's epistemology *per se* and cognitive-propositionalism is a form of rationalism or foundationalism.

EPISTEMOLOGY PER SE

The first criticism presented against Henry's method comes from postmodern theologians Stanley Grenz and John Franke. Not only do they use postmodernism to criticize Henry's epistemology *per se*, Grenz and Franke also use it to criticize his hermeneutic as epistemology and methodology too. In their book titled, *Beyond Foundationalism*, Grenz and Franke label Henry as a foundationalist.[5] They claim,

> In the mid-twentieth century, the classic Protestant scholastic approach to theology found an able advocate in the renowned evangelical theologian Carl F. H. Henry. Henry asserts that the sole foundation of theology rests on the presupposition that the bible [sic], as the self-disclosure of God, is entirely truthful in

---

historical background of foundationalism to Enlightenment foundationalism. He believes that Henry's epistemology is derived from rationalism and a result of foundationalism (again, terms he uses interchangeably). Webber believes that Henry's cognitive-propositional method illustrates the rationalist method best. He suggests that Henry's insistence on a literal interpretation of Scripture is an overflow of his epistemology and view of propositional revelation. Webber, *The Younger Evangelicals*, 94–98.

4. The reason this section will only investigate the claims that Henry is a modernist and/or rationalist and his view of propositional revelation is because those are the two most pertinent critiques of his view. Others such as R. C. Sproul and John Gerstner have charged Henry with being a fideist; however, this claim applies to his overall apologetic methodology not his hermeneutic as epistemology or methodology. Furthermore, some theologians charge Henry with not being modern enough for not endorsing contemporary forms of biblical exegesis. Many of these critiques label Henry as a modernist who works out that method into his overall hermeneutic approach. However, this is merely another way of labeling Henry as a rationalist.

5. Grenz and Franke, *Beyond Foundationalism*, 7, 14, 61. For a working definition of foundationalism, see, Blackburn, *Oxford Dictionary of Philosophy*, 145.

propositional form. Therefore, the task of theology is simply 'to exhibit the content of biblical revelation as an orderly whole.'[6]

According to Grenz and Franke, Henry's method is in the scholastic theological tradition that understands the Bible primarily as rational and cognitive- propositional revelation.[7] They claim A. A. Hodge and B. B. Warfield are the historic advocates of this rational view of Scripture. Grenz and Franke believe the scholastic approach views the Bible as primarily a storehouse of theological facts with a collection of true statements. Unsurprisingly, Grenz and Franke believe Henry's approach is a recapitulation and a throwback to pre-Enlightenment epistemology and theology. They claim that the hermeneutical methods of scholastic theologians, the Princetonians, and Henry are ultimately based on rationalist epistemologies.[8]

The second criticism against Henry's method comes from Alister McGrath, who affirms a critical-realist epistemology and believes Henry's methodology (e.g., epistemology *per se*, hermeneutic as epistemology, apologetic methodology and so forth) has been influenced by rationalism.[9] McGrath also believes Henry and other American evangelicals, such as John Warwick Montgomery, Francis Schaeffer, and Norman Geisler, have been influenced by Princetonian rationalism continuing the epistemological preconceptions of rationalistic philosophy.[10] McGrath claims Henry is the main representative of this trend. He writes,

> Thus even Carl Henry can offer such hostages to fortune as his affirmation of belief in a 'logically consistent divine revelation.' In the end, Henry risks making an implicit appeal to a more fundamental epistemological foundation in his affirmation of the authority of Scripture, leading to the conclusion that the authority of Scripture itself is derived from a more fundamental

6. Ibid., 14.
7. Ibid., 61.
8. Ibid.
9. McGrath, *A Passion For Truth*, 106. He traces the rationalistic spirit in American evangelicalism through the Princetonian use of "Scottish-realism" or "Common-sense philosophy." The effect has been that American evangelicalism has responded to theologies like neo-orthodoxy and created an apologetic that stresses the informational content of revelation. Ibid., 106. McGrath claims, "The result is that forms of American evangelicalism which have been especially influenced by rationalism, such as that associated with Carl Henry, have laid too much emphasis upon the notion of a purely propositional biblical revelation." Ibid.
10. Ibid., 170.

authority. Thus for Henry, 'without noncontradiction and logical consistency, no knowledge whatever is possible.'[11]

McGrath believes the danger of Henry's approach is it reduces Scripture to a type of "code book." It makes the truth of divine revelation dependent on fallen human reason. McGrath claims evangelicalism cannot allow revelation to be imprisoned by fallen reason. It cannot allow the extra-biblical use of evangelical rationalism to validate or judge the Scriptural witness.[12] McGrath attempts to trace the effects of this type of rationalist approach back to the early church. He believes Tertullian pointed out the danger of this rational method.[13] It seems like McGrath is trying to claim that Henry's use of rationalist ideals renders evangelicalism to affirm heretical positions in order to preserve "logic." This is said in such a way so as to convey the idea that "logic is the supreme authority over divine revelation."[14] However, as will be seen later; McGrath, much like Kevin Vanhoozer, seems to be misreading Henry and possibly reading him in the worst possible light.[15]

"Evangelicalism," according to McGrath, "if it were to follow Henry's lead at this juncture, would set itself on the road that inevitably allows fallen human reason to judge God's revelation, or become its ultimate foundation."[16] McGrath believes evangelicalism cannot go down this road, even if it did at one point and time offer a short-term apologetic advantage within the culture of the Enlightenment worldview. He goes on to say, "Today, evangelicalism is free to avoid the false lure of foundationalism, and to maintain the integrity of divine revelation on its own terms and in its own categories. Let Scripture be Scripture!"[17] McGrath

11. Ibid.

12. Ibid.

13. Ibid., 171.

14. However, what is McGrath's response to the notion of logical consistency and divine revelation? McGrath claims, "If divine revelation appears to be logically inconsistent on occasion (as it undoubtedly does: witness the doctrine of the two natures of Christ), this cannot be taken to mean that the doctrine in question is wrong, or that the doctrine is not divine revelation on account of its 'illogical' character. Rather, this merely illustrates the fact that fallen human reason cannot fully comprehend the majesty of God. This point was made regularly by Christian writers as diverse as Thomas Aquinas and John Calvin." Ibid.

15. Thornbury, *Recovering Classic Evangelicalism*, 107.

16. McGrath, *A Passion For Truth*, 171.

17. Ibid., 172.

returns to Henry, suggesting he has fallen prey to the rationalist ideals characteristic of the Enlightenment. He writes,

> The theological style adopted by Henry also gives the impression of preferring to deal with general principles or 'objective facts' (a characteristic Enlightenment notion) rather than with the historical narrative of revelation. Henry insists, in true Enlightenment fashion, that each and every aspect of the Bible may be reduced to first principles or logical axioms. 'Regardless of the parables, allegories, emotive phrases and rhetorical questions used by these [biblical] writers, their literary devices have a logical point which can be propositionally formulated and is objectively true or false.' Henry adopts an approach which Hans Frei discerned as characteristic of rationalism: the extraction of logical propositional statements from an essentially narrative piece of writing.[18]

McGrath seems to propose that Henry's hermeneutic as epistemology has been taken hostage by Enlightenment philosophy. In turn, his doctrine of divine propositional revelation and hermeneutics as methodology are the logical extensions of these rationalistic ideals.[19]

COGNITIVE-PROPOSITIONALISM

Kevin Vanhoozer, another generally speaking critical-realist, concurs with the claim that Henry affirms the Enlightenment philosophy of A. A. Hodge. In his address to the Evangelical Theological Society, Vanhoozer wrote an article titled, "Lost In Interpretation? Truth, Scripture, and Hermeneutics."[20] In that article, he includes a section titled, "'Mining

---

18. Ibid.
19. Ibid.
20. Vanhoozer, *Lost in Interpretation*, 89–114. Vanhoozer claims, "In the big geopolitical picture, postliberals and evangelicals are allies: postliberals are generously orthodox, trinitarian, and Christocentric. But they are not so sure about us. Hans Frei, for example, worries that Carl Henry is a closet *modernist* because of his commitment to truth as historical factuality. For Frei, it is the biblical narrative itself, not its propositional paraphrase, that is the truth-bearer. Whereas for Henry doctrines state the meaning of the narratives, for Frei we only understand the doctrine by understanding the story. Emergent evangelicals have similar questions about their conservative counterparts. Raschke, for example, says, 'Inerrantism amounts to the rehellenizing of the faith and a retreat from the Reformation.'" Ibid., 99–100.

the deposit of truth': The Hodge-Henry hypothesis."[21] In his book titled, *The Drama of Doctrine,* Vanhoozer claims Henry's type of cognitive-propositionalism characterizes not only Aquinas, but also the scholastic tradition, the Princetonians, and older forms of evangelicalism (e.g., what Thornbury labels as "classic evangelicalism").[22] He goes on to note,

> Carl F. H. Henry's magisterial defense of propositional revelation follows in the same tradition. He defines a proposition as 'a verbal statement that is either true or false.' The Scripture, says Henry, contain a divinely given body of information actually expressed or capable of being expressed in propositions. Those parts of the Bible that are not already in the form of statements may be paraphrased in propositional form. In Henry's words: 'Christian theology is the systematization of the truth-content explicit and implicit in the inspired writings.' In what we may call the Hodge-Henry (H-H) hypothesis, doctrine is the result of biblical induction and deduction, a capsule summary of the meaning of Scripture 'taken as a set of propositional statements, each expressing a divine affirmation, valid always and everywhere.' Propositionalist theology tends to see Scripture in terms of revelation, revelation in terms of conveying information, and theology in terms of divine information-processing.[23]

Vanhoozer represents the H-H hypothesis as a view that portrays language as "*Correspondence as a picture relation.*"[24] That term means the H-H hypothesis is primarily concerned with stating truth, which in turn is a function of describing and representing the world.[25] He critiques the H-H view of language for its similarities to Wittgenstein's picture theory of language. Vanhoozer believes both approaches fail to account for the ways people *use* language, and finally ". . . in seeking propositional restatements of Scripture it [cognitive-propositionalism] implies that there is something inadequate about the Bible's own forms of language and literature."[26] Vanhoozer calls for evangelicalism to move beyond this

---

21. Ibid., 94.

22. Vanhoozer, *The Drama of Doctrine,* 267.

23. Vanhoozer, *Lost In Interpretation,* 95.

24. Ibid.

25. Ibid. Vanhoozer claims, "Meaning here becomes largely a matter of ostensive reference, a matter of indicating objects or statements of affairs. The biblical text is a mirror of nature, history, and even eternity to the extent that I can state universal truths about God's being." Ibid.

26. Ibid., 96.

type of "molecular hermeneutics."[27] He claims that *texts* are not simply bundles of propositions, but new kinds of entities with emergent properties.[28] Vanhoozer's main problem with the H-H hypothesis and the picture theory of meaning is it seems inadequate for *textual* meaning.[29]

Vanhoozer suggests Henry claims those parts of the Bible that are not already in propositional statements, may be summarized in propositional form.[30] He praises Henry for desiring to stress the cognitive content of Scripture; however, Vanhoozer believes his insistence on the complete propositional nature of special revelation does not do justice to the Bible's various genres. Vanhoozer agrees with the claim that Henry advocates a version of the "heresy of propositional paraphrase."[31] He suggests Henry preserved the propositional nature of revelation due to a fear that theologians might utilize theories of interpretation to "neutralize" inerrancy.[32]

Vanhoozer believes the way forward for evangelicalism is not to retreat to propositionalist theology, but to find out the *kind* of truth

27. Ibid.
28. Ibid.
29. Ibid.
30. Vanhoozer claims in the corresponding footnote, "Henry comes close to what literary critics call the 'heresy of propositional paraphrase' when he suggests that the truth expressed in literary forms such as poetry and parable may be expressed in 'declarative propositions' (*God, Revelation and Authority*, 3.463). Even speech acts such as promising and commanding can be 'translated into propositions' (p. 477). Such paraphrases and translations are necessary because 'the primary concern of revelation is the communication of truth' (p. 477)." Ibid., 95, fn. 21.

31. Vanhoozer claims in the corresponding footnote, "Henry comes close to what literary critics call the 'heresy of propositional paraphrase' when he suggests that the truth expressed in literary forms such as poetry and parable may be expressed in 'declarative propositions' (*God, Revelation andAuthority*, 3.463). Even speech acts such as promising and commanding can be 'translated into propositions' (p. 477). Such paraphrases and translations are necessary because 'the primary concern of revelation is the communication of truth' (p. 477)." Vanhoozer, *Lost in Interpretation*, 95, fn. 21.

32. Ibid., 97. Vanhoozer claims, "The Lausanne Covenant (1974) and the Chicago Statement (1978) use similar formulations to define biblical inerrancy, the one saying the Bible is 'without error in all that it affirms,' the other that 'it is true and reliable in all matters it addresses' (Art. XI). Strictly speaking, however, 'it' neither affirms nor addresses; *authors* do. Interestingly, Carl Henry worries that too great a focus on authorial intention detracts from inerrancy, since 'some commentators seem to imply that the biblical writers need not always have intended to teach truth.' for example, does the author of Josh 9:13 intend his statement about the sun standing still to contradict a heliocentric world view? Was Melanchthon right to attack Copernicus for suggesting that it is the earth, not the sun, that moves?" Ibid., 106.

the Bible has and *how* it speaks about truth.³³ Vanhoozer interacts with Henry at this point suggesting,

> Carl Henry was absolutely right to stress the cognitive content of Scripture and doctrine over against those who sought to make revelation a non-cognitive experience. Is it possible, however, that in so focusing on biblical *content* he, and other conservative evangelicals, have overlooked the significance of biblical literary *form*? We shall return to this point below. The immediate point is this: of all theological traditions, evangelicals must respect the nature of the biblical books they interpret. It is no service to the Bible to make a literary-category mistake. At least on this point, I agree with James Barr: 'Genre mistakes cause the *wrong kind of truth values* to be attached to the biblical sentences.' The dialogue between conservative and emergent evangelicals could be helped by a recognition of the cognitive significance of Scripture's literary forms.³⁴

In the end, Vanhoozer believes speech-act-theory offers evangelicals a more theologically robust and coherent corrective to the propositionalist theologies of Hodge and Henry.³⁵

Vanhoozer labels himself as a "modified propositionalist."³⁶ He desires to recognize the cognitive significance not only of statements and

33. Ibid., 100.

34. Ibid. Immediately following these remarks Vanhoozer claims, "To interpret the Bible truly, then, we must do more than string together individual propositions like beads on a string. This takes us only so far as fortune cookie theology, to a practice of breaking open Scripture in order to find the message contained within. What gets *lost* in propositionalist interpretation are the circumstances of the statement, its poetic and affective elements, and even, then, a dimension of its truth. We do less than justice to Scripture if we preach and teach only its propositional content. Information alone is insufficient for spiritual formation. We need to get beyond 'cheap inerrancy,' beyond ascribing accolades to the Bible to understanding what the Bible is actually saying, beyond professing biblical truth to *practicing* it." Ibid.

35. Vanhoozer suggests that speech acts are able to understand better whether or not the authors intended their sentences to be assertive, factual, commanding, etc. Vanhoozer points out that Henry was leery of suggesting that the biblical authors did not always intend to teach truth. Ibid., 107. However, Vanhoozer suggests, "*The cognitive contribution of literary forms: the literary sense is the literal sense.*" Ibid. Vanhoozer interprets this statement to mean, "The Bible proposes things for our consideration not just via individual assertions but in 'many and diverse ways' that derive from its diverse literary forms (as well as from its diverse illocutionary forces, as we have just seen). The form of what Scripture says is not merely incidental to its truth." Ibid.

36. Ibid. See chapter three for Henry's response to Vanhoozer-like approaches that attempt to diminish or deny the plenary cognitive status of divine revelation.

propositions, but of *all* the Bible's figures of speech and literary forms.[37] Vanhoozer believes his approach resists the temptation to "dedramatize—to de-form" the biblical text in order to abstract a revealed truth.[38] He concludes by saying, "My approach to theology—call it 'postconservative'—does not deny the importance of cognitive content, but it does resist privileging a single form—the propositional statement—for expressing it."[39] Vanhoozer calls for a new understanding of biblical inerrancy, where the *literal* sense is understood to be the *literary* sense.[40] He distinguishes his view of inerrancy from the "cheap inerrancy" view of Henry and the Chicago Statements on Biblical Inerrancy and Hermeneutics.[41]

ANALYSIS OF NEGATIVE RESPONSES

Now that Grenz, Franke, McGrath, and Vanhoozer, have been able to level their charges against Henry's method, it is time to evaluate their claims.[42] This second section will respond to their charges by analyzing four areas of Henry's epistemology and cognitive-propositionalist method: (1) It will analyze different views on faith and reason to show that Henry is not a rationalist; (2) It will: (a) analyze the secondary sources defending Henry against the claim that he is a rationalist; (b) explore Henry's self-testimony that he adheres to an Augustinian epistemology vs. a Cartesian form of rationalism, and explain his criticisms of rationalism; (3) It will analyze the claim that Henry is a classic (e.g., Cartesian) foundationalist; and (4) It will analyze the charges leveled against Henry's cognitive-propositionalism.

Faith and Reason

Norman L. Geisler and Paul Feinberg in their book titled, *Introduction to Philosophy*, explain rationalism and how it interacts with different views of faith and reason.[43] In their chapter titled, "The Relationship Between

37. Ibid., 107–108.
38. Ibid., 108.
39. Ibid.
40. Ibid.
41. Ibid., 108–109.
42. These claims come from the scholarly publications listed above.
43. Geisler and Feinberg, *Introduction to Philosophy*, 110.

Faith and Reason," they offer five different solutions to the debate on the relationship between faith and reason.[44] Geisler and Feinberg note, "The solutions to the issue of which method is a reliable source of truth are divisible into five basic categories: (1) revelation only; (2) reason only; (3) reason over revelation; (4) revelation over reason; and (5) revelation and reason."[45] These five solutions offer a paradigm to explain the relationship between rationalism and varying views of faith and reason.

One possible objection against the proposed method for defending Henry against the charge that he is a rationalist is Henry does not use Geisler and Feinberg's categories of faith and reason. While it is true Henry never *explicitly* utilizes Geisler and Feinberg's five categories to discuss faith and reason, however, a thorough reading of his books (especially *Toward a Recovery*), indicate Henry does employ *similar* categories to discuss and analyze faith and reason.[46] With that being said, the following section is going to: (1) Briefly allow Geisler and Feinberg to explain these five categories of faith and reason; and (2) Use Geisler and Feinberg's categories of faith and reason to show that Henry does not affirm a rationalist method or rationalist view of faith and reason; instead, he is Augustinian in his method and approach to faith and reason.

Geisler and Feinberg list Sören Kierkegaard as the main advocate of the "revelation only" approach. They claim, "According to Sören Kierkegaard (1813–1855), the father of modern existentialism, the human is wholly incapable of discovering any divine truth."[47] Karl Barth is the

---

44. Ibid., 255.

45. Ibid.

46. Henry, *Toward A Recovery*. For example: (1) Revelation only, Henry claims, "More properly labeled as fideists are Soren Kirkegaard and certain neo-orthodox theologians who dismiss public reason and rational tests as irrelevant to religious truth claims." (Ibid., 39); (2) Reason only, Henry claims, "The negative impulse of the Enlightenment aimed to promote human reason by stifling supernatural revelation" (Ibid., 70). (3) Reason over revelation, Henry claims, "But the Enlightenment managed to suffocate both reason and revelation, instead of recognizing that reason is the ally and not the enemy of divine revelation" (Ibid.); (4) Revelation over reason, Henry claims, ". . . but equally much with the so-called Tertullian formula *credo quia absurdum* ('I believe what is absurd'). The modern neo-orthodox revival of Tertullian's slogan was not unrelated to existentialist insistence on the ultimate absurdity of the world, a notion that is neither biblical nor evangelical." (Ibid., 40); (5) Revelation and reason, Henry claims," One must contrast the Augustinian formula *credo ut intellegam* ('I believe in order to understand') not only with Thomas Aquinas's formula ('I understand in order to believe') . . ." (Ibid).

47. Geisler and Feinberg, *Introduction to Philosophy*, 256.

second example of the "revelation only" approach, who like Kierkegaard, argues that God is "Wholly Other" and can be known only by divine revelation.[48] The second view they list is the "reason only" approach. They list Immanuel Kant and Benedict Spinoza as the main advocates of this view. These two philosophers did not believe anything about God was known by revelation; instead, only reason is the final test for religious truth. Geisler and Feinberg note that Kant went so far as to claim agnosticism about the knowledge of God. Geisler and Feinberg list the Alexandrian Fathers and Modern Higher Criticism as advocates of the "reason over revelation" approach. For example, they claim, "Justin Martyr believed in divine revelation, but in addition to the Bible he held that 'reason is implanted in every race of man.' In view of this he held that those among the ancient Greeks who 'lived reasonably are Christians, even though they have been thought atheists.' This included men such as Heraclitus and Socrates."[49]

The fourth view is the "revelation over reason" approach. They list Tertullian and Cornelius Van Til as the two main advocates of this method.[50] Geisler and Feinberg claim,

> Perhaps the best example among contemporary evangelical thinkers of one who exalts revelation over reason is the Reformed theologian and apologist, Cornelius Van Til (b. 1895). His view is often called *presuppositionalism* because it strongly stresses the need to 'presuppose' the truth of revelation in order for reason to function. For if there were no God—who created and sustains the very laws and processes of reason, then thinking itself would be impossible. Reason, for Van Til, is radically and actually dependent on revelation.[51]

The final view Geisler and Feinberg list is the "revelation and reason" approach. They claim Saint Augustine and Thomas Aquinas are the main advocates of this method. Geisler and Feinberg note that Augustine attempts to reason about, within, and for revelation; but never against it.[52]

With these categories in place, it helps to set the stage for a discussion of the charge that Henry is a rationalist. It seems like the charges

---

48. Ibid., 258.
49. Ibid., 261.
50. Ibid., 262–263.
51. Ibid., 263.
52. Ibid., 265.

labeled against Henry claim he is advocating for either the "reason only" or "reason over revelation" approaches. However, there is no warrant for this claim in any of Henry's writings.[53] Moreover, just because Henry labels himself as a presuppositionalist and argues for a deductive method, does not entail that he is a rationalist. It should be noted that in chapter two on Henry's epistemology the second principle of his approach is, "Human reason is a divinely fashioned instrument for recognizing truth; it is not a creative source for truth."[54] Rationalist approaches on the other hand argue that reason is the creative source for truth, even determining the validity of divine revelation.[55] Henry dismisses the claim that an appeal to rationale and use of the laws of logic is a form of rationalistic philosophy.[56] He criticizes rationalism, claiming, "What is objectionable about rationalism is not reason, however, but human reasoning deployed into the service of premises that flow from arbitrary and mistaken postulations about reality and truth."[57]

---

53. Geisler and Feinberg note that a rationalist approach seeks justification in reason alone. Methodologically, rationalists operate from a certain starting point and deduce all other truths about reality. Furthermore, in the five different views of faith and reason, it is becomes apparent that the "reason only" and "reason over revelation" approaches were the only two that seem to meet the rationalist definition and methodological criteria. These approaches either downplayed or degraded the role of revelation in light of the authority of reason. The "revelation over reason" approach of Cornelius Van Til seems to operate according to a rationalist methodology, in that it allows for a certain starting point, and it allows for a deductive method. However, it does not meet the rationalist definition because it does not claim that reason is superior or degrades revelation; instead, revelation is superior and even degrades fallen human reason. The "revelation and reason" approach still allows for certain starting points and a deductive method. It allows for humanity to base their knowledge as the starting point of revelation and in rational categories. Human thinking is able to make inferences to the nature of God, and deductions from the nature of truth to the existence of God. However, reason does not trump revelation, and revelation does not override reason. Geisler and Feinberg suggest, "'Revelation and reason' . . . properly assigns a role to each and shows their interrelationship. One should reason about and for revelation, otherwise he has an unreasonable faith. Likewise, reason has no guide without a revelation and flounders in error." Ibid., 270.

54. Henry, GRA, 2:223. He emphatically favors the necessity of rationale within a Christian worldview. Henry's insists on rationale to the point in which he claims, "The Christian faith emphasizes that one has nothing to gain and everything to lose by opposing or downgrading rationality." Ibid., 2:225

55. Ibid.
56. Ibid., 2:226.
57. Ibid.

Henry neither resembles the definition of the rationalist method, nor does his method come to the same conclusions of Kant and Spinoza or the Alexandrian Fathers and Higher Critics (e.g., the two examples listed by Geisler and Feinberg of the "reason only" and "reason over revelation" approaches).[58] Henry's method may utilize a deductive approach; however, it is grounded within a revelational theistic framework, in which the two axioms are the existence of God and the Bible as the starting points of all theology. If anything, Henry's method has a different starting point because it does not allow for reason to override revelation, however, it does not allow for revelation to override reason. Instead, his method argues for the compatibility of faith and reason. In the end, much like his epistemological forefather in the faith; Henry, like Augustine, develops a method in which faith utilizes and harmoniously employs reason, not one in which reason is the creative source for all truth.

Rationalism and Augustinianism

G. Wright Doyle has an entire chapter in his book responding to the charge that Henry is a rationalist.[59] He alludes to M. J. Ovey, who claims that "rationalism" still carries many negative overtones in many communities. Doyle distinguishes between rationalism and a commitment to being rational, with the latter being the process of providing reasons for ones beliefs and a commitment to the validity of the laws of logic.[60] He suggests some scholars understand rationalism to be a view claiming that human reason is the supreme and only means of arriving at truth, divine truth included. Furthermore, they understand rationalism to be a sterile, passionless, anti-supernatural method, contrary to Christian theism and the Bible as divine revelation.[61] Doyle claims, "When Henry's opponents brand his theological method as 'rationalism,' they score a rhetorical victory without really having to substantiate their charge."[62] He believes

---

58. Ibid.

59. He cites C. Stephen Evans, who claims, "Rationalism has been defined as a 'conviction that reason provides the best or even the only path to truth. . . . In theology the term rationalism often designates a position that subordinates revelation to human reason or rules out revelation as a source of knowledge altogether.'" Doyle, *Carl Henry*, 107. Evans, "Approaches to Christian Apologetics," 98–99.

60. Doyle, *Carl Henry*, 108.

61. Ibid., 108–109.

62. Ibid., 109.

if Henry's critics can merely associate his approach with a "rationalist" method, they have already won the rhetorical battle. Doyle offers three reasons why Henry is not a rationalist:

> 1. *Carl Henry's thought does not fit in any sense the standard definitions of rationalism given above.* That is, he does not believe that reason alone can ascertain ultimate truth; he does not give reason priority over God's revelation in the Bible; he does not believe that rational evidence alone will persuade anyone to believe in Christ.... 2. *Some of the charges of a sort of 'Christian rationalism' leveled against Henry by fellow Christians seem to be based either on ignorance of misunderstanding.* Even a cursory reading of *God, Revelation and Authority* will show they lack foundation. 3. *It seems to me that accusations that Henry is a 'rationalist' sometimes proceed from premises that are false or internally contradictory.*[63]

Doyle goes on to explain his second objection by appealing to the fact that in Henry's section titled, "Four Ways of Knowing," he critiques the rationalist method. Henry's criticism of the rationalist method is not to say that he did not validate a *type* of rational intuition. Doyle explains,

> Still, there is a kind of 'rational intuitionism' held by Augustine, Calvin, and others, including Henry, which believes that 'human beings know certain propositions immediately to be true, without resort to inference.' These would include the existence of God and the sense of right and wrong, the awareness of self, the laws of logic, and truths of mathematics. According to this view, the categories of thought are aptitudes for thought implanted by the Creator and synchronized with the whole of created reality.[64]

Doyle is correct when he insists that Henry's method is not derived from modern rationalism; instead, Revelational Theism finds its origin in Augustine's theory of knowledge. Doyle stresses that Henry's method is not a rationalistic approach because human reasoning is not the only reliable and valid source of knowledge. Revelation is the only reliable and valid source of knowledge, and human reason is fashioned to recognize God's revelation.[65]

---

63. Ibid., 109–110.

64. Ibid., 111.

65. Henry's Revelational Theistic epistemology insists that the Logos of God is both the creator and sustainer of reality. The Logos is both the salvific and epistemological

Chapter two discusses *how* Henry argues for a Revelational Theistic epistemology (e.g., Augustinian) by incorporating its views of reason and revelation. Furthermore, it notes where Henry argues against rationalism; however, a few points need to be made to distinguish Henry's epistemology from rationalism. First, Henry makes a distinction between the use of reason and rationalism. According to Henry, reason simply refers to "... man's intellect, mind or cognitive powers."[66] Furthermore, when discussing the relationship between reason and revelation, he claims,

> Divine revelation is the source of all truth, the truth of Christianity included; reason is the instrument for recognizing it; Scripture is its verifying principle; logical consistency is a negative test for truth and coherence a subordinate test. The task of Christian theology is to exhibit the content of biblical revelation as an orderly whole.[67]

In this quote, Henry makes the distinction between, "Divine revelation is the source of all truth" and "reason is the instrument for recognizing it [truth]." This distinction between the source of truth and the instrument for recognizing truth distinguishes Henry from rationalism.[68] Furthermore, Henry notes that this distinction between revelation and his use of reason distinguishes Revelational Theism from rationalism. He claims, "The rationalistic approach subordinates the truth of revelation to its own alternatives and has speculated itself into exhaustion. If we are again to speak confidently of metaphysical realities, the critically decisive issue is on what basis—human postulation or divine revelation?"[69] In brief, Henry favors Revelational Theism (e.g., Augustinianism) over and above rationalism.

---

mediator, who reveals Himself in creation and in Scripture. Doyle claims that Henry utilizes a deductive method; however, the purpose is to demonstrate that humanity is able to make legitimate inferences. The starting point of theology is the Bible, not human reason. Our knowledge of God does not arise from human speculation, but from divinely revealed truths. Finally, Doyle notes that Henry recognizes the necessity of the Holy Spirit to illumine the mind of believers, enabling them to understand and believe what they have learned. In these respects, Doyle is correct in his assessment that Henry is not a rationalist. Instead, Henry, like Augustine and Calvin, utilizes reason in accordance with revelation.

66. Ibid., 1:225–226.
67. Henry, *GRA*, 1:215.
68. Ibid.
69. Ibid., 1:95.

The following quote by Henry illustrates *why* he favors a revelational approach. Henry claims, "The revelational alternative can lift the philosophical enterprise once again above theories that are essentially irrational, and can restore reason to indispensable importance, without abetting rationalism; it can overcome the current addition to the nonobjectivity of knowledge . . ."[70] Considering these types of comments from Henry, it is evident he favors a revelational approach to epistemology because it grounds knowledge in God (e.g., ontological axiom) and Scripture (e.g., epistemological axiom), over and against speculative philosophical approaches grounded in the non-God (e.g., their ontological axiom) and the postulations of human reason (e.g., their epistemological axiom).

A second distinction between Henry's method and rationalism is found in volume one, chapter four of *God, Revelation and Authority*, titled, "The Ways of Knowing."[71] There he correlates rationalism with Descartes and criticizes the rationalist (e.g., Cartesian) method. However, in chapter nineteen Henry includes a chapter titled "The Philosophical Transcendent A Priori (II)." In that chapter, Henry offers some of his most explicit criticisms of rationalism, especially Cartesian rationalism, which are: (1) Rationalism offers a wholly philosophical approach to epistemology (whereas Henry believed in a revelational approach to epistemology);[72] (2) Rationalism falsely makes human reason the starting point for epistemic investigation (whereas Henry made God, his ontological axiom, and the Bible, his epistemological axiom, the starting points for epistemic investigation);[73] (3) Henry distinguishes Descartes's view from Augustine's. Henry claims,

> Augustine had not only recognized God as the source of all being and true knowledge, but viewed all knowledge also as in some sense the revelation of the one ultimate Spirit to created spirits. Descartes's philosophy develops quite out of touch with this revelational setting. As speculative, his near-pantheistic schema is, of course, projected as an alternative to the revelational theism which Christianity grounds in principle of supernatural disclosure. In Descartes's approach, with its emphasis on

---

70. Ibid.
71. Ibid., 1:70–95.
72. Ibid., 1:302.
73. Ibid.

human initiative, one finds little to suggest any direct interest in divine revelation, whether particular or universal.[74]

In summary, the research indicates that Henry distinguishes his Revelational Theistic epistemology from rationalism; however, contrary to the claims of his critics, Henry's distinction is not a distinction without a difference.

The differences between Henry's epistemology and rationalism boil down to differences on the following points: (a) the definition of reason and the relationship between reason and revelation; (b) the primacy of revelation in the epistemological process; (c) the priority of the divine vs. the human initiative in the knowing process. The final reason Henry should not be considered a rationalist is because according to his own self-testimony he claims to follow a form of Revelational Theism in the Augustinian tradition, not a version of Cartesian rationalism.

Foundationalism

The second charge against Henry's epistemology claims his method endorses a version of strong foundationalism.[75] In particular, this section is going to use Chad Brand's article titled, *Is Carl Henry a Modernist?*, in order to analyze and respond to the claim that Henry is a strong foundationalist.[76] The analysis of Brand's article will address: (1) Brand's distinction between strong (e.g., classic) foundationalism and soft (e.g., fallibilist) foundationalism; and (2) Brand's claim that Henry affirms a form of soft (e.g., fallibilist) foundationalism to overcome the charge that Henry is a strong (e.g., classic) foundationalist.[77]

Brand addresses the question, "Is Henry a foundationalist?" by claiming, "If one means by 'foundationalist,' the search for Cartesian certainty through the discovery of indubitable and noninferrential truth claims arrived at through reason or reflection, then the answer is a resounding, 'no.'"[78] Brand goes on to claim,

---

74. Ibid., 1:303.
75. Audi, *Epistemology*, 216.
76. Brand, *Is Carl Henry a Modernist?*, 44–60.
77. Ibid., 52–53.
78. Ibid., 52.

> It might be correct, on the other hand, to call Henry a scriptural foundationalist, a term used by Nancey Murphy in her discussion of Donald Bloesch. Henry is clearly a biblical foundationlist in that his entire edifice is founded upon a rock-ribbed conviction that the Bible is to be trusted, while all philosophical systems are suspect, even Platonism, Aristotelianism and, certainly, Cartesianism.[79]

Brand admits he pushes the description of Henry's foundationalism a bit further to include the notion of "biblical foundationalism."[80] The reason he labels Henry a "biblical foundationalist," is because Brand believes Henry must affirm a form of foundationalism in order to preserve his commitment to the inerrancy of Scripture and adherence to the law of non-contradiction.[81] Still, even by labeling Henry a "biblical foundationalist," Brand believes this label distinguishes Henry from the charges he is a "strong foundationalist."

In order to maintain the claim that Henry is not a strong foundationalist, Brand appeals to Robert Audi and makes the following point. He writes, "Robert Audi has recently argued that foundationalism is not the great Satan of contemporary thought, but rather, that a certain form of foundationalism is virtually required of anyone who does not wish to fall into pure subjectivism and relativism."[82] Brand goes on to say, "A commitment to foundationalism, then does not necessarily imply a commitment to indubitable and noninferential truths. There is, for instance, such a thing as fallibilist foundationalism."[83] At this point, Brand seems to claim there are at least three types of foundationalism: (1) strong foundationalism; (2) fallibilist foundationalism; and (3) biblical foundationalism. Apparently Brand believes by making these kinds of distinctions between these three views, he can overcome the charge that Henry is a strong foundationalist.

Brand believes these types of distinctions are able to free Henry's epistemology from the charges that it is a version of strong foundationalism because: (a) there are different types of foundationalism; and (b) it is a rhetorical device to label Henry as a foundationalist (insisting that he is a strong foundationalist) because of the negative overtones associated

79. Ibid., 52–53.
80. Ibid., 53.
81. Ibid.
82. Ibid.
83. Ibid.

with strong foundationalism.[84] With these two points in mind, Brand suggests that contemporary scholars should not oppose all types of foundationalism; instead, they should only oppose Cartesian foundationalism because of its criterion for indubitable and noninferrential truths. He also believes soft foundationalism (or as he labels it "fallibilist foundationalism") is able to overcome the charges to strong (e.g., Cartesian) foundationalism. With these distinctions in place, Brand claims,

> While Henry certainly believes the truths of Scripture are indubitable, he recognizes that human knowledge is always subject to error and revision. In regards to Scripture, Henry is certainly a firm, biblical foundationalist; in regards to the outworking of the theological implications of biblical asseverations, it appears that Henry is a soft foundationalist, one who is willing to admit that all our claims to understand are subject to the eternal bar of God's judgment.[85]

With Brand's categories clearly laid out on the table, a few comments in response to his points are necessary in order to continue the dialogues about Henry's epistemology.

First, Brand correctly notes that Henry opposes rationalism, especially Cartesian rationalism. In that sense, Brand and Doyle seem to be in agreement over their assessment of Henry's approach to rationalism. However, one of the difficulties with Brand's assessment is he discusses Henry's epistemology in categories Henry never explicitly used. One would be hard pressed to find in any of Henry's literature a discussion on the distinctions between different types of foundationalism (e.g., strong, soft, fallibilist, biblical, and so forth). The present researcher believes one reason is because classic evangelicalism seems to discuss theories of knowledge in different categories than contemporary forms of evangelicalism. For that reason, there are times when classic evangelicals and present-day evangelicals are sometimes two ships passing in the night. For example, classical evangelicals seem to use the terms relativism and subjectivism interchangeably; whereas some present-day evangelical approaches make a distinction between them. In addition, many present-day evangelicals seem to have different categories for discussing

---

84. Ibid.
85. Ibid.

epistemology (e.g., strong foundationalism, soft foundationalism, and so forth), than classic evangelicals.[86]

Nonetheless, just because Henry does not utilize the same language and categories of thought does not mean Brand and subsequent philosophers cannot place Henry into these epistemic categories.[87] In fact, the distinction Brand makes between strong (e.g., Cartesian) and soft (e.g., fallibilist) foundationalism rightly captures one aspect of Henry's epistemology *per se* and hermeneutic as epistemology. This is because Henry claims human knowledge is subject to error and revision; however, unlike subjectivist approaches to knowledge, he does not believe subjectivity undermines the objective nature of divine revelation or the universal laws of logic.[88] That being said, Brand's distinction between strong and soft foundationalist is a category used by contemporary epistemologists and it seems to rightly vindicate Henry from the charge of being a strong foundationalist. In that respect, Henry's epistemology is markedly different than strong foundationalist epistemologies because his epistemology, like that of soft foundationalism, includes criteria to account for error and revision (unlike strong foundationalism).

The second distinction Brand makes is one between strong foundationalism and biblical foundationalism. While Brand does not offer an explicit definition of the term "biblical foundationalism," he does suggest it entails that the Bible is to be trusted over and above all philosophical systems. Brand's labeling of Henry as a "biblical foundationalist," while not a term used by Henry about his own method, seems to grasp one of the key points of Henry's epistemology; namely, his belief that the Bible is the epistemological axiom for all knowledge. This entails: (a) epistemologists should not allow nonbiblical (e.g., alien categories) categories to

86. This comment on the different categories for discussing epistemology and the language used in that conversation could be a book in and of itself. The justification comes from personal experience and observation. In my experience, in my experience many classic evangelicals (e.g., Norman L. Geisler, Carl F. H. Henry, R. C. Sproul, J. I. Packer) use a historical approach to epistemology. For example, they study Augustinianism, Thomism, Hume, and Kantianism as such; however, they do not discuss these figures in terms of foundationalism, warrant, justification and so forth. Whereas many present-day evangelicals will read those same figures, but use different categories and language in their conversations.

87. In fact, in many respects academic disciplines attempt to explain previous theories through the lenses of present day approaches, categories, and methods.

88. This claim will be further discussed in chapter six on Henry's analysis of critical realism. In particular, it will discuss Henry's analysis of Bernard Lonergan and Alister McGrath's use of critical realism and theological method.

frame the conversations and categories of epistemological dialogues and conclusions; (b) epistemologists should use the Bible to frame the conversations and categories of epistemological dialogue and conclusions; (c) all theological doctrine should find their origin in Scripture, not in the non-God (e.g., ontological axioms contrary to Christian theism) or in speculative human reason (e.g., non-biblical theories of knowledge or secular epistemological axioms).[89]

In the final analysis, the present researcher believes Brand's distinction between strong foundationalism and soft foundationalism (e.g., fallibilist foundationalism), seems to be a good way to distinguish Henry's epistemology from the charge that he is a strong foundationalist. In Brand's opinion, the key distinction is that strong foundationalism requires indubitability and certainty, whereas Henry's epistemology allows for fallibility and error. The second thing to notice is Brand's analysis rightly captures the fact that Henry is a type of foundationalist, namely a soft foundationalist and biblical foundationalist. Henry believes there are certain unproven truths that ground other truth claims, and that valid inferences from those foundational truth claims provide certain conclusions; however, those truths find their origin in Scripture, not speculative human reason. In these respects and with Brand's categories in place, Brand's distinctions seem to provide a way to overcome the charges made by Grenz, Franke, and McGrath that Henry is a foundationalist (e.g., strong foundationalist).

Cognitive-Propositionalism

After considering the works of Vanhoozer, three characteristics can be identified to summarize his criticisms of Henry's view of language. First, Vanhoozer suggests that Henry's method resembles Wittgenstein's picture theory of meaning. He believes the failure of referential approaches to meaning is that language does more than refer. Second, Vanhoozer claims Henry's approach downplays or diminishes the various genres of Scripture. Third, Vanhoozer believes Henry's epistemology and religious language cannot account for the different *types* of truth. Each of these criticisms have been addressed in chapters two and three. However, a few comments will suffice to indicate *why* Vanhoozer's charges are

---

89. See chapter two.

actually misrepresentations of Henry's hermeneutic as epistemology and methodology.

Vanhoozer's first criticism is that Henry's philosophy of language resembles referential theories of meaning. However, Vanhoozer appears to misunderstand the nature of truth as correspondence to reality. He seems to have been misled by Wittgenstein's criticism that correspondence is the "picture" theory wherein a statement corresponds to the facts if it mirrors them. But this is not what "correspondence" means. Correspondence means a statement (or expression) must *match* reality, not necessarily *mirror* it. It must correctly *reflect* reality, but not necessarily *resemble* it. It must properly *represent* reality, not *reproduce* it. A statement corresponds to reality when it correctly signifies, conforms to, or agrees with reality, not when it is a mirror image of it.[90]

Vanhoozer's second criticism is that Henry's cognitive-propositional method downplays or diminishes the various genres of Scripture is inaccurate. Thornbury claims, "As is the case with other figures in the critical reception of Henry, Vanhoozer reads Henry in the worst possible light, namely, that Henry claims no more than one way to read a text of Scripture."[91] Paul Helm also recognizes that Vanhoozer has characterized and misrepresented the H-H hypothesis on genre and propositional truth.[92] Henry's emphasis on propositional revelation should not be seen as downgrading or diluting the various genres of Scripture. In chapter three of the present research, Henry is quoted saying,

> By its emphasis that divine revelation is propositional, Christian theology in no way denies that the Bible conveys its message in many literary forms such as letters, poetry and parable, prophecy and history. What it stresses, rather, is that the truth conveyed by God through these various forms has conceptual adequacy, and that in all cases the literary teaching is part of a divinely inspired message that conveys the truth of divine revelation. Propositional disclosure is not limited to nor does it require only one particular literary genre. And of course the expression of truth in other forms than the customary prose does not preclude expressing that truth in declarative propositions.[93]

90. Geisler and Roach, *Defending Inerrancy*, 139.

91. Thornbury, *Recovering Classic Evangelicalism*, 103.

92. See Paul Helm, "Vanhoozer's Remythologizing Theology," Helm's Deep, entry posted May 1, 2010, http://paulhelmsdeep.blogspot.com/search?.q=Remythologizing+Theology. Helm, *Faith, Form, and Fashion*.

93. Henry, *GRA*, 3:463.

A straight forward reading of Henry's *God, Revelation and Authority*, reveals he affirms the Bible's various uses of genre. One of the key points of difference between Henry and Vanhoozer centers on the nature and purpose of genre. Vanhoozer believes propositional theology downplays the Bible's various genres. Whereas, Henry believes propositional theology affirms the Bible's various genres. Vanhoozer appears to suggest that genre determines meaning. In this sense, genre criticism operates as the best way to understand the *way* the various writers of Scripture are communicating the different *types* of truth. Henry, on the other hand, claims genre does not determine meaning; instead, it enhances meaning and magnifies truth.

Vanhoozer's third charge is Henry's view of epistemology and religious language cannot account for the different *types* of truth. Chapter two demonstrates that for Henry, because all of humanity equally bears the image of God, each individual has the same rational faculties. The continuity of rationale in humanity entails there are not different *types* of truth. There is only *one* truth and logic in all of humanity. Chapter three establishes how Henry taught that the plurality of genres in Scripture are each capable of grasping and communicating this *one* truth in a *variety* of literary forms.[94] Just like different cultures throughout the world do not create different minds, so too, the different genres of Scripture do not create different kinds of rationale and truth.[95]

As chapter two argues, Henry affirms a correspondence view of truth (e.g., where correspondence takes ontological priority over a coherence test for truth; however, coherence is a subtest for truth).[96] All views of truth have an inherent correspondence to reality, because the proponents believe their view corresponds to reality.[97] Most basic of all is the fact that the correspondence view of truth is literally undeniable for the very denial of it purports to correspond to reality. Without a correspondence view of truth, there is no basis for knowing an error (e.g., there is nothing in reality to which the claim must be made to correspond). Almost any-

---

94. This aspect of Henry's language theory was explained in chapter three under the sections titled, "The Logic of Religious Language," "Linguistic Analysis and Propositional Truth," and "The Bible as Propositional Revelation."

95. See the section in chapter three titled, "The Bible as Propositional Revelation." Also, the section in chapter four titled, "The Grammatical-Historical Method of Interpretation."

96. See chapter two.

97. Geisler and Roach, *Defending Inerrancy*, 139.

thing could be true if one starts redefining the nature of truth claiming there are different *types* of truth (e.g., personal vs. correspondence). It is a misnomer to speak of "relational" or "personal" truth. There are truths about relationships and truths about persons in Scripture, but truth itself is not relational or personal. Truth is propositional, that is, it makes a statement that affirms or denies something about reality. Norman Geisler and I in our book, *Defending Inerrancy*, claim,

> . . . Vanhoozer's own description [of epistemology and propositional revelation] admits, he is diminishing much of the history of Christianity from the first century to our time. Even he acknowledges that 'for large swaths of the Western tradition, the task of theology consisted in mining propositional nuggets from the biblical deposit of truth' (LI? 94). He admits that the roots of this go back to the New Testament where 'the Pauline shaft in particular was thought to contain several rich doctrinal lodes' (94). He also correctly observes that this carried into the Middle Ages. He wrote: 'According to Thomas Aquinas, Scripture contains the science of God: the unified teaching from God about God. . . . doctrine is essentially sacred teaching, a divinely revealed informative proposition about an objective reality' (94). Following this, in '19th-century Princeton, A. A. Hodge and B. B. Warfield laid the groundwork for conservative evangelical theology by insisting on the importance of propositional truth' (94). In short, Vanhoozer's view is against the mainstream of Christianity for the last two thousand years!⁹⁸

Henry's revelational hermeneutic defends the traditional view of truth. The Bible calls for Christians to use reason (Isa. 1:18: 1 Pet. 3:15). Indeed, the use of the mind is part of the great commandment, which includes loving God with both the "mind" as well as the "heart" (Matt. 22:37). Surely Vanhoozer does not want to remove the laws of logic from the task of thinking. The apostle Paul admonishes for Christians to "avoid . . . contradictions" (1 Tim. 6:20). Even the Westminster Confession of Faith (which is a classic confession in Vanhoozer's Reformed tradition) encourages the use of logic in theology and speaks of "the whole counsel of God . . . either expressly set down in Scripture, *or by good and necessary consequence may be deduced from Scripture*."⁹⁹ Using logic to deduce truths from Scripture (which is the basis of these truths) is

---

98. Ibid., 141.
99. Schaff, *Creeds of Christendom*, 3:603, Emphasis added.

not basing truths on logic. Logic is only the rational instrument (coming from a rational God and inherent in the rational creatures made in his image) that enables humanity to discover certain truths that are implied in Scripture.

CONCLUSION

The research from this chapter indicates that the claim "Henry is a rationalist" is misguided because he neither meets the standard definition of a rationalist nor does he employ a rationalist method. Instead, Henry affirms an Augustinian epistemology and presuppositional methodology. Furthermore, the charges by Kevin Vanhoozer are a misrepresentation of Henry's actual position. Henry does not meet the criterion for affirming early Wittgenstein's theory of referential meaning. Moreover, instead of diminishing the Bible's various genres, Henry affirms that each one of them is important and essential for a proper exegesis of Scripture. And lastly, Henry believes there is a single type of truth given by God which is displayed in both general and special revelation. The final chapter of this book will attempt to incorporate Henry's analysis of hermeneutics as epistemology and methodology into the current conversations in hermeneutics.

6

Carl F. H. Henry's Revelational Hermeneutic in the Current Conversation

INTRODUCTION

IF HISTORIC CHRISTIANITY IS again to compete as a vital world identity, evangelicalism must project a solution for the most pressing problems in epistemology. Given the growing public nature of epistemology, and the unique challenge it poses for hermeneutics, the need is for evangelicals to frame their hermeneutic with the pressing challenges of epistemology in mind. Now is the time for Christian theologians to put their best foot forward by outflanking competing hermeneutics at their philosophical core, and replace them with biblically based first principles.

The vital issue at stake involves a choice between critical hermeneutics and the historical-grammatical method of interpretation. In many evangelical and non-evangelical divinity schools, a critical approach to hermeneutics prevails that is remarkably naïve to its hidden presuppositions about biblical interpretation. By leaping over any sustained discussion over its own assumptions, such schools of thought attempt to claim their methods and philosophical axioms are in alignment with the Protestant Reformers and classic evangelicalism.[1] But if anything should

1. Geisler and Roach, *Defending Inerrancy*. Examples include: Clark Pinnock, Bart Ehrman, Peter Enns, Kenton Sparks, Kevin Vanhoozer, Andrew McGowan, Stanley Grenz, Brian McLaren, Darrell Bock, and Robert Webb. See also Walton and Sandy, *The Lost World of Scripture*; Blomberg, *Can We Still Believe the Bible?*.

be clear from a reading of the Reformers and classic evangelicals, it is surely they were not adherents of critical hermeneutics, either wittingly or unwittingly.

Carl F. H. Henry is considered to be an indispensable figure of classic evangelicalism and a prevailing figure in twentieth century hermeneutics, who foresaw these coming trends in hermeneutics, and attempted to address them at their philosophical starting points.[2] This book contends that Henry's epistemology is foundational to his hermeneutic offering present-day evangelicals an epistemologically justified approach to hermeneutics as epistemology and methodology. This final chapter will (1) Reintroduce and summarize the key points why epistemology is the decisive issue for hermeneutics; and (2) Discuss the ways Henry's method is able to offer present-day evangelicals an epistemologically justified approach to hermeneutics, while remaining faithful to classic evangelicalism and the axiom that all knowledge starts with the God who freely chose to reveal himself.

EPISTEMOLOGY AND HERMENEUTICS

Classic Reformed epistemology and hermeneutics lost its hold in the western world as the premises of modernity collectively brought epistemology and hermeneutics into the age of "critical philosophy," requiring both secular and religious theories of interpretation to engage with the science of linguistic understanding and the hermeneutical problem.[3] Not that modern epistemology is a one-colored cloak; unquestionably, it is a coat of many colors. One color is the development of the concept of the "hermeneutical spiral" in hermeneutics by individuals such as Friedrich Schleiermacher to explain the "art of understanding" the facet of human knowledge known as *understanding*.[4] Another color is the development

---

2. This is a point argued by R. Albert Mohler at the Carl F. H. Henry Centennial Address on 9-26-2013: http://www.youtube.com/watch?v=8rHg2RE2-tY.

3. Helm, *Faith, Form, and Fashion*. Frei, *The Eclipse Of Biblical Narrative*; Palmer, *Hermeneutics*; Grondin, *Introduction to Philosophical Hermeneutics*; Thiselton, *New Horizons in Hermeneutics*; Osborne, *The Hermeneutical Spiral*. In this context, the term "collectively" is used to describe the fact that no one epistemology acted alone in forming what has been deemed the "hermeneutical problem." Furthermore, the term "critical-philosophy" refers to the concept to describe the Greek word that means "to sort" or "to sift out." Lawhead, *The Voyage of Discovery*, 327.

4. Ibid.

of phenomenology and historical understanding, primarily represented by Martin Heidegger and Hans-Georg Gadamer. Shades of these colors are manifest in the theories of hermeneutics and theological methods of the 19th and 20th centuries, especially amongst present-day innovative approaches to hermeneutics.[5]

Gregory Alan Thornbury in his book titled, *Recovering Classic Evangelicalism*, argues that Henry's project in *God, Revelation and Authority*, was to develop an epistemology to undergird classic evangelical theology and to combat the philosophical presuppositions of Roman Catholicism, Protestant liberalism, and neo-orthodoxy.[6] Thornbury believes scholars from these spectrums of thought have incorporated the innovations of modern and contemporary epistemology into their hermeneutics as epistemology and methodology.[7] Henry also sought to interject an evangelical epistemology into these dialogues in epistemology and hermeneutics. Thornbury claims, "He [Henry] committed himself to the task of showing the strength of evangelicalism at the level of epistemology—in its presuppositions, claims, and understanding of divine revelation."[8] Moreover, as Daniel Treier in his article titled, *Scripture and Truth*, notes, "Evangelicals such as Carl F. H. Henry likewise maintained an identity of the Bible with God's Word along with the 'propositional' character of divine revelation: Scripture contains cognitive content, claims that are either true or false."[9] These insights by Thornbury and Treier are important for this project because they indicate Henry believes that from evangelicalism's inception, it offered the watching world not only the unvarnished Protestant gospel, it also sought to propose an epistemology to undergird a theology of revelation distinct from the dominant theologies and epistemologies of his day. Henry believes it is the duty of evangelical theologians to criticize opposing theories of knowledge, faithfully proclaim the gospel, and defend an evangelical view of Scripture.[10]

---

5. See chapter one of the present research. See also: Addinall, *Philosophy and Biblical Interpretation*; Barton, *The Cambridge Companion to Biblical Interpretation*; Bernstein, *Beyond Objectivism and Relativism*; Bleicher, *Contemporary Hermeneutics: Hermeneutics as Method*; Gerald Bray, *Biblical Interpretation Past and Present*; Gerald L. Bruns, *Hermeneutics: Ancient and Modern*.

6. Thornbury, *Recovering Classic Evangelicalism*, 202.

7. Ibid.

8. Ibid.

9. Trier, "Scripture as Communication," 85.

10. See the following paragraph as it explains Henry's six principles.

In *God, Revelation and Authority*, Henry elaborates upon the confrontational nature of evangelical epistemology and theology. His sixth principle is, "*The theology of revelation requires the apologetic confrontation of speculative theories of reality and life.*"[11] Henry explains this sixth principle claiming,

> By applying the laws of logic, the Christian apologist will mount internal criticism of contrary positions and expose the contradictions inherent in the axioms of secularism; he will thereby reduce to absurdity the successively proffered alternatives to Christian theism and force the intellectual abandonment of speculative views. At the same time, he will exhibit the internal consistency of the Christian axiom and show that evangelical truth far better accounts for any desirable facet or proffered alternative while also avoiding its logical inconsistencies.[12]

Each of Henry's six principles are axiomatic for his hermeneutics as epistemology.[13] His method, theological and hermeneutical method included, seeks to confront opposing theories of knowledge.[14] In a similar respect, Henry attempts to develop and exhibit the internal consistency of Revelational Theism over and against speculative theories of knowledge and diverse views of hermeneutics.

The following section will discuss and incorporate the spirit of Henry's sixth principle, namely, the confrontational nature of revelational epistemology, in order to explain: (1) The ways Henry believes Revelational Theism provides a superior account of epistemology; (2) How Revelational Theism influences Henry's hermeneutics as epistemology and hermeneutics as methodology; and (3) How Henry uses Revelational Theism when interacting with opposing theories of hermeneutics as epistemology and methodology.[15]

11. Henry, *GRA*, 1:241.

12. Ibid.

13. The six principles are: (1) God in his revelation is the first principle of Christian theology, from which all truths of revealed religion are derived; (2) Human reason is a divinely fashioned instrument for recognizing truth; it is not a creative source for truth; (3) The Bible is the Christian's principle of verification; (4) Logical consistency is a negative test of truth and coherence a subordinate test; (5) The proper task of theology is to exposit and elucidate the content of Scripture in an orderly way; (6) The theology of revelation requires the apologetic confrontation of speculative theories of reality and life.

14. Ibid.

15 R. Albert Mohler discusses the integral nature of revelational epistemology in

REVELATIONAL THEISM AND HERMENEUTICS

Of the foregoing assumptions that undergird Henry's hermeneutic is the epistemological framework of Revelational Theism.[16] Henry believes since the advent of the Christian church, theologians have used biblical revelation to frame their conversations in the various disciplines of thought, ranging from theology to philosophy and ethics.[17] It was against this backdrop Henry sought to engage speculative theories of knowledge in the twentieth century. Revelational Theism is his epistemology of choice, because he believes it is epistemologically justified and views it as the prevailing theory of knowledge in the history of Christian thought, affirmed by noted theologians such as: Augustine, Anselm, Luther, and Calvin.

Furthermore, Revelational Theism is operant in Henry's approach because he believes it provides a more consistent account of epistemology than empirical and rationalist approaches to knowledge.[18] In particular, Henry adopts a revelational epistemology because he believes it provides a more consistent explanation of epistemology by which to frame his theory of hermeneutics as epistemology than other theories of knowledge (e.g., rationalist, empirical, and so forth).[19] Moreover, he incorporates Revelational Theism in order to fulfill his sixth principle of confronting speculative theories of knowledge and to demonstrate the superiority of

---

the current dialogues of hermeneutics using the language of and logic of Henry. See, Gundry, *Five Views On Biblical Inerrancy*, 31.

16. See chapter two in order to know the details of a Revelational Theistic epistemology. Some of the foregoing assumptions include: (1) The belief that revelation should frame the discussions of epistemology; (2) The role of reason and the relationship of reason and revelation; (3) An Augustinian epistemology, in particular the immediate and *a priori* knowledge of God; (4) The role of presuppositions and axioms of verification in the discipline of epistemology; (5) The role of the Logos and the image of God in epistemology; (6) A theistic view of language.

17. Henry, *GRA*, 1:323–343.

18. Ibid., 1:70–93. The researcher believes there is justification to label Augustine, Anselm, Luther and Calvin and philosopher-theologians because each of them tackled difficult questions of metaphysics and epistemology during their respective time periods. However, each of them are known best for their contributions to theology; nevertheless, their theological contributions have influenced the development of Revelational Theism.

19. It should be noted that in this context Revelational Theism and Revelational epistemology are two terms being used synonymously. Revelational Theism is used to depict the fact that a theistic God has revealed Himself to humanity. Revelational epistemology is a term to describe the overall process of Revelational Theism.

his hermeneutic as epistemology and methodology.[20] With this historical background in mind, the next section will discuss the implications of Henry's revelational epistemology, and the reasons it is able to provide a more consistent hermeneutic as epistemology and methodology than other approaches in the current dialogues in hermeneutics.[21]

Augustinian Epistemology

Methodologically, Henry adopts Augustine's Revelational Theistic epistemology to substantiate his hermeneutic as epistemology. He believes Augustine's epistemology is preferable to modern and contemporary approaches to knowledge for a number of reasons.[22] First, Augustinian epistemology grounds knowledge in the paradigm of Trinitarian theism and allows biblical revelation to frame the conversations in epistemology. As chapter two notes, Henry demands that alien categories (e.g., non-revelatory and/or non-biblical categories) and probabilistic methods not take precedence over the categories of biblical revelation. For example, in his book, *Toward A Recovery*, Henry claims,

> Empiricism has been much the vogue of recent evangelical theology. While it is not pressed the length of making sensory observation and laboratory verification the only reliable way of knowing, it nonetheless encourages a theological appeal to particulars in search of a universal, rather than postulating a universal explanatory principle subject to testing. Any deductive exposition of Christianity is therefore disparaged.[23]

In light of the influence of empiricism, alternatively, Henry affirms an *a priori* and deductive method in his approach to knowledge.[24] Henry claims it was not until Thomas Aquinas proposed an empirical and inductive alternative in the twelfth century was the deductive method seriously disputed.[25] He acknowledges the Protestant Reformers employed a

---

20. Ibid., 1:241.

21. See chapter four of the present book under the section "Hermeneutics as Epistemology."

22. See chapter two under the section titled, "Augustinian Epistemology." Especially footnote one hundred and fourteen.

23. Henry, *Toward A Recovery Of Christian Belief*, 37.

24. Ibid., 61–96.

25. Ibid., 38.

deductive method, whereas empirical approaches to knowledge following in the Thomistic tradition, start with induction by employing proofs found in natural theology.[26] In that sense, Henry believes a deductive method preserves the Reformed methods of interpretation, which allows the Bible to be the source criterion of knowledge.[27]

Henry critiques many modern and contemporary philosophers for grounding their epistemology in empirical and inductive approaches to knowledge.[28] He believes empirically based approaches to knowledge will only be able to provide probabilistic accounts of knowledge, and are unable to overcome some form of epistemological subjectivity.[29] Henry urged the evangelicals of his day to cross the Tiber from epistemological empiricism to epistemological *a priorism*, because empiricism appeals to particulars subject to revision and tentative conclusions.[30] One of the benefits of this move to deductive *a priorism*, according to Henry, is it provides for the possibility of grounding epistemology in the categories of biblical revelation, rather than alien categories of thought (e.g., secular or the non-God).

Consequently, Henry believes if evangelicals adopt and consistently employ a classic understanding of revelational epistemology, they can deduce a more coherent framework to undergird their hermeneutic as epistemology and methodology, than empirical and inductive theories of knowledge. For Henry, Revelational Theism provides a coherent paradigm to affirm epistemological objectivity and overcome hermeneutical nihilism and metaphysical anti-realism.[31]

---

26. Ibid.

27. Ibid. It should be noted that no theologian, Carl Henry included, operates according to either a purely deductive or inductive method. Each method offers a valid approach to knowledge providing sound syllogistic reasoning. However, in this instance, Henry is noting that the inductive method became the dominant method by late Medieval, modernistic, and contemporary approaches to epistemology. In that respect, he believes methodologically, inductivism gave way to the tentative nature of epistemology. Furthermore, he believes that the Reformers emphasized a deductive method in order to combat this epistemological trend and to ground knowledge in biblical revelation.

28. Henry, *GRA,*, 1:70–93.

29. Ibid.

30. Henry, *Toward a Recovery*, 37.

31. Henry, *GRA*, 4:129–475.

Epistemological Certainty

By affirming an Augustine's Revelational Theistic epistemology, Henry believes he is able to give an account of knowledge that provides at least in theory, for the possibility of absolute epistemological certainty. He claims, "The philosophical foes of Augustine were the skeptics of the New Academy who allowed no knowledge beyond probability, and the sensationalists who professed to derive everything in the intellect from sensation alone."[32] B. B. Warfield elaborates on Augustine's notion of epistemological certainty, noting, "And not only is this standard, the *verum*, certainly in the possession of every man and instinctively employed by him; but no one can by any means rid himself of it."[33] Augustine argues that reason ought to withdraw its primary attention from the external world and focus on the inner consciousness.[34] There Augustine (and Henry) asserts truth can be found. Those who seek knowledge from the external world *alone*, never attain to it; for according to Augustine, knowledge begins in the inner man and makes its dwelling there.[35] This claim should not be interpreted as insisting that Augustine and Henry deny ontological realism; instead, it is to emphasize the fact they ground their epistemology in an *a priori* vs. *a posterori* theory of knowledge.

Henry believes Augustine's notion of revelational epistemology, offers a way for evangelicals to develop a unified theory of knowledge between the intellect and the sense world.[36] Within Augustine's theory of knowledge, the soul was created to exist in a dual environment: the world of the senses and the world of the intellect. The role of the senses is to link

---

32. Ibid., 4:129–475; 1:325. B. B. Warfield comments on this aspect of Augustine's doctrine of knowledge pointing out that, "They [the Academicians] asserted that we can never get beyond suspense because we lack all criterion of truth. The best we can do is to say that this or that looks like truth; that it is *verisimile* or *probabile*: we can never affirm that it is truth, *verum*; though, of course, we can as little affirm that it is not truth. Lacking all *signum* we are left in utter hopeless uncertainty. Augustine, on the contrary, in the apodeictic certainty of, say, mathematical formulas, was in possession of a sure criterion on the basis of which he could confidently assert truth.... In other words, in every department of investigation there is attainable real and clear, if somewhat roughly measured, knowledge." Warfield, *Tertullian and Augustine*, 137.

33. Ibid.
34. Ibid.
35. Ibid.
36. Henry, *GRA*, 1:325.

man to the objective world of sense perception, while the intellect links man to the objective world of intellection.[37] Henry claims,

> The certitude of consciousness involves at the same time certitude of the external world. The Creator's determination constantly maintains man in this joint relationship to the rational and phenomenal worlds, and to the Creator himself as decisive for all. The soul, like the sense world in which man is placed, has in God its constant support and direction.[38]

According to Henry, the benefit of Augustine's epistemology in its ability to overcome epistemological subjectivity by offering objectivity to both the intellectual and sense worlds.[39] Warfield explains Augustine's precise notion of epistemological certainty. He writes,

> Do what we will, we cannot help knowing that the world is either one or not one; that three times three are nine; and the like; that is to say the principles which underlie, say for example, logic and mathematics.... If the mind did not exist, it could not even doubt. The act of doubt itself becomes, thus, the credential of certitude. It is impossible even to doubt unless we are, and remember, and understand, and will, and think, and know, and judge: so that he that doubts must not and cannot doubt of these things, seeing that even if he doubts he does them. Even he who says, 'I do not know,' thereby evinces not only that he exists and that he knows that he exists, but also that he knows what knowing is and that he knows that he knows it. It is impossible to be ignorant that we are; and as this is certain, many other things are certain along with it, and the confident denial of this is only another way of demonstrating it.[40]

Henry's use of Augustine's epistemology is what makes his hermeneutic as epistemology unique in the current dialogues in hermeneutics. In particular, Henry's claims to epistemological certainty and objectivity run distinctly contrary to the subjectivist epistemologies that seem to dominate present-day hermeneutics as epistemology.[41]

---

37 Ibid.

38. Ibid.

39. Ibid. Henry does not specifically define subjectivity. As has been noted elsewhere, Henry like many classic evangelicals seems to use subjectivity and relativity interchangeably.

40. Warfield, *Tertullian and Augustine*, 138–139.

41. A critic of Henry's position could argue that Henry affirms a fideistic position.

Henry believes Augustine's epistemology is suited best to confront what he considers to be the errors of epistemological subjectivists, who commitment their epistemologies to secular (e.g., non-biblical) categories.[42] According to Henry, subjectivist epistemologies err because their theories are typically grounded in empirical approaches to knowledge.[43] He believes empirical approaches can only offer knowledge claims that comes in degrees of probability and allow for the possibility of biblical revelation to be overturned in light of new evidence and discoveries. Henry believes both of these options run contrary to an evangelical bibliology and revelational epistemology.

In contradistinction with many present-day approaches, Henry believes Augustine's Revelational Theism is superior to empirical and subjectivist accounts of knowledge because it attempts to ground knowledge in Trinitarian theism and in the categories of revelational epistemology. Augustine's revelational epistemology is operant in and undergirds Henry's hermeneutic as epistemology by providing the appropriate axioms to validate interpretation and offer a paradigm to affirm objectivity in biblical interpretation.[44] Moreover, it allows the Bible to be the judge of secular theories of knowledge. Revelational Theism also places biblical revelation over extra-biblical evidence and it does not allow it to nullify in the slightest degree the truthfulness of any text in all the text asserts and claims.

The Logos and *Imago Dei*

Henry also makes a valuable contribution to evangelical epistemology and hermeneutics by reintroducing and emphasizing the theological concepts of the Logos doctrine and the *imago Dei*. In particular, according

---

This is because there is a distinction between biblical and secular categories. Henry responds to this charge in *Toward a Recovery*, 38–49.

42. See chapter two under the sections titled "Augustinian Epistemology" and "Presuppositional Method."

43. As has been noted in chapters two and four, it ought to be emphasized that Henry and many classic evangelicals tend to use the terms subjectivist and relativistic interchangeably. In this sense, however, subjectivist theories of knowledge are those that claim individuals are not able to overcome the personal aspects of knowledge which influence the knowing process.

44. See chapter four under the headings titled, "Hermeneutics as Epistemology" and "Hermeneutics as Methodology."

to Henry's epistemology, these two concepts serve to ground the fixed nature of meaning and human nature regardless of geographical, historical or sociological conditioning.[45] Chapter two argues that for Henry, the Logos fulfills two important mediating roles.

The first is a salvific mediating role; whereby, the Word of God made flesh mediates salvation between God the Father and humanity. The second is an epistemological mediating role; whereby, the Word of God, serving as the agent of revelation, mediates between the mind of God and the mind of humanity.[46] Henry suggests that one of the prevalent issues in modern epistemology is "anti-intellectual" and "anti-Logos" epistemologies. Subsequently they deny the rational and cognitive elements of divine revelation. In doing so, however, anti-Logos epistemologists reduce the Logos to a non-cognitive category. The epistemological implication of these epistemological approaches is the Logos is no longer able to act as a rational mediator between the mind of God and the mind of humanity; instead, the Logos must be understood in non-rational and relational categories.[47] However, if the Logos is rational, he can serve as the epistemological mediator between the mind of God and the mind of humanity.

Henry continues to discuss the rise of "phantom logos" (e.g., false logos or fake logos doctrines) theologies and epistemologies, and how they have affected epistemology. The reason Henry brings up opposing "phantom-logos" doctrines is because he believes there is a long intellectual stream of thought in Western philosophy that has sought to produce an assortment of conjectural alternatives to the Logos, culminating in the contemporary abandonment of the Logos. Bob Patterson explains what Henry believes are the effects of this abandonment. He writes,

> This desertion of the Logos of revelation, says Henry, has led to an intellectual disaster, the loss of fixed meaning of existence, and the giving up on the enduring worth of man. 'If we can learn anything from these speculative or mythological *logoi* of rationalistic philosophy and religious theory, it is simply that each and every such phantom-*logos* has its day and is soon spent.' The alternatives are either nihilism or the Nazarene.[48]

---

45. See chapters two and three of the present research.

46. Patterson, *Carl F. H. Henry*, 97.

47. Henry believes the downplay of a rational Logos by neo-Protestant theologians affects the understanding of the Bible as the propositional Word of God.

48. Patterson, *Carl F. H. Henry*, 98.

Patterson rightly notes Henry believes the only way to reestablish fixed meaning is to reintroduce the Logos into contemporary epistemology. In contradistinction to many proponents of the phenomenological and existential streams of the hermeneutical problem, Henry argues that the Logos provides the framework to ground theories of linguistic meaning and ontology.[49] Furthermore, Henry uses the Logos doctrine to oppose those who claim different cultures and historical situations manufacture different types of "logics" in humanity. For Henry, there is no such thing as a "human logic" and a "divine logic;" neither is there any such thing as a "Hebrew mind" and a "Greek mind." Instead, for Henry, there is only one logic between God and man, the Logos, Christ Jesus.[50]

Like Augustine, Henry claims the image of God in humanity enables humanity to directly receive revelation from the Logos of God. This knowledge of God is innate, rational, and coherent. Furthermore, since each individual bears the image of God, all of humanity has the ability to use the canons of logic.[51] In contradistinction with post-modern and existential epistemologists and theologians, who claim there are no universal canons of logic and truth, Henry suggests the *imago Dei* entails that all of humanity operates according to the same rational faculties.[52] This is important for Henry's hermeneutic as epistemology because it demands that the rational criterion for validity are the same for all of humanity, regardless of geographical or sociological influences.[53]

For example, in their book, *Philosophy for Understanding Theology*, Diogenes Allen and Eric O. Springsted include a chapter where they discuss the effects of existentialism and phenomenology on hermeneutics.[54] When discussing Heidegger, they claim,

> *Being and Time* is thus preparatory study, for Heidegger's interest is not in human beings as such. It is simply that we are

---

49. Ibid.

50. See chapter three of the present research under the section titled "The Logic of Religious Language."

51. See chapter two of the present research under the heading titled, "Sub-Axioms of Revelational Theism."

52. For example, John Franke in his chapter in the book *Five Views on Biblical Inerrancy*, argues for a post-modern approach to the nature of truth and the role of reason. See Gundry, *Five Views on Biblical Inerrancy*, 259–287.

53. See chapter four of the present research under the heading titled, "The Role of Reason."

54. Allen and Springsted, *Philosophy for Understanding Theology*, 187–209.

already concretely involved by our very existence with the question of Being because we need to *become* something. This inescapable involvement Heidegger calls the 'existentiall [sic] question.'. . . . An existential analysis shows the distinctive characteristics that mark us off from other kinds of beings. Among them are (1) to exist is to be 'on the way,' never complete, but to be constituted by possibilities (the possible ways of existing are called the 'existentialia'), (2) to exist is to choose to be oneself—hence to be always incomplete—or to lose oneself by submerging oneself in the conventions of society.[55]

Henry believes Revelational Theism's metaphysical and epistemological realism is able to overcome the idealistic *becoming* of Heidegger's phenomenological and existential situatedness.[56] Furthermore, it is able to overcome Gadamer's historical situatedness by providing a more coherent explanation of continuity (e.g., metaphysical, epistemological, linguistic, and historiographical) than "fusion of horizons" theories.[57] This is because according to Henry's understanding of revelational epistemology, speculative theories of ontology and epistemology are unable to alter the image of God in humanity.[58] The *imago Dei* remains the unchanging ontological and epistemological point of contact between individuals separated by the proposed ontological distance and historical situatedness (as proposed by the phenomenological and existential wings of the hermeneutical problem).[59]

Consequently, due to the transcultural nature of the *imago Dei*, and the faculties of universal reason, Henry believes theologians should employ revelation to confront culture, and not allow culture to confront revelation.[60] Contrary to the claims of many postmodern and post-liberal theologians, Henry argues the Bible presents only one true theology, and there are not many "gospels," each conditioned by a different sociology of knowledge. Instead, joining with the Apostle Paul, Henry's view seems to insist there is "One Lord, one faith, one baptism, one God and Father of

---

55. Ibid., 193–194.

56. Ibid.

57. See chapter four of the present book titled "Gadamer."

58. See chapter two of the present research under the section titled, "Image of God."

59. Ibid.

60. This point is best substantiated by the totality of Henry's fifteen theses published in his work *God, Revelation and Authority*.

all, who is over all and through all and in all" (Eph. 4:17).[61] Evidently for Henry, the Logos and the *imago Dei* serve as an ontological and epistemological ground to unify theological truth and ensure the transcultural communication of *the* gospel of Jesus Christ.

A Theistic View of Language

In addition to its epistemological strengths, Henry believes Revelational Theism also makes significant contributions in the arena of religious language. As chapter three argues, Henry's view of propositional revelation is consistent with his epistemology and functions within the framework of a theistic view of language. For Henry, a theistic view of language recognizes that God is the source, origin, and designer of human language. Furthermore, a theistic view of language is the result of God's desire to reveal himself to humanity through the agency of cognitive revelation.[62] Because of this claim (e.g., that it is God's desire to cognitively reveal himself to humanity), chapter four argues that for Henry to affirm a "cognitive-propositionalist" view of revelation means, as Henry claims, "That divine disclosure is cognitive and intelligible—hence a mental activity—intrinsic to Judeo-Christian revelation."[63]

By repositioning religious language within the framework of a theistic view of language, Henry's method provides a more consistent and comprehensive approach to language than many of the modern and contemporary linguistic theories (e.g., analytic philosophy, analogical predication, conventionalism, and so forth).[64] While Henry discusses several views of religious language and the nature of meaning, this current project has only discussed his analysis of logical positivism and conventionalism. Henry rejects both of these linguistic approaches because he believes

---

61. The reason for this claim is because different cultures do not create different theologies or different gospels. There is not a French gospel vs. an American gospel; instead, there is only one gospel. The varying cultures of the world do not create localized theological truths. The task of the theologian is to bring the different world cultures under the authority of Scripture through the task of preaching and discipleship.

62. See chapter three under the section titled, "A Theistic View of Language."

63. Henry, *GRA*, 3:481.

64. The research indicates that both secular and Christian philosophers began to incorporate various theories of meaning in order to accommodate their linguistic theory to the predominant views of epistemology in the universities and seminaries. Thiselton, *New Horizons in Hermeneutics*.

they are unable to substantiate the classic evangelical belief in the Bible as both cognitive and propositional revelation.[65] In particular, he critiques a conventionalist theory of meaning for its insistence on the non-cognitive aspects of language and how it downplays the rational structure of divine revelation.[66]

Furthermore, even though Henry's view is already framed within the context of Revelational Theism—in light of the fact that he affirms a cognitive-propositional view of revelation and allows for an Augustinian worldview to frame his philosophical categories—Henry shows how a theistic view of language is able to provide a much more consistent account of linguistic meaning than other views of language prevalent in the current dialogues in hermeneutics.

First among these advantages is Henry's claim that a theistic view of language entails that a rational and verbal God is the ground of all linguistic communication.[67] God is the Creator of language; however, he is not the Creator of all words or uses of language. Henry's second point suggests,

> In the theistic view, language is possible because of man's God-given endowment of rationality, of *a priori* categories and of innate ideas, all of which precondition his ability to think and speak. Since every mind is lighted by the Logos or Reason of God, thought stands behind language. . . . The Bible depicts man as specially equipped by God for the express purposes of knowing God's rational-verbal revelation, of communicating with God in praise and prayer, and of discoursing with fellow-men about God and his will.[68]

The implication of this second point is language is no longer dependent upon social structures or conventional approaches to linguistic meaning; instead, by the design of God, the rational faculties of man (due to the *imago Dei* and Logos) are able to serve (with God as the ultimate source, of course) as the source criterion and originator of language.[69]

A third advantage of Henry's view of language, and one of his most significant contributions to theories of meaning and hermeneutics, is his

---

65. See chapter three of the present research.
66. Henry, *GRA*, 3:235.
67. Ibid., 3:388.
68. Ibid., 3:389.
69. Ibid.

twenty one statements on a "theistic view of language." A few comments will help to summarize the implications of Henry's twenty one statements on a theistic view of language for the current dialogues in hermeneutics.[70]

First of all, Henry grounds his theory of language in the belief that God appears in the Bible from the very beginning to be a God who speaks, and who declares before he acts, and speaks in intelligible linguistic propositional form.[71] This belief not only distinguishes Henry's view from non-cognitive and paradoxical approaches to language and revelation, it also provides a model consistent with his revelational epistemology that claims when God reveals himself to humanity in special revelation, he does it through the agency of cognitive revelation. Henry believes he provides strong exegetical support to substantiate the claim that God uses intelligible and propositional revelation to communicate. Henry first goes to the creation account to demonstrate that from the very beginning meaningful words have been the divine precedent.[72] In addition, Henry notes that God continues to use rational language to communicate the words of creation and the Word of God. The purpose is to emphasize the intelligible nature of language and reiterate his insistence on the rational Logos of God.

Henry also addresses the nature of language before and after the fall. He claims before the fall God addressed both Adam and Eve through the agency of intelligible and propositional special revelation.[73] According to Henry, the superiority of a theistic view of language is that it not only has exegetical justification, it also reiterates the fact that it was God's design from the very beginning to communicate through the instrumentality of cognitive-propositional revelation.[74] Henry notes that after the fall, God continues to address humanity through cognitive-propositional revelation.[75] Subsequently, the noetic and moral aspects of the fall did not completely obliterate either in Adam or Eve (or the rest of humanity) the ability to receive and understand God's special revelation.[76] The fall may have corrupted human language, but it neither destroys human language

70. Ibid.
71. Ibid., 3:390.
72. Ibid., 3:391.
73. Ibid.
74. Ibid.
75. Ibid., 3:392.
76. Ibid.

nor alters the divine precedent to address humanity through the agency of rational and propositional revelation.[77]

Another advantage Henry believes a theistic view of language is able to offer is a more coherent explanation for the multitude of human languages than secular, positivistic, or evolutionary accounts of language. In particular, Henry traces the variety of languages (e.g., Hebrew, Aramaic, Greek, French, German, English, and so forth) back to the tower of Babel and views the diversity of languages as a result of human rebellion.[78] Modern linguistic theorists err because they attempt to explain the biblical drama apart from the Bible's own depiction of human history and rebellion.[79] For Henry, the Bible paints the picture that the various human languages arose, not out of some convoluted structuralist or conventionalist theories of meaning; instead, they are the result of humanity's rebellion against divine authority and revelation.[80] However, even in the midst of human rebellion, God is still able to use human language to communicate cognitive-propositional revelation.[81]

In the final analysis, Henry's Revelational Theistic approach has many advantages in the contemporary dialogues in hermeneutics for the following reasons. First of all, as chapters three and five argue, contrary to many of his critics, Henry believes his view of cognitive-propositionalism adequately accounts for the Bible's various genres.[82] His insistence on the propositional nature of revelation does not diminish his belief that the Bible contains various types of literature.[83] Henry's view of cognitive-propositionalism stands against his critics such as Kevin Vanhoozer, who claims it is the task of the interpreter to understand *how* the Bible presents various *types* of literature in order to communicate different *types* of truth. For Henry, there is only one type of truth; however, that single truth can be displayed in a variety of ways and a plurality of genres.

The second advantage of Henry's linguistic approach is it provides a view of language grounded in the framework of Christian theism derived

---

77. Ibid.
78. Ibid.
79. Ibid.
80. Ibid.
81. Ibid., 3:395.
82. See chapter three under the section "The Bible as Propositional Revelation."
83. Henry, *GRA*, 3:463.

from an exegetical study of the Bible.[84] Henry provides present-day evangelicals a coherent framework to uphold the long history of linguistic realism. Classic evangelicalism has always opposed non-cognitive and modified propositional accounts of special revelation.[85] Henry's linguistic model seems to offer a more coherent explanation of the origin of language and the nature of religious meaning than non-realistic, non-cognitive, structuralist, conventional, and speech-act theories of language.[86]

The final advantage of Henry's linguistic theory and how it affects evangelical hermeneutics as methodology (as chapters three and four have argued), is it stands alongside both the Reformers and classic evangelicalism by affirming the literal interpretation of Scripture.[87] Both the Reformers and classic evangelicalism recognize that a literal interpretation of Scripture must take into account the Bible's use of metaphors and various genres.[88] The literal method does not dismiss the plain sense of Scripture by allegorizing the text or explaining away the clear meaning of the Bible by appealing to Jewish or Greco-Roman genres of literature or methods of interpretation.[89] This methodological point is especially important because it serves as both a reminder and a corrective to many present-day evangelicals who are quick to use genre criticism to dismiss the literal meaning of Scripture in favor of new and innovative approaches in hermeneutics.[90]

REVELATIONAL THEISM: HERMENEUTICS AS EPISTEMOLOGY AND METHODOLOGY

In Thornbury's book, *Recovering Classic Evangelicalism*, he writes about a time when Henry addressed the issue of evangelical hermeneutics as

---

84. Ibid.

85. Geisler, *Biblical Errancy*, 163–204.

86. Geisler, *Biblical Errancy;* Sproul, *Explaining Inerrancy.*

87. George, *Reading Scripture With The Reformers*; Ramm, *Protestant Biblical Interpretation*; Thomas, *Evangelical Hermeneutics.*

88. Packer, *'Fundamentalism' and the Word of God*, 101–114.

89. Gundry, *The New Testament Use Of The Old Testament*

90. Walton and Sandy, *The Lost World of Scripture;* Sparks, *God's Word In Human Words;* Stark, *The Human Faces of God;* Licona, *The Resurrection of Jesus;* Enns, *The Evolution of Adam;* Beale, *The Erosion of Inerrancy in Evangelicalism.*

epistemology at The Southern Baptist Theological Seminary in 1997.[91] The title of Henry's unpublished lecture is "The Instability of 20th Century Theology."[92] Thornbury reflects on the symposium remembering that the tone of Henry's address was one of both grace and gentle regret.[93] He also notes that at this symposium Henry made some of his final comments on evangelical hermeneutics before succumbing to spinal stenosis which kept him from public ministry until his death in 2003.[94]

Thornbury remarks that Henry showed signs of regret because ". . . 'mediating evangelicals' were exchanging their heritage for a mess of postmodern pottage."[95] In particular, Henry laments that "mediating evangelicals" were seeking to synthesize narrative theology and postliberalism with an evangelical view of Scripture, because he believes these new approaches undermine the classic evangelical doctrines of inspiration and inerrancy.[96] These innovative approaches undermine the inerrancy of Scripture because they weaken propositionalist theology and downplay the need to insist upon the historical and factual character of Scripture. Henry mourns the fact "mediating evangelicals" are turning away from the classic evangelical insistence that through the divinely revealed Scriptures, Christians have access to biblical history much more than historical methods can offer. The Bible tells more than the "history-likeness" of the resurrection or other biblical events; instead, it communicates in propositionally revealed truths, both the historical factuality of the events and their eternal significance for human history.[97]

Thornbury's comments are important to the overall discussion of the implications of Henry's hermeneutic in the current dialogues because he notes the stark differences between what he labels as "classic evangelicalism" and "mediating evangelicalism."[98] In particular, Thornbury points out,

> Henry refused to be sanguine about the theological choices of younger evangelicals, and wondered aloud which 'drummer'

---

91. Thornbury, *Recovering Classic Evangelicalism*, 203.
92. Ibid., 205; Henry, *The Instability of 20th Century Theology*.
93. Thornbury, *Recovering Classic Evangelicalism*, 204.
94. Ibid.
95. Ibid.
96. Ibid.
97. Ibid.
98. Ibid.

might be leading the parade next. He expressed some incredulity and perhaps a bit of hurt to see the epistemological, metaphysical, and ontological program that he and so many of his colleagues had outlined so carefully in scores of monographs, courses, and confessions of faith left in favor of less weighty hermeneutical options. 'What is wrong with classic evangelicalism?' we can almost hear him say.[99]

By following Henry, Thornbury believes classic evangelicalism offers an epistemology markedly different than the options offered by present-day evangelical epistemologies and hermeneutics as epistemology and methodology, included.

In view of this, the following section will make some critical observations regarding the influence of Henry's revelational epistemology and the effects it has for the current dialogues in hermeneutics as epistemology and methodology. This should not be considered an exhaustive list; however, it serves as a way to illustrate some of the implications of Henry's method in contradistinction to other evangelical (possibly mediating evangelical) options.

Since Thornbury has already applied a "Henry-esque" critique to Hans Frei's narrative theology, George Lindbeck's postliberalism, and Kevin Vanhoozer's canonical-linguistic approach; the following section will offer a "Henry-esque" critique of: (1) Alister McGrath and Bernard Lonergan's use of critical-realism; and (2) The hermeneutical implications of Peter Enns' book, *Inspiration and Incarnation* and historical criticism.[100] These figures have been chosen because they illustrate best two areas where Henry's hermeneutic is able to interact with two of the current innovative hermeneutical methods prevalent amongst present-day evangelical hermeneutics as epistemology and methodology.

McGrath and Lonergan

Before his death in 2003, Henry was able to engage with Alister McGrath's book, *The Genesis of Doctrine*.[101] He agrees with McGrath that

---

99. Ibid., 205.

100. This notion is derived from Thornbury's approach to analyzing present-day hermeneutical approaches.

101. McGrath, *The Genesis of Doctrine*.

theologians should base doctrine on Scripture, not a set of prevailing concepts or "alien conceptualities."[102] However, Henry goes on to say,

> But one is left wondering about the role of objective Scriptural truths [in McGrath's *The Genesis of Doctrine*]. The Scriptural narrative, we are told must be allowed 'to generate its own framework of conceptualities.' But what then is the role of logical consistency and of Scriptural verification in the identification of revelation? Doctrines define God, we are told, 'not in order that God might be comprehended' but that 'the believer may relate to God in faith' (p. 78). 'Reason' and 'Revelation' are both subject to the limits of historicity' (p. 90).[103]

Henry continues to evaluate McGrath's thesis charging him with denying the objective nature of truth. This is because in *The Genesis of Doctrine*, Henry believes McGrath accommodates to a subjectivist scheme by claiming non-believers will continue to interpret Jesus according to rival theories of truth and reason, whereas the community of faith will continue to view him as an object of worship. Henry goes on to say,

> And can McGrath seal off from the universal historical location doctrinal formulations of his own preferred option? What are the implications for evangelism and apologetics of the thesis that 'only by standing within the Christian tradition' can the 'full depth and meaning of its symbols and doctrines be understood' (p. 199)?[104]

McGrath claims his critical-realist method is following in the tradition of Bernard Lonergan and Roy Bhaskar.[105] Henry believes the error of critical-realist approaches is they "seek in advance a method common to all of the sciences, theology included," which undermines the classic evangelical insistence on "objective truth and knowledge."[106] When speaking about Lonergan's critical-realist epistemology, Henry suggests,

> Rather than permitting theological subject matter to determine its own relevant method, Bernard J. F. Lonergan (*Method in*

---

102. Henry, *The Genesis of Doctrine*, 101.

103. Ibid. Note: This quote is directly cited by Thornbury in *Recovering Classic Evangelicalism*, 36.

104. Henry, *The Genesis of Doctrine*, 103. Note: This quote is also directly cited by Thornbury. See, Thornbury, *Recovering Classic Evangelicalism*, 36–37.

105. McGrath, *A Scientific Theology*, 195–244.

106. Henry, *GRA*, 1:195–196.

Theology) seeks in advance a method common to all sciences, theology included. He therefore risks the subsumption of some subject matter, especially theology, to other sciences. Lonergan affirms only the '*virtually* unconditioned' (hence highly probable, yet not beyond possibility of revision), and hence is indifferent to Scripture as a basic instrument of final truth. But a theological method derived from other sciences really adjusts theology to a general methodology that denies to theology its own distinctive object and subject matter. If the attempt to discuss God's nature is confined to theological statements related to objects within the field of other subjects, God will remain a mystery. Current religious knowledge-theory is historically conditioned by modern scientific controls and imposes upon theology an ideal borrowed from Leopold von Ranke's scientific historiography. Theology is not to be chained in advance to the method of other sciences. Does not a scholar like Lonergan, who can write almost interminably on epistemology and not mention God, need to reconsider the relation between revelation and reason? Nobody should be overwhelmed by a discovery that we cannot reach the Christian doctrines by Lonergan's method.[107]

In this assessment, one of evangelicalism's leading theologians opposes both Lonergan and McGrath's critical-realist hermeneutical method because he believes it accommodates Scripture to non-biblical categories and a probabilistic-empirical epistemology. While praising Lonergan and McGrath for their commitment to metaphysical realism, Henry believes they have accommodated their hermeneutical method to a false subjectivist approach to epistemology. In other words, Henry claims they have been profoundly impacted by the probabilistic nature of empirical epistemologies that undergird many present-day theories of hermeneutics.

In disagreement with critical-realism, Henry believes Revelational Theism provides a superior account for hermeneutics as epistemology and methodology because it overcomes the probabilistic and tentative

107. Ibid. Thornbury notes, "If Henry were still with us, one wonders what he would make of McGrath's recent attempt to construct a 'scientific theology'" based upon the verities of rational discourse into the nature and the elegant ways of God in the cosmos. Although I will return at the end of the next chapter to hiss poor reception among evangelicals currently involved in the field of hermeneutics, what I intend to indicate by drawing attention to Henry's review of McGrath's *Genesis of Doctrine* is that the leading evangelical theologian of our time was always interrogating the matter of epistemology—the grounds for belief and knowledge." Thornbury, *Recovering Classic Evangelicalism*, 37.

nature of empirical approaches to knowledge. It also provides a framework to engage hermeneutics in a way that preserves both the Protestant principles of interpretation and addresses the influence of epistemology in hermeneutics, without allowing the predominant method of present-day theories of hermeneutics to dominate its theological method and doctrinal conclusions. It ought to be remembered that chapters two and four discuss Henry's axioms of validation and the role of presuppositions in epistemology and hermeneutics. Henry claims presuppositions affect interpretation, and for that reason, his method cannot be labeled as a "naïve" or "pre-critical" approach to hermeneutics. However, Henry believes if Revelational Theism is the operant epistemology, then biblical categories and presuppositions are allowed to frame and govern the exegetes task. In short, Revelational Theism provides at least in theory, for the possibility of an epistemology and hermeneutic that allows for objectivity in biblical interpretation.[108]

Peter Enns

Back in 2005, former professor of Old Testament at Westminster Theological Seminary, Peter Enns, published his book titled, *Inspiration and Incarnation*.[109] In *Inspiration and Incarnation*, Enns claims, "The purpose of this book is to bring an evangelical doctrine of Scripture into the conversation with the implications generated by some important themes in modern biblical scholarship—particularly Old Testament scholarship—over the past 150 years."[110] In his publications, Enns attempts to synthesize a doctrine of Scripture with Second Temple hermeneutics.

After the publication of Enns' book *Inspiration and Incarnation*, a fire storm of controversy broke out at Westminster and in the greater evangelical world over the relationship between critical scholarship and a high view of Scripture.[111] One result of this controversy was the publication of *The Erosion of Inerrancy In Evangelicalism* by G. K. Beale.[112] Beale's book serves as a response to Enns' theses in *Inspiration and*

---

108. See chapter four of the present research. Also, Radmacher and Preus, *Hermeneutics, Inerrancy, & the Bible*, 916.
109. Enns, *Inspiration and Incarnation*.
110. Ibid., 13.
111. Geisler and Roach, *Defending Inerrancy*, 99–111.
112. Beale, *The Errosion of Inerrancy in Evangelicalism*.

Incarnation.¹¹³ Since 2005, Enns has also published a hotly debated book titled, *The Evolution of Adam*.¹¹⁴ In *The Evolution of Adam*, Enns applies the same method found in *Inspiration and Incarnation* to the question of human origins and the historical Adam.¹¹⁵

Enns presents a unique and most pressing challenge to classical evangelicalism. In many respects, Enns believes evangelicals are left asking the questions: "*Is the Bible still the word of God?*"¹¹⁶ How does the traditional view of creation and the flood reconcile with *Enuma Elish, Arthasis,* and *Gilgamesh*—the so-called parallel biblical accounts? Is revelation unique? Is the Bible able to communicate actual history or is all historiography biased and therefore subjective? Enns answers these questions by claiming the Bible is still the "word of God" (lower case); however, he radically departs from the traditional view of inspiration, inerrancy, and historical factuality by synthesizing (e.g., incarnating) Scripture with parallel mythological accounts.¹¹⁷

During the second summit meeting of the *International Council on Biblical Inerrancy* (ICBI), Henry offered the concluding message. In many respects Henry's address was a charge to his fellow evangelicals on the way(s) to interact with critical scholarship and hermeneutics as epistemology. In his message, Henry suggests,

> In challenging the concessive mode of the day we must avoid certain temptations. One temptation is to overstate the strength of the critical camp and to under-represent the evangelical enterprise as but a corporal's guard or Gideon's band. Among teachers and clergy the defections from a fully authoritative Bible may be disconcertingly numerous. But the great masses of active churchgoers take the Bible as its word. There is no firm consensus or stability of outlook among those who hold a broken and inconstant view of biblical authority.¹¹⁸

Henry's first point of advice to his evangelical colleagues, when interacting with scholars such as Enns, is pay close attention to the lack of

---

113. Beale summarizes Enns' work in *Inspiration and Incarnation*. Beale, *The Errosion of Inerrancy*, 44–45.
114. Enns, *The Evolution of Adam*.
115. Ibid., xi.
116. Enns, *Inspiration and Incarnation*, 39.
117. Geisler and Roach, *Defending Inerrancy*, 99–111.
118. Radmacher and Preus, *Hermeneutics, Inerrancy, & the Bible*, 917.

unanimity amongst critical scholars and critical scholarship. While individuals such as Enns claim critical scholars speak with a unified voice on these matters, the fact is regardless of what they claim, there is no consensus amongst critical scholars and the topics of critical scholarship.

The second point of advice from Henry to the ICBI, after reminiscing about his address before the American Theological Society (which he claims "consider the survival of biblical inerrantists as viable as that of dinosaurs"),[119] is that the real objections to biblical inerrancy by critical-scholars are, "... philosophical and speculative, thus no amount of resolution of particular problems will serve to reinstate the evangelical view."[120] Henry's advice is instructive to present-day evangelicalism. He notes that regardless of the amount of exegetical work done on a particular passage, the vast majority of critical scholars will not change their views because their metaphysic and epistemology has already committed them to their exegetical conclusions.[121]

Henry not only opposes the speculative epistemologies supporting Enns' views of hermeneutics as epistemology, he also opposes Enns' views of critical scholarship including his redaction criticism and the role of ancient Near Eastern approaches to biblical interpretation. Henry reiterates the fact that a correspondence view of truth entails that the truth value of the proposition is equal to the truth value of the historical event. Consequently, Henry believes a correspondence view of truth is important for exegetes because interpreters such as Enns, attempt to relegate the Bible to one type of truth and factual history to another type of truth. As was seen in chapters two and three, according to Henry, if anyone claims there are "different types of truth," that claim should be seen as a fallacious bifurcation because it manufactures a pseudo dichotomy (e.g., between relational and propositional truth; biblical history and actual history; ancient history and modern history) with only rhetorical value, not factual value.[122]

By using an Old Testament illustration, Henry charged his colleagues at the ICBI with a third word of advice about evangelical engagement with critical methodologies using the following Moses-like pronouncement. He declared,

---

119. Ibid.
120. Ibid., 918.
121. Ibid.
122. Radmacher and Preus, *Hermeneutics, Inerrancy, & the Bible*, 163–216.

God said, 'Let my people go,' meaning free them from bondage and let them take the place in the world that I seek for them. "Let it go' seems now to say to us, 'Let my Bible go': go beyond the limitations imposed by critics, beyond the walls of cloisters and churches, beyond even evangelical reticence and timidity; give it free and full scope in the world. *Let the earth hear my voice*. . . . Somehow we must relate the witness of the inerrant Bible to the world for which God has intended it. Our concern to attest to an inerrant Bible must lead beyond our Essene community into the cultural mainstream, there to confront our contemporaries with the right questions until they reach for the supreme answer.[123]

If Henry were alive today he would most likely be charging "mediating evangelicals" to return to the legacy of their evangelical forefathers. In many respects, Henry is still a voice crying out in the wilderness "Let my Bible go!" Let my Bible go from the speculative epistemologies and relativistic hermeneutical nihilism. Let my Bible go from the non-cognitive and mythological forms of language and neo-Protestant views of revelation. Let my Bible go from historiographical and critical views that attempt to neutralize the historical factuality of Scripture. Let my Bible go from narrative theology, speech-act theory, and genre criticism. Henry's final charge before the ICBI still rings true for present-day evangelicals is: "Let my Bible go" and "Remember Jesus Christ, risen from the dead. The Word of God is not bound."[124] In effect, for Henry, the Bible is not bound by mediating evangelical epistemologies or critical theories of interpretation.

HENRY'S METHOD AND THE FUTURE OF EVANGELICAL HERMENEUTICS

Timothy George in his article with *First Things* titled, "*The Awesome Disclosure of God*," discusses the legacy and future of Henry's project for present-day evangelicals.[125] George notes that during the Reformation Martin Luther engaged the theological landscape with ninety-five theses, whereas Henry engaged twentieth century evangelicalism and

---

123. Ibid., 918–919, 920.
124. Ibid., 921.
125. http://www.firstthings.com/onthesquare/2013/10/the-awesome-disclosure-of-god. Accessed 10/10/2013.

non-evangelicalism with fifteen theses.[126] George believes what is axiomatic to Henry's project is his first thesis claiming that revelation is a divinely initiated activity.[127] He reiterates Henry's contribution to evangelical scholarship. George also praises the renaissance taking place among present-day evangelicals to reengage with Henry's vision and method through conferences, books, articles, dissertations, and so forth. He goes on to say, "I applaud and welcome the Henrician renaissance now under way. . . . a renewed commitment to doing theology in the service of the church, and to doing it with a Henry-like passion for truth, and with love for the God who is both the source and object of truth."[128] That being said, many theologians such as George and Thornbury note that some scholars (both evangelical and non-evangelical) have failed to even engage with Henry's hermeneutic as epistemology and methodology. However, the research in this book suggests ways Henry's method is able to address the pressing topics in the current dialogues in hermeneutics.

The primary reason Henry's method offers present-day evangelicals an epistemologically justified approach to hermeneutics is because he is committed to revelational epistemology. His hermeneutic is rooted in the longstanding Augustinian tradition and it incorporates the enduring Protestant principles of interpretation. He does not shy away from engaging in philosophical hermeneutics. In fact, Henry directly interacts with the main figures in order to claim that evangelicals are not required to affirm epistemological relativism or hermeneutical nihilism. When addressing the role of revelational epistemology in present-day conversations on epistemology and hermeneutics, R. Albert Mohler claims,

> The way out of hermeneutical nihilism and metaphysical antirealism is the doctrine of revelation. It is indeed the evangelical, biblical doctrine of revelation that breaks this epistemological impasse and because the foundation for a revelatory epistemology. This is not foundationalism in a modernist sense. It is not rationalism. It is the understanding that God has spoken to us in a reasonable way, in language we can understand, and has given us the gift of revelation, which is his willful disclosure of himself, the forfeiture of his personal privacy.[129]

---

126. Ibid.
127. Ibid.
128. Ibid.
129. Gundry, *Five Views On Biblical Inerrancy*, 31.

Mohler's comments serve as a reminder that present-day evangelicals should not succumb to the pressure to forego the time honored legacy of revelational epistemology and hermeneutics, in order to march to the same drum-beat as present-day theories that incorporate mediating epistemologies into their hermeneutical approaches. Henry's Revelational Theism provides evangelicals an epistemologically justified approach to epistemology and hermeneutics in that it affirms ontological realism along with epistemological and hermeneutical objectivity.

CONCLUSION

The question facing present-day evangelicals is: How will they do hermeneutics in light of the public nature of epistemology and the challenges epistemology poses for hermeneutics? This book argues that in order to represent their evangelical tribe well, present-day evangelicals should not forego the wisdom and vision of classic evangelicalism. Moreover, this book argues that in order for present-day evangelicals to move forward in the conversations of hermeneutics as epistemology and methodology, they must first look back upon their classic evangelical heritage; in particular, the heritage paved by one of the grandfathers of the movement, Carl F. H. Henry. Henry's revelational epistemology provides a way for present-day evangelicals to engage rightly in the task of philosophical hermeneutics, without abandoning the Protestant principles of interpretation, a literal interpretation of the Scripture, or the inerrancy of the Bible. In light of the contemporary negligence of Henry's literature and misrepresentations of his epistemology and hermeneutic, the final word of advice to present-day evangelicals about Henry's revelational epistemology and hermeneutic is: *tolle lege*! (Take up and read!).

BIBLIOGRAPHY

Addinall, Peter. *Philosophy and Biblical Interpretation: A Study in Nineteenth-Century Conflict.* Cambridge: Cambridge University Press, 1991.
Adler, Mortimer. *The Difference of Man and the Difference It Makes.* New York: Fordham University Press, 1967.
Allen, Diogenes. *Philosophy for Understanding Theology.* Atlanta: John Knox, 1985.
Aquinas, Thomas. *Summa Theologicae.* 5 vols. Translated by Fathers of the English Domican Province. Allen: Christian Classics, 1948.
Audi, Robert. *Epistemology: A Contemporary Introduction to the Theory of Knowledge.* New York: Routledge, 2011.
Austin, J. L. *How to Do Things with Words.* Oxford: Oxford University Press, 1979.
Bhaskar, Roy. *From East to West: Odyssey of a Soul.* New York: Routledge, 2000.
Barr, James. *Fundamentalism.* London: SCM, 1977.
———. *The Semantics of Biblical Language.* Oxford: Oxford University Press, 1961.
Barth, Karl. *Church Dogmatics.* Edinburgh: T & T Clark, 1936.
———. *The Word of God and the Word of Man.* Translated by Douglas Horton. Grand Rapids: Zondervan, 1935.
———. *Nein!* [No!]. Eugene: Wipf & Stock, 2002.
Bartholomew, Craig G. "Postmodernity and Biblical Interpretation." In *Dictionary for Theological Interpretation of the Bible*, edited by Kevin J. Vanhoozer, 600–607. Grand Rapids: Baker, 2005.
Barton, John, ed. *The Cambridge Companion to Biblical Interpretation.* Cambridge: Cambridge University Press, 1998.
Beale, G. K. *The Erosion of Inerrancy in Evangelicalism: Responding to New Challenges to Biblical Authority.* Wheaton: Crossway, 2008.
Behr, John. *Formation of Christian Theology.* New York: St Vladimir's Seminary, 2004.
Berkouwer, G. C. *Holy Scripture.* Studies in Dogmatics. Translated by Jack B. Rogers. Grand Rapids: InterVarsity, 1994.
Bernstein, Richard. *Beyond Objectivism and Relativism.* Philadelphia: University of Pennsylvania Press, 1988.
Bhaskar, Roy. *From East to West: Odyssey of a Soul.* New York: Routledge, 2000.
Blackburn, Simon. *Oxford Dictionary of Philosophy.* New York: Oxford University Press, 1994.
Bleicher, Josef. *Contemporary Hermeneutics: Hermeneutics as Method: Philosophy and Critique.* London: Routledge, 1980.

Bloesch, Donald. G. *A Theology of Word and Spirit: Authority and Method in Theology.* Downers Grove: InterVarsity, 1992.

Blomberg, Craig. *Can We Still Believe the Bible? An Evangelical Engagement with Contemporary Questions.* Grand Rapids: Baker, 2014.

Boa, Ken D. and Robert M. Bowman Jr. *Faith Has Its Reasons: Integrative Approaches to Defending the Christian Faith.* Waynesboro: Authentic, 2006.

Bowald, Mark A. "Objectivity." In *Dictionary for Theological Interpretation of the Bible*, edited by Kevin J. Vanhoozer, 544–546. Grand Rapids: Baker, 2005.

Brand, Chad Owen. "Is Carl Henry a Modernist? Rationalism and Post-War Evangelical Theology," SBJT 8/4 (2004), 44–60.

Bray, Gerald. *Biblical Interpretation Past and Present.* Downers Grove: InterVarsity, 1996.

Brunner, Emil. *Revelation and Reason: The Christian Doctrine of Faith and Knowledge.* Translated by Olive Wyon. Philadelphia: Westminster, 1946.

Bruns, Gerald L. *Hermeneutics: Ancient and Modern.* New Haven: Yale University Press, 1992.

Bultmann, Rudolf. *Existence and Faith.* Translated by Schubert M. Ogden. New York: Living Age Books/Meridian Books, 1960.

Calvin, John. *Institutes of the Christian Religion.* Peabody: Hendrickson, 2008.

Campbell-Jack, W. C., and Gavin J. Mcgrath., eds. *New Dictionary of Christian Apologetics.* Downers Grove: InterVarsity, 2006.

Caputo, John D. *Radical Hermeneutics: Repetition, Deconstruction, and the Hermeneutic Project.* Bloomington: Indiana University Press, 1987.

Carson, D. A. *Exegetical Fallacies. The Gagging of God: Christianity Confronts Pluralism.* Grand Rapids: Zondervan, 1996.

Carson, D. A ., John D. Woodbridge, and Carl. F. H. Henry, eds. *God and Culture: Essays in Honor of Carl F. H. Henry.* Grand Rapids: Eerdmans, 1993.

Carswell, Justin. "A Comparative Study of the Religious Epistemology of Carl F. H. Henry and Alvin Plantinga." PhD diss., The Southern Baptist Theological Seminary, 2007.

Cayhill, Howard. *A Kant Dictionary.* Oxford: Blackwell, 1995.

Chomsky, Noam. *Aspects of the Theory of Syntax.* Cambridge: Massachusetts Institute of Technology, 1965.

Clark, Gordon. *A Christian View of Men and Things.* Grand Rapids: Eerdmans, 1952.

———. *Karl Barth's Theological Method.* Philadelphia: Presbyterian and Reformed, 1963.

———. *Religion, Reason, and Revelation.* Philadelphia: Presbyterian and Reformed, 1961.

Collier, Andrew. *Critical Realism: An Introduction to Roy Bhaskar's Philosophy.* London: Verso, 1994.

Copleston, Frederick J. *A History of Philosophy.* 9 vols. New York: Image Books, 1994.

Cotterell, Peter and Max Turner. *Linguistics and Biblical Interpretation.* Downers Grove: InterVarsity, 1989.

Demarest, Bruce A. *General Revelation: Historical Views and Contemporary Views.* Grand Rapids: Zondervan, 1982.

Dorrien, Gary. *The Remaking of Evangelical Theology.* Louisville: Westminster John Knox, 1998.

Doyle, G. Wright. *Carl Henry-Theologian for All Seasons: An Introduction and Guide to God, Revelation, and Authority.* Eugene: Pickwick, 2010.

Dulles, Avery. *Models of Revelation.* Garden City: Double Day, 1983.

Duvall, J. Scott and J. Daniel Hays. *Grasping God's Word.* Grand Rapids: Baker, 2005.

Elwell, Walter A., ed. *Evangelical Dictionary of Theology.* Grand Rapids: Baker, 1984.

Enns, Peter. *Inspiration and Incarnation: Evangelicals and the Problem of the Old Testament.* Grand Rapids: Baker, 2005.

———. *The Evolution of Adam: What The Bible Does And Doesn't Say About Human Origins.* Grand Rapids: Brazos, 2012.

Erickson, Millard J. *Christian Theology.* Grand Rapids: Baker, 1998.

Evans, Stephen C. "Approaches to Christian Apologetics. " In *new Dictionary of Christian Apologetics*, edited by W. C. Campbell-Jack and Gavin J. McGrath, 15-21. Downers Grove: InterVaristy, 2006.

Falk, Darrell R. *Coming to Peace with Science: Bridging the Worlds between Faith and Biology.* Downers Grove: InterVarsity, 2004.

Fee, Gordon D. and Douglas Stuart. *How to Read the Bible for all Its Worth.* 3rd ed. Grand Rapids: Zondervan, 2003.

Feinberg, John S. "Non-Cognitivism: Wittgenstein." In *Biblical Errancy: An Analysis of its Philosophical Roots*, edited by Norman L. Geisler, 163–201. Eugene: Wipf and Stock, 1981.

Feurbach, Ludwig. *The Essence of Christianity.* Translated by Marian Evans. New York: Harper and Row, 1957.

Fish, Stanley. *Is There a Text in This Class?: The Authority of Interpretive Communities.* Cambridge: Harvard University Press, 1980.

Frame, John M. *Apologetics to the Glory of God: An Introduction.* Phillipsburg: Presbyterian and Reformed, 1995.

———. Frame, John. "Presuppositional Apologetics." In *New Dictionary of Christian Apologetics*, edited by W. C. Campbell-Jack and Gavin J. McGrath, 575–578. Downers Grove: IVP, 2006.

———. *The Doctrine of the Knowledge of God: A Theology of Lordship.* Philadelphia: Presbyterian and Reformed, 1987.

Franke, John. *The Character of Theology: An Introduction to Its Nature, Task, and Purpose.* Grand Rapids: Baker, 2005.

Frei, Hans. *The Eclipse of Biblical Narrative: A Study of Eighteenth and Nineteenth Century Hermeneutics.* New Haven: Yale University Press, 1974.

Gadamer, Hans-Georg. *Truth and Method.* New York: Continuum, 1975.

Geisler, Norman L. *Baker Encyclopedia of Christian Apologetics.* Grand Rapids: Baker, 1999.

———, ed. *Biblical Errancy: An Analysis of its Philosophical Roots.* Eugene: Wipf & Stock, 1981.

———, ed. *Inerrancy.* Grand Rapids: Zondervan, 1980.

———. *Systematic Theology: In One Volume.* Minneapolis: Bethany House, 2011.

Geisler, Norman L, and Paul Feinberg. *Introduction to Philosophy: A Christian Perspective.* Grand Rapids: Baker, 1980.

Geisler, Norman L, and William C. Roach. "Defending Inerrancy: A Response to Methodological Unorthodoxy." *Journal of the International Society of Christian Apologetics*, 5 (2012) 61–87.

———. *Defending Inerrancy: Affirming the Accuracy of Scripture for a New Generation.* Grand Rapids: Baker, 2011.
George, Timothy. "Carl Henry." In *God and Culture: Essays in Honor of Carl F. H. Henry*, edited by D. A. Carson and John D. Woodbridge, 78–112. Grand Rapids: Eerdmans, 1993.
———. "Daddy Evangelical: Why some think it's time to make Carl Henry cool again." *Christianity Today* (2013).
———. *Reading Scripture With The Reformers.* Downers Grove: IVP Academic, 2011.
George, Timothy, and David S. Dockery, eds. *Theologians of the Baptist Tradition.* Nashville: Broadman and Holman, 2001.
Greco, John., and Ernst Sosa. *The Blackwell Guide To Epistemology.* Malden: Blackwell, 1999.
Grenz, Stanley J. *A Primer on Postmodernism.* Grand Rapids: Eerdmans, 1996.
Grenz, Stanley J., and John Franke. *Beyond Foundationalism: Shaping Theology in a Postmodern Context.* Louisville: Westminster John Knox, 2000.
Grenz, Stanley J., and Roger Olson. *20th Century Theology: God & The World in a Transitional Age.* Downers Grove: InterVarsity, 1992.
Grondin, Jean. *Introduction to Philosophical Hermeneutics.* Translated by Joel Weisheimer. New Haven: Yale University, 1994.
Grudem, Wayne A. *Systematic Theology: An Introduction to Biblical Doctrines.* Grand Rapids: Zondervan, 1995.
Gundry, Stanley N., ed. *Five views On Biblical Inerrancy.* Grand Rapids: Zondervan, 2013.
———, ed. *Three Views On: the New Testament Use Of The Old Testament.* Grand Rapids: Zondervan, 2008.
Halliday, Steve, and Al Janssen, eds. *Carl Henry at His Best: A Lifetime of Quotable Thoughts.* Portland: Multnomah, 1989.
Hegel, Georg Wilhelm F. *The Christian Religions: Lectures on the Philosophy of Religion: the Revelatory, Consummate, Absolute Religion.* Edited and translated by Peter C. Hodgson. Based on the edition by Georg Lasson. Missoula: Scholars Press, 1979.
Helm, Paul. *Faith, Form, and Fashion: Classical Reformed Theology and Its Postmodern Critics.* Eugene: Cascade, 2015.
———. "Vanhoozer's Remythologizing Theology," Helm's Deep, entry posted May 1, 2010. http://paulhelmsdeep.blogspot.com/search?.q=Remythologizing+Theology.
Henry, Carl F. H. *Confessions of a Theologian: An Autobiography.* Waco: Word Books, 1986.
———. *Faith at the Frontiers.* Chicago: Moody Press, 1965.
———. *Frontiers in Modern Theology.* Chicago: Moody, 1965.
———. *gods of this Age or . . . God of the ages?* Edited by R. Albert Mohler. Nashville: Broadman and Holman, 1994.
———. *God, Revelation and Authority.* 6 vols. Waco: Word Books, 1976–1983. Reprint, Wheaton: Crossway Books, 1999.
———. *Remaking the Modern Mind.* Grand Rapids: Eerdmans, 1948.
———. Henry, Carl F. H. "Review of *The Genesis of Doctrine*, by Alister McGrath." *Journal of the Evangelical Theological Society*, 38 (1995).
———. Henry, Carl F. H. "The Instability of 20th Century Theology." Unpublished manuscript, 1997.
———. *The Protestant Dilemma.* Grand Rapids: Zondervan Publishing House, 1946.

Hirsh, E. D. *Validity in Interpretation*. New Haven: Yale University Press, 1967.
Hodge, Charles. *Systematic Theology*. Grand Rapids: Eerdmans, 1946.
Hoitenga, Dewey J. *Faith and Reason from Plato to Plantinga: An Introduction to Reformed Epistemology*. Albany: University of New York Press, 1991.
Horton, Michael S. *Covenant and Eschatology: The Divine Drama*. Louisville: Westminster John Knox, 2002.
Howe, Thomas. *Objectivity in Biblical Interpretation*. Advantage Books, 2004.
Hume, David. *Dialogues Concerning Natural Religion*. Edited by Norman Kemp Smith. New York: Macmillan, 1947.
Jewell, Elizabeth. *The Oxford: American Desk and Dictionary Thesaurus*. New York: Berkley, 2001.
Kaiser, Walter C., Jr., and Moises Silva. *An Introduction to Biblical Hermeneutics*. Grand Rapids: Zondervan, 1994.
Kant, Immanuel. *The Critique of Pure Reason*. New York: Cambridge, 1995.
Kapic, Kelly, and Bruce L. McCormick, eds. *Mapping Modern Theology: A Thematic and Historical Introduction*. Grand Rapids: Baker, 2012.
Kelsey, David H. *Proving Doctrine: The Uses of Scripture in Recent Theology*. Edinburgh: T&T Clark, 1999.
Kenny, Anthony. *The God of The Philosophers*. New York: Oxford University Press, 1987.
Klein, W. William, Craig L. Blomberg, and Robert L. Hubbard Jr. *Introduction to Biblical Interpretation*. Revised edition. Nashville: Thomas Nelson, 2005.
Körner, Stephen. *Kant*. London: Penguin Books, 1955.
Lauber, David. "Yale School." In *Dictionary for Theological Interpretation of the Bible*, edited by Kevin J. Vanhoozer, 859–861. Grand Rapids: Baker, 2005.
Lawhead, William F. *The Voyage of Discovery: A Historical Introduction to Philosophy* 2nd ed. Belmont: Wadsworth, 2002.
Licona, Michael R. *The Resurrection of Jesus: A New Historiographical Approach*. Downers Grove: InterVarsity, 2010.
———. http://www.risenjesus.com/images/stories/pdfs/2011%20eps%20saints%20paper.pdf.
Lindbeck, George. *The Nature of Doctrine: Religion and Theology in a Postliberal Age*. Philadelphia: Westminster, 1984.
Lindsell, Harold. *The Bible in the Balance*. Grand Rapids: Zondervan, 1979.
Lonergan, Bernard. *A Second Collection*. Philadelphia: Westminster, 1974.
Longman, Tremper. *How to Read Genesis*. Downers Grove: InterVarsity, 2005.
Maier, Gerhard. *Biblical Hermeneutics*. Translated by Robert W. Yarbrough. Wheaton: Crossway, 1994.
Marsden, George M. *Fundamentalism and American Culture*. New York: Oxford University Press, 2006.
———. *Reforming Fundamentalism: Fuller Seminary and the New Evangelicalism*. Grand Rapids: Wm. B. Eerdmans,1995.
———. *Understanding Fundamentalism and Evangelicalism*. Grand Rapids: Eerdmans, 1991.
Matthews, Gareth B. *Thought's Ego In Augustine And Descartes*. Ithaca: Cornell University Press, 1992.
McGrath, Alister. *A Passion for Truth: the Intellectual Coherence of Evangelicalism*. Downers Grove: InterVarsity Press, 1996.
———. *A Scientific Theology*. London: T & T Clark, 2012.

———. McGrath, Alister. "Engaging the Great Tradition." In *Evangelical Futures*, edited by John G. Stackhouse Jr., 78–112. Grand Rapids: Baker, 2000.

———. *Historical Theology: An Introduction to the History of Christian Thought*. Malden: Blackwell Publishing, 1998.

———. *Reality*. Grand Rapids: Eerdmans, 2002.

———. *The Genesis of Doctrine: A Study in the Foundations of Doctrinal Criticism*. Oxford: Blackwell, 1990.

———. *The Open Secret: A New Vision for Natural Theology*. Oxford: Blackwell, 2008.

McKim, Donald K. *A Guide to Contemporary Hermeneutics: Major Trends in Biblical Interpretation*. Grand Rapids: Eerdmans, 1986.

———, ed. *Historical Handbook of Major Biblical Interpreters*. Downers Grove: InterVarsity Press, 1998.

Meyer, Ben F. *Critical Realism & The New Testament*. Allison Park: Pickwick, 1989.

Meyer, Raymond K. "An Evangelical Analysis of Critical Realism and Corollary Hermeneutics of Bernard Lonergan With Application For Evangelical Hermeneutics." PhD diss., Southeastern Baptist Theological Seminary, 2007.

Mohler, Jr., R. Albert. "The Devil Is In the Details: Biblical Inerrancy and the Licona Controversy." Accessed 6/10/2013. http://www.albertmohler.com/2011/09/14/the-devil-is-in-the-details-biblical-inerrancy-and-the-licona-controversy.

———. "The Life and Legacy of Carl F. H. Henry." Accessed on 4/17/2013. http://www.albertmohler.com/2003/12/09/the-life-and-legacy-of-carl-f-h-henry-a-rembrance/.

Montgomery, John W. *Faith Founded on Fact: Essays in Evidential Apologetics*. Nashville: Thomas Nelson, 1978.

Mortiz, Thorsten. "Critical Realism." In *Dictionary for Theological Interpretation of the Bible*, edited by Kevin J. Vanhoozer, 147–150. Grand Rapids: Baker, 2005.

Mueller-Vollmer, Kurt, ed. *The Hermeneutics Reader*. New York: Continuum, 1994.

Muller, Richard A. *The Study of Theology: From Biblical Interpretation to Contemporary Formulation*. Grand Rapids: Zondervan, 1991.

Murphy, Nancey. "Epistemology." In *Dictionary for Theological Interpretation of the Bible*, edited by Kevin J. Vanhoozer, 191–194. Grand Rapids: Baker, 2005.

Naselli, Andrew Davis, and Collin Hansen, eds. *Four Views On: The Spectrums of Evangelicalism*. Grand Rapids: Zondervan, 2011.

Nash, Ronald H. *Faith and Reason*. Grand Rapids: Zondervan, 1988.

———. *The Light of the Mind: St. Augustine's Theory of Knowledge*. Lexington: University Press of Kentucky, 1969.

———. *The Word of God and the Mind of Man: The Crisis of Revealed Truth in Contemporary Theology* (Grand Rapids: Zondervan, 1982).

Osborne, Grant. *The Hermeneutical Spiral: A Comprehensive Introduction to Biblical Interpretation*. Downers Grove: InterVarsity, 2006.

Packer, James I. *A Quest For Godliness: The Puritan vision of the Christian Life*. Wheaton: Crossway, 1990.

———. *Beyond the Battle for the Bible*. Westchester: Cornerstone Books, 1980.

———. *Fundamentalism and the Word of God: Some Evangelical Perspectives*. Grand Rapids: Zondervan, 1959.

Palmer, Richard E. *Hermeneutics*. Evanston: Northwestern University Press, 1969.

Patterson, Bob E. *Makers of Modern Theological Mind: Carl F. H. Henry*. Peabody: Hendrickson Publishing, 1983. .

Pinnock, Clark. *Tracking the Maze: Finding Our Way Through Modern Theology from an Evangelical Perspective*. San Francisco: Harper & Row, 1990.
Plantinga, Alvin. *Warrant and Proper Function*. New York: Oxford University Press, 1993.
———. *Warrant: The Current Debate*. New York: Oxford University Press, 1993.
———. *Warranted Christian Belief*. New York: Oxford University Press, 2000.
Pojman, Louis J. *What Can We Know? An Introduction to the Theory of Knowledge*. Belmont: Waldworth, 2001.
Polyani, Michael. *Personal Knowledge: Towards a Post-Critical Philosophy*. Chicago: The University of Chicago Press, 1958.
Porter, Stanley E. and Beth M. Stovell. *Biblical Hermeneutics: Five Views*. Downers Grove: InterVarsity, 2012.
Quarles, Charles L. "Review of Michael R. Licona, *The Resurrection of Jesus: A New Historiographical Approach*." *Journal of the Evangelical Theological Society*, 54 (2011) 839–44.
Radmacher, Earl D., and Robert D. Preus, editors. *Hermeneutics, Inerrancy, and the Bible: Papers from ICBI Summit II*. Grand Rapids: Zondervan, 1984.
Ramm, Bernard. *Protestant Biblical Interpretation: A Textbook of Hermeneutics*. Grand Rapids: Baker, 1970.
Richard, Rorty. *Objectivity, Relativism, and Truth: Philosophical Papers I*. Cambridge: Cambridge University Press, 1991.
Ricoeur, Paul. *Interpretation Theory: Discourse and Surplus of Meaning*. Fort Worth: The Texas Christian University Press, 1976.
———. *The Conflict of Interpretation*. Evanston: Northwestern University Press, 1974.
Rogers, Jack B., and Donald K. McKim. *The Authority and Interpretation of the Bible: An Historical Approach*. San Francisco: Harper and Row, 1979.
Ryken, Leland. *How to Read the Bible as Literature*. Grand Rapids: Zondervan, 1984.
Schaff, Phillip. *The Creeds of Christendom*. 3 vols. Grand Rapids: Baker, 1993.
Schaeffer, Francis A. *The God Who Is There*. Downers Grove: InterVarsity, 1982.
Schleiermacher, Frederich. *Hermeneutics and Criticism: And Other Writings*. Translated by Andrew Bowie. Cambridge: Cambridge University Press, 1998.
———. *The Christian Faith*. Translated by H. R. Mackintosh and J. S. Stewart. Edinburgh: T&T Clark, 1968.
———. *On Religion: Speeches to Its Cultured Despisers*. Translated by John Oman. New York: Harper, 1958.
Searle, John. *Speech Acts: An Essay in the Philosophy of Language*. Cambridge: Cambridge University Press, 1969.
Shipway, Brad. "The Theological Application of Bhaskar's Stratified Reality: The Scientific Theology of A. E. McGrath, "*Journal of Critical Realism* 3 (2004): 191–203.
Sparks, Kenton L. *God's Word in Human Hands: An Evangelical Appropriation of Critical Biblical Scholarship*. Grand Rapids: Baker, 2008.
Sproul, R. C., John Gerstner and Arthur Lindsley, *Classical Apologetics*. Grand Rapids: Zondervan, 1984.
Sullivan, Daniel J. *An Introduction to Philosophy: The Perennial Principles of the Classical Realist Tradition*. Rockford: Tan Books, 1957.
Tekippe, Terry. *What is Lonergan Up To in Insight?* Minnesota: The Liturgical, 1996.

Thiselton, Anthony C. *Hermeneutics and Philosophical Description with Special Reference to Heidegger, Bultmann, Gadamer, and Wittgenstein.* Grand Rapids: Eerdmans, 1980.

———. Thiselton, Anthony C. "Hermeneutical Circle" In *Dictionary for Theological Interpretation of the Bible*, edited by Kevin J. Vanhoozer, 281–282. Grand Rapids: Baker, 2005.

———. Thiselton, Anthony C. "Hermeneutical Spiral." In *Dictionary for Theological Interpretation of the Bible*, edited by Kevin J. Vanhoozer, 283–287. Grand Rapids: Baker, 2005.

———. *Interpreting God and the Postmodern Self: On Meaning, Manipulation and Promise.* Grand Rapids: Eerdmans, 1995.

———. *The Two Horizons: New Testament Hermeneutics and Philosophical Description.* Grand Rapids: Eerdmans, 1980.

———. *New Horizons in Hermeneutics: The Theory and Practice of Transforming Biblical Reading.* Grand Rapids: Zondervan, 1992.

Thomas, Robert L. *Evangelical Hermeneutics: The New Versus the Old.* Grand Rapids: Kregel, 2002.

Thornbury, Gregory Alan. *Recovering Classic Evangelicalism: Applying the Wisdom and Vision of Carl F. H. Henry.* Wheaton: Crossway, 2013.

Torrance, Thomas F. *Theological Science.* New York: Oxford University Press, 1969.

Trier, Daniel J. "Scripture as Communication." *Mapping Modern Theology: A Thematic and Historical Introduction*, edited by Kelly M. Kapic and Bruce L. McCormack, 67–96. Grand Rapids: Baker, 2012.

Trueman, Carl R. "Admiring the Sistine Chapel: Reflections on Carl F. H. Henry's God, Revelation and Authority," *Themelios*, 25 (2000): 48–58.

Vanhoozer, Kevin J., editor. *Dictionary for Theological Interpretation of the Bible.* Grand Rapids: Baker, 2005.

———. "Lost in Interpretation? Truth, Scripture, and Hermeneutics." *Journal of the Evangelical Theological Society*, 48 (2005) 89–115.

———. *The Drama of Doctrine: A Canonical Linguistic Approach to Christian Theology.* Louisville: Westminster John Knox, 1998.

———. *Is There a Meaning in This Text? The Bible, the Reader, and the Morality of Literary Knowledge.* Grand Rapids: Zondervan, 1998.

———, ed. *The Cambridge Companion to Postmodern Theology.* Cambridge Companions to Religion. Cambridge: Cambridge University Press, 2003.

———. Vanhoozer, Kevin J. "Ricoeur, Paul." In *Dictionary for Theological Interpretation of the Bible*, edited by Kevin J. Vanhoozer, 692–695. Grand Rapids: Baker, 2005.

———. "Theology and Apologetics." Pages 35–43 in *New Dictionary of Apologetics.* Edited by W. C. Campbell-Jack and Gavin McGrath. Downers Grove: InterVarsity, 2006.

Van Til, Cornelius. *A Christian Theory of Knowledge.* Phillipsburg: Presbyterian and Reformed, 1969.

———. *Christian Apologetics.* New Jersey: Presbyterian and Reformed, 2003.

Waltke Bruce, and Charles Yu, *An Old Testament Theology: An Exegetical, Canonical, and Thematic Approach.* Grand Rapids: Zondervan, 2007.

Walton, John. *Ancient Near Eastern Thought and the Old Testament: Introducing the Conceptual World of the Hebrew Bible.* Grand Rapids: Baker, 2006.

———. *The Lost World of Genesis One: Ancient Cosmology and the Origins Debate.* Downers Grove: InterVarsity, 2009.

Walton, John H., and D. Brent Sandy. *The Lost World of Scripture: Ancient Literary Culture and Biblical Authority.* Downers Grove: InterVarsity, 2013.

Warfield, Benjamin B. *The Works of Benjamin B. Warfield: Studies In Tertullian and Augustine.* Grand Rapids: Baker, 2003.

Webber, Robert E. *The Younger Evangelicals: Facing the Challenges of the New World.* Grand Rapids: Baker Books, 2002.

Westphal, Merald. "Hermeneutics as Epistemology." In *The Blackwell Guide to Epistemology*, edited by John Greco and Ernest Sosa, 415–435. Malden: Blackwell, 1999.

White, James Emery. *What is Truth?: A Comparative Study of the Positions of Cornelius Van Til, Francis Schaeffer, Carl F. H. Henry, Donald Bloesh, Millard Erickson.* Nashville: Broadman and Holman, 1994.

Wittgenstein, Ludwig. *Philosophical Investigations.* Translated by G. E. M. Anscombe. New York: Macmillan, 1953.

Wolterstorff, Nicholas. *Divine Discourse: Philosophical Reflections of the Claim that God Speaks.* Cambridge: Cambridge University Press, 1995.

Wright, N. T. *The New Testament and the People of God: Christian Origins and the Question of God.* Vol. 1. Minneapolis: Fortress, 1992.

Index

a priori, 75-80, 81-11, 263
a posteriori, 72-75, 263
Adam, 137, 140
Adler, Mortimer, 122
agnosticism, 6, 12
Albright, William F., 149
Alexandrian Fathers, 241, 243
Alitzer, Thomas J., 116-118
Allen, Diogenes, 267
Althusser, Louis, 125
American Theological Society, 280
Ames, William 64
analytic philosophy, 129-34
Anselm, 76
Aquinas, 72, 110, 236, 241, 261-62
Aristotle, 72, 117, 152, 155
Audi, Robert, 248
Augustine, 76, 81, 83-91, 110, 241, 243, 263-65, 267
Augustinian epistemology, 83-89, 178, 195, 239, 243-47, 261-65, 282
Austin, J. L., 53-55, 130, 153, 165-66
authorial intention, 179, 187-92
Ast, Friedrich, 10-11
Ayer, A. J., 128, 130
Bacon, Francis, 36
Barr, James, 145, 149-50, 193, 227-28
Barth, Karl, 30, 101, 136, 160, 163, 184-85, 240-41
Bartholomew, Craig, 33-34
Bavinck, Herman, 64
Beale, G. K., 278-79
Bergson, Henri, 174
Berkeley, George, 34
Bhasker, Roy, 39, 276

Bible as Propositional Revelation, 159-70
biblical theology, 148-49
Blaikie, Robert, 120-22
Bloesch, Donald, 63
Boa, Kenneth, 95
Boice, James Montgomery, 59, 227
Bowman, Robert, 95
Brand, Chad, 247-51
Brown, Colin, 63
Brunner, Emil, 30, 101
Buddhism, 118
Bultmann, Rudolf, 30, 102
Calvin, John, 64, 81
canonical-linguistic, 56-57
Carnap, Rudolf, 128
Carnell, E. J., 63
Carson, D. A., 59, 217-18
Carswell, Justin, 72-73, 75, 81-83, 90-91, 100, 103
Catholicism, Roman, 146
Chicago School of Interpretation, 30-34, 53
Childs, Brevard, 31, 149
Christianity Today, ix
Chomsky, Noam, 122
Clark, Gordon, 95, 101, 134-35
Cleobury, F. H., 132
cognitive-propositionalism, 55-56, 63, 74-75, 113, 115, 231-55
Colsen, Charles, ix
Comte, Auguste, 104
conventionalism, 118-19, 152-59
crisis of truth, 2
critical philosophy, 14, 77

296 INDEX

critical-realism, 30, 39–44
Darwin, Charles, 173
dasein, 19–20, 22, 108
Dilthey, Wilhelm, 18–19, 28, 175
Demarest, Bruce, 63
Derrida, Jacques, 6, 34–35
Descartes, Rene, 5, 70, 76, 82, 87, 246–47, 249–50
Dewey, James, 70
dialecticalism, 6
Doyle, G. Wright, 61, 66–67, 193, 243–47
Durkheim, Emile, 70
Ebling, Gerhart, 30
Ebner, Ferdinand, 174
Edwards, Jonathan, 64
empiricism, 67, 72–75
Enns, Peter, 191, 209–11, 275, 278–81
epistemological concerns, 66–80
epistemological nihilism, 3
epistemology, 60–61, 65–66
epistemology and hermeneutics, 257–73
epistemology and language, 114–70
epistemology and methodology, 207–10
Erickson, Millard, 63
Euclidian, 21
Evangelical Theological Society, 208, 235
Evans, C. F., 150
existence precedes essence, 19
Existentialism, 19–20
faith and reason, 239–43
fallibility of the exegete, 192–98
Feinburg, Paul, 239–247
Feuerbach, Ludwig, 26
Fichte, Johann, 126
final truth, 60
Fish, Stanley, 49
Foncault, J. B., 125
Foucault, Michael, 34
foundationalism, 65, 247–51
Franke, John, 35–39, 63, 114, 231–33, 239
Frei, Hans, 12, 15–17, 31–32, 34, 214–22, 275
Freud, Sigmund, 26
Fuchs, Ernst, 30

Fuller Theological Seminary, ix
fusion of horizons, 23, 180–81
Gadamer, Hans Georg, 6, 22–24, 34, 175, 177–81, 183–86, 258, 268
Geisler, Norman, 55, 59, 63–65, 227, 233, 239–247, 254
Geisteswissenschaften-Phenomenology-Existentialism, 17–25
genre, 158–59, 164–65
George, Timothy, 59–60, 281–82
Graham, Billy, 59
grammatical-historical, 205, 222–28, 256
Greco-Roman biography, 47–48, 142, 273
Grenz, Stanley, 35–39, 63, 114, 231–33, 239
Grondin, Jean, 13, 22
Grudem, Wayne, 64
Gundry, Robert, 221–22, 224–25
Harlow, Daniel, 191
Heidegger, Martin, 6, 19–24, 34, 174–77, 183–86, 258, 267
Hegel, Georg, 6, 26, 34, 71, 76–80, 87, 117, 121–22, 126
Helm, Paul, 55, 252
Henry's epistemology, 80–111
Henry-Hodge, 55, 236–39, 252–55
Henry's six principles 92–99, 259
Hermeneutical arc, 25–26
hermeneutical circle, 14–17, 204
hermeneutical nihilism, 3–4, 174, 185–86, 222–223
hermeneutical problem, 28–29, 175–82, 205
hermeneutical spiral, 48–53, 73–75, 182–86, 204, 257–58
hermeneutics, 4
hermeneutics as a system of interpretation, 25–28
hermeneutics as epistemology, 61, 173–204, 260–61
hermeneutics as methodology, 61, 204–228
higher-criticism, 192, 194
Hirsch, E. D., 23, 154, 181, 187–88
history-likeness, 215–16
historical-critical method, 205–207

historical horizon, 23
historical interpretation, 19
historical understanding, 18-19, 24
Hodge, A. A., 29, 233, 235-37, 254
Hodge, Charles, 29, 55
Holy Spirit and interpretation, 201-04
Homer, 141
horizons of understanding, 22, 108
Horton, Michael, 64
human defection from truth, 3
human understanding, 24
Hume, David, 70, 73, 122-23, 128, 159
Husserl, Edmund, 19
idealism, 66
illumination, 201-04
image of God, 108-111, 194-95, 265-69
inerrancy, 30
International Council on Biblical Inerrancy, 62, 118, 189, 223-24, 279
intuition, 68-71
Kaiser, Walter, 192
Kant, Immanuel, 5, 12-14, 17, 21, 26, 70-71, 76-80, 82, 111, 126-27, 159-60, 173, 241, 243
Kantzer, Kenneth, x, 59, 63, 146
Kelsey, David, 31-33, 216
Kierkegaard, Soren, 94, 106-07, 173, 240-41
Kittle, Gerhard, 150
Krugar, Arthur, 154
Lauber, David, 31-34
Lawhead, William, 34, 129-30
Leibniz, Gottfried, 76, 82
Lessing, Gotthold, 173
Lewis, Gordon, 63
Licona, Michael, 44-48, 57, 189-90, 191
Lindbeck, George, 31-32, 34, 275
Lindsell, Harold, 59
linguistic analysis and propositional truth, 151-59
linguistic turn, 129-30
Locke, John, 5, 122-23
logic of religious language, 115-22
logical positivism, 75, 128-29
logos, 100-08, 147-48, 194-95, 265-69

Lonergan, Bernard, 39, 41, 75, 275-78
Luther, Martin, 282
Lutherans, 72
Lyotard, Jean-Francoisem, 35
MacKay, Donald, 123-24
Manicas, Peter, 154
Marsden, George, 63
Marx, Karl, 26
Mascall, E. O., 132
McGrath, Alister, 39-40, 114, 231-35, 275-78
McLaren, Brian, 35
meaning and religious language, 127-34
Metzger, Bruce, 150
Meyer, Ben, 41-42
modified-propositionalist, 55
Mohler, R. Albert, 60, 282-83
Montgomery, John Warwick, 233
Moore, G. E., 130
Mortiz, Thorsten, 40-44
Murphy, Nancey, 65
mysticism, 68-69, 72
narrative theology, 214-22
Nash, Ronald, 159-62, 169
Nicole, Roger, 59
Nida, Eugene, 147
Niebuhr, Richard, 160
Nietzsche, Friedrich, 26, 34, 70
noetic effects of sin, 88-89
objectivity, 196-98
Ockenga, Harold, 59
Olsen, Roger, 114
Ovey, M. J., 243
ontologically subjective, 19
origin of language, 122-27
Osborne, Grant, 44, 48-53, 57, 193-94
Packer, J. I., 1-2, 59
Palmer, Richard, 7-29, 102, 143-44, 175, 188
Patterson, Bob, 72, 84, 89, 266-67
Patterson, Paige, 59
Phenomenology, 19
Philological Methodology, 9-11
Pinnock, Clark, 98
Plato, 70, 88, 152
Polkinghorne, John, 39, 42
Polyani, Michael, 39

Protestant principles of interpretation, 2
Plantinga, Alvin, 82
presuppositional axioms, 90–92
presuppositional principles, 92–99
presuppositional method, 89–99
post-Gadamerian hermeneutics, 24
post-liberalism
post-modernism, 30
Puritans, 1
Ramm, Bernard, 2, 63, 225–27
rationalism, 67, 76, 94, 246–47
rationalism and Augustinianism, 243–247
revelation and myth, 210–14
revelational theism, 67, 85–89, 99–111
revelational theism and hermeneutics, 260–73
Ricoeur, Paul, 25–27, 51
Ritschl, Albrecht, 159–60
Roach, William, 55, 254
Robinson, John, 149
role of reason, 198–201
Rorty, Richard, 5–6, 34
Russell, Bertrand, 130
Ryle, Gilbert, 130
Sapir, Edward, 122
Satan, 139
Schaeffer, Francis, 59, 120–21, 227, 233
Schleiermacher, Friedrich, 10–12, 14–17, 23, 28, 69, 73–75, 159, 173, 175–76, 183–86, 257–58
Schneider, John, 191
Schubert, Ogden, 163
science of linguistic understanding, 11–17
Searle, John, 53–55
self-understanding, 25
six definitions, 7–29
Sola Scriptura, 4, 37
speech-act-theory, 53–57, 164–71, 238–39
Spinoza, Baruch, 76, 200, 241, 243
Springsted, Eric O., 267
Sproul, R. C., 59, 227
square of opposition, 160, 169
Strauss, Levi, 125–27
Strong, Augustus, 66

sub-axioms of revelational theism, 99–111
Sullivan, Daniel J., 138–39
tabula rasa, 123
Tertullian, 241
The Southern Baptist Theological Seminary, 274
theism, 93–94
theistic view of language, 134–51, 269–71
theological interpretation, 30
theological transcendent a priori, 81–111
theory of biblical exegesis, 8–9
Thiselton, Anthony, 18, 23–24
Thornbury, Gregory Alan, 54–55, 61–64, 66, 108, 114–115, 164, 178, 190–91, 236, 258, 273–75
Tillich, Paul, 160, 163
Torrance, Thomas, 105–07
tradition, 37–38
Trier, Daniel, 23, 25, 30, 32, 258
Trueman, Carl, 62
truth, 97–99, 216, 251–55
Tucker, Aliezer, 46
Vanhoozer, Kevin, 25–26, 44, 53–57, 63, 114–115, 164–65, 168–70, 190–91, 232, 234–39, 251–55, 275
Van Til, Cornelius, 95–96, 110, 241
Vatican II
Warfield, 29, 233, 254, 263–64
ways of knowing, 67–68, 244
Webber, Robert, 34–35, 65–66, 114
Westminster divines, 1
Wesphal, Merold, 5, 21
Westminster Shorter Catechism, 1
White, James Emery, 93–99
Wisdom, John, 128
Wittgenstein, Ludwig, 104, 130, 150, 153, 165–66, 236, 253
Wolf, August, 10–11
Wolterstoff, Nicholas, 114, 166–68
Wright, N. T., 41–44
Yale Divinity School, 30
Yale School of Interpretation, 30–34, 53

www.ingramcontent.com/pod-product-compliance
Lightning Source LLC
Chambersburg PA
CBHW061429300426
44114CB00014B/1607